THE CHARTER OF
THE ISLAMIC CONFERENCE

The Charter of

The Islamic Conference

and

Legal Framework of Economic Co-operation among its Member States

A study of the Charter, the General Agreement for Economic, Technical and Commercial Co-operation and the Agreement for Promotion, Protection and Guarantee of Investments among Member States of the OIC

HASAN MOINUDDIN

CLARENDON PRESS · OXFORD
1987

Oxford University Press, Walton Street, Oxford OX2 6DP
Oxford New York Toronto
Delhi Bombay Calcutta Madras Karachi
Petaling Jaya Singapore Hong Kong Tokyo
Nairobi Dar es Salaam Cape Town
Melbourne Auckland
and associated companies in
Beirut Berlin Ibadan Nicosia

Published in the United States
by Oxford University Press, New York

British Library Cataloguing in Publication Data
Moinuddin, Hasan
The Charter of the Islamic Conference and legal framework of economic co-operation among its member states: a study of the charter, the General Agreement for Economic, Technical and Commercial Co-operation and the Agreement for Promotion, Protection and Guarantee of Investments among Member States of the OIC.
1. Islamic law 2. Islamic countries—Economic integration
I. Title
342.3'7'0917671 [LAW]
ISBN 0-19-825524-1

Library of Congress Cataloging in Publication Data
Moinuddin, Hasan.
The Charter of the Islamic Conference.
Based on author's thesis (doctoral—Ruhr University Bochum)
Bibliography: p.
Includes index.
1. Organization of Islamic Conference. 2. Islamic countries—Economic integration. 3. Commercial law—Islamic countries. I. Title.
DS35.3.M64 1986 341.24'77 86-802
ISBN 0-19-825524-1

Typeset by Joshua Associates Limited, Oxford
Printed in Great Britain
at the University Printing House, Oxford
by David Stanford
Printer to the University

To my mother, Dr Noor Begum,
in deep gratitude and affection

Preface

RECENT focus on 'Islamic resurgence' and politico-economic developments in Islamic countries has led to a renewed debate on the relevance of religion in modern state and society. Whereas specialized country studies or general monographs on the political, economic, and religious dimensions of Islam abound, little work has yet been done on organizations dealing with the institutionalization of Islamic co-operation on the international plane. This humble contribution, which is an enlarged version of my doctoral thesis submitted to the Faculty of Social Sciences at the Ruhr University, Bochum, West Germany, focuses on the Organization of the Islamic Conference (OIC) as a forum of political and economic co-operation among its Member States. My main purpose is to provide a specifically legal analysis of the Charter of the OIC and other relevant economic agreements, thus references to the political and economic position of the Islamic States are made solely for contextual purposes. The legal basis of Islamic co-operation in the modern world must be surveyed in its proper historical perspective, however. Part I of this book is therefore a historical and comparative introduction, and it is followed in Part II by an analysis of the Charter of the OIC and other relevant agreements dealing with economic co-operation among the Member States.

I take this opportunity to thank all the friends and reviewers who helped me with their suggestions and criticisms. In particular, I should like to thank Professor Knut Ipsen, Professor Helmut Rumpf, Dr Erhard Liemen, and Dr Volker Nienhaus of Ruhr University, Bochum for their valuable suggestions and institutional support. Of course I am entirely responsible for any errors and inaccuracies that may still persist. A special word of thanks is due to the former Director of the Department of Economic Affairs at the OIC in Jeddah, Dr Ashraf-uz-Zaman and the Assistant Director, Mr Naeem-ul-Hasan for their kind help in my research efforts.

I am also grateful to the Friedrich Naumann Foundation in Bonn, West Germany, for extending generous financial support throughout my studies. Last but not least I thank my wife, Jolanta, for her untiring encouragement and patience without which this study could not have been brought to a successful conclusion.

H. M.

Bochum, West Germany
27 December 1984

Contents

Abbreviations

ABAJ	*American Bar Association Journal*
AdV	*Archiv des Völkerrechts*
AJCL	*American Journal of Comparative Law*
AJIL	*American Journal of International Law*
AH	anno Hijra
AWD	Außenwirtschaftsdienst des Betriebberaters
Ber.	Berichte
BfAI	Bundesstelle für Außenhandelsinformation
BGBl.	*Bundesgestzblatt*
BSOAS	*Bulletin of the School of Oriental and African Studies*
BYIL	*British Yearbook of International Law*
CMLR	*Common Market Law Review*
COLJTL	*Columbia Journal of Transnational Law*
CYIL	*Canadian Yearbook of International Law*
DEG	Deutsche Gesellschaft für wirtschaftliche Zusammenarbeit (Entwicklungsgesellschaft) mbH
DGes.VR	Deutsche Gesellschaft für Völkerrecht
Doc.	Document(s)
EB	*Encyclopaedia Britannica*
ECDC	Economic Co-operation among Developing Countries
ECOSOC	Economic and Social Council
EEC	European Economic Community
EI	*Encyclopaedia of Islam*
EWG	Europäische Wirtschaftsgemeinschaft
FAO	Food and Agriculture Organization
FAZ	*Frankfurter Allgemeine Zeitung*
FRG	Federal Republic of Germany
GATT	General Agreement on Tariffs and Trade
HWI	*Handwörterbuch des Islam*, eds. A.J. Wensinck and J.H. Kramers (Leiden, 1941)
ICE	Islamic Council of Europe
ICFM	Islamic Conference of Foreign Ministers
ICJ	International Court of Justice
ICJ Rep.	*International Court of Justice Reports*
ICLQ	*International and Comparative Law Quarterly*
IDB	Islamic Development Bank
IJIL	*Indian Journal of International Law*

IJMES	*International Journal of Middle East Studies*
ILC	International Law Commission
ILM	*International Legal Materials*
ILQ	*International Law Quarterly* (see *ICLQ*)
ILR	*International Law Reports*
IMF	International Monetary Fund
Int. Aff.	*International Affairs*
IO	International Organization
IQ	*Islamic Quarterly*
Isl. Lit.	*Islamic Literature* (Lahore)
Isl. Rev.	*Islamic Review*
Isl. Stud.	*Islamic Studies* (Islamabad)
IYIA	*Indian Yearbook of International Affairs*
JAOS	*Journal of American Oriental Society*
JECIC	*Journal of Economic Co-operation Among Islamic Countries*
JIR	*Jahrbuch für internationales Recht*
JPHS	*Journal of the Pakistan Historical Society*
JPL	*Journal of Public Law*
JZ	*Juristenzeitung*
MEJ	*Middle East Journal*
MW	*Muslim World*
NATO	North Atlantic Treaty Organization
NIEO	New International Economic Order
NILR	*Netherlands International Law Review*
NYIL	*Netherlands Yearbook of International Law*
OAPEC	Organization of Arab Petroleum Exporting Countries
OAS	Organization of American States
OAU	Organization of African Unity
OECD	Organization for Economic Co-operation and Development
OIC	Organization of the Islamic Conference
OPEC	Organization of Petroleum Exporting Countries
ÖZöR	*Österreichische Zeitschrift für öffentliches Recht*
PCIJ	Permanent Court of International Justice
PCIJ Rep.	*Permanent Court of International Justice Reports*
PLD	All Pakistan Legal Decisions
PLO	Palestine Liberation Organization
Proc. ASIL	*Proceedings of the American Society of International Law*
Q	*The Holy Koran*
RdC	*Recueil des Cours* (of the Hague Academy of International Law)
Rev. Egypt.	*Revue égyptienne de droit international*
SCOR	Security Council Official Records
Trans. Grot. S.	*Transactions of the Grotius Society of International Law*
UN	United Nations

UNCIO	United Nations Conference on International Organization
UNCTAD	United Nations Conference on Trade and Development
UNDP	United Nations Development Programme
UNGAOR	*United Nations General Assembly Official Records*
UNGA Res.	*United Nations General Assembly Resolutions*
UNICEF	United Nations International Children's Emergency Fund
UNIDO	United Nations Industrial Development Organization
UNRIAA	*UN Report of International Arbitral Awards*
UNTS	*United Nations Treaty Series*
UNYB	*United Nations Yearbook*
VJIL	*Virginia Journal of International Law*
WHO	World Health Organization
WVR	*Wörterbuch des Völkerrechts*, eds. K. Strupp and H. J. Schlochauer (1960-2) (see also Bibliography)
WINS	*Die Welt des Islam* (neue Serie)
YBLIC	*Yearbook of the International Law Commission*
ZaöRV	*Zeitschrift für ausländisches öffentliches Recht und Völkerrecht*

Table of Cases

References to the following cases may be found either in the text directly or in the annotations on the pages cited.

PART I

A Historical-Legal Introduction

I

Introduction

A WELL-ESTABLISHED trend among Islamic States today is the full acceptance of and active participation in the United Nations system in order to promote the development of universally acceptable principles of international law. Even the basis of interregional co-operation among Islamic States within the OIC could be said to consist of well-recognized and established general principles of international law (see Chapter 3).

In spite of these developments, the recent political resurgence of Islam (in Iran and Pakistan) has conjured up a general picture of militant Islam on the march. Fuel has been added to this fire by work done by serious scholars,[1] who have always taken great pains to show that according to the classical Islamic conception of external relations, Jihad (legally defined as 'holy war') is the *only* basis of international relations between Islamic and non-Muslim States or entities and have compared Islamic with Socialist (Soviet) legal theories of international law.[2] Attempts by modern Muslim scholars[3] to show that Jihad is *not the only* basis of international relations between Islamic and non-Muslim States or entities have been termed as 'apologetic' in nature, 'sweeping' and amounting to 'no more than gratuitous and non-committal slogans'.[4] The problem is not only one of academic value but has serious practical implications if Islamic political resurgence means the application of a revitalized theory of external relations by Islamic States based on the concept of Jihad. That this would be the case has already been contended by Western scholars.[5]

On the other hand, it has been contended that the only option open to a Muslim State in international affairs is a secular one.[6] Recent political developments seem to indicate otherwise. The process of decolonization has inevitably set free the forces required to achieve political, social, religious and cultural rehabilitation of the total Islamic community. Political resurgence within individual Islamic States and Islamic 'solidarity' without are two sides of the same picture; contrary to earlier beliefs, held by some,[7] of an increase in secularism and secularist power in the Muslim world and driven by the urge to remain aloof from Super Power entanglements between Capitalist and Socialist countries, the Islamic States have, in the spirit of non-alignment, taken the first step towards creating a 'third force'[8] resolved to 'preserve Islamic spiritual, ethical, social, and economic values'.[9]

This study of the Charter of the Islamic Conference will pursue three major queries in order to establish a general international legal framework of inter-Islamic solidarity and co-operation and a particular legal framework of economic co-operation among Member States of the OIC. These queries are:

(*a*) what is the legal basis of external relations in Islam?
(*b*) what is the legal basis of inter-Islamic co-operation today?
(*c*) what are the salient features embodied in the legal framework of economic co-operation among Member States of the OIC?

Part I gives an historical-legal background to the theoretical and practical aspects of external relations in Islam, and we have countered contentions put forward by Western scholars by showing in Chapter 2.4 that Jihad is *not the only* basis of international relations in Islam. Some misconceptions about the doctrine of Jihad prevail, and by using methodological arguments and adducing evidence from the international legal practice of Muslim States we have tried to expose the critical errors to which classical Muslim authorities and, following them, modern Western scholars have fallen prey.

Part II, which deals with the substance of Islamic co-operation, begins with an examination of the Charter of the Islamic Conference in order to establish the legal basis of contemporary inter-Islamic relations. This is followed by an examination of those multilateral agreements which purport to establish a legal framework of economic co-operation among Islamic States, thus underlining the growing emphasis on economic co-operation and regional integration among developing states.

1.1. REGIONAL INTEGRATION AND ECONOMIC CO-OPERATION

The establishment of the United Nations Organization and the admittance of so-called 'new' African and Asian States to the UN has wrought tremendous changes in the structure and content of modern international relations which are 'reflected in more diversified patterns of modern international law'.[10] The quest for regional international co-operation and organization is one of the patterns which has led to far-reaching reorientation in the conception and study of contemporary international law.[11] Thus the developing States of Asia, Africa, and Latin America are increasingly favouring the development of international law on a regional basis.[12] The necessity of regional co-operation among developing states cannot be overemphasized. UNCTAD has continuously and increasingly stressed the importance of trade expansion, economic co-operation, and regional integration among developing countries.[13] This reorientation has led to a flood of multilateral and bilateral economic co-operation agreements and attempts at regional integration among Asian, African, and Latin American States.[14] This general tendency towards regional economic integration has been accelerated by the efforts of developing States to achieve 'self-reliance' and an improvement in their ever deteriorating economic conditions. The basis of such co-operation, however, is the legal and institutional framework,[15] built on common political, social, economic, cultural, and, perhaps, moral values.

1.2. ISLAMIC STATES AND ECONOMIC CO-OPERATION

The OIC, based on the Charter of the Islamic Conference,[16] is an expression of interregional co-operation among Islamic States. In order to lend impetus to economic co-operation, the OIC has worked out a set of multilateral treaties such as the 'General Agreement for Economic, Technical, and Commercial Co-operation Among Member States of the Islamic Conference'[17] and the 'Agreement for Promotion, Protection, and Guarantee of Investments Among Member States of the Islamic Conference'[18] to provide a legal framework of co-operation. The establishment of an Islamic Development Bank (IDB) in pursuance of the Declaration of Intent issued by a Conference of Finance Ministers of Islamic Countries held in Jeddah in December 1973[19] further augments the financial aspects of co-operation.

The study of economic co-operation among Islamic States in the field of public international law is interesting for several reasons. The Islamic States belong to that group of 'uncommitted'[20] Asian and African States which have challenged the 'traditional' law of responsibility of States for injuries to aliens[21] as a product of exploitative capitalist imperialism designed to favour investors at the expense of capital-importing countries.[22] These States have been fiercely vocal in supporting the call for a New International Economic Order[23] and in adopting the Charter of Economic Rights and Duties,[24] which contains some highly controversial demands on the part of the developing countries. On the other hand, the international legal practice of a majority of these states, as highlighted by their entering into a series of bilateral agreements[25] with some principal capital-exporting states to ensure a sustained flow of capital, is diametrically opposed to their attitude of confrontation in international forums, thus underlining their ambivalent stand on these issues.[26]

In the light of this it is interesting to compare rules governing inter-Islamic protection and guarantee of investments as embodied in the 'Agreement for Promotion, Protection, and Guarantee of Investments' with those applicable and (still) valid in contemporary international law. Do these rules reflect traditionally established principles of international law covering protection of foreign investments and expropriation or do they diverge considerably from them? In the case of diverging norms, do they create 'new' international legal rules applicable within an interregional framework composed of Islamic Member States of the OIC? These are the basic questions with which the subsequent examination of the legal framework of Islamic economic co-operation is concerned.

1.3. BASIC DEFINITIONS OF LEGAL CONCEPTS

Before we proceed further with our examination, however, a clarification of certain terminologies and definitions used throughout the text is essential.

1.3.1. The *Shariʿah*

It would be a mistake to assume that the *Shariʿah* (Islamic law) is a purely 'religious' law such as Canon Law or *Kirchenrecht* pertaining to Church matters, priesthood, and spiritual affairs. The *Shariʿah* encompasses not only religious duties and obligations but also secular aspects of law (substantive and procedural) regulating human acts; the first class called *ʿibadāt* (ritual) deals with purely religious matters and the second class called *muʿamalāt* (transactions) deals with subjects which normally form the substance of legal systems such as Common Law.[27] Since the *Shari'ah* regulates religious as well as secular matters, it indicates 'not only what the individual is entitled or bound to do in law, but also what he or she ought, in conscience, to do or refrain from doing'.[28] This leads to an elaborate value-scale attached by Islamic law to human acts comprising of five values; an act may be mandatory, prohibited, or indifferent; if it falls into the last category it may be simply indifferent, praiseworthy, or blameworthy.

Although the term *Shari'ah* generally means a 'course' or 'path',[29] the Koran uses the words *Shir'ah* and *Shari'ah* as meaning a clear path of commandments revealed to the Holy Prophet Muhammad or a law or institution prescribed by God revealing the right way or mode of action.[30] In the early days of Islam *Shari'ah* did not carry the specific meaning of law and Islamic jurists defined it variously as meaning performatory duties or as a sense of institution.[31] In contrast to *Shari'ah* the term *fiqh* (law) was gradually narrowed down to apply to legal problems and even legal literature.[32] Today the term *Shari'ah* is an all-embracing concept; it covers the basic tenets of religion (*din*) as well as law (*fiqh*). Thus the *Shari'ah* is the wider circle which embraces all human actions and *fiqh* is the narrow one which deals with legal acts.[33] Since the *Shari'ah* means the path laid down by God as revealed to the Prophet, the *fuquha* (jurists) expound and deduce the law by drawing upon the sources of *'ilm* (knowledge). Thus *fiqh* has been defined by a medieval Islamic jurist as 'the science of ascertaining religious commands (regarding practical affairs of life) by means of their detailed guides (sources)'.[34]

1.3.2. Sources of the *Shari'ah*

According to the classical legal theory the sources of the *Shari'ah* are the Koran, the *Sunnah* (model behaviour of the Prophet), *ijma'* (consensus) and *qiyās* (analogical reasoning).[35] Muslim scholars are unanimous on the point that the authority of the Koran is binding on all Muslims. The authority of the Prophet comes next only to the Koran because the Koran itself bestows legislative and interpretive authority upon the Prophet.[36] Thus the Koran stipulates obedience to the Prophet.[37]

Sunnah means 'a way, course, rule, mode, or manner of acting or conduct of life' and in the Koran, where it often appears, it means established course of rule, mode of life, and line of conduct.[38] *Sunnah* of the Prophet means mode of life of the Prophet or model behaviour which is to be found in the *hadith*, i.e., the narration of the life of the Prophet.[39] However, a widely held belief among Orientalists as well as some Muslim scholars is that the *ahadith* (plural) must be regarded as inventions and inauthentic.[40] These erroneous beliefs have been challenged and after exhaustive study adequately refuted by Muslim scholars.[41] Some *ahadith* may have been inventions or of spurious origins. This does not require us arbitrarily to label each and every piece of *hadith*, or in short the entire corpus of *ahadith*, as inauthentic and an invention. Each *hadith* stands and falls on its merit.

In addition to the Koran and *Sunnah* of the Prophet, the primary sources of the *Shariʿah*, there are *qiyas* (analogical reasoning) and *ijmaʿ* (consensus) which are auxiliary sources. These are simply methodological legal devices to help jurists extract and posit legal rules from the primary sources. *Qiyas* only conditions independent reasoning (*ijtihad*) which was a well-known practice in the various schools of Islamic jurisprudence. The difference of opinion which resulted from the exercise of *ijtihad* led to the necessity of instituting *ijmaʿ* (consensus). Both these auxiliary sources are interrelated and complementary.[42] *Ijmaʿ* was a mechanism to integrate divergent opinions either by evidence of universal acceptance, in the case of obligatory duties, by the entire community, or, in matters of intricate legal details, by consensus among the scholars.[43] *Ijmaʿ*, according to the classical theory, evolved in the process of time, and the failure of the classical Islamic jurists to provide organized machinery for its implementation is its basic weakness.

From the superficial description of the sources of Islamic law given above, one may, nevertheless, discern that Islamic law (*Shariʿah*), though divine in origin, is not immutable and rigid as it is generally believed to be. As far as norms are set forth in the Koran these are immutable. But the Koran is not an all-embracing legislative code setting out each and every norm precisely. In essence it is a divine message containing very few 'legal' (in the sense of secular) provisions. The *Sunnah* of the Prophet reflects decisions rendered or conduct followed by the Prophet in certain given situations. This conduct was, however, subservient to and in accordance with Koranic provisions and spirit. By exercising *ijtihad* within the general guidelines laid down by the Koran and *Sunnah*, the Koran and *Sunnah* have been extended and applied to fresh situations as circumstances arose which tested the interpretation of the text.[44] *Qiyas* (analogy) restricted the exercise of *ijtihad* in order to prevent contravention of the general Koranic provisions. Divergent interpretations were subjected to an evolutionary consensus (*ijma*ʿ). Thus a large body of rules incorporated in the *Shariʿah* are primarily deduced from the sources but are, in effect, man-made.

The *Shariʿah* does not, therefore, simply consist of 'Koranic' laws, a widespread misconception which often leads to wilful distortions. Just as the Koran is not a comprehensive legal code so it is not a compendium containing an all-embracing political or economic system. It does, however, lay down broad outlines,[45] supported by ethical rules of conduct, appealing directly to Man to act with reason and moderateness, righteously and justly. These ethical-legal norms restrict the development of political and economic theory within a general framework which could be labelled 'Islamic'. Attempts by contemporary Muslim scholars to define and posit theoretical outlines of an Islamic economic system and highlight various economic aspects of Islam[46] are to be seen as the exercise of *ijtihad* within the general framework laid down by the Koran and *Sunnah.* Erroneous beliefs that no such system could be specifically defined as 'Islamic' have been sharply criticized.[47]

1.3.3. Enforceability and Application of the *Shariʿah*

The Koran is primarily directed at Man (in his individual and collective capacity) and hence each and every believer tries to conform to its legal and ethical injunctions, even without imminent fear of compulsion by the State. Although enforceability is not an essential attribute of the *Shariʿah*, an Islamic State remains principally under the obligation to enforce not only the corpus of the *Shariʿah* (as far as legal injunctions are concerned) but also other administrative measures, ordinances and by-laws in accordance with the spirit of Koranic provisions and not in contravention of them. In a very early stage of political development in the city-state of Medina the 'rule of law' was acknowledged as a fundamental principle of State and administration of justice made independent of subservience to executive authority.[48] Thus even if the *Shariʿah*, in its application to Muslims, is a personal law, i.e. it binds individuals and not territorial groups and, accordingly, believers must observe the law even if they happen to be in non-Muslim territory,[49] it gains territorial application within the confines of the Islamic State. That part of the *Shariʿah* called *Muʿamalat* (transactions) would apply equally to Muslims as well as non-Muslims living under the protection of the Muslim State with the exception of prohibited acts and transactions of a purely religious character such as drinking alcohol or business transactions involving wine and pork which are solely applicable to Muslims.[50]

1.3.4. 'Islamic' State: Problems of Definition

In modern times a group of Asian and African States have emerged which are successor States of the Islamic world extant during the medieval age. These States are members of the UN and its multifarious agencies, and subjects of international law. However, the criteria which could prove useful in determining the 'Islamic' character of such States are controversial.

In the classical Islamic theory of external relations the world was split into two divisions: the territory of Islam (*Dar al-Islam*) and the territory of war (*Dar al-harb*). The *Dar al-Islam* was based on the theoretical concept of *ʿumma* (one Islamic community) *vis-à-vis* other non-Islamic political entities.[51] The concept of *ʿumma* inevitably gave rise to a controversy between two schools of thought, one advocating central authority and a unified Islamic State under one Caliph, the other arguing for a pluralistic community of more than one Islamic State.[52] The factual split-up of the Islamic world into more than one independent state demarcated by separate territory, population, and government gave practical relevance to the school advocating a pluralistic Islamic community.[53] The legal position of a territory, however, depended on the allegiance of its people to Islam, on the observance of Islamic law (*Shariʿah*) and custom, on the freedom of religious practice, i.e. Islamic rituals, on the regular holding of public prayers such as Friday prayers and *ʿīd* (feast-day) prayers, and on the prevalence of Muslim authority over non-Muslim subjects of State.[54]

The contemporary emergence of a number of Asian and African States claiming to be successor States of the traditional Islamic world and resolved to promote 'Islamic solidarity'[55] has renewed the controversy concerning the nature of an 'Islamic' State. A State may be defined as 'Islamic' in which Islam is expressly or implicitly declared to be the religion of the State.[56] Although a number of surveys concerned with the constitutions of some Arab and Muslim States do adduce evidence of constitutional incorporation of Islam as a State religion,[57] an exhaustive study of the subject would, because of reasons of unstable political and constitutional development in Asian and African States, hardly provide a definitive answer, far less a conclusive one. While some take the distribution of population, according to religious confessions, as a basic criterion for describing a state as 'Islamic',[58] others have suggested the list of States participating in the Islamic Foreign Ministers' Conference.[59] Whereas the criterion of population cannot be taken as the sole indicator of determining the point at issue, the suggested list of participant States inevitably includes some States which have a Muslim population of less than 40 per cent as 'Islamic'.[60] As the present examination is concerned with the legal framework of inter-Islamic economic co-operation and investment, however, reference to 'Islamic' States shall mean those countries which are Member States of the OIC.

1.4. *SHARIʿAH* AND THE ISLAMIC STATES

The ideals of Islam and the Islamic States of the contemporary world, including Iran, Saudi Arabia, and Pakistan, diverge considerably in various ways. It has been pointed out that Saudi Arabia comes closest to maintaining a 'pure' Islamic legal system,[61] a statement which would be vehemently contested by supporters of the Islamic Republic of Iran. The point overlooked by many ardent supporters of Islam, however, is that the rule of law, one of the main contentions of the *Shariʿah*,[62] is often ignored by the all-powerful state machinery in these States. This can only be explained by the fact that the latter are passing through a state of transition; in their search for political, economic, and cultural identity the peoples of these States are experiencing a phase of turmoil and structural change, in the aftermath of colonialism, the outcome of which is far from certain.

Colonial encroachment and the emergence of independent national States following the break-up of the Ottoman Empire at the end of the First World War has wrought tremendous changes in the application of the *Shariʿah* in the Islamic world. The modern period, that from the close of the First World War to the present time, could be divided into two unequal phases. The first phase which roughly lasts up to the early 1970s is distinguished by a trend of Westernization of law in the Islamic countries,[63] whereas the second phase, dating from the period slightly prior to the overthrow of the Shah of Iran and continuing into the 1980s, is marked by a trend of Islamic 're-assertion'.[64]

It is possible to divide up the States within the Islamic world into four different groups according to the legal policy and orientation followed by each of them during the first phase. Turkey, the only State rejecting Islamic law openly, followed a path of total secularization.[65] The disintegration of the Ottoman Empire led to the emergence of a number of Middle Eastern States called the modernist Islamic States led by Egypt which enacted codes derived from the Western world indicating Islamic law as a subsidiary source of law. This group could be contrasted with States of traditionalist orientation led by Saudi Arabia, where the only law applicable is the *Sharīʿah* (in the case of Saudi Arabia it is the *Hanbali* school which is officially followed) and where the sovereign is given exclusive competence on matters of public administration (*siyâsa sharʿiyya*) in a way that does not contradict the *Sharīʿah*.[66] Finally, the Islamic States of Asia and Africa previously colonized by the English and French retained the Common Law or Civil Law systems introduced during the colonial period after their emergence as independent states. This division of the prevailing legal systems in the Islamic world is reflected in its linguistic manifestations; Art. 13 of the Charter of the Islamic Conference recognizes Arabic, English, and French as the official languages of the Conference.

The first phase of legal development in the Islamic world was increasingly characterized by the modernization of legal systems on the pattern of Western models and the limitation of the *Sharīʿah* in a circumscribed manner to personal matters such as wills, succession, divorce, and the like.[67] Such a development had already taken place in Asian and African States under colonial domination where, as in the case of India, Islamic legal rules were retained in personal status cases involving Muslims.[68] In matters of commercial legislation the importance of the *Sharīʿah* was gradually reduced in proportion to the express promulgation of commercial codes,[69] enacted on the Egyptian pattern, which were a synthesis of Islamic and modern European legal principles.[70] In view of these developments the general outcome was thought to be the gradual replacement of the *Sharīʿah* as a source of law by codified (even secular) laws of the State.[71]

The second phase of legal development that started in the 1970s, however, has ushered in a critical mood of introspection and a review of the total, unquestioning acceptance of Western legal concepts. This 're-assertive' mood has led to dramatic events in Iran and certain developments in Pakistan[72] which are part of this reviewing process.

Kuwait set up a committee in 1977 'to amend and develop the Kuwaiti legislation in accordance with provisions of the Islamic Shariah',[73] and Saudi Arabia requires (since 1978) companies which opt for settlement of disputes by international arbitration to insert an express clause stating that settlement must not be contrary to Islamic law.[74]

Whether the *Shariʿah* would experience a total comeback or would be checked by so-called considerations of 'practical sanctions' is a matter which only time can decide. At present, however, Islamic law exists in the contemporary Islamic states in one form or another and can be categorized as follows:[75]

(*a*) an underlying corpus of principles applicable in the absence of statute or used to assist in the interpretation of statutory law;[76]

(*b*) 'modern' legislation which presents 'statutory' provisions of one or another school of Islamic jurisprudence, primarily in the areas of personal status (marriage, divorce, guardianship), inheritance, and *waqf*;[77]

(*c*) the jurisprudence of one of the schools of the *Shariʿah*, applicable in its entirety, as in Saudi Arabia;

(*d*) customary law followed in defiance of modern legislation, as in Turkey,[78] or followed with the acquiescence of the State, as in the Bedouin communities, and

(*e*) a parallel system covering particular areas of law (again, usually personal status) for a specific group of people, as in the jurisdiction given to the *Shariʿah* courts.

2

Islam and International Law

PERCEIVED from a geographic and demographic point of view, the Islamic States make up a sizeable portion of the world community. They could, if united in purpose, exert considerable influence and emerge as a political and economic entity to be reckoned with. Thus the recent waves of political resurgence in the Islamic world raise some fundamental questions about the attitude of Islamic States towards the present international legal order in general, and towards international law in particular. Does internal political resurgence among the Islamic States mean the reactivation of an Islamic theory of external relations based on the doctrine of Jihad? The general view in Western countries (which we have already mentioned in the introduction to Chapter 1) seems to be that a politically resurgent Islam would inevitably lead to a revitalized Islamic theory of external relations in all its classical ramifications, which could be comparable to the Socialist (Soviet) theory of international law. This view is, in our opinion, untenable.

In this chapter we shall endeavour to show that it is a misconception to believe that the doctrine of Jihad is the sole basis for external relations in Islam; that the centuries of interaction in the past between the Islamic world and non-Muslim States or entities on the international plane was based solely on unilateralism; and that by agreeing to conduct their relations with other States on the basis of equality and reciprocity, Islamic States have abandoned a fundamental, theological, and legal doctrine. Such a doctrine called for a refusal to recognize non-Muslim States as equals and hence subjects of international law, and it is thought that a so-called politically resurgent 'fundamentalist' Islamic State might seek to reintroduce it into its external relations. Thus our treatment of the legal basis of international relations in Islam (in sections 2.4-2.4.8) should be considered as one compact unit seeking to expose misconceptions about the doctrine of Jihad and the divergence between the legal theory and practice of Islamic States, which attempts to trace the development of the external relations of Islamic States from the time of the Prophet

Muhammad up to the modern period. For the sake of clarity, a brief comparison is made (in section 2.4.3.4) between the legal strictures on war and self-defence in Islam and the prohibition on resorting to force in contemporary international law.

Since the present study is also concerned with the protection of inter-Islamic investments, we have endeavoured to give a short introduction (in sections 2.6-2.6.4) to the concept of property and its legal protection in Islam and briefly compare rules governing expropriation of property and payment of compensation in Islam and international law.

2.1. CLASSICAL CONCEPTION OF EXTERNAL RELATIONS IN ISLAM (THE *SIYAR*)

The classical conception of external relations in Islam has been subjected to detailed treatment.[1] The classical conception, which was developed as a separate branch of the *Shariʿah* called *Siyar*,[2] only regulated relations of the Islamic State with non-Muslim States. The scope of the *Siyar*, it is claimed by some, did not include the external conduct of the Muslim State *vis-à-vis* other Muslim States, which, though falling under the legal definition of *Dar al-Islam*[3] (territory of Islam), already existed as separate territorial entities.[4] The relations between Muslim States were hardly subsumed under *Siyar* and thus could be termed as part of inter-Islamic relations,[5] based on a special relationship built on the concept of *ʿummah* (one Islamic community) and Islamic solidarity. Other authorities, however, are of the opinion that 'Muslim international law is not confined to the intercourse of Islam with other peoples. It also embraces the inter-Islamic relations.'[6]

2.2. SOURCES OF THE *SIYAR*

In addition to the primary sources of the *Shariʿah*–the Koran and the *Sunnah*–several other sources have been invariably used by Muslim jurists to construct the classical edifice of the *Siyar*. Just as the practice of the Prophet, preserved in the *Sunnah*, is deemed by Muslim jurists to be a material source supplementing the Koran, the practice of the first four Caliphs (Abu Bakr, Umar, Uthman, and Ali), generally known as the 'rightly guided Caliphs', is also considered an additional 'primary' source of the *Siyar*.[7] There are strong reasons to accept the practice of the rightly guided Caliphs as precedents of the *Siyar* and recognize their legal authority. These Caliphs, being among the foremost companions of the Prophet, were in a position to know his practice in matters of the *Siyar* more thoroughly than others. Secondly, they strictly followed the *Shariʿah* in letter and spirit during their own Caliphates, diverging from it only when strong reasons backed by legal evidence were to be found.[8] In contrast to the practice of the first four Caliphs of Islam, the practice of other later Muslim rulers does not possess, in matters of *Siyar*, such legal authority.[9] Acceptance of the latter-day practice of Islamic rulers and States is conditioned by their non-contravention of the primary sources.

Methodologically, the primary sources of the *Siyar* are followed by a number of subsidiary sources which go beyond the conventional sources of the *Shariʿah*.[10] These include treaties and agreements made by Muslim rulers with non-Muslims,[11] official instructions of the Caliphs given to the commanders in the field and other State officials,[12] juristic writings of eminent Muslim jurists embodying legal opinion on matters of *Siyar*,[13] arbitral awards,[14] internal legislation of the Muslim State regulating matters of the *Siyar* and unilateral declarations of the Muslim State with regard to *Siyar*,[15] and custom and usage.[16]

It has also been contended that the sources of *Siyar*, if interpreted in modern terms, conform generally to the same categories defined by modern jurists and specified in Art. 38 (1) of the Statute of the ICJ, namely, agreement, custom, authority, and reason, whereby the Koran, the Prophet's utterances, and the Caliphs' decisions and instructions represent authority; principles derived from treaties fall in the category of agreement; local practice is equivalent to custom; and juristic writings of Muslim jurists, consisting of independent opinions (*ijtihad*) based on various forms of juristic reasoning and analogical deductions, represent reason.[17] If, however, we examine Art. 38 (1) of the Statute of the ICJ, we find that the Court's function is to decide disputes which are submitted to it in accordance with international law by applying:

(*a*) international conventions, whether general or particular, establishing rules expressly recognized by the contesting parties;
(*b*) international custom, as evidence of a general practice accepted as law;

(*c*) the general principles of law recognized by civilized nations;
(*d*) subject to the provisions of Art. 59, judicial decisions and the teachings of the most highly qualified publicists of the various nations, as subsidiary means for the determination of rules of law.

From the wording of Art. 38 (1) cited above it is difficult to perceive any 'source' which could be equivalent to 'authority'. If it could be assumed that Professor Khadduri seems to suggest 'judicial decisions ... [as] sources of legal authority'[18] by the term 'authority', then the recognition of such decisions as 'authority' for the law is limited by the effect of Art. 59 of the ICJ Statute which provides that 'the decision of the Court has no binding force except between the parties and in respect of that particular case'. If, however, we were to take 'the general principles of law recognized by civilized nations', as constituting 'authority' in the sense used by Khadduri, then it must be noted that the 'source' appearing in Art. 38 (1) *c* is rather controversial[19] and is said to add nothing to what is already embodied in treaties and custom. At most, the 'source' mentioned in Art. 38 (1) *c* may be considered to be a 'reservoir of principles which an international judge is authorised ... to apply' but in the application of which the ICJ has exercised considerable restraint.[20]

Furthermore, if we may consider 'reason', as mentioned by Professor Khadduri, to be equivalent to teachings of the most highly qualified publicists of the various nations, it would be appropriate to note that these teachings are mentioned as a 'subsidiary means' of determining the law. At present, the role of publicists in international law seems to be diminishing,[21] although they probably continue to influence its further evolution indirectly.[22] In the Islamic *Shariʿah*, the juristic commentaries of text writers, as well as other utterances and opinions based on analogical reasoning, are considered to be auxiliary sources of the law which can supplement the primary sources, the Koran and the *Sunnah* of the Prophet.[23] Despite their methodological status as a secondary 'source' of the *Shariʿah*, these law books and commentaries, opinions and digests have, as correctly pointed out by Khadduri, influenced both the development of the law generally and the Islamic law of nations particularly, as this was 'derived from custom and reason' rather 'than from the other conventional sources'.[24] Similarly, the contribution of writers was much more important in the formative period of modern international law than it is thought to be today.

2.3. SCOPE OF THE *SIYAR*–PAST AND PRESENT

The classical concept of *Siyar* dealt with a limited number of subjects, such as the doctrine of Jihad, treaties, safe-conduct, etc., which were of a purely international character. Certain other matters, which would properly belong to the sphere of private international law, or conflict of laws, were also treated by Muslim jurists under the head of *Siyar*.[25]

In the past the classical concept of *Siyar* was applied, at least theoretically, to all matters appertaining to relations between Muslims and non-Muslims. A cursory perusal of the treaties 'Abwāb al-Siyar fi Ard al Harb' (translated as 'Chapters on the *Siyar* in the Territory of War')[26] by Shaybani (AH 132/AD 750-AH 189/AD 804), who is considered to be the founder of the science of *Siyar*, shows that it deals with situations arising from war, rights relating to captured persons and property, the treatment of prisoners and the wounded, contraband trade, principles of *pacta sunt servanda* and postliminy, peace treaties, and safe-conducts.[27] There are also discussions on the rights and obligations of non-Muslims permanently resident in the territory of Islam and the subject of apostasy receives detailed treatment.

Contemporary Islamic States have generally discarded the classical concept of *Siyar* and rules governing the treatment of aliens or non-Muslim subjects are no longer derived from the classical concept of the *Siyar*. Islamic States have joined the UN and have accepted international law as the basis of relations between States in the contemporary world. Even the basis of regional co-operation among Islamic States seems to be based on well-recognized and established general principles of international law.[28]

Islamic 're-assertion' could possibly lead to the reinstatement by Islamic States of certain concepts which have their origin in the classical *Siyar* albeit in a totally renewed form and context. The contention that 'classical Islamic theories of international relations will remain irrelevant and inapplicable to the actual conduct of Muslim statesmen'[29] has been strongly countered by others[30] with evidence of growing political and economic consciousness in the Islamic world. No doubt there has lately been an increasing trend in the Islamic States towards critical self-inspection and moves to 're-assert' Islamic values in order to check the secularist tide. In the sphere of international relations, however, the 're-assertion' of Islamic values does not necessarily mean the reintroduction of classical doctrines of *Siyar*; it is, rather, the reinforcement of general principles of law with ethical content.

Thus the value of the body of the *Siyar* and other general principles of the *Shariʿah* could be considered to be prominent in the area of comparative legal studies and the possible postulation of general international principles with a common basis. In a period of direct political and economic confrontation it is all the more essential that we seek a wider basis of authority for the fundamentals of the existing law and acknowledge the need for a reasonable measure of flexibility.[31] At a time when developing States in Africa, Asia, and Latin America are demanding structural adjustments in the international economic and legal order in order to accommodate changed political, economic, and social realities, it is all the more imperative to seek for a common basis of co-operation, and, particularly in the international legal field, for common principles of a general nature, in order to avoid the impression that the primary function of international law is to protect vested interests. It is, rather, the adjustment of conflicting interests on a basis sufficiently reasonable and broad to command the support of a universal community,[32] that is the primary function of international law.

2.4. LEGAL BASIS OF INTERNATIONAL RELATIONS IN ISLAM

Following expositions by classical Muslim jurists on the legal basis of relations between Muslims and non-Muslims, modern Western scholars have represented the doctrine of Jihad as the pivot of Islamic international relations and conduct.[33] Consequently, the objective of the *Siyar*, as defined by classical Muslim jurists and faithfully restated by modern Western scholars,[34] was to achieve the universal rule of Islam, and, thereby, deploy Jihad (meaning holy war) as an instrument of the Islamic State, whenever peaceful methods failed.

The claim by Islam to universal rule, and the subsequent legal development of the doctrine of Jihad as a state instrument to achieve this aim, has, however, been challenged by modern Muslim scholars.[35] The classical conception of *Siyar* has been criticized as reflecting the impact of socio-political circumstances on the understanding of jurists, particularly under the Abbasids.[36] Furthermore, it is argued that the development of the classical doctrine of Jihad was made possible because of the manner in which jurists interpreted the texts of the Koran and the *Sunnah*. If these texts are examined with due regard to the letter and spirit of what the whole body of the Koranic message represents and in the light of modern tenets, they could provide Muslims with solutions to cope with the needs of present international relations.[37] As a consequence Muslim scholars[38] have argued that certain Koranic injunctions recognize the equality of all mankind and try to show how far the *Shariʿah* accepts the principle of legal equality between States and peaceful relations as the *normal* state of external relations in Islam.

These theoretical attempts at evolving a modern Islamic theory of external relations have been strongly criticized by non-Muslim scholars.[39] The attitude of Muslim scholars is said to be ambiguous because on the one hand they depart from the classical doctrines of *Shariʿah* by reinterpreting and rearranging, and on the other hand retain the definition of Muslim international law as an internal law for Muslims in their relations with non-Muslims, irrespective of whether the latter accept its obligatory character or not.[40] These charges are, however, utterly baseless. They are based on the premiss that the classical theory of external relations, as developed by Islamic jurists of the Abbasid period, an inalienable part of the *Shariʿah*. This would only be the case if the classical concept of external relations is entrenched in the primary sources of the *Shariʿah*–the Koran and *Sunnah*. This is certainly not the case, however, as the Koran and *Sunnah* (as recorded in the body of *hadith*) are far from being elaborate legal codes.[41] Furthermore, since Islamic law is not a written law and its provisions are to be sought first and foremost in the teachings of 'authoritative' jurists,[42] every legal concept developed by them seems sacrosanct and gains the sanctity of *Shariʿah*, irrespective of its legal and ethical validity in the light of the entire body of the Koran and *Sunnah*. Thus misconceptions about the *Siyar* in general, and the doctrine of Jihad in particular, have misled and still mislead scholars into arbitrary pronouncements.

2.4.1. Misconceptions about the *Siyar*

As far as the classical conception of *Siyar* is concerned, the effort of searching for its basic tenets in the teachings of 'authoritative' jurists has been a source of great confusion for non-Muslim scholars. For the classical conception of external relations 'is found neither in the Quran nor in the Prophet's utterances, although its basic assumptions were derived from these authoritative sources; it was rather the product of Islamic juridical speculation at the height of Islamic power.'[43] As a matter of fact, the twofold division of the world into *Dar al-Islam* (territory of Islam) and *Dar al-harb* (territory of war) which, never occurred in the Koran or *hadith*, are an innovation of the Abbasid legists and thus reflect the realities of those times.[44] Other examples from *Siyar* also demonstrate the lack of a unified classical legal code[45] even in the early period. According to al-Thawri,[46] 'Fighting against the associators [meaning non-believers, i.e., those who associate others with God's Divinity] is not an obligation unless they start the fight, then it is an obligation to fight back.'[47] Early Hanafi jurists and others such as Awzāʿi[48] and Malik[49] have not stated explicitly that Jihad was a war to be waged against unbelievers solely on account of their disbelief (*Kufr*).[50] In contrast to these opinions Shafiʿi held that 'the Jihad, and rising up in arms in particular, is obligatory for all able-bodied believers'[51] and was to be waged on the unbelievers for their disbelief and not merely when they entered into conflict with Islam.[52] The impact of Shafiʿi's Jihad doctrine was a split between the Hanafi jurists into two groups, the one adhering to the doctrine that fighting was enjoined only in a conflict with unbelievers, to which Tahawi (d. AH 321/AD 933)[53] subscribed, and the other, to which Sarakhsi[54] belonged, accepting the Shafiʿi doctrine that fighting the unbelievers was 'a duty enjoined permanently until the end of time'.[55] The most appropriate argument, however, harmonizing the Koranic message and the spirit of the Jihad injunction, was offered by Ibn Taymiya[56] who held that unbelievers who made no attempt to encroach upon the *Dar al-Islam* would not have Islam imposed upon them by force for he said 'if the unbeliever were to be killed unless he becomes a Muslim, such an action would constitute the greatest compulsion in religion' which would run contrary to the Koranic rule:

> There is no compulsion in religion (*Q* 2: 256)[57]

Thus the idea advanced by some classical Muslim jurists and taken by non-Muslim scholars to be *the* 'Islamic' objective of external relations, that the *Dar al-harb* be converted to Islam so that the only peaceful arrangement between these territories must of necessity be shortlived, does not comply with the strict legal provision of the Koranic rule mentioned above. We shall, therefore, proceed in the following section to give a definition of Jihad and sketch out the manner of interpretation used by classical Islamic jurists to build up the legal edifice of Jihad as a holy war by citing Koranic verses on the subject.

2.4.2. Definition of Jihad

The word Jihad is derived from the verb *jahada* which means to strive, labour, toil, or exert oneself. The term Jihad thus signifies the exertion of one's power to the utmost.[58] Another conventional legal term, *ijtihad*, is also derived from the same root meaning to exert the faculties (of the mind) to the utmost for the purpose of forming an opinion in a case of law.[59] Hence, a Muslim jurist who exercises *ijtihad* is known as a *Mujtahid*, in contrast to the *Mujahid* who exerts his utmost in the cause of God.[60] The Koran uses the word *Quʿud* (sitting) as an antonym to Jihad (striving) to emphasize the difference between those believers who prefer to sit at home, risking nothing and receiving no harm, to those *Mujahidun* 'who strive and fight in the cause of God with their goods and their persons'.[61]

Fighting in the way of God, however, denotes only one aspect of Jihad which encompasses the struggle against evil in whatever form or shape.[62] In this context the Jihad against one's self (*nafs*) for the attainment of moral and religious perfection has been called the 'Jihad-i-Akbar, the greatest of Jihads'.[63]

In legal literature Muslim jurists used the word Jihad as a synonym for the word *qital* (fighting).[64] By interpreting the word in a narrow sense to mean a war to be waged permanently against non-believers, and by underlining the obligatory nature of Jihad for Muslims individually and collectively,[65] the doctrine of Jihad came to hold a central position in the exposition of *Siyar*. According to the classical doctrine developed by Muslim jurists, the Jihad had an offensive as well as a defensive character; the defensive type of Jihad was called *ribat*, meaning the safeguarding of frontiers usually undertaken by isolated groups or individuals settled on the frontiers of Islamic territory.[66]

2.4.3. Legal Foundations of the Doctrine of Jihad

Since the basic assumptions of Jihad are derived from the Koran and the Prophet's *Sunnah*, classical Muslim jurists, in expounding the doctrine of Jihad, draw upon several verses of the Koran to show evidence of the validity of their teaching. Confronted with several conflicting verses of the Koran on the subject they resort to the doctrine of abrogation (*naskh*), which holds that several verses of the Koran were of relevance only for certain periods of time and these were later abrogated by others.[67] Thus classical commentators made out five successive periods in the development of the commandment to wage Jihad against the non-believers as represented in the Koranic verses.[68]

Furthermore, Muslim jurists quote verses of the Koran by isolating them from their context and without paying due regard to the remainder of the text.[69] We have, therefore, elaborated upon these points to show that the doctrine of abrogation (*naskh*) cannot be applied to interpreting Koranic verses on the subject of Jihad and that the manner of citation of the relevant verses is in breach of fundamental rules of interpretation.

2.4.3.1. *Doctrine of Abrogation (*naskh*)*

Mention of abrogation has been made in the following Koranic verse:

> Such of Our revelations as We abrogate or cause to be forgotten, We bring (in place) one better or the like thereof. (*Q* 2: 106)[70]

This verse is to be read in the context of other verses which precede it and in which a controversy between the Prophet and the Jews of Medina is mentioned, whereby the latter rejected the Koranic revelation which supplanted the Law of the Torah. The most widely accepted interpretation of the verse cited above is that the Koran speaks of the abrogation of previous Scriptures and not the abrogation of any passage of the Koran itself.[71]

The classical theory of abrogation cannot be traced back to the Prophet as we find no information from the Prophet clarifying the existence of abrogated verses.[72] A serious bone of contention is that if the Koran is said to be eternal and its injunctions valid for all ages, how is it possible that some of its passages lost their practical value and were, nevertheless, allowed to remain posited alongside other 'abrogating' verses?[73] Furthermore, the Koran itself rejects the notion that the passages contained therein are full of inconsistencies:

> Will they not then ponder on the Quran? If it had been from other than Allah they would have found therein much incongruity. (*Q* 4: 82)[74]

And since we possess neither explicit nor implied authority from the Prophet regarding abrogated verses, what are the criteria to select them and who determines them authoritatively? With the death of the Holy Prophet revelation came to an end and no Muslim theologian nor jurist could claim to interpret the Koranic verses as authoritatively and finally as the Prophet himself. In fact, there is no general agreement as to which verses were actually abrogated,[75] and modern writers on the subject deny the abrogation of Koranic verses.[76]

2.4.3.2. *Interpretation and Manner of Citation*

The classical doctrine of abrogation is inseparably linked with the habit of out-of-context citation of Koranic verses on Jihad. The doctrine of abrogation enabled classical Islamic legists to argue in support of an aggressive doctrine of Jihad by citing such verses as:

Warfare is ordained for you, though it is hateful unto you. (*Q* 2: 216)

and

Slay the idolators wherever ye find them. (*Q* 9: 5)

without paying due regard to the condition imposed on the permission to fight as in:

Sanction (permission to fight) is given unto those who fight because they have been wronged. . . . Those who have been driven from their homes unjustly only because they said: Our Lord is Allah. (*Q* 22: 39-40)

By ignoring the causes of immediate warfare between the nascent Muslim community and the polytheist Meccans as explicitly stated in the Koran, and by totally overlooking the earlier belligerent state of relations between the Muslims of Medina and the other hostile non-Muslim tribes or communities living in Arabia, classical Muslim jurists argued for the establishment of the universal rule of Islam by deploying Jihad and quoted, *inter alia*, the following Koranic verse in support of their view:

And fight them (the unbelievers) until persecution is no more, and religion is for Allah. (*Q* 2: 193)[77]

Here the establishment of 'religion for Allah' has been taken to be the establishment of Islam in the world, if necessary by force. This is a typical example of an out-of-context citation of a Koranic verse and a misleading interpretation. We shall now give the full context of the passage from which the verse mentioned above has been isolated. Verse 193 belongs to *Surah al-Baqara* and forms the last of a number of verses granting the Muslims permission to fight the unbelievers.

190. Fight in the way of Allah against those who fight against you, but begin not hostilities. Lo! Allah loveth not aggressors.

191. And slay them wherever ye find them, and drive them out of the places

whence they drove you out, for persecution is worse than slaughter. And fight not with them at the Inviolable Place of Worship until they first attack you there, but if they attack you (there) then slay them. Such is the reward of disbelievers.

192. But if they desist, then lo! Allah is Forgiving, Merciful.

193. And fight them until persecution is no more, and religion is for Allah. But if they desist, then let there be no hostility except against wrongdoers.

From the full context of the Koranic verses 190-3 we perceive that permission to fight is given to Muslims against 'those who fight against you'. Muslims are not allowed to commit aggression,[78] and the ethical-legal sanction of this rule lies in the admonishing sentence 'Allah loveth not aggressors.' However, permission to fight is further qualified by reference to 'persecution'. It has been allowed that Muslims only fight 'against those' who have been persecuting them,[79] the reason being 'persecution is worse than slaughter'. Moreover, permission to fight the persecutors does not mean indiscriminate killing even after the enemy surrenders. Surrender by the enemy or the phrase 'if they desist' has a twofold meaning. The first meaning as set forth in verse 192 is the surrender to God, which is the acceptance of the Will of God and the recognition of the Prophet as His Messenger; in this case God is Forgiving and Merciful. The second meaning is laid down in verse 193 which stipulates that if the enemy desists, the Muslims are to cease hostilities. Only the wrongdoers, i.e., the transgressors and those who have committed excesses are to be punished. Religious sanction of these norms lies in the approval or disapproval of God expressed in such phrases as 'Allah is Forgiving, Merciful' and 'Allah loveth not aggressors'.[80]

It is clear from the textual analysis rendered above that the command to fight is not an unconditional one for a Muslim; he may not begin hostilities unless the enemy fights him;[81] he must cease hostilities if the enemy does. And the reason for fighting is to free himself from persecution. If the sole reason for fighting were to establish Islam's supremacy on earth, then the command to cease hostilities 'if they desist' from persecution tends to detract from the achievement of this objective through violent means. If we accept the phrase 'and religion is for Allah' to mean the establishment of Islam's supremacy, then total subjugation of the enemy may, at times, favour a more thorough achievement of this objective. It is, however, clear that in the context cited above the expression means the practice of religion free of persecution.[82]

As mentioned earlier Sufyan al-Thawri has held that Jihad becomes obligatory only when the enemy attacks the Muslims.[83] This is said to have been overruled by another 'authoritative interpretation'[84] which holds that verse 190 of *Surah al-Baqara* has been abrogated by *Q* 9: 5.[85] If, however, the latter verse is also subjected to a critical textual analysis and reviewed within the context from which it is usually dislocated, it yields similar results.[86] The basis of so-called 'authoritative interpretation' is weak as it draws upon the theory of abrogation of certain Koranic verses on the subject of Jihad for its support. But we submit that the doctrine of abrogation, as far as the repeal of certain Koranic verses on Jihad by others is concerned, is a legal fiction. In addition, the citation of Koranic verses out of context in support of an aggressive doctrine of Jihad is flagrantly in breach of the rules of interpretation[87] and totally repugnant to the spirit of the Koranic message.

Having established the fact that Koranic verses do not support the theory of Islam achieving supremacy over unbelievers by force or compulsion, it cannot be maintained that the Jihad, in the form of a permanent war, 'is a sanction against polytheism and must be suffered by all non-Muslims who reject Islam, or in the case of the dhimmis (Scriptuaries), refuse to pay the poll tax'.[88] There is no doubt that the institution of Jihad exists in Islamic theological and legal doctrine, and there is equally no doubt about its mention in the Koran and the *hadith* of the Holy Prophet. However, the precise scope and concrete application of the doctrine has, in our opinion, been a matter of great controversy and, perhaps, even misinterpretation. From the foregoing discussion of the basic Koranic provision on warfare it has become clear that the Koran does not sanction a state of permanent warfare against the non-Muslim world. Thus, in order to establish the precise contours of Jihad, it is necessary to examine whether the Jihad could be considered to be the *bellum justum* of Islam.

2.4.3.3. *Jihad as the* bellum justum *of Islam*

War has been the natural state of affairs in human society. Just as Plato called this 'natural state of war' everlasting,[89] the Muslim historian and sociologist, Ibn Khaldun (1332-1406), was of the opinion that war had existed since Creation.[90] The idea that a distinction between just and unjust warfare could be made has persisted since antiquity: it may be traced back to Aristotle who reasoned that 'against men who, though intended by nature to be governed, will not submit . . . war . . . is naturally just',[91] and the *jus fetiale* instituted by the Romans, which had to conform to certain rules in order to qualify as *justum* and *pium*.[92] In medieval times the doctrine of *bellum justum* was further developed by St Augustine and St Thomas Aquinas who justified certain kinds of wars as a means of solving the problem of a Christian participating in war without committing a sin. Thus, according to St Augustine, 'it is the wrong-doing of the opposing party which compels the wise man to wage a just war'.[93] In similar terms, St Thomas Aquinas, by citing the Bible (Deut. 20: 10) in support of his opinion, maintained that the (Divine) Law 'commanded that war should be declared for a just cause'.[94] Thus the Catholic doctrine of *bellum justum* stipulates several conditions in order to establish an objectively just cause of war. According to St Thomas Aquinas, three factors are essential: the authority of the sovereign by whose command the war is to be waged; a just cause, namely, that those who are attacked should be attacked because they deserve it on account of some fault; and a right intention, so that they intend the advancement of good or avoidance of evil.[95] Thus the essence of the doctrine is that war can be waged in self-defence against the unjust enemy or aggressor, for the enforcement of one's right, and for the punishment of wrongs; in all cases it is immaterial whether it is waged offensively or defensively.[96] This doctrine was further absorbed into the natural law theories of the sixteenth, seventeenth, and eighteenth centuries and consolidated by Victoria, Suarez, and others and finally secularized to some extent by Gentili, Grotius, and their successors.[97]

Islamic law prohibits all kinds of warfare except the Jihad waged in the cause of God.[98] Hence Muslim jurists have introduced a technical distinction between the words *harb* (war) and Jihad (Holy Struggle or War). Ibn Khaldun, who has noted four different kinds of wars existing in Islamic history, namely tribal warfare, feuds and raids, wars prescribed by the *Shariʿah*, such as Jihad, and, finally, wars against rebels and dissenters, contends that the first two are unjustified and the latter two are just wars.[99] It has already been shown that classical Muslim jurists generally interpreted the doctrine of Jihad as a permanent war or struggle to be waged with the objective of establishing Islam's supremacy in the territory of war. Since there existed no consistent unanimity on the question whether the armed struggle of Jihad was to be an offensive instrument or a defensive one to be invoked only on the actual encroachment of Islamic territory by non-Muslims, the controversy could be reduced to reasonable general propositions by direct reference to provisions contained in the Koran.

From the foregoing analysis (in section 2.4.3.2) of some central Koranic verses on the subject of fighting, it is possible to draw the following general propositions governing the scope and application of Jihad:

(*a*) that fighting in the cause of Allah is basically sanctioned by the Koran;
(*b*) that the permission to fight has been granted to the Muslims because they have been wronged or persecuted on the grounds of religion; hence warfare is permitted if Muslims are persecuted, because persecution is worse than slaughter;
(*c*) that sanction to wage warfare is, however, given against those who fight the Muslims; it is also conditioned by the stipulation that Muslims are not to begin hostilities or commit aggression;
(*d*) that fighting may be continued until persecution ceases or the persecutors desist.

Thus the basic assumptions derived from the Koranic obligation to wage Jihad in the form of armed struggle qualify it to be considered as the *bellum justum* of Islam because it is to be waged for a just cause as a consequence of some wrong or injury inflicted upon the Muslims; it includes the inherent right of self-defence; and it must be conducted in accordance with upright intentions and not for material gains or the sake of glory and power. On the other hand, the duty to wage Jihad, that is, a perpetual struggle against all that is evil and against disbelief distinct from armed struggle, remains.

The right to invoke and wage Jihad in the form of an armed struggle by modern Islamic States has undergone fundamental changes in the light of contemporary international law which prohibits the threat or use of force in international relations. It is, therefore, necessary to examine the scope of Jihad in the light of these modern developments.

2.4.3.4. *Jihad and the Prohibition of Force in Contemporary International Law*

The nineteenth century could be said to mark the abandonment of the distinction between 'just' and 'unjust' wars. For it was argued that international law had 'no alternative but to accept wars, independently of the justice of its origin, as a relation which the parties to it may set up if they choose'.[100] Although the right to go to war was considered to be an attribute of the sovereign State, as the doctrine of war as an ultimate means of enforcing legal rights, in the event that peaceful modes of settlement failed, developed in practice, States resorting to force did not generally rely on an arbitrary right to do so, but most frequently sought to justify the use of force on grounds of self-preservation, security, and necessity.[101] By the beginning of the twentieth century two diametrically opposed views competed to gain prominence: the first contended that war was not forbidden in general international law, and was, therefore, legally admissible as an instrument for altering existing rights;[102] the second, which was indeed a variation of the concept of *bellum justum* couched in positivistic terms, held that war, being forbidden in principle, was permitted only as a reaction against an illegal act.[103] Attempts to limit the right of war were made at the Hague Conferences of 1899 and 1907, but it was not until the end of the First World War that significant changes could be initiated. These changes, which finally led to the formulation of the prohibition of resort to force in Art. 2 (4) of the UN Charter, could be said to be chiefly reflected in the Covenant of the League of Nations (1919) and the General Treaty for the Renunciation of War (1928), also known as the Pact of Paris, the Kellogg-Briand Pact, or the Kellogg Pact.

The Covenant of the League of Nations[104] did not purport to prohibit war, but restricted the right to resort to war in some cases and, in others, made it conditional on the principal obligation to seek settlement of disputes by peaceful means. Although the Covenant did not restrict the freedom of action of States if certain conditions had been satisfied (Art. 12) or the machinery for effecting a peaceful settlement had failed (Art. 15 (7)), it did make war between States a matter of international concern (Art. 11 (1)) and imposed a legal obligation in Art. 10 'to respect and preserve as against external aggression the territorial integrity and existing political independence of all Members of the League . . .'. Attempts made to remove apparent 'gaps' in the Covenant on the regulation of the use of force by the 'Protocol for the Pacific Settlement of International Disputes' (also known as the Geneva Protocol of 1924) and the Locarno Treaties of 1925 were supplemented and superseded by the 'General Treaty for the Renunciation of War' signed on 27 August 1928. Whereas, by virtue of Art. I of the Treaty, the High Contracting Parties 'condemn recourse to war for the solution of international controversies, and renounce it as an instrument of national policy in their relations with one another', Art. II stipulates that 'settlement or solution of all disputes or conflicts of whatever nature or of whatever origin they may be, which may arise among them, shall never be sought except by pacific means'.[105] By the beginning of the Second World War, the provisions of the Kellogg Pact could be considered to have represented 'universal' obligations as those States not bound by the Treaty were bound by the Saavedra Lamas Pact of 1933.[106] Taking the practice of States between 1928 and 1945 and the nearly universal binding character of the Kellogg Pact into consideration, Professor Brownlie maintains that by 1939 an international customary rule to the effect 'that the use of force as an instrument of national policy otherwise than under a necessity of self-defence was illegal, had emerged.[107] Although there was some controversy about the question whether the Kellogg Pact also prohibited resort to force short of war, which has at present lost significance in the light of the comprehensive prohibition of the use of force embodied in the Charter of the UN, the assertion put forward by Brownlie could be supported without reserve.

The prohibition of resort to the use of force in contemporary international law is embodied in Art. 2 (4) of the UN Charter which stipulates that:

> All Members shall refrain in their international relations from the threat or use of force against the territorial integrity or political independence of any state, or in any other manner inconsistent with the Purposes of the United Nations.

Whereas previous attempts to regulate the use of force were concerned with the right of States to resort to war, Art. 2 (4) of the UN Charter represents a fundamental break from the past: in its comprehensiveness, the prohibition of 'threat or use of force' has brought about a shift of emphasis from the freedom of action of States to that of collective use of 'armed force' only in the common interest in order to maintain international peace and security.[108] The prohibition is regarded as a cardinal principle of international law possessing the character of a principle of general and customary international law binding even on non-Member States of the UN.[109] The inherent exception to the comprehensive prohibition of the use of force is that which is resorted to in the exercise of the right of self-defence. Art. 51 of the UN Charter stipulates:

> Nothing in the present Charter shall impair the inherent right of individual or collective self-defence if an armed attack occurs against a Member of the United Nations, until the Security Council has taken measures necessary to maintain international peace and security. Measures taken by Members in the

exercise of this right of self-defence shall be immediately reported to the Security Council and shall not in any way affect the authority and responsibility of the Security Council under the present Charter to take at any time such action as it deems necessary in order to maintain or restore international peace and security.

Art. 51 has effected some significant changes in the law existing prior to the UN Charter; first, an essential distinction is drawn between the right of self-preservation and the right of self-defence, the latter being embodied in Art. 51;[110] secondly, the right of individual self-defence is enlarged by including that of collective self-defence;[111] and thirdly, an individual State is not the sole judge to determine in a given case whether it is exercising its right of self-defence, even if in the first instance it invokes such a right by taking measures, as the primary authority and responsibility of maintaining international peace and security rests with the Security Council.[112] In practice, however, the controversy has largely centred around two issues:[113] whether Art. 51 restricts the exercise of the right of self-defence to cases in which 'an armed attack occurs', and, therefore, excludes the right of 'anticipatory' self-defence recognized in traditional international law; and whether, in the case of the ineffectiveness of the Security Council to take appropriate measures or otherwise, the right of self-defence permits a State to use force against the territorial sovereignty of another State in exercising protection over its nationals and their property.

Islamic States today have widely accepted the general prohibition of 'threat or use of force' in international relations, as embodied in Art. 2 (4) of the UN Charter. The question whether it curtails the scope and application of Jihad may be considered as follows:

(*a*) as the obligation to wage Jihad, in the form of an armed struggle, underlies the Koranic injunction 'not to begin hostilities' and the ethical admonishment 'Allah loveth not aggressors' (*Q* 2: 190), the prohibition of resorting to the use of force in contemporary international law does not represent an antithesis to the Islamic obligation of Jihad;

(*b*) since Jihad, in the form of an armed struggle, is a collective obligation, and its invocation lies within the authority, judgement, and discretion of the head of State or responsible State institutions, the Membership of contemporary Islamic States in the UN system and their undertaking to resort to force only in accordance with international law has limited the right of invoking Jihad to cases of self-defence;

(*c*) nevertheless, the 'right' to wage Jihad in cases of religious persecution, as expressly sanctioned by the Koran, or in cases of colonial oppression and self-determination, as interpreted in modern times, has been vigorously asserted; it is, therefore, necessary to discuss it in some detail.

In the course of the nineteenth century calls for waging Jihad in the form of armed struggle against colonial forces of aggression were widespread in the Islamic world.[114] Following the Second World War and the establishment of the UN in 1945, the decolonization movement gathered momentum and culminated in the UN General Assembly 'Declaration on the Granting of Independence to Colonial Territories and Peoples' (Res. 1514 (xv) of 14 December 1960). Third World States in general, and Islamic States in particular, supported by Soviet bloc countries, have generally asserted that resort to the use of force in the exercise of the right of self-determination by colonial peoples represents a lawful use of force, as, in the assertion of their rights, the colonial peoples are acting in self-defence. Hence this constitutes an exception to the prohibition of force in Art. 2 (4) of the UN Charter.[115] This viewpoint is usually rejected by scholars in Western countries[116] on the grounds that the application of the prohibition of resort to force, as embodied in Art. 2 (4) of the UN Charter, is comprehensive and absolute; that even the most widest interpretation of Art. 51 would not justify the use of force by colonial peoples; and to insist upon the right of dependent peoples to the use of force, in accordance with the right of self-defence, is a step backward in the traditional, pre-UN Charter direction of *bellum justum* (just war) and thus contrary to Art. 2 (4).

The stand taken by Third World States on this issue is an uncompromising one; in fact, they have not only insisted on the legal arguments and political needs of supporting colonial peoples in their struggle for self-determination, in practice they have always supported wars of liberation materially and morally. It is worth noting that whenever the Super Powers have felt their own interests to be at stake, they have usually joined the fray. The uncompromising stand taken by Third World States and scholars is based on the premiss that a colonial situation is an 'illegal' situation and, as a consequence, colonial peoples may legitimately resort to arms to secure the full exercise of their right to self-determination.[117] It has also been argued that colonial situations pose a threat to peace.[118] But the crux of the matter is that colonialism is not only to be abhorred and condemned morally as an obsolete form of exercising power in the international community, it is, in the legal sense, a kind of 'permanent aggression' against colonial peoples and territories.[119] It follows that peoples under colonial rule were free and sovereign prior to the advent of colonialism; that colonial powers subjugated them by the use of force against the wishes of the people; and that the struggle waged by dependent peoples against the colonial powers was, at the beginning of colonial aggression, and is still, waged by virtue of the 'inherent' right of self-defence which existed as a legal right even prior to the very formulation of Arts. 2 (4) and 51 of the UN Charter. An overwhelming majority of States have recognized the 'right' of colonial peoples to self-determination, and the language used in UN General Assembly resolutions, in spite of being hortatory and vigorously condemnatory, is unequivocal in its call for a speedy end to colonialism. The ICJ has itself determined on two different occasions that the right of self-determination is applicable to colonial peoples.[120] Indeed, as the Court had occasion to state forcefully in its 'Advisory Opinion on Legal Consequences for States of the Continued Presence of South Africa in Namibia (South West Africa)' in 1971,[121] 'The member States of the United Nations are ... under obligation to recognize the illegality and invalidity of South Africa's continued presence in Namibia.' Thus, the most pertinent question arising in the context of such a manifestly 'illegal' situation is concerned with the method of bringing it to an end. The ICJ further pointed out in its Advisory Opinion on the Legal Consequences Case (1971),[122] that

> The precise determination of the acts permitted or allowed–what measures are available and practicable, which of them should be selected, what scope they should be given and by whom they should be applied–is a matter which lies within the competence of the appropriate political organs of the United Nations acting within their authority under the Charter.

It is thus up to the Security Council to decide and take appropriate measures to end 'illegal' situations arising from colonial encroachment. The Security Council has generally failed to live up to its responsibilities, however. And since the Security Council, in view of its present composition and the power structure which bestows the right of veto upon some former colonial powers, is crippled when called to take action, hardly ever being in a position to take unanimous and effective action, colonial peoples have reverted to the exercise of the right of self-defence. It is because of the special nature of this problem that the 'Declaration on Principles' (1970) stipulates that it is the duty of every State 'to refrain from any forcible action which deprives (dependent) peoples . . . of their right to self-determination and freedom and independence'. For that matter, every State has a duty to promote the realization of the self-determination of colonial peoples. The OIC Charter confirms this stand by stating as one of its basic objectives the 'endeavour to eliminate racial segregation, discrimination and to eradicate colonialism in all its forms'.

2.4.4. External Relations between Muslims and Non-Muslims during the Lifetime of the Prophet: Origin of the *Siyar*

So far the discussion has focused mainly on the legal basis of external relations in Islam as expounded and developed by Muslim jurists under the Abbasids. Thus the classical conception of the *Siyar* was based upon the doctrine of Jihad which was said to have been, *inter alia*, deduced from Koranic verses. In our foregoing discussion of the legal foundations of the doctrine of Jihad, we have attempted to show that the deductions made and the assumptions drawn by classical Muslim jurists cannot be supported if the relevant Koranic verses are examined within their proper context. Our contention is, however, that the Jihad cannot be considered to be the sole basis of external relations; that several passages of the Koran explicitly support and encourage the maintenance of peaceful relations with non-Muslims; and, above all, the practice of the Prophet bears testimony to the fact that relations between Muslims and non-Muslims were not *solely* conducted on the footing of belligerency and war but also included peaceful relations. In order to establish this contention it is essential to trace the origin of the *Siyar* and its theoretical development and systematization. By doing so, we shall show that the divergence between the classical concepts of *Siyar* and Jihad, as developed by Muslim jurists under the Abbasids, and the practice of Muslim States is not only apparent in latter-day State practice but also in the early period in Medina.

In order to establish the legal basis of external relations in Islam it is imperative to consider the regulation of external relations between Muslims and non-Muslims during the lifetime of Prophet

Mohammed. For the Prophet's practice in such matters could be considered to be the origin of rules pertaining to the *Siyar*. Although the theoretical development and systematization of the *Siyar* flowered under the Abbasids, elementary principles and general rules governing Islamic external relations have existed in a rudimentary form since the very lifetime of the Prophet. The Islamic 'city-State' of Medina organized by the Prophet in AD 622 emerged in a society which already knew such independent States as Persia, Abyssinia, and Byzantium[123] and which possessed its own particular system of international law. The city-States and tribal confederacies of pre-Islamic Arabia also entered into peaceful, hostile, and neutral relations with each other and with the neighbouring States. As a consequence, certain prominent legal institutions, such as the system of escort, the system of alliances and pacts, the system of arbitration, the sending and receiving of legations and the laws of war,[124] emerged as part of the customary law (known commonly as *Sunnah*) of those times.

It has been contended that the Prophet was endowed with international personality even before his emigration to Medina as he enjoyed the passive and active right of legation and concluded treaties and covenants in his name and personal capacity.[125] Although in the past individuals were recognized as possessing international personality, in modern times the practice of States is evidence for the proposition that recognition of the individual as an international person is extremely restrictive, only given in exceptional cases. Following the Prophet's emigration to Medina, however, he may be deemed to have acted as head of the nascent Islamic State.

Arriving with his followers in Medina[126] in AD 622 (which dates the beginning of the Islamic calendar and corresponds to AH I (*anno Hijra*)) direct persecution of the Muslims by the Meccans changed to open hostilities. As long as the Prophet lived in Mecca, harassment and persecution of the Muslims by the Meccans was thought to be the internal affair of that city and its inhabitants. With the establishment of an Islamic political community in Medina, however, the situation was no longer that of persecution of a religious minority but the problem of extending recognition to another Arab city-State which came to be controlled by undesirable and, for the Meccans, politically dangerous elements. Failing to achieve the deportation of Muslims from Medina a state of belligerence ensued.[127] Thus began several years of incessant hostility, consisting of numerous skirmishes and raids carried out by both parties and several major battles, only temporarily interrupted by the truce agreed upon by the Meccans and the Muslims in AD 629 at Hudaibiyah. The Treaty of Hudaibiyah[128] may be taken to be a formal recognition of the Islamic City-State of Medina by the Meccans as the Treaty was concluded between two equals with acknowledgement of the Prophet's political power in Medina.[129] Violation of its provisions by the Meccans[130] within a short time of its conclusion, however, led to the conquest of Mecca by the Muslims in AD 630.

This protracted period of hostility gave rise to the adoption in pre-Islamic Arabia of some customary rules applicable in war which were then supplemented with some new rules that emerged from Koranic stipulations and the Prophet's practice. It is in this context that the prevailing customs and rules relating to the conduct of warfare were imbued with humanitarian elements such as prohibition of the killing of non-combatants (women, children, the old, the sick, and those living in religious seclusion) and the wanton destruction of enemy property.[131] The development of rules regulating the conduct of the Islamic State were not limited to warfare, however; the Prophet's practice also included peaceful relations with those tribes and political communities that were either friendly to the Muslims or chose to remain neutral.

The subject of peaceful relations with non-Muslims has been dealt with explicitly in the Koran:

> God forbids you not, with regard to those who fight you not for (your) faith nor drive you out of your homes, from dealing kindly and justly with them: for God loveth those who are just. (*Q* 60: 8)[132]

Furthermore, the Koran exhorts the Muslims to honour treaties concluded with those polytheists who remained peaceful or neutral towards the Muslims. Thus, after the violation of the Treaty of Hudaibiyah by the Meccans, the Koran proclaims freedom from obligation towards these idolators (i.e., the Meccans and their allies),

> Excepting those of the idolators with whom ye (Muslims) have a treaty, and who have since abated nothing of your right nor have supported anyone against you. [As for these] fulfil their treaty to them till their term. Lo! Allah loveth those who keep their duty [unto Him]. (*Q* 9: 4)[133]

Soon after migrating to Medina the Prophet embarked on a policy of entering into alliances with non-Muslim Arab tribes. Treaties of mutual aid and neutrality were concluded with the Banu Damrah, the Banu Ghifar, the Banu ʿAbd ibn ʿAdīy, and the Jewish tribes living in and around Medina.[134] The Prophet also 'gave his safeguard to the Christians of Najran, the Jewish Governor of Taima and prolonged a treaty of protection for Yuhanna, the Patriarch of Willah on the Gulf of ʿAqaba'.[135] The Prophet's guarantee (*amānah*) of protection to Yuhanna was given on the payment of the *jizya* (poll-tax) by the latter.[136] Thus the *jizya* came to be 'levied from the People of the Book as protected communities under a covenant (*dhimmah*), hence the term *ahlu'l-dhimmah* for the Christians, Jews, and certain others, tolerated under Muslim law and practice'.[137] The payment of *jizya* was not in lieu of political or military subjugation, however; the payment of *jizya* enabled the *dhimmis* to be exempted from military service and was exacted in return for full guarantee of protection and security.[138]

In conformity with Koranic injunctions various aspects of external relations, such as the laws of war, treaties, diplomatic envoys, and neutrality, had been subjected by the Prophet to the formulation of general principles, the rendering of decisions, and the adoption of customary rules as Islamic State practice. But the systematization of these rules into a separate and independent subject of study followed much later. In the earliest extant treatises and compilations dealing with Islamic law[139] the subject was treated under special headings, such as '*Kitab as-Siyar*', 'Jihad', '*al-Ghanimah*' (Booty), and '*Amān*' (safe-conduct).[140] Theoretical development and systematization of the *Siyar* is attributed to Abu Hanifah (d. AH 150/AD 767), his pupils Abu Yusuf (d. AH 182/AD 798) and Muhammad al-Shaybani (d. AH 189), and his contemporaries Malik (d. AH 179), and Al-Awzāi (d. AH 157).[141] It is in this formative period of theoretical-legal speculation that the doctrine of Jihad emerged to become the pivot of external relations in Islam. Latter-day Muslim jurist-theologians conformed to the classical doctrine developed under the Abbasids. In fact, Muslim jurists have continued to adhere to the classical doctrine of Jihad right up to the middle of the nineteenth century[142] without paying heed to the tremendous political changes which had already precipitated changes in Islamic State practice.

2.4.5. Divergence between Legal Theory and State Practice

The theoretical development, systematization, and codification of the rules of *Siyar* was undertaken by individual jurist-theologians who had established themselves as recognized and independent teachers and expounders of the law in large towns and centres situated in the Hijaz, Syria, and Iraq. Their pupils adhered to the basic doctrines expounded by them and succeeded in establishing various rites (*madhab*) or schools of jurisprudence.

Though the theoretical framework of the *Siyar* was derived from Koranic provisions and the utterances of the Prophet, the manner of interpretation and the doctrinal development supported by legal and methodological arguments rendered by the jurists left flexible room for expansion or critique.[143] Thus the exposition of the rules of *Siyar*, which is a branch of the *Shariʿah*, by Muslim jurists was dictated neither by the needs of the Islamic State nor officially promoted by it. On the contrary, it was the individual and independent effort of Muslim jurists of the second and third century after *Hijra* to expound the Divine law. The *Shariʿah* was deemed binding on the rulers of the Islamic State, but they were free to give preference to the opinions of any one of the prevailing schools of jurisprudence. In practice, the rulers deviated from strict adherence to the *Shariʿah*[144] whenever political self-interest dictated such a course. The theoretical development of the doctrine of Jihad by Muslim jurists displays a lack of appreciation of the international practice of the Islamic State which often entered into alliances with non-Muslim States or conducted foreign relations on the basis of equality and reciprocity.

Thus the mutual and friendly relations cultivated and maintained by the Abbasid Caliph Harun al-Rashid (AD 786-809) with Charlemagne[145] stood in contrast to the hostile attitude of the Islamic State towards Byzantium.[146] At a time when the Abbasids entered into an alliance with the 'Franks', the Umayyads in Spain, who had succeeded in establishing a rival Caliphate, pursued a militant policy towards their Christian neighbours and the Franks.[147] In expounding the theoretical legal framework of Islamic international relations Muslim jurist-theologians of the Abbasid era failed to evaluate these historical facts.[148] This divergence between legal theory and Islamic State practice was perpetuated throughout the age of the Crusades, during which military alliances and commercial relations were maintained with the Crusaders.[149]

Under the Ottoman Turks the so-called counter-crusade (Jihad) launched by the Muslims reached its final peak in the second siege of Vienna in 1683. This precipitated another European coalition (the Holy Alliance) against the Ottoman Empire that was strong enough to inflict severe military defeats upon the Ottomans culminating in the Treaty of Carlowitz (1699).[150] Thus Carlowitz marks the end of Ottoman expansion in Europe and the rise of European military expansion and domination of the Muslim East.

Peaceful contacts and relations between the Islamic rulers and 'Christian' Europeans (known to the Muslims as 'Franks') were maintained throughout this period, however, despite occasional military action. The growth of commercial relations between the Italian cities on the Mediterranean and Muslim Spain, Egypt, and Syria led to the granting of commercial privileges (also known as capitulation) by Islamic rulers to the Europeans.[151] The granting of commercial privileges by Islamic rulers was based on the Islamic legal concept of *amān* (safe-conduct)[152] which was, with a few exceptions, of a unilateral character. Thus commercial privileges were granted in the treaty of 1489 concluded between the Republic of Florence and the Mamluk Sultan Qaʿitbay.[153] In granting capitulations to non-Muslims, the Ottomans usually endeavoured to conform to the prescriptions of the *Shariʿah*.[154] Thus under the Ottomans Genoa was the first European power to obtain such privileges.[155] At the height of Ottoman expansion into Europe King Francis I of France sought an alliance with the Ottoman Sultan Süleyman I (1520-66) as well as a direct capitulation for France, and his efforts resulted in a Draft Treaty of Amity and Commerce drawn up in AD 1536.[156] Although the Treaty was never confirmed by Sultan Süleyman I, in accordance with the provisions of Art. XVI, he nevertheless reconfirmed pre-Ottoman French capitulatory privileges in Egypt and later permitted France to enjoy these privileges throughout his empire.[157]

It could, however, be argued that centuries of peaceful contacts and commercial relations between Islamic and non-Islamic States prior to the admittance of the Ottoman Empire to the European Concert in 1856 had led to the emergence of a body of 'regional' or 'Islamic' customary rules which provided the underlying basis of such relations. Consideration of international customs as a 'source' of international law has been provided for in Art. 38 (1) *c* of the ICJ Statute which qualifies such customs 'as evidence of a general practice accepted as law'. However, reference to 'a general practice' does not necessarily limit the validity of those customs within the context of 'general' and wide practice, but could and does include, as the ICJ has had occasion to confirm,[158] local or regional customs amongst a group of States or even just two States. Thus, in order to establish the emergence or existence of 'regional' or 'Islamic' customs underlying the basis of relations between Islamic and non-Islamic States prior to 1856, it is essential to show that such customs could be considered to have represented 'a constant and uniform usage practised by the states in question', which had become binding on the parties.[159] The application of such (modern) criteria to determine the question whether customary rules could be said to have been the basis of relations between Islamic and non-Islamic States in the medieval age is beset with insurmountable difficulties. To show conclusively that Islamic as well as non-Islamic States, by complying with certain common rules, followed them out of conviction of an *opinio juris sive necessitatis*, i.e., in the belief that such compliance amounted to legal obligation, is a virtually impossible task. Notwithstanding these formal obstacles, it could still be argued that regular peaceful contacts throughout the ages, whether on the basis of unilateralism or principles of equality and reciprocity, provided a fertile ground for the eventual development of a consistent legal policy applied by Islamic States in their external relations with other States. This legal policy, which was reflected in treaty relations between Islamic and non-Islamic States and which was based on principles of equality and reciprocity, could be said to have become a general and widely practised 'customary' policy by 1856.

2.4.6. Treaty Relations between Islamic and Non-Islamic States in the Period 1700–1856

The dichotomy between doctrinal aspects of the *Siyar*, as developed by early Muslim jurists, and the practice of Islamic States, as evidenced in the maintenance of treaty relations between Islam and non-Islamic States, became prominently registered in the eighteenth and early nineteenth centuries. The Treaty of Carlowitz concluded in 1699 was rapidly surpassed by a number of peace treaties concluded by the Ottoman Empire with Russia[160] and Austria.[161] The Treaty of Peace signed at Kücük Kaynarca in 1774, which ended a six-year war between Tsarist Russia and the Ottoman Empire, surpassed in significance all other treaties between the two States, fixing the pattern of their relations until the outbreak of the First World War. Art. I of this treaty, purporting to establish 'perpetual peace', reads thus:

> From the present time all the hostilities and enmities which have hitherto prevailed shall cease for ever, and all hostile acts and enterprises committed

on either side, whether by force of arms or in any other manner, shall be buried in an eternal oblivion without vengeance being taken for them in any way whatever; but, on the contrary, there shall always be a perpetual, constant, and inviolable peace, as well by sea as by land.[162]

Even if lip service were given to the maintenance and upholding of the doctrine of Jihad in external relations, the fact cannot be overlooked that the phrase 'perpetual, constant, and inviolable peace' which was to exist between Tsarist Russia and the Islamic Ottoman Empire by virtue of this treaty was everything other than the perpetual struggle (war) of Islam against the non-believers. Apart from peace treaties, the granting of commercial privileges to the European States by the Ottoman Empire,[163] Persia,[164] the Garrison of Algiers,[165] Morocco,[166] Tunis,[167] and Muscat[168] from the sixteenth to the beginning of the nineteenth century increased at an unprecedented rate. As a result of fierce competition and commercial rivalry between European States, a 'most-favoured-nation' clause, which had begun to figure in capitulations as early as 1580,[169] began to appear in capitulatory grants and treaties. These increasing grants of commercial and extra-territorial privileges to European powers proved, however, to be detrimental to the political and economic interests of the Islamic States. The growing military capability of Europe was used as an instrument of pressure against the already weakened Ottoman Empire and other Islamic rulers in order to maintain, extend, and even perpetuate the abuse of privileges granted.[170]

The Ottoman Empire gradually acquiesced to the conclusion of agreements with European States on the basis of equality and reciprocity in the conduct of its foreign relations. Internal pressures and external realities also led to efforts by Ottoman Sultans to introduce institutional reforms which transformed traditional structures of the State in a profound manner. In response to the disruptive impact of European powers and to keep pace with the accelerating tempo of diplomatic affairs, Sultan Selim III took, in 1793, 'the epoch-making step of attempting, for the first time in Ottoman history, to set up a system of permanent diplomatic representation in European capitals'.[171] The internal transformation of the Ottoman Empire had already begun to take place due to the impact of internal socio-economic and political factors long before the impact of European pressures from outside.[172] European influence only helped accelerate this transformation which, as we have mentioned above, had begun with Carlowitz and culminated in the Europeanization of Ottoman diplomacy in the nineteenth century.[173] With the signing of the Treaty of Paris in 1856 terminating the Crimean War the Sublime Porte (Ottoman Empire) was formally 'admitted to participate in the advantages of the public law and system (concert) of Europe' (Art. VII).

The Treaty of Paris did not change the legal status of the Sublime Porte as it had only a declaratory effect; it merely took formal note of what had already become a fact with the conclusion of the London Convention for the Pacification of the Levant in 1840 between Austria, Great Britain, Prussia, and Russia, and the Ottoman Empire.[174]

Thus the Treaty of Paris marks the beginning of the end of duality in the Islamic conduct of external relations. The dichotomy between the Islamic legal theory of *Siyar* and Islamic State practice finally subsided with the latter emerging triumphant. As we have already shown the diverging practice of Islamic States grew out of the political interests of the rulers and the necessities of the age. In our treatment of the substantive issues of the doctrine of Jihad we have attempted to show that appropriate and relevant Koranic verses on Jihad do not substantiate the coherency of the doctrine of Jihad as developed by classical Muslim jurists. We have also adduced evidence from Islamic State practice to show that peaceful relations with other non-Muslim political entities were not uncommon. The Treaty of Paris was for the Islamic State nothing more than a formal recognition of a well-established practice in external relations which could be traced back to the very beginning of the Ummayad Caliphate.[175] Thus the development of Islamic legal theory in matters of *Siyar* had drawn a full circle to come back to the Koranic reminder that Mankind is one community (*Q* 2: 213) and nations and tribes have been created so that we may distinguish one another (*Q* 49: 13). However, with the entrance of the Ottoman Empire to the European Concert and public law, the exclusive 'Christian' and 'European' character of the latter was finally abandoned.[176]

2.4.7 *Siyar* and the Evolution of Modern International Law

Though its roots go far back into history, the evolution of modern international law is usually dated from the rise of the European nation-state.[177] In fact, 'the history and practice of international law in the Eastern countries (like ancient India, China, and the Muslim countries) reveal some interesting and instructive anticipation of rules and institutions usually considered as the exclusive contributions of the Western nations'.[178] Claims by Muslim scholars[179] that modern international law has *inter alia* been influenced by, and is the result of, centuries of interaction between European 'Christian' States and 'Islamic' States have been labelled by others as a gross exaggeration.[180] Attempts on our part to support or oppose any contention would be a futile academic exercise as such assertions would be difficult to prove conclusively. However, if due consideration is given to the centuries of interaction between Islam and Christendom, not only in the form of conflict and competition but also in the context of cultural and educational transmission, one may go so far as to contend that such contacts could not have remained fruitless and without some sort of lasting impact or influence on both sides. If the exchange of general information concerning the norms and customs of both Islamic and Christian worlds was deemed to have been possible during the medieval age, then the diffusion of technical and other knowledge (concerning military institutions, tactics, and general rules of conduct during warfare) from the conquerors to the conquered was most probable. And since the intermittent struggle for supremacy between Islam and Christian powers in the medieval age led to alternating victories and defeats for both sides, diffusion of knowledge from an advanced and, for the standards of those days, sophisticated culture to a developing one was inevitable. Thus the assertion that the influence of Islam on Western 'founders' of international law was, in the given historical circumstances, highly probable does not altogether stand on weak assumptions.

With the rise of Muslim power in the middle of the seventh century and its initial expansion into territories traditionally held by Christian Byzantium in the East and Christian Spain in the West, Christian Europe learned, through fear of Muslim domination, to unite both during the Crusades and subsequently.[181] Thus in 1538, 1571, and again in 1684, alliances entitled Holy Leagues were formed to oppose the advances of the Ottoman Empire in the Mediterranean and in central Europe.[182] Military campaigns and periods of expansion were, however, usually followed by the establishment of peaceful contacts made initially for the purposes of trade, exchange of prisoners, and the sending of envoys. The main centres of Muslim cultural diffusion in the West, namely Spain,[183] Sicily,[184] and southern parts of Italy and its ports, functioned as focal points of cultural osmosis long before European Crusaders came into direct contact with Islam.[185]

Thus any consideration of the movement of ideas between Islam and the West and of any positive acquisitions made by the latter from Islamic law and legal institutions has to be made against this general background. It is difficult in this present study to give a detailed examination and list all possible Western legal institutions which might possibly be traced back to Islamic sources. But in the face of technical difficulties, such as lack of direct evidence as European writers of the medieval age rarely referred to their sources of information, a few examples might, perhaps, suffice to show that assertions of Islamic influence on certain Western institutions are not entirely remote and unfounded.

Commenting on law and society in Islam, the late Professor David de Santillana,[186] after praising Islamic law as 'immeasurably superior to the barbarous practices and crude formalism of early feudal law, with which its floruit was contemporaneous', asserted,

> Among our positive acquisitions from Arab law, there are legal institutions such as limited partnership (*qirād*), and certain technicalities of commercial law. But even omitting these, there is no doubt that the high ethical standard of certain parts of Arab law acted favourably on the development of our modern concepts; and herein lies its enduring merit.

In the absence of 'direct' evidence, Marcel Boisard[187] adduces weighty 'circumstantial' evidence to show that the influence of Islamic ideas and legal principles on the 'founders' of modern international law is far from remote; it is not only theoretically possible, but, in fact, most probable. In a detailed study, Theodor Landscheidt[188] has convincingly argued that the development of the *temperamenta belli* in European international law did not remain without decisive influence from Islam. It is against this general background of research already done on the subject and in the light of historical contacts that the 'probable' influence on the evolution of modern international law is to be considered. It has been contended that contact between Islam and Christendom, which also promoted a free flow of ideas and the transmission of ancient knowledge as well as an originality of spirit, had a profound effect on the development of ideas in medieval Christian Europe by such luminaries as Thomas Aquinas, Vittoria, Las Casas, and Suarez.[189] Even Grotius, who remained faithful to a medieval conception of public law, had knowledge of Islamic law as he was astonished to find the principle of postliminium therein.[190] However, evidence of direct Islamic legal influence may be discerned in parts of

Las Siete Partidas pertaining to the codification of rules applicable in armed conflict and the whole *Siete* itself is the first codified volume of laws drawn up in Europe under the patronage of the Castilian King Alphonse X.[191] Not only does the basic content of this document, which, *inter alia*, deals with considerations of a 'just' war, military organization, and rules applicable in armed conflict, sound like a Muslim treatise of *Siyar*,[192] but the Islamic principle of religious tolerance towards its non-Muslim subjects was incorporated into the *Siete Partidas* at a time when the Augustinian principle of *compelle intrare* reigned supreme in *Orbis Christianus*.[193]

Even if we may not consider the *Siete Partidas* of King Alphonse X, the *Arbre des bataille* written by Honoré Bonet and most probably influenced by the *Siete Partidas*,[194] and writings by Vittoria, Belli, and Gentili as codification or expositions of 'European' international law, they have, nevertheless, contributed to the development of the *temperamenta belli* of the European laws of war.[195]

Furthermore, several concepts of modern international law may be traced back to international relations maintained throughout the modern period between Asian and European nations which were based on equality and in accordance with rules of a 'universalist law of nations',[196] thus providing some evidence of a common basis of relations in practice. Despite evidence of such practice and contrary to the original idea of universality as propagated by Gentili, Grotius, Pufendorf, Vattel, and Bynkershoeck[197] international law was conceived by Western writers of the nineteenth century[198] as being of European and 'Christian' origin and hence limited to them. The idea of universality which faded and changed into an exclusive European concept after the Congress of Vienna started regaining its lost position with the entrance of Turkey to the European Concert in 1856. However, present efforts at codification and other developments in the field of public international law have lent support to the assertion that 'law in the large has a certain unity, and no body of law is an island complete unto itself'.[199]

2.4.8. Islamic Conception of International Law

International political realities of the age and the present international practice of Islamic States has given rise to modern Islamic conceptions of international law. Factually, the Islamic world may be split up into various nation-States, but in reality they have inherited the vast legacy of the classical Islamic world; Muslims, collectively and individually, have usually 're-asserted' Islamic principles in order to preserve Islamic values and way of life. It is in this sense that 'Muslim' international law has been defined by a modern Muslim scholar as 'that part of the law and custom of the land and treaty obligations which a Muslim *de facto* or *de jure* state observes in its dealings with other *de facto* or *de jure* states'.[200] Superficially, this definition seems to repeat the unilateral character of the *Siyar* as undue emphasis placed upon the word 'Muslim' State might tend to exclude a body of general legal principles which have gained universal legal validity. However, a closer scrutiny of the definition reveals that 'Muslim' international law essentially consists of the following characteristics:

(*a*) it is part of the law of the land in the sense of general positive law;
(*b*) which includes custom of the land;
(*c*) and treaty obligations;
(*d*) that are *observed* in the Muslim State's dealings with other *de facto* or *de jure* States.

These points require further elaboration:

(*a*) The *Siyar* is a branch of the *Shariʿah* and hence rules pertaining to the *Siyar* are part of Islamic law. This was specifically underlined by Sole Arbitrator Dr Mahmassani in the LIAMCO Award,[201] who pointed out, 'that Islamic law treats international law (the law of *Siyar*) as an imperative compendium forming part of the general positive law, and that the principles of that part are very similar to those adopted by modern international legal theory'. As a consequence there was never any hesitation among Muslim jurists about the binding quality of rules of *Siyar* and its obligatory character for the Islamic State. As far as the content of rules of *Siyar* were concerned, these were based on the primary sources of Islamic law and supplemented to a great extent by custom and the legal reasoning of jurists.

(*b*) Apart from the rules of positive law derived from the primary sources, Islamic law recognizes custom as a source of law which complements or explains contents to be found in various legal instruments. Several Islamic legal maxims read thus:

- 'Custom is authoritative';
- 'What is customary is deemed as if stipulated by agreement';
- 'A matter established by custom is like a matter established by law'; and

– 'Public usage is conclusive and action may be taken in accordance therewith.'[202]

Thus relations between Islamic and other States based on rules derived from customary law would be equally authoritative and binding in Islamic law and would be deemed to have been stipulated by agreement.

(*c*) From its very inception as a community the Islamic 'city-State' of Medina entered into treaty relations with other communities and entities. In Islamic law treaty obligations are generally regarded as contractual obligations which are governed by two fundamental principles: that the basic freedom to contract is guaranteed except in cases where such transactions are proscribed by the *Shariʿah*; and that all contractual obligations must be observed in good faith.

In accordance with the first principle, an Islamic State may not be a party to provisions repugnant to the basic prescriptions of the Koran and the *Sunnah*. This may seem to pose a basic legal problem, at least theoretically, in cases where the *Shariʿah* and the principles of international law may clash, but in practice the effect has been nominal if not virtually non-existent. For instance, a treaty of alliance supporting aggression could be said to be repugnant to the Koranic stipulation

And help one another in righteousness and piety, and do not help one another in sin and aggression. (*Q* 5: 2)[203]

Just as any consent to treaties by a State requires ratification through its legislative organs before it is deemed to have gained binding force, so the consent given to treaties by any Islamic State requires ratification, which is actually the proper place to examine the treaty as to its consistency or repugnancy with principles of the *Shariʿah*.

The second principle is concerned with the sanctity of contracts which is emphasized, *inter alia*, in the following Koranic verses:

Fulfill the covenant of Allah when ye have covenanted, and break not your oaths after the assertion of them, and after ye have made Allah surety over you. Lo! Allah knoweth what ye do.

And be not like unto her who unravelleth the thread, after she hath made it strong, to thin filaments, making your oaths a deceit between you because of a nation being more numerous than (another) nation. Allah only trieth you thereby, and He verily will explain to you on the Day of Resurrection that wherein ye differed. (*Q* 16: 91-2)[204]

Since Islamic law does not make any distinction between a treaty and a contract in civil or commercial law, as far as its binding force is concerned, such undertakings 'are viewed by Moslem jurists as agreements or pacts which must be observed, since God is a witness to any contract entered into by individuals or by collectivities'.[205] The Koranic stipulation to abide by treaties and pacts entered into by Muslims supersedes even the obligation of rendering mutual assistance to fellow brethren. This may be noted in the following verse:

> But if they seek your aid in religion, it is your duty to help them, except against a people with whom ye have a treaty of mutual alliance. (*Q* 8: 72)[206]

Only under special circumstances may a treaty be fairly repudiated. One of the conditions allowing for such repudiation is stated in the following verse:

> If thou hast reason to fear treachery from people (with whom thou hast made a covenant), cast it back at them in an equitable manner: for, verily, God does not love the treacherous! (*Q* 8: 58)[207]

Thus the principle of *pacta sunt servanda* is entrenched, as a religiously sanctioned norm, in the primary source of the *Shariʿah*–the Koran. In its international relations, an Islamic State is not only bound by the international legal norm of abiding by treaties to which it is a party, but it is also under the strict legal obligation to honour its treaty obligations in accordance with its internal laws which are governed by the *Shariʿah*. Hence, if an Islamic State has given its consent to treaties and conventions, it is legally bound to honour them in international law as well as the *Shariʿah*.

(*d*) The key to the interpretation of 'Muslim' international law as incorporating principles of general international law lies in the verb 'observes' used in the definition mentioned above. According to modern conceptions, Muslim international law is that which the Islamic State observes towards other States. So far, Islamic States have generally adhered to those established principles of international law which could be said to have gained universal acceptance. Continuous adherence to such principles may have been by virtue of express consent or tacit approval.[208] Islamic States have also observed customs, whether general, regional, or local, and entered into treaty relations with other States. Thus observance of 'Muslim' international law, at least in the modern period, is not based on unilateralism but reciprocity. This, in essence, puts in a nutshell the answer to all theoretical objections.

It may, nevertheless, be argued that, if Islamic States have accepted international law as an obligatory system, what is the essential purpose of designating such principles as 'Muslim' international law as there cannot be said to be anything specifically Islamic which is not common to other legal systems and philosophies? The explanation lies in the problem of ascertaining the basis of legal obligation in international law. The definition of those principles accepted by Islamic States as 'Muslim' international law underlines the Islamic philosophy and conception of 'law' as such, and the place of international law within that system. Islam subscribes to the theory of universality of law, whereby rules of Islamic law applicable internally and externally in the conduct of a Muslim State are part of a universal legal order. The Islamic theory is partly identical to the monist doctrine concerning the relationship of international law to municipal law in so far as the universality of law is concerned. Monism is not simply a theory of the relationship of international law and municipal law but rather tries to explain the underlying basis of legal obligation, i.e., authority and legal duty are alike subject to the universality of natural law.[209] Whereas the monist doctrine had its origin in the Middle Ages and Renaissance philosophies of the unity of Western Europe and was supported by the naturalist doctrine, Islam looks upon the *Shariʿah* (Islamic law) as Divine law containing precepts with universal application, i.e., for mankind in general. In Islamic legal theory, the *Shariʿah* does not simply regulate the normative relations between national and international law but also provides the underlying basis of obligation. The ultimate sanction of law in general, and international law in particular, for the Muslim State as well as individual Muslims lies in the *Shariʿah*.

On the basis of obligation in international law we find several theories offered as explanation: there is the classical positivist theory of consent (as expounded by Bergbohm, Jellinek, Zorn, Wenzel), generally known as the *Selbstverpflichtungslehre* (self-limitation), which is said to have been mitigated by the *Vereinbarungslehre* (as expounded by Triepel, Bindung, Walz);[210] there is Kelsen's 'normative theory' resorting to the fundamental assumption of a 'basic norm' which 'is not created by acts of will of human beings' but 'is presupposed by the jurists interpreting legally the conduct of states',[211] there are the natural law thinkers searching for an independent *Wertordnung* (value order) in the rational and social behaviour of mankind or in general norms of justice and morality;[212] and finally the sociological-political objectivist theories seeking to find the basis of legal obligation in the fulfilment of a community purpose or simply pointing towards its necessity.[213] Although these theories have been criticized as being unable to provide conclusive answers,[214] they have proved invaluable in providing an insight into the complex nature of international law and its basis of obligation.[215] At present, however, most publicists perceive in the practice of States wide acceptance and recognition of the validity of international law as an obligatory system[216] and have, as a consequence, abandoned the efforts of enquiring about the basis of obligation in international law.

Notwithstanding such developments, the positivist theory of consent still remains the most fundamental assumption of the basis of obligation in contemporary international law. This was succinctly formulated by the Permanent Court in the Lotus as follows:[217]

> International law governs relations between independent States. The rules of law binding upon States therefore emanate from their own free will as expressed in conventions or by usages generally accepted as expressing principles of law and established in order to regulate the relations between these co-existing independent communities or with a view to the achievement of common aims.

Recent changes in the classical positivist theory of consent have led to two major viewpoints. One, which is actually a variation of the classical doctrine underlining the sovereignty of states, holds that nothing but the express consent of the State binds it to any principle of international law as may be embodied in treaty or customary international law. This contention has generally received strong support from publicists of the Soviet Union[218] and the Third World.[219] In its proper implication the notion of consent would create the legal possibility for a State to reserve to itself the right to be bound only by those rules which it clearly accepts.[220] As a matter of fact, the so-called 'new' Asian and African States have basically relied on the consensus theory of legal obligations in order to reject some parts of 'traditional' international law.[221] Although a fundamental objection to this attitude may be that a 'new' State in asserting the faculties of statehood is actually accepting the existing structure and system of international law and may not, therefore, pick and choose the acceptable institutions,[222] in the case of the Asian and African States, however, it has been argued that since these States had usually risen from colonial servitude to political independence, the obligation to accept the structure and the system of that law which they find in operation at the time of their admission does not necessarily mean that every norm or rule of that law is sacrosanct.[223] It could not reasonably be expected of the 'new' Asian and African States that they continue to adhere to inequitable rules arising from a past colonial relationship in the wake of newly gained political independence and territorial sovereignty.[224] Thus the doctrine of consent, taken in its classical ramifications and as supported by the publicists of the Soviet Union and the Third World, does create the dilemma of each state exercising its right to withdraw from implied or presupposed consent.

The other version of the consensual theory of obligation in international law has found expression in the doctrine of 'common consent', which, according to Oppenheim and Lauterpacht,[225] 'can . . . only mean the express or tacit consent of such an overwhelming majority of the members, that those who dissent are of no entity in contradiction to the wills of its single members'. The doctrine of 'common consent' has been criticized for several reasons.[226] It is maintained that the doctrine resorts to a 'fiction' by assuming that customary law is actually recognized–expressly or tacitly–by all states since a customary rule is not observed because it has been consented to, but because it is believed to be binding. This is especially true for 'new' States which are not required to give express or tacit consent to customary rules already in existence, but their admittance is deemed to include 'the duty to submit to all the rules in force'.[227] As we have already noted above, the 'new' States have raised serious objections to this assumption. Another significant objection to the doctrine of 'common consent' emanates from the argument concerned with customary law, specifically that dealing with the principle of *pacta sunt servanda*.

A treaty is generally valid if express consent is given to it by the parties concerned. However, as Sir Gerald Fitzmaurice[228] correctly points out, a treaty derives its binding force not from the instrument itself 'but from the principle *pacta sunt servanda*–an antecedent general principle of law. The law is that the obligation must be carried out, but the obligation is not, in itself law.' Thus consent to treaties can create obligations and duties, i.e., rules of law, but it cannot create the binding force of the law.[229] If we consider the principle of *pacta sunt servanda* to be a rule of customary international law and, therefore, based on consent of States, it is not quite clear at what point of time in history express consent was actually given to this principle. Even the exponents of the doctrine of 'common consent' admit that 'the binding effect of that rule rests in the last resort on the fundamental assumption, which is neither consensual nor necessarily legal, of the objectively binding force of International Law.'[230] As Brierly also notes:[231]

> To say that the rule *pacta sunt servanda* is itself founded on consent is to argue in a circle. A consistently consensual theory again would have to admit that if consent is withdrawn, the obligation created by it comes to an end. Most positivist writers would not admit this, but to deny it is in effect to fall back on an unacknowledged source of obligation, which, whatever it may be, is not the consent of the state, for that has ceased to exist.

In reality, however, the principle *pacta sunt servanda* draws its validity from the fact that it constitutes and has always constituted an integral part of most legal systems, including those based on Roman law, the Napoleonic Code, and other European civil codes, the Common Law system, and Islamic Jurisprudence (*Shariʿah*).[232] It is, therefore, one of those principles which have been described by Art. 38 (1) *c* of the ICJ Statute as constituting 'general principles of law recognized by civilized nations'. Thus, a treaty is capable of having binding effect because of the underlying general rule *pacta sunt servanda* and speaking of a legal obligation as consensual means only that the occasion out of which it arose is a consensus but not 'intending to imply that its ultimate basis, the rule of law which gives binding effect to the consensus is itself consensual in character'.[233]

The problem of the obligatory character of international law is only one aspect of the problem of the obligatory character of law in general. This clearly manifests itself in the various theories concerned with the explanation of the legal basis of obligation. The answer to the problem cannot be provided 'by a merely juridical explanation'[234] but must be sought outside the law. Whereas Kelsen's 'basic norm' rests on a fundamental hypothesis, the explanation offered by Brierly rests on the inherent nature of man, whether taken as a single individual or associated with other men in a State, who 'is constrained, in so far as he is a reasonable being, to believe that order and not chaos is the governing principle of the world in which he has to live'.[235]

On the other hand, Islamic legal theory seeks a basis of legal obligation in moral and ethical postulates of a general nature as expounded in the primary sources of the *Shariʿah*, just as the natural law thinkers have tended to find an explanation in morality and principles of justice. This is why Muslim jurists have usually refrained from emphasizing any clear distinction between law and morality. Even

Brierly has sought to underline the interrelationship between the two on the premiss that too much emphasis on the distinction between law and morality tends to blur the intrinsic connection between the two because 'the ultimate basis of the obligation to obey the law cannot be anything but moral'.[236] Muslim scholars, whose duty it is to uphold the *Shariʿah*, would probably have no difficulty in subscribing to this view. Thus any effort to describe international law principles which are binding on an Islamic State as 'Muslim' international law and, therefore, an integral part of the Islamic legal system, is nothing other than the assertion of an Islamic basis of legal obligation in international law.

2.5. CONCEPT OF SOVEREIGNTY IN ISLAM

Consent to treaties and conventions is only given by virtue of sovereignty, whereby the State limits its sovereign rights and undertakes to be bound by legal obligations of an international nature.

In Islam sovereignty is nominally vested in God[237] and Man acts only as His vicegerent.[238] In real terms it means that sovereignty is delegated to Man who is to use this power on earth within the constraints of law. Thus for legal purposes sovereignty is located in Man which could find expression in the power of a single ruler or institution. In the classical period the power to exercise sovereignty was thought to have rested with the Imam or Caliph.[239] The reigning Caliph or Imam exercised the rights of sovereignty by virtue of delegation and his powers were limited by the Divine law. The people appointing the Caliph owed allegiance to him so long as he faithfully enforced the Divine law,[240] and rules in consultation with others.[241] Though deriving his authority from the law the Imam could not arbitrarily assert his power in an autocratic manner.[242] The ruler of an Islamic State is not above the law and hence violation of his obligations meant forfeiture of his right to remain as Imam.[243] However, classical Islamic jurists failed to indicate the legal machinery to remove such a ruler.[244]

The concept of sovereignty in Islam is not an absolute one. It is not based on the concept of popular sovereignty but is one of limited sovereignty. This does not necessarily hamper the State in its external conduct. In international relations the Islamic State may and does consent to rules of international law based on reciprocity. In consenting to be bound by certain rules of international law a Muslim State is in a similar legal position as any other sovereign State. Since by virtue of its consent the Islamic State limits its sovereignty and observes certain rules towards other States, it could be argued that the acceptance of international law depends wholly and solely upon the will of the Islamic State.[245] Thus an Islamic State acceding to the UN Charter accepts its provisions by explicitly giving its consent to abide by it. Once consent has been given in good faith the Islamic State becomes legally bound to honour the provisions not only in the light of international law as such, but also in accordance with the provisions of the *Shariʿah*.

As a corollary of its limited sovereignty, however, the Muslim State, as we have pointed out above,[246] does not possess absolute freedom to consent to rules or legal provisions which are repugnant to the fundamental tenets of Islam as embodied in the Koran and *Sunnah*.[247] This legal position may be contrasted with the 'positivist' view of the absolute nature of sovereignty in international law which is only qualified by the principle of 'auto-limitation' (*Selbstbeschränkung*).[248] Only in extreme situations and driven by necessity may the Muslim State acquiesce as long as the necessity prevails. This doctrine, aptly called the rule of necessity and need[249] and drawing sanction from the Koran,[250] is to be interpreted, as in the case of exceptions to the rule, cautiously, narrowly, and strictly. In contrast to the rule of necessity and need, the doctrine of public interest (*al-masalihuʾl-mursalah*) in Islam, also developed by Muslim scholars,[251] provides a rather unrestricted field of interpretation as public interest could also go against some fundamental tenets of Islam and thus legalize acts absolutely prohibited as falling within the interests of the Islamic community. The path would be opened for rampant legislation on unlimited topics which could be diametrically opposed to Islam. On the other hand, the rule of necessity and need would not restrict the number of subjects open for discussion but the manner of interpretation would have to take the general framework of the *Shariʿah* into consideration.

2.6. CONCEPT OF PROPERTY AND ITS PROTECTION IN ISLAM

The concept of property in Islamic law is central to our basic examination of the protection and guarantee of inter-Islamic investments.

2.6.1. Definition of Property

The proper subject-matter of ownership (*milk*) in Islamic law is not confined to physical objects but covers a wide range of ideas.[252] Property (*mal*) has been defined by Islamic jurists as 'that which can be hoarded or secured for use and enjoyment at a time of need or that to which a man's desires incline and which men are in the habit of giving away . . . and of excluding others therefrom'.[253] This definition, however, has been qualified by an additional condition of 'its being fit for the use and advantage of men and not in the power of the owner to destroy it'.[254] Islamic law does not permit the exclusive appropriation of certain things such as air, light, fire, grass, water of the sea, rivers, streams, public roads, common pasturing grounds, etc., which are for common use and hence non-disposable.[255]

Another criterion of defining property has been the application of taxable categories of property. Since Islam stipulates the payment of *zakah* (a tax levied on property) to the poor and the needy,[256] property was divided, for the purpose of calculating the amount of *zakah* payable, into three categories, the first consisting of gold and silver and the profits of trade, the second category being cattle and other domestic animals, and the third being agricultural and farming produce.[257] Property assessed for levying *zakah* had to be in excess of the basic needs of the owner and could be termed as that portion of property which could be called 'surplus wealth'. It has been held that in modern times the categories of property defined in the early days of Islam would have to be extended to include industrial machinery, banknotes, and profits accrued from the pursuance of various professions and trades.[258]

2.6.2. Concept of Ownership

There is a general agreement among Muslim scholars[259] that there is no place for the concept of absolute ownership of property in Islam as Man holds property as a trust, the true owner being God.[260] And because Man's position as trustee brings with it conditions of trust such as moral and legal constraints,[261] the institutions of private property as well as public ownership have received a fair amount of attention in Islamic law. Islamic jurisprudence treats definitions, norms relating to acquisition, disposal, sale, purchase, and inheritance of property in a detailed manner.[262] However, the most controversial differences concern: the central position of private ownership; the relative scope of public and private ownership; and the degree of social control on private ownership rights and the circumstances justifying abrogation or abridgement of such rights.[263] Some claim a central place for individual ownership of property,[264] others confine the institution of property to articles of consumption, living quarters, etc.,[265] while a third group regards individual, State, and communal ownership as three forms existing parallel to one another.[266]

As far as the scope of curtailment of private ownership rights is concerned, this is to be governed by public interest and for the social good.[267] A general consensus exists on the necessity of State intervention in order to ensure the fulfilment of the basic needs of each and every individual.[268] Some even advocate limits or ceilings on agricultural and urban property.[269] Despite Koranic injunctions on the sanctity of property and the explicit prohibition of devouring the property of believers wrongfully except by way of trading on the basis of mutual consent[270] or utterances of the Prophet to that extent[271] most modern Muslim scholars[272] have succeeded in opening wide the door of State intervention in the economic life of the Islamic State generally, and the institution of private property particularly, contrary to practice extant in the Islamic world during the medieval age.[273] This, however, may be seen as 'an irreversible trend reflecting the changing conditions of modern economic life which is becoming more complex and interdependent'.[274]

In the past Islamic legal theory did not restrict ownership of property to any selected group or class of subjects in the Islamic State. Although Islamic legal theory differentiated between Muslims and non-Muslims (*dhimmis*) permanently resident in the territory of Islam, the latter were recognized as subjects of the Islamic State and not as aliens. On the payment of an annual capitation tax (*jizyah*), which was exacted only from able-bodied males and ranged between 48 and 12 *dirhams* in accordance with their economic means, the *dhimmis* received a pledge of security and protection from the Islamic State, and were exempted from the payment of the surplus tax (*zakah*) and conscription.[275] By virtue of this pledge or covenant, which was of a permanent nature and could be said to have possessed the character of a constitutional charter,[276] the *dhimmis* were recognized as subjects of the Islamic State enjoying security of life and protection of property.

In contrast to the *dhimmi*, the non-Muslim alien could, by virtue of a pledge of *amān* (safe-conduct), take up temporary residence in the territory of Islam. Although there was some difference of status and privileges between the non-Muslim subject (*dhimmi*) and the non-Muslim alien (*Musta'min*), the scope of the pledge of *amān* was not significant for the protection of alien property and, therefore, requires further consideration.

2.6.3. The Scope and Application of *amān* to the Protection of Alien Property

The *Musta'min* was a natural person fully recognized by Islamic law as capable of having rights and being liable to duties.[277] In contrast to the *dhimmi*, the *Musta'min*'s status was regulated by the pledge of *amān*[278] with a maximum duration of one year.[279] *Amān* could be granted by individual Muslims as well as the Imam (ruler) of the State. Any adult believer, male or female, free or slave, could grant an *amān* to the non-Muslim which enabled him to travel freely within the territory of Islam during the prescribed period, own property, carry on business transactions, or pursue any peaceful purposes. Protection of his life and property was guaranteed by the State so long as he did not violate the conditions of *amān*. Even if the *Musta'min* died in the territory of Islam, the *amān* granted was still valid for his property and his heirs could claim it and, if they desired, remove it or its value from the territory of Islam. On expiry of the permitted period of stay the *Musta'min* could choose to become a subject of the Islamic State by paying the capitation tax (*jizyah*) and becoming a *dhimmi* or he could be safely conducted to the borders of the Islamic State in order to return to his place of origin.

The Imam or his representative granted *amān* either in a personal capacity or by virtue of a treaty (*muwadaʿa*).[280] The procedure of granting personal *amān* (i.e., by individuals), in contrast to the treaty, was a simple one; once the non-Muslim's intention of requesting *amān* was known, it could be granted by any word or sign, in any language and in any manner. Even an unintentional sign or word understood wrongly by the non-Muslim to mean a pledge of *amān* was held to be valid and irrevocable.

The usefulness of the legal device of *amān* in bygone days cannot be underestimated. It was important both for Muslims and non-Muslims as it served as a 'passport' to facilitate contacts and exchange of goods. Muslims wishing to travel in non-Muslim lands received a similar pledge of *amān* to pursue their journey without hindrance. The Islamic State meted out reciprocal treatment to non-Muslims in matters of customs duties, trade facilities, and other privileges. Despite protracted periods of war or state of belligerence existing between Islamic and Christian lands in the medieval age, and especially during the Crusades and after, Muslim and non-Muslim traders and other travellers used the device of *amān* to promote and maintain some sort of trade and cultural relations. *Amān* could be cancelled on the authority of the Imam if the *Musta'min* failed to comply with terms of the *amān* or acted in a manner harmful or dangerous to Islamic interests. Penal offences were, however, no grounds for cancellation of *amān* as the offending *Musta'min* could be prosecuted in the Islamic courts. Even the resumption of active hostilities between the Islamic State and the *Musta'min*'s State of origin was no reason to declare him an 'enemy alien', cancel his *amān*, and confiscate his property so long as he did not openly help the enemy. In this case 'assistance' would, *inter alia*, mean spying for the enemy or exporting weapons, war materials, goods, and war animals to strengthen the enemy.

The extent and far-reaching nature of the provisions of *amān* can be seen from a recent decision rendered by the High Court of Pakistan[281] which applied the classical concept of *amān* as part of the body of the *Sharīʿah*, in addition to the express statutory provisions which failed to cover the facts of the case adequately. Thus the Pakistan High Court referred to a body of *Sharīʿah* rules as a subsidiary source of law in a case where the statutory provisions were limited in scope. The outbreak of war between India and Pakistan in 1965 led to the proclamation of a state of emergency in Pakistan which resulted in the confiscation of property belonging to 'enemy aliens'. The State Bank of India, having succeeded the Imperial Bank of India, which had acquired 'rights and assets' in the territory of Pakistan before the partition of British India in 1947, claimed the aforementioned by suing the Custodian of Evacuee Property, who had, in the meantime, become legally responsible for the administration of these 'rights and assets'. However, by virtue of 'Emergency laws' passed in 1965 the lower court found the State Bank of India as falling under the definition of 'alien enemy' and thus possessing 'no *locus standi* to prosecute and continue the writ petitions'.[282] On appeal, the High Court of Pakistan reversed the decision of the lower court and, applying 'the law of war and peace with special reference to enemy subjects' in Islamic jurisprudence, held that *amān* 'is a pledge of security by virtue of which an enemy alien would be entitled to protection, while he is in the *dar al-Islam* (territory of Islam)'; that 'no procedural technicality can take away the rights of a *Musta'min*';[283] and 'that enemy aliens when under express or implied *amān* cannot be deprived of their rights as to property and to deal with it . . . subject, of course, to the condition that the exercise of such rights does not directly or indirectly add to the war potential of the enemy'.[284] The Court ruled that the State Bank of India had the status of a *Musta'min* and without having violated the conditions of *amān* possessed *locus standi* to prosecute and continue the writ petitions.

The importance of this decision lies not only in the remarkable application of classical concepts of *Siyar* in modern times [285] but also in the manner in which statutory provisions have been glossed over and supplemented by Islamic legal provisions which are wider in their application, providing a far better protection for the individual against arbitrary acts of the State than those Common Law concepts prevailing in the legal system. After the partition of British India into two independent and sovereign States, namely, India and Pakistan, the 'rights and assets' of the Imperial Bank of India situated in the territory of Pakistan were taken over and administered by the Custodian of Evacuee Property only on the abandonment of these (rights and assets) by the employees of the Imperial Bank and their flight to India. At the time of reclamation by the State Bank of India, the Pakistan Government, relying on the strength of 'Emergency' laws, refused to grant the Bank's request and deemed the position of the Bank to be that of a non-resident and enemy alien. That the High Court of Pakistan held the State Bank of India to be a *Musta'min* and thus entitled to enjoy all the rights appertaining to that status, although it was never expressly granted an *amān* by the Government of Pakistan, is a proof of the wide latitude of the concept of *amān*. The Court relied on the fact that since the State Bank of India was a successor of the Imperial Bank of India, acquisition of assets by the latter in the territory of Pakistan and its status therein prior to partition were automatically transferred to its successor. In this case the State Bank of India enjoyed the benefits of an implied *amān* and could be defined as a *Musta'min.*

The significance of this decision also lies in the fact that Islamic law is still considered part and parcel of the law of the land and may even override statutory provisions in order to fill in gaps. Even in situations of conflict, where statutory provisions fail to provide adequate protection to the weaker party and the rules of *Shariʿah* cover the case, it seems that the latter would triumph.[286]

2.6.4. Expropriation and Payment of Compensation

In Islamic legal theory the right of property ownership and its inviolable character is based, *inter alia*, on the following Koranic verse:

> And eat not up your property among yourselves in vanity, nor seek by it to gain the hearing of the judges that ye may knowingly devour a portion of the property of others wrongfully. (*Q* 2: 188)[287]

The Koranic injunction expressly prohibits 'wrongful' appropriation of property belonging to others and its squandering in vanity. The general rule articulated by Muslim jurists has found expression in Art. 97 of the Ottoman Majallah Code which states:[288]

> One is not allowed to take another's property without legal cause.

As we have already noted elsewhere (see 2.6.2) the jurisdiction of the Islamic State to interfere with private property and set limits to it whenever public interest for the social good or public benefit of the Islamic community demands, has been generally conceded by Muslim scholars. The legal basis of interference with private property is said to be justified under the *Shariʿah* rule:

> Private damage has to be suffered in order to fend off public damage.[289]

This overriding right of the Islamic State to interfere with private property has to conform to other general principles of the *Shariʿah*, however, and cannot be invoked in an arbitrary manner. The general rule, in cases where private owners of property are deemed to have been expropriated with a 'legal cause', is that such 'harm is not to be removed by harm'.[290]

Thus the originally 'harmful' act, i.e., the expropriation of private property, is rendered permissible under two conditions:

(*a*) that these acts are deemed beneficial for the community and hence undertaken in the public interest;
(*b*) that expropriationary acts, i.e., the legally permissible 'harmful' acts, are 'not removed by harm'.

It is only in this sense that Islamic law regards the act of expropriation as a 'compulsory sale' (*ikrah hukmi*).[291] Thus Islamic law recognizes the obligation to pay compensation in lieu of property expropriated. However, a general right of confiscation by the State without payment of compensation exists in cases of wrongful acquisition of property by individuals.[292]

It is also essential to distinguish between expropriation of private property and the abrogation of 'concessionary rights' bestowed by the State upon private persons for the exploitation of public property. Islamic law generally recognizes the jurisdiction of the State over its territory and what lies above it and below it.[293] It does, however, distinguish between physical objects which are intended for common use and those which have not been secured as property, such as waste land (*mawat*), game (*sayd*, i.e., animals in a state of nature), fish in the sea, river, or deep tank, trees of forests, etc., and, therefore, open to the use of all.[294] These objects of nature, generally called *mubahat* (or *res nullius*), may be secured by any man as his property by the employment of skill or labour. Thus waste land, which does not belong to any community (village, or other local institution), may be secured as private property by any one who revives it (*yahi*) with the sanction of the head of the State.[295] In the case of natural resources (such as mines, and other underground resources) which are not to be found on the premises of private owners of land,[296] it is generally agreed that these are owned by the entire community of Muslims, and hence property of the State.[297] It is, therefore, questionable whether, by authorizing private persons (whether natural or juridical, national or alien) to exploit natural resources, the State could be considered to have transferred 'ownership' of the resources to the concessionaire or simply contracted to transfer certain 'incorporeal' property rights.

In the ARAMCO Arbitration,[298] the Tribunal, after considering the fact that the concessionaire's (Aramco) 'right of ownership in the oil it extracts and the oil derivatives it produces is not expressly mentioned in the 1933 Concession Agreement'[299] and further referring to certain correspondence in which the Government of Saudi Arabia was said to have recognized this very 'right of ownership', came to the conclusion that 'in Saudi Arabian law as in the laws of Western Countries, the oil concession is an institution which implies an authorization by the State, on the basis of a statute or of a contract, and necessarily entails the grant to the concessionaire of property rights in oil'.[300] This conclusion of the Aramco Tribunal may, however, be contrasted with the opinion of Sole Arbitrator Lagergren in the BP Award,[301] who expressed doubts about the Claimant's (i.e. British Petroleum) contention of 'ownership' in oil extracted from the area of the Concession Agreement before and after the nationalization as 'the fact that ownership of the oil in its natural strata is vested in the State of Libya under the Petroleum Law of 1955 does not argue in favour of the Claimant'.[302] Further clarification may be sought by reference to the LIAMCO Award in which Sole Arbitrator Mahmassani expressed the view that 'Concession rights, as those of the present dispute, may be included under the class of incorporeal property.'[303] In Islamic law 'incorporeal' property rights are recognized as *Manfaʿah* (benefice, usufruct) and also classified by some under *ijara* contracts.[304] Hence it is arguable that the nationalization of such (incorporeal) property rights belonging to a concessionaire cannot be termed, strictly speaking, an act of expropriation as the real ownership of the resources lies in the community as represented by the State. If, in asserting its rights of ownership and in the exercise of its unilateral act of sovereignty, an Islamic State abrogates or terminates rights of the concessionaire, it commits a breach of the terms of the concessionary contract. For the nature of such concessionary rights is essentially contractual. This was confirmed by the Tribunal in the ARAMCO Arbitration which held that: 'Aramco's Concession must be considered as an "unnominated" contract *sui generis*. This conception of Saudi Arabian law is related to that which is accepted in many other civilized States, but with one distinctive feature: the contractual character of the concession in Saudi Arabian law is unquestionable.'[305]

Even if under certain legal systems such concession contracts could be considered to be 'administrative contracts',[306] the essential consequence of breach or premature termination of such contractual obligations is indemnification or damages,[307] and cannot be considered to be a restitution of those rights abrogated, as public interest overrides purely private interest. Thus violation of contractual obligations which are committed by the State under the compulsion of necessity and within the public interest cannot be considered to be an expropriation of ownership of property, which is in any case vested in the State, but a breach of a private contract in the form of a premature termination of a concessionary contract that entails the obligation to pay compensation.

On the question whether the Islamic State is under a legal obligation to pay compensation in cases of expropriation, the difference of opinion is not one of principle but of degree: some declare it to be 'just compensation';[308] others call it 'suitable compensation';[309] and still others label it 'due compensation'.[310] All these definitions fail to consider whether compensation due includes loss of profits (*lucrum cessans*) which might have accrued to the owner in the absence of expropriation or breach of contract. However, in the classical teachings of some leading expounders of Islamic law the quantum of damages due in cases of wrongful expropriation or usurpation (*ghasb*) included pecuniary valuation of incorporeal property rights or the value of any beneficial use (*manfaʿah*) which may have accrued if the contract had not been prematurely terminated, or property expropriated.[311] Even if expropriation is justified under the heads of public interest and social good of the community, the principle of compensatory payment for property taken cannot be denied. In fact, modern Islamic States have not denied outright the duty to pay compensation in lieu of expropriation or nationalization of alien property.[312] These States have, however, disputed over the actual amount to be paid and have generally refused to comply with the obligation of compensatory payment in an effective manner. In any case, the amount of compensation would have to revolve around the value of property taken in order to be 'just' and 'due'. Since 'harm cannot be removed by the infliction of harm' compensation payable for property taken cannot be less than what is fair and equitable.

In international law the subject of expropriation of property has received extensive treatment. The term 'expropriation' is understood to mean a compulsory acquisition or 'taking' of property by the State.[313] It inevitably includes all types of 'takings', such as nationalizations or requisitioning of private property by the State.[314]

The principle that every State possesses the sovereign right of expropriating property, whether belonging to its own or foreign nationals, situated within its territorial jurisdiction does not seem to have been firmly established at the beginning of the twentieth century. Whereas in 1926 in the Certain German Interests in Polish Upper Silesia Case,[315] the PCIJ acknowledged that 'expropriation for reasons of public utility, judicial liquidation and similar reasons' was permissible in international law, in the Chorzow Factory Case,[316] the Court considering the Polish act of expropriation to be in violation of the Geneva Convention of 1922, insisted that the action 'is a seizure of property rights and interests which could not be expropriated even against compensation', and, as a consequence, the reparation to be paid 'must, as far as possible, wipe out all the consequences of the illegal act and reestablish the situation which would, in all probability, have existed if that act had not been committed'. The basic legal propositions that may be deduced from these pronouncements are: that foreign-owned property cannot be 'taken' except for reasons of public utility;[317] that property taken for reasons other than public utility and in violation of treaty provisions are illegal acts; that the appropriate remedy for 'illegal' acts of expropriation is not compensation but *restitutio in integrum*. These propositions have undergone fundamental changes which have been effected by subsequent developments, such as large-scale expropriationary measures and nationalizations in the inter-war period and in the years following the Second World War. As a result of the continuous and consistent practice of States resorting to expropriation of foreign-owned property irrespective of existing treaty obligations to the contrary,[318] and in the light of lukewarm reactions offered by affected capital-exporting States which have never disputed the exercise of sovereignty,[319] the sovereign right of every State to expropriate or nationalize property situated within its territory is generally recognized.[320]

Whereas a considerable number of publicists and governments in Western industrialized nations deem an act of expropriation or nationalization of foreign property to be wrongful unless it is for reasons of public utility and followed by payment of 'prompt, adequate, and effective' compensation,[321] a majority of States, including Islamic States, accept the obligation to pay compensation but reject the formula of 'prompt, adequate and effective' as a binding rule of law.[322] Furthermore, the usefulness of the rule of public utility, which occurs in the UN General Assembly Resolution on Permanent Sovereignty over Natural Resources[323] and is considered to reflect existing law,[324] has been seriously questioned by some[325] because of the problems of objectively determining the invalidity of the public purpose or utility of the expropriating State. In contemporary international law, the essential distinction between lawful and unlawful expropriation seems to be conditioned by the obligation to compensate for the 'taking' and the prohibition of discrimination.[326] As far as the formula of compensation is concerned, present practice of States seems to confirm the contention that the classical formula of 'prompt, adequate and effective' compensation represents a standard of preference rather than a rule of international law.[327]

2.7. CONCLUSIONS

In the preceding introductory sections of our examination we have attempted to trace the evolution and development of international relations between Islamic States and other political entities, beginning with the days of the Holy Prophet and ending with the gradual emergence of a consensus on general principles of international law which finally led to the foundation of a universal community of nations after the Second World War.

In our historical treatment of the subject we have also tried to reconstruct a legal basis of international relations in Islam. By rejecting certain widely held and still prevailing misconceptions about the objectives of the Islamic *Siyar* in general, and the concept of Jihad in particular, we have tried to reconstruct a legal basis of international relations in Islam which is in accord and harmony with the spirit of the message of the Koran.

By adducing methodological arguments and evidence from the practice of Islamic States, we have tried to show the underlying theoretical basis of external relations in Islam which later enabled a substantial number of 'new' Asian and African Islamic States to accept a universal community of nations based on universally recognized general principles of international law. Their acceptance of the Charter of the United Nations is evidence of the fact that the principles embodied therein are generally recognized by the Islamic States to be of universal binding force. Adherence to principles of equality and reciprocity among nations does not detract in any manner from the Islamic basis of external relations. In fact, common principles of law are to be found both in the Islamic theory of international relations and in public international law, which, given the centuries of interaction between Islamic and other States, is hardly surprising. Furthermore, these common principles have been embodied in the Charter of the Islamic Conference which lays the foundation of inter-Islamic solidarity and co-operation in the present age.

It would, therefore, be appropriate to conclude,

(*a*) that the theory of Jihad cannot be recognized as the 'sole' basis of external relations in Islam as it is neither warranted by any provisions contained in the Koran nor was it explicitly recognized as such in the practice of the Holy Prophet;

(*b*) that acceptance of and adherence to general principles of international law by Islamic States is not contradictory with the legal basis of external relations in Islam;

(*c*) that on the other hand acceptance of general principles of law by the Islamic States does not provide any evidence of their Europeanization, Westernization, or secularization as similar general principles of law are common to Islam and other legal systems, religions, and philosophies.

PART II

Substance of Islamic Co-operation

3

Forum of Islamic Co-operation: The OIC

3.1 THE EMERGENCE OF THE OIC

THE OIC consists of forty-five Member States[1] and is based on the Charter of the Islamic Conference which came into force on 28 February 1973.[2] It is an institutionalized instrument of Islamic States to achieve Islamic solidarity and co-operation among a substantial number of African and Asian nations whose 'common belief constitutes a strong factor for rapprochement and solidarity'.[3] The OIC is a heterogeneous assembly of States which could not justifiably be called a 'regional' organization; the geographical distances separating Mali from Malaysia and Iraq from Indonesia have certainly contributed to diverse political, social, economic, and cultural factors which have been conditioned by the individual historical developments in these States. The common cohesive political, economic, social, and cultural factors deemed to be essential preconditions for regional 'integration' could be said to be 'absent' in this case.

All the Member States of the OIC belong to the group of States commonly called 'developing States', however.[4] This factor is augmented by the sharing of a colonial or semi-colonial past and the present state of political, economic, and social transition and re-orientation. The alien structures implanted in the Member States of the OIC during the colonial period have failed to cater to the needs of a majority of the people; the colonial system of education and administration which introduced alien values and outlook has estranged the majority of the masses from their rulers. Thus, internally, these States are coming under increasing pressure to effect imminent structural changes in order to correct imbalances. Externally, the historical bond of Islam, which integrated these various States within a common ideological whole, was severed by colonial intrusion and occupation for protracted periods of time. After the emergence of national entities and new forms of political and economic dependence a need for *rapprochement* and solidarity between the Muslim populations of these States was badly felt. A renewal of historical and ideological ties was gradually seen as a necessary first step towards achieving political and economic strength.[5]

3.1.1. The First Call for Islamic Unity

The first call for a summit meeting of Muslim Heads of State was formulated during a non-governmental 'Islamic Conference' held from 16-20 May 1962 (during the annual Hadj Season) in Mecca.[6] The idea of Islamic co-operation was not only supported by various Islamic institutions and organizations but by the leaders in several parts of the Muslim world.[7] At the end of 1964 another Islamic Conference, convened in Mogadishu, Somalia, by various groups and organizations, officially adopted and communicated the call of the Somali President Adam Othman 'for the convening of an Islamic Summit conference to be attended by all Kings and Presidents of the Muslim Countries' to all leaders of the Muslim world.[8]

At this stage the political atmosphere of the Arab world was hardly conducive to such ventures. The Arab world was divided into blocs and involved in a 'cold war' of its own, with the so-called 'conservative' bloc consisting of Jordan, Kuwait, Libya, Morocco, and Saudi Arabia on the one extreme and the 'revolutionary' bloc of Algeria, Egypt, Iraq, Syria, and Yemen on the other.[9] Whereas the official call for an Islamic summit made by the Somali President hardly excited any attention in the Arab world, a new dimension was added when, during the inaugural meeting of the General Islamic Conference (2nd Session) held from 17-22 April 1965 in Mecca, the late King Faisal of Saudi Arabia officially declared his intention to 'hold an Islamic Summit Conference'.[10]

A first step towards realizing this intention was King Faisal's meeting with the Shah of Iran on 7 December 1965 in Tehran. A joint communiqué was issued at the end of the visit approving 'the call for convening an Islamic Summit Conference which will provide an opportunity for discussing matters of concern to Muslim States, a springboard towards their unity and safeguarding their interests'.[11] Certain interpretations of this meeting, as an attempt to form an 'Islamic Alliance'[12] or 'Islamic Pact'[13] between conservative monarchs of the region hostile to Communism and interested in putting a check to the Socialist tide around them, unleashed an unprecedented uproar in the Arab world,[14] which finally culminated in President Nasser's well-known Unity Day Speech (22 February 1966) vilifying the meeting of the monarchs as imperialist-reactionary plotting aimed at propagating the idea of Islamic unity in order to confront Arab unity and directed at the destruction of Arab nationalism.[15]

As a consequence, a fresh wave of bitter political squabbles broke out giving rise to several years of political propaganda in the form of open mud-slinging among Arab leaders, countless charges of serving foreign interests followed by vehement denials and counter-charges, and delicate political balancing acts; in short, a war of words. It left deep scars on the morale of the Islamic world as a whole and demonstrated the inherent political and intellectual weakness of the Arab world in being unable to sort out the conflict in regional terms.[16]

The main dividing line between the 'revolutionary' and 'conservative' Arab States, which now crystallized into the supporters of the idea of Islamic solidarity opposing the supporters of Abdul Nasser's call for Arab nationalism,[17] continued throughout 1966 until the disastrous Arab-Israeli war in 1967. Though the summit of Muslim Heads of State that was so long demanded and eagerly sought after did not materialize in 1966, the drastic changes wrought by the 1967 war and the incident of the burning of Al-Aqsa Mosque[18] in Jerusalem finally smoothed the way for convening the first Islamic Summit Conference of the Kings and Heads of State and Government of Islamic Countries in Rabat (Morocco) from 22-25 September 1969.[19] The foregoing incidents had brought about a new tide of opinion which reversed the position held by some leaders in 1966.[20]

3.1.2. The First Islamic Summit Conference and after

The First Islamic Summit Conference, convened as a gesture of Islamic unity in reaction to the profanation of Al-Aqsa,[21] was attended by Heads of State and Representatives from twenty-four countries, with the PLO as observers. Although the deliberations of the summit centred around the act of arson in the Al-Aqsa Mosque, the occupation of Arab territories and Jerusalem by Israeli military forces, and the liberation of Palestine, the major outcome of the summit was the resolution of the Governments to promote 'between themselves a close co-operation and mutual assistance in the economic, scientific, cultural and spiritual fields'.[22] In fact, the First Summit paved the way for further meetings at Foreign Minister level which set the machinery of Islamic co-operation in motion.

At the first Islamic Conference of Foreign Ministers held 23-5 March 1970 in Jeddah, the representatives of the participating States decided to create a permanent Secretariat responsible for contacting governments participating in the Conference and co-ordinating their activities.[23] This Secretariat was to act as a liaison between the participating States, prepare and organize Conference sessions to be held annually and to follow up the implementation of decisions taken by the Conference.[24]

The second ICFM held 26-8 December 1970 in Karachi deliberated upon the formulation of its basic principles and objectives and recognized the need of a detailed and formal statement of these principles.[25] It requested the Secretary-General to circulate a draft memorandum and organize a meeting to study the document. Thus the second ICFM came a step further by facilitating the preparation of a draft Charter of the Islamic Conference to be submitted to the third ICFM for its consideration.[26]

The third ICFM held 29 February-4 March 1972 in Jeddah plunged into a lengthy discussion of the various articles, effected a few minor changes in the draft,[27] and finally came up with a Charter of the Islamic Conference acceptable to all parties.[28] From the initial conception of the Conference as a forum of co-operation and consultation[29] for all Muslim countries, the third ICFM had, in its wisdom, come a long way to establish the Organization of the Islamic Conference.[30]

3.2. THE CHARTER OF THE OIC

In its role as a constitutional instrument, the Charter of the Islamic Conference documents the consensual legal basis of inter-Islamic solidarity and co-operation. The Charter establishes an interregional organization of Islamic States whose principal policy-making bodies are constituted in the form of 'conferences'. In our examination of its contents our endeavour shall be to answer some fundamental questions concerning

(*a*) the objectives of the OIC Charter;
(*b*) the legal basis of inter-Islamic solidarity and co-operation today;[31]
(*c*) the legal character of the Organization, i.e., whether the OIC is an 'international' or a 'supranational'[32] entity? In other words, can the

OIC be seen as a closely knit organization bestowing rights and duties and imposing sanctions[33] upon its Member States, or may it be seen as a loose forum of consultation and co-operation?

In the interpretation of the OIC Charter it is essential to have recourse to rules of treaty interpretation that have received general consideration in the deliberations of international tribunals,[34] are widely recognized and endorsed,[35] and have been embodied in Art. 31 and 32 of the Vienna Convention on the Law of Treaties.[36] In accordance with the provisions of Art. 31 (1) of the Convention a treaty is to be interpreted 'in good faith in accordance with the ordinary meaning to be given to the terms of the treaty in their context and in the light of its object and purpose'. This 'general rule of interpretation', which is in fact an amalgamation of various approaches,[37] is further augmented by Art. 32 which permits recourse to preparatory work[38] of the treaty as a supplementary means of interpretation.

The OIC Charter does not contain any provisions on 'rules' or methods of interpreting the instrument. During the general debate preceding the adoption of the OIC Charter, however, a controversy arose involving Art. XII, which provides for the peaceful settlement of disputes that may arise in the interpretation, application, or implementation of any article in the Charter, and which originally contained two paragraphs. Paragraph (*a*) stipulated: 'This Charter shall not contain any matter which contradicts with the Charter of the United Nations or infringes on the rights of the member States and their obligations toward it.'[39] Initially inserted on the request of Iran, the rather unhappy and, perhaps, even provocative wording of the paragraph led to serious objections being raised by Saudi Arabia[40] to the effect that such a conditioning clause was uncalled for and lacked precedents. These objections were supported by Morocco, Algeria, and Guinea. Thus, despite Iran's insistence on keeping it,[41] it was finally agreed that paragraph (*a*) be deleted as the Preamble of the Charter reaffirms its commitment to the UN Charter. The position taken by Iran on this legal issue is difficult to support. It may have had some extra-legal reasons and motivations, but a clause such as Iran insisted on inserting into the Charter is unwarranted due to the fact that under Chapter VIII of the UN Charter all regional arrangements and their activities are to be pursued consistent with the purposes and principles of the UN (Art. 52). In the case of the OIC this rule is implicit and since Art. 103 of the UN Charter is generally applicable in relation to Art. 52, there is no need to give express mention to it in the OIC Charter. Thus Art. XII of the OIC Charter was confined to the following text: 'Any dispute that may arise in the interpretation, application or implementation of any Article in the present Charter shall be settled peacefully, and in all cases through consultations, negotiations, reconciliation or arbitration.'

As the title of the Organization suggests, the Charter institutionalizes a series of conferences on different levels. The word 'Conference' throws some light on the loose character of the OIC. The convening of conferences for the purpose of consultations tends to conjure up the impression that the only purpose of Member States of the Islamic Conference is to indulge in aimless talk at the highest level. This first impression is, however, unjustified. As an international organization, the OIC is comparable to any other intergovernmental institution. In its emphasis on promoting *rapprochement* and solidarity between Islamic peoples, the Charter of the OIC may be compared with the Charter of the Organization of African Unity which emphasizes brotherhood and solidarity 'in a larger unity transcending ethnic and national differences'.[42] Whereas the OAU Charter refers to a compact geographical area,[43] the Charter of the OIC refers to States which had participated in the First Islamic Summit Conference in Rabat (1969) and to every 'Muslim State' which is eligible to join the Islamic Conference upon expressing its desire and preparedness to adopt the Charter (Art. VIII).[44]

The Preamble of the OIC Charter reaffirms the commitment of its Member States 'to the UN Charter and fundamental Human Rights, the purposes and principles of which provide the basis for fruitful co-operation amongst all people'. This formal commitment to the UN Charter is similar to the reaffirmation contained in the Preamble of the OAU Charter and may be deemed to be nothing more than a reiteration of a basic formula to which every signatory to the UN Charter is bound. On the other hand, one could interpret the commitment of the OIC Member States to the UN Charter to mean their commitment to international legal principles embodied in that Charter and the value of this statement also lies in the formal recognition of the UN Charter by a solemn and representative body of States claiming to be Islamic. Mention has already been made of the reference to 'fundamental Human Rights' in the Preamble of the OIC Charter. Similarly, the OAU Charter mentions as one of its purposes the promotion of international co-operation 'having due regard to the

Charter of the United Nations and the Universal Declaration of Human Rights'.[45] The latter statement seems to carry a stronger legal significance because of its incorporation as one of the basic purposes of the OAU and its reference to a specific General Assembly Resolution, while the OIC Charter does not reiterate the formula used in the Preamble elsewhere in the Charter and refers only to 'fundamental Human Rights' which could carry different meanings for different States in different circumstances.

3.2.1. The Objectives of the Charter

The objectives of the OIC Charter encompass three distinctive sets of relationships. The first set comprises relationships among Member States, and hence may be termed internal objectives. The second set of objectives are directed towards particular states. And the third set of objectives are general commitments to uphold peace and promote co-operation. The latter may be termed external objectives of the OIC. In our subsequent examination we have discussed them according to the contents of the provisions and major policy issues.

3.2.1.1. *International Co-operation and Understanding*

In their relations with other states OIC Member States are interested in creating a suitable atmosphere 'for the promotion of co-operation and understanding' (Art. II (*A*) 7). Thus their primary intention is to create and maintain peaceful relations as well as intensify these relations through mutual co-operation.

3.2.1.2. *International Peace and Security*

The gist of international relations, as envisaged by Art. II, paragraph (*A*) 4 of the OIC Charter, also includes the achievement and maintenance of 'international peace and security'. In this respect, Member States of the OIC are prepared 'to take necessary measures to support international peace and security' but not at the cost of justice. Art. II (*A*) 4 is conspicuous for two reasons: first, it reiterates the principal purpose of the UN Charter as laid down in Art. 1 (1), which is to 'maintain international peace and security'. And the OIC Member States are clearly willing to support the UN in its objective of maintaining international peace and security. Secondly, these measures are to be taken, as Art. 1 (1) of the UN Charter stipulates, 'in conformity with the principles of justice and international law', whereby Art. II (*A*) 4 of the OIC Charter is conspicuous for its omission of the term 'international law'. This, however, cannot be construed to mean that the OIC Charter deliberately attaches undue emphasis to the concept of justice at the expense of totally ignoring the principles of international law. Both the Preamble of the OIC Charter, which reaffirms its commitment to the UN Charter, and Art. II (*B*), which testifies to the obligation of Member States of the OIC to adhere to general principles of international law,[46] help to refute such a construction. The answer lies in the fact that in the spirit of Art. 1 (1) of the UN Charter, the OIC Charter emphasizes the concept of justice (or the principles of justice) as something distinct from international law. This view was endorsed by the San Francisco Conference in 1945 introducing into the international sphere the notion that provisions of the law may clash with the most elementary principles of conscience and justice.[47] Thus for a substantial number of States in the international community strict adherence to the letter of the law, in cases where clashes with moral and ethical dictates arise, would be extremely difficult to uphold and justify. In Art. II (*A*) 4 of the OIC Charter reference to the Middle East situation in general, and the Palestine Question in particular, is implicit as a peaceful solution of both these problems would positively contribute towards the enhancement of principles of justice and international law and the maintenance of 'international peace and security'.

3.2.1.3. *Elimination of Racial Discrimination and Eradication of Colonialism*

In its endeavour 'to eliminate racial segregation, discrimination and to eradicate colonialism in all its forms' (Art. II (*A*) 3), the Charter of the OIC upholds two major legal principles which have recently gained considerable support and recognition. The first principle is concerned with a basic human right, namely, the principle of racial non-discrimination, which has been held by a majority of the Judges in the Barcelona Traction case (Second Phase)[48] to be an obligation *erga omnes.* The objective of eliminating racial segregation and discrimination embodied in Art. II (*A*) 3 of the OIC Charter also reflects the purpose of the International Convention on the Elimination of all Forms of Racial Discrimination (1966), which defines 'racial discrimination' in Art. 1 (1) as: 'any distinction, exclusion, restriction or preference based on race, colour, descent, or national or ethnic origin which has the purpose or effect of nullifying or impairing the recognition, enjoyment or exercise, on an equal footing, of human rights and fundamental freedoms in the political, economic, social, cultural or any other field of public life.'[49] Thus reference to South Africa's policy of Apartheid and its actions in Namibia are implicit in the wording of Art. II (*A*) 3 of the Charter.

The OIC Charter objective of eradicating colonialism in all its forms is the application of the principle of self-determination to colonial situations and peoples.[50] The principle of self-determination has found expression in the UN General Assembly 'Declaration on the Granting of Independence to Colonial Countries and Peoples' (Res. 1514 (XV) of 14 December 1960), which is said to be 'in the form of an authoritative interpretation of the (UN) Charter',[51] and in the 'Declaration on Principles of International Law Concerning Friendly Relations and Co-operation among States' (Annex to *UNGA Res.* 2625 (XXV) of 24 October 1970), which explicitly endorses the duty of every State 'to bring a speedy end to colonialism'.[52] The International Court of Justice has, on more than one occasion, confirmed the existence and application of the 'right' of self-determination in the context of non-self-governing territories.[53] Thus the Charter of the OIC endorses the struggle to eradicate colonialism, which is the typical hallmark of Afro-Asian solidarity, and which enjoys a wide spectrum of support in the international community. Whether the phrase 'colonialism in all its forms' could be read so as to include the term 'neo-colonialism', generally applied to the continuing political and economic domination of ex-colonial territories even after their attaining independence, is difficult to say. Although the wording of Art. II (*A*) 3 of the OIC Charter does not give express mention to the term, as the OAU Charter does,[54] the phrase could, nevertheless, be interpreted as including all kinds of modern variations of colonialism.[55] On the other hand, if Art. II (*A*) 3 is read as a whole, the phrase 'in all its forms' could apply not only to colonialism alone, but also to racial segregation and discrimination 'in all its forms'.

3.2.1.4. *Promotion of Islamic Solidarity*

As far as internal objectives are concerned, primary importance has been laid on the objective of promoting Islamic solidarity among Member States of the OIC as stipulated by sub-paragraph 1 of Art. II (*A*). While the content of Art. II (*A*) sub-paragraphs 5 and 6 are peculiar to the OIC, the objectives calling for the promotion of solidarity and co-operation are similar to those of the OAU Charter[56] and the Pact of the Arab League.[57] Whereas the Charter of the OAU speaks of promoting unity and solidarity among African States[58] and the Pact of the Arab League refers to the co-ordination of political activities of Member States with the aim of realizing a close collaboration between them,[59] the OIC Charter mentions the promotion of 'Islamic solidarity' without providing specific elaboration or meaning of the term 'Islamic'. In order to understand the modern implications of the term, however, some understanding of the roots of modern reform movements in the Islamic world of the nineteenth century is called for. In this context the pan-Islamic movement and its association with the name of Jamal al-Din al-Afghani (1839-97), one of the foremost propounders of the political concept of Islamic unity and solidarity in the face of European encroachment and colonialism, has left an indelible mark.[60] Islamic solidarity is to be understood as the collective effort of Islamic States to preserve Islamic values and foster greater understanding, *rapprochement*, and brotherhood among themselves[61] with the ultimate objective of achieving a high degree of integration. This objective is to be achieved by the consolidation of co-operation among Member States in the economic, social, cultural, and other vital fields. In the economic field co-operation among Islamic States has led to the formulation of basic policy measures endorsed by the 'General Agreement for Economic, Technical and Commercial Co-operation among Member States of the Islamic Conference', and emphasis on the transfer of capital resources within the OIC for purposes of economic development has led to the creation of a legal framework for the promotion, protection, and guarantee of investments.[62]

Solidarity also includes the mobilization of collective support for broad policy measures and positions to be represented in international organizations. Hence the second part of sub-paragraph 2 of Art. II (*A*) of the Charter underlines the importance of carrying out consultations among Member States in international organizations.

3.2.1.5. *The Palestine Issue*

The main expression of Islamic solidarity in political terms is the support of the struggle of the people of Palestine as stipulated in sub-paragraph 5 of Art. II (*A*). The Palestine issue and the Jerusalem Question is central to the Charter of the OIC. It should be recalled that the immediate catalyst which helped precipitate the first Islamic Summit Conference in Rabat (1969) was the incident of the burning of the Al-Aqsa Mosque. Even before the existence of the OIC as a forum of Islamic solidarity and co-operation, the Palestine issue commanded wide sympathy and support in the Islamic world. Incorporation of the Palestine issue in the OIC Charter shows that it is not only a regional issue or a particular problem of the Arab States, but is a priority concern of all Islamic States. It is, therefore, necessary to expose the basic political and legal attitudes on this issue which are prevalent in the Islamic world. An examination of the contents of Art. II (*A*) 5 of the OIC Charter would by necessity be subjective as it involves a discussion of what the wording of the provision actually stands for. An exhaustive, objective examination of the issue is not intended here as it is beyond the scope of the present study.

It should, however, be noted that the Palestine issue is intrinsically connected with the principle of self-determination as applicable to territories and groups of people previously under the League of Nations mandate. In its advisory opinion on the Namibia (South West Africa) case, the International Court of Justice has held the principle of self-determination to be applicable to all non-self-governing territories.[63] Seen in this light the Palestine issue gains significant relevance if it is realized that the Mandatory Power did not discharge its legal obligation to the people of Palestine and abandoned them to the fate they are suffering today. Thus Art. II (*A*) 5 is concerned with the political issue of self-determination and the religious issue of the status of Jerusalem, both of which are interrelated. Sub-paragraph 5 calls for co-ordination of efforts for the safeguarding of the Holy Places, thus giving expression to a religious sentiment shared by all Muslims. The attachment of Muslims all over the world to the Holy City of Jerusalem is deeply rooted in their religious and political history.[64] The Charter of the OIC refrains from mentioning the City of Jerusalem in sub-paragraph 5 of Art. II (*A*) and limits itself to the mention of 'Holy Places', which would include not only the Al-Aqsa Mosque in Jerusalem but also other Holy Places. The Charter does perceive the City of Jerusalem to be under military occupation, however, and, accordingly, refers in Art. VI (5) to the establishment of the headquarters of the Secretariat General of the OIC in Jeddah, 'pending the liberation of "Bait Ul Maqdis" (Jerusalem)'.

Added to this religious sentiment of the Muslims is the political aspiration of the Palestinians to regain their political sovereignty and liberty. Sub-paragraph 5 of Art. II (*A*) speaks of the 'rights' of the Palestinians and pledges support 'to liberate their land'. The Declaration of Rabat issued by the First Summit in 1969 also confirmed its full support to the Palestinian people for the 'restitution of their rights' on the standpoint that these 'rights' were usurped–a basic legal contention which is endorsed by Art. II (*A*) 5 of the Charter on the premiss that the legal sovereignty of Palestine still lies 'in the original inhabitants of the country as they existed at the time of the detachment of Palestine from Turkey at the end of the First World War'.[65] By virtue of Art. 16 of the Treaty of Lausanne, Turkey agreed to the settlement of the future of territories priorly governed by the Ottoman Empire by the parties concerned. Even though Turkey relinquished claims of sovereignty over these Arab territories, it did not expressly transfer sovereignty and title to the British forces occupying Palestine. Thus it is argued that sovereignty reverted to the original inhabitants of these territories and neither the invalid Zionist claim to an historic title to Palestine[66] nor their reliance on the Balfour Declaration,[67] which was endorsed by the League of Nations' Mandate over Palestine,[68] can legally effect any transfer of sovereignty.[69] Sovereignty in the case of a mandated territory is clearly vested in the inhabitants of the mandated territory.[70] Even the General Assembly of the UN did not possess legal competence to recommend the partition of Palestine or the creation of a Jewish State[71] and thereby encroach upon the sovereignty of the people of Palestine in violation of the Covenant of the League of Nations and the UN Charter.[72] Thus, in the face of gross injustice and flagrant breach of international law Muslims all over the world have, from the very beginning of political conflict in Palestine, solidarized with the Palestinians in rejecting the Balfour Declaration, the League of Nations' Mandate over Palestine and the UN General Assembly Resolution recommending partition. Following its creation in 1922, the Supreme Muslim Council of Jerusalem sent various delegations to Arab and other Islamic countries in order to mobilize support and funds for the safeguarding and restoration of Al-Aqsa.[73] Popular outbreaks of violence and disturbances[74] in Palestine were echoed by protests from all over the Islamic world condemning British policies in Palestine and Zionist encroachment and declarations of solidarity could be heard not only from Baghdad, Cairo, and Damascus in the Arab world but also from the Muslims of India, the Dutch East Indies, Zanzibar, and parts of Yugoslavia.[75]

The question of Islamic solidarity, as expressed in the Charter of the OIC, is consistent with the historical and political response of Muslims all over the world to the Jerusalem Question and the Palestine issue. In the debate preceding the adoption of the OIC

Charter an objection to Art. II (*A*) sub-paragraph 5 was raised by the representative of Sierra Leone on the grounds that the Charter, being the constitution of the OIC, may not be specific on any issue, and since mention of the Palestinian case was made in the draft Charter to the exclusion of other Muslim peoples, he suggested that the objective be reformulated so as to read 'to support the struggle of all Muslims under oppression and help them to regain their legitimate rights and liberate their lands'.[76] However, Saudi Arabia countered that the Palestine Question was a unique one because it had never happened before in the history of humanity[77] and for this very reason Palestine had been singled out. This position was supported by Syria, Algeria, Mauritania, Egypt, and the representative of the PLO and thus a separate sub-paragraph was incorporated in the Charter (Art. II (*A*) 6) calling for efforts 'to strengthen the struggle of all Moslem peoples with a view to safeguarding their dignity, independence, and national rights'.[78]

Even if we concede the factual existence of Israel, which can hardly be denied, and recognize the effectiveness of its government and control over its territory and population, the question of recognition of the State of Israel would, as far as the Islamic States and the Palestinians are concerned, surely revolve round the principle of legitimacy. Can a State, which excluded and still excludes a substantial part of the original inhabitants of its territory from all sorts of political participation and refuses their right to political self-determination, be recognized as legitimately founded and constituted? Recognition of Israel without the simultaneous recognition of the rights of the Palestinians to return to their homeland and freely determine their future by Israel would be tantamount to rewarding its aggressive use of force and legitimizing its territorial gains. This would be contradictory to the principles of the UN Charter whose purpose is to condemn violations of international law by refusal to recognize a *fait accompli*. Once the rights of the weaker party have been established and evidenced by historical facts and points of law it would be a gross injustice to reward the wrongdoer by recognizing his claims as equally legitimate, thus rewarding him by failing to question territorial acquisitions by force. In such cases even the most efficient effectiveness of the State's establishment and organization does not warrant the abandoning of legal and just claims unless and until a mutual settlement is reached between the parties concerned.

3.2.1.6. *Support of the Struggle of Moslem Peoples*

Art. II (*A*) 6 was not originally envisaged by the drafters of the OIC Charter but was inserted on the objections raised by the representative of Sierra Leone, as mentioned above, in order to include 'the struggle of all Moslem peoples' as an objective worthy of support. Since sub-paragraph 6 mentions 'Moslem peoples', as being distinct from Muslim States, it may be read in conjunction with the general objective of achieving Islamic solidarity, as laid down in Art. II (*A*) 1 of the Charter, or even a translation of the principle of self-determination into practice if Art. II (*B*) 2 is to be interpreted in that sense. The kind of struggle which the Charter deems as worthy of support is that waged 'with a view to safeguarding their dignity, independence and national rights'. This, however, would be a strict reading of the provision and other possible interpretations could be advanced in support of a wider construction. We shall proceed by dwelling briefly on the terms 'dignity', 'independence' and 'national rights' as they occur in sub-paragraph 6 of Art. II (*A*) and then discuss the problems involved in defining 'Moslem peoples' in order to lend content and meaning to the provision and its application in practice.

The term 'dignity' in legal language means 'incorporeal hereditament';[79] in the context of sub-paragraph 6 it probably implies some sort of (intangible) rights or legal interests enjoyed by Moslem peoples, which have been either expressly granted to them or acquired by prescription. However, 'dignity' ordinarily means elevation of rank or place. Hence the term could mean the dignity or rank of the Moslem peoples. The phrase 'safeguarding their dignity' would mean the protection, and in the case of infringements, restoration of such rights enjoyed by the Moslem peoples. 'Independence' may be construed to mean political independence. And 'national rights', in contrast to 'dignity', are the fundamental requirements on which the claim to the right of self-determination is based.

It seems, however, that sub-paragraph 6 does not envisage three distinct situations, each concerned with one or more of these types of rights, in which struggles by Moslem peoples may be waged, but mentions them together with the conjunction 'and' instead of 'or', which usually denotes alternatives. Thus any struggle waged by Moslem peoples 'with a view to safeguarding their dignity, independence, and national rights' may be construed as meaning one and the same case and thus deemed worthy of support by the OIC Member States in the light of Art. II (*A*) 6 of the Charter.

The crucial problems involved in the interpretation of sub-paragraph 6 revolve around the definition of the term 'Moslem peoples' and the application of the principle of self-determination to any groups claiming such rights within the present territorial delineations existing in the Member States of the OIC. A literal definition of 'Moslem peoples' would include populations professing the Islamic faith and inhabiting the territories of Member States as well as constituting religious minorities in non-Islamic countries. Thus, in accordance with this definition, the term would include Muslim minorities in non-Member States of Asia, Africa, and Europe (such as the Philippines, India, Burma, Ethiopia, Albania, Yugoslavia, the USSR, and the People's Republic of China) as well as 'Moslem peoples' claiming 'national rights' in such Member States of the OIC as Morocco, Algeria, Pakistan, Iran, Iraq, and Turkey. The latter groups would be excluded from the definition as the Charter itself draws a distinction between the Islamic Conference consisting of Member States and the 'Moslem peoples' whose struggle the Member States are individually and collectively called upon to strengthen. It is, therefore, logical that no Member State, made up of various national groups, would willingly consent to strengthen and support dissident 'Moslem' groups, or for that matter any group, claiming 'national rights' distinct from those enjoyed under the prevalent constitutional system, and thereby preside over the dismemberment of its territorial integrity. Thus the term 'Moslem peoples' may be construed to mean

(*a*) Moslem peoples under colonial rule or military occupation;
(*b*) Muslim minorities permanently resident in non-Muslim States.

As far as the nature or type of support deemed appropriate for the purpose of Art. II (*A*) 6 is concerned, a clue may be derived by comparing its wording with that of sub-paragraph 5. Whereas sub-paragraph 5 refers to 'support' of a 'struggle' already being waged by the people of Palestine and calls for help and support which is to be rendered by Member States of the OIC so that the Palestinians may 'regain their rights' by liberating their land, sub-paragraph 6 restricts itself to the word 'strengthen' without elaborating the manner of support. Art. II (*A*) 5 contains a stronger wording than Art. II (*A*) 6 and also implies the use of force to 'liberate' the land of the Palestinians. Thus the nature of support to be given to strengthen the struggle of 'Moslem peoples' may be political, moral, material, or otherwise. The question whether or not the lending of such support by

Member States of the OIC in order 'to strengthen the struggle of Moslem peoples' in non-Muslim States constitutes an intervention in the internal affairs of the latter is the subject-matter of the discussion of the principles of self-determination and non-intervention below.

3.2.2. Principles of the Charter

The principles laid down in Art. II, paragraph (*B*) constitute a central subject of our study of the OIC Charter. In order to realize the objectives of the Charter, Member States have undertaken to be 'inspired and guided by the following principles':

1. total equality between member States;
2. respect of the right of self-determination, and non-interference in the domestic affairs of member States;
3. respect of the sovereignty, independence, and territorial integrity of each member State;
4. settlement of any conflict that may arise by peaceful means such as negotiation, mediation, reconciliation, or arbitration;
5. abstention from the threat or use of force against the territorial integrity, national unity, or political independence of any member State.

These principles, which enjoy the unequivocal and collective endorsement of Islamic States, could be said to form the basis of inter-Islamic relations today. The subsequent discussion purports to show whether these principles are also widely recognized as general principles of international law.

3.2.2.1. *Preliminary Considerations*

Before going into a detailed examination of these principles some preliminary questions arise about their obligatory character for Member States of the OIC.

Art. II, paragraph (*B*) speaks of inspiration and guidance to be sought by Member States from these principles. The phrase 'shall be inspired and guided' does not seem to create legal obligation in express terms. This position may be contrasted with the wording of Articles III and VI of the OAU Charter.[80] Art. III of the OAU Charter enumerates seven principles to which the Member States 'solemnly affirm and declare their adherence'. Art. VI of the same Charter reinforces this solemn intention of adherence by categorically stating that 'Member States pledge themselves to observe scrupulously the principles enumerated in Art. III of the present Charter.' Thus, in contrast to the OAU Charter, Member States of the OIC neither give any solemn affirmation or declaration of adherence to principles stipulated in Art. II (*B*) of the Charter, nor do they pledge themselves to observe these scrupulously.

The principles stipulated in Art. II (*B*) of the OIC Charter may be said to possess binding force if they are of a normative character and purport to establish legal obligations, the violations of which are covered by the imposition of sanctions,[81] or if they generally reflect established principles of customary international law, the reiteration of which in any regional, constitutive instrument may be deemed to have a declaratory effect.[82] Following precedents of other regional organizations,[83] the OIC Charter does not contain any express provisions on the imposition of sanctions. The absence of any provision of the OIC Charter relating to the imposition of sanctions in case of violations, however, does not detract, in any manner, from the value of these principles as normative statements. The principles inspiring and guiding Member States of the OIC are indeed a reiteration of general principles embodied in international instruments of a universal or quasi-universal character. The contents of Art. II (*B*) of the OIC Charter generally reflect some fundamental principles embodied in Art. 2 of the UN Charter and further elaborated in the *UNGA* 'Declaration on Principles of International Law Concerning Friendly Relations and Co-operation among States' (Res. 2625 (XXV), 24 Oct. 1970).[84] And as Article 2 of the UN Charter is of fundamental importance and constitutes the legal obligations and rights[85] of the Member States of the United Nations, a restatement of principles enshrined in Art. 2 by Member States of the UN in a regional or interregional instrument (such as the OIC Charter) can be construed as possessing normative character. Furthermore, if the principles embodied in the OIC Charter could be said to possess binding force by virtue of their being rules of customary international law, their incorporation in the Charter may be deemed to have a declaratory character. In the subsequent discussion the legal character of these principles will be examined and the results summarized below.[86]

In our interpretation of the principles of the OIC Charter we have generally drawn upon the UN Charter and the UN Declaration on Principles (1970) as 'material sources' helpful in the proper understanding of these principles.[87] Whereas principles incorporated in the UN Charter have legal binding force, the obligatory character of the elaboration of these principles in the UN Declaration on Principles is still open to question. The reason for dismissing outright the Declaration as a binding legal instrument[88] is based on the general rule that *UNGA Resolutions per se* are not binding on its Members–a point which has been and most probably will continue to be the subject of controversial debate.[89] The Declaration on Principles cannot, however, simply be regarded as just another Resolution of the General Assembly; its legal value and significance may be determined by the following facts: that it provides 'evidence of the consensus among Member States of the United Nations on the meaning and elaboration of the principles of the Charter';[90] that it embodies a reiteration of general principles enshrined in the UN Charter as well as contained in rules of customary international law;[91] and because of the very nature of its formulations, the Declaration may be conceived to be 'a material "source" of international legal or public policies'.[92] While some Afro-Asian and Latin American States and countries of the Soviet bloc held (and still hold) the view that the Declaration contains an authentic interpretation of established principles of international law, and is, therefore, deemed legally binding,[93] Western States were not prepared to accept the Declaration as a legally binding instrument.[94] However, the legal effect of the Declaration lies between these extremes and was aptly stated by the Italian delegate to the UN Special Committee on Friendly Relations, Arangio-Ruiz, as follows: 'The principles embodied in the declaration are principles of international law in so far as they exist as customary international law, or as part of other binding international instruments, or can be deduced therefrom.'[95]

Even if we adhere to a stricter view that *UNGA Resolutions* have, as such, no binding force and the Declaration on Principles may be regarded as a 'material source' of international law only if the content of the Declaration is embodied in a treaty or recognized in practice by States as constituting rules of customary international law [96] it remains to be seen whether Member States of the OIC have given recognition to the contents of the Declaration by embodying its elaborated principles in the Charter.

3.2.2.2. *Principle of Total Equality*

Sub-paragraph 1 of Art. II (*B*) lays down the principle of total equality between Member States. The wording of this principle differs from that of Art. 2 (1) of the UN Charter which refers to the principle of sovereign equality. The principle of sovereign equality, which has been commonly interpreted to mean juridical equality,[97] combines two different principles, that of equality and sovereignty, in a 'problematical manner'.[98] Art. II (*B*) 1 of the OIC Charter makes a formal distinction between the principles of equality and sovereignty by enumerating them separately in sub-paragraphs 1 and 3 of Art. II (*B*) respectively. Sub-paragraph 1 refers to 'total equality' which may be construed as a comprehensive concept. It would include juridical as well as voting equality.[99] As a consequence the principle of total equality attaches importance to the rule of unanimity in voting procedures if decisions and resolutions are to have any binding effect on the Member States, and no obligation arises for a Member State from such decisions and resolutions of the Organization which it does not support. An interpretation of the principle of sovereign equality, as set forth in the Declaration, is that all States 'have equal rights and duties and are equal members of the international community, notwithstanding differences of an economic, social, political or other nature'.[100] This interpretation of Article 2, paragraph (1) of the UN Charter ignores the fact that privileges conferred by the UN Charter upon permanent members of the Security Council are incompatible with the doctrine of equality of States.[101] In contrast, the principle of total equality, as contained in sub-paragraph 1 of Art. II (*B*) of the OIC Charter underlines equality before the law as well as factual equality within the Organization. However, as far as equal duties are concerned, the OIC Charter seems to have made an exception in Art. VII which deals with the financial obligations of Member States. Art. VII of the OIC Charter stipulates that all expenses are to be borne 'by Member States according to their national incomes'.

3.2.2.3. *Principles of Self-determination and Non-intervention*

According to sub-paragraph 2 of Art. II (*B*) Member States of the OIC are to show 'respect of the right of self-determination, and non-interference in the domestic affairs of Member States'. Appearing in the context of sub-paragraph 2 both the principles seem to be inter-related and complementary in their application. A proper understanding and interpretation of this principle may be achieved by a brief survey of various connotations attached to the principle of self-determination.

The principle of self-determination is, *inter alia*, mentioned in Art. 1 (2) of the UN Charter,[102] in Art. 1 of both the International

Covenants,[103] in the *UNGA* 'Declaration on the Granting of Independence to Colonial Countries and Peoples'[104] (Res. 1514 (XV), 14 Dec. 1960), and in the 'Declaration on Principles of International Law Concerning Friendly Relations and Co-operation Among States'.[105] For the sake of clarity we may distinguish two periods during which the principle of self-determination is said to have become operative as a 'legal right'.[106] The first period began at the close of the First World War with the proclamation of the right of self-determination in universal terms by the US President Wilson, and to which substantial consideration was given by the drafters in drafting Article 22 of the Covenant of the League of Nations.[107] The 'right' of self-determination claimed by the Palestinians in Palestine and the Namibians in Namibia can be traced back to this period. The second period of operativeness begins at the end of the Second World War and seems to have culminated in the 'Declaration on Granting of Independence to Colonial Countries and Peoples' (1960). Those who are inclined to accept the right of self-determination as a legal right,[108] usually qualify it to be applicable to colonial countries and peoples. This has been confirmed by the 'Declaration on Principles' (1970) which explicitly refers to the duty of every State to promote the realization of the principle of equal rights and self-determination in order 'to bring a speedy end to colonialism, having due regard to the freely expressed will of the peoples concerned'.[109] The exercise of the right of self-determination by colonial peoples was understood to be equated with complete independence,[110] although certain exceptions were possible. However, the Declaration on Principles has clearly stated the modes of implementing the right of self-determination as being the 'establishment of a sovereign and independent state, the free association or integration with an independent state or the emergence into any other political status freely determined'.[111]

The crucial question is whether the right of self-determination is applicable to all peoples or is limited to colonial situations and peoples? If it applies as a legal right to all peoples, then does it include the right to secession? This raises some fundamental problems for most Third World States which have usually asserted the limitations of the right of self-determination, despite widely held views to the contrary.[112] The insertion of the right of self-determination in the Declaration on Principles may give rise to assumptions that the principle has been finally accepted as a 'legal' right universally acceptable, but such hopes are unwarranted and unsupported by State practice. In the Nigerian conflict over Biafra and the attempted Katangan secession from the Congo, the UN[113] and the OAU[114] upheld the principle of territorial integrity instead of the right of self-determination. The only successful case of the application of the right of self-determination applied to a non-colonial situation, also held to be legitimate because of the deprivation of fundamental human rights, is that of Bangladesh. It may be argued that the exercise of the right of self-determination in Bangladesh is a special case which approaches the parameters of a colonial situation because of the precision of definition of the group of people to which this right applied.[115] Even if we hold the case of Bangladesh to be a legitimate exercise of the right of self-determination, it raises the difficult question of aid by the armed forces of a third State, in the case of Bangladesh India, which seems to open up the possibilities of armed intervention on the basis of humanitarian policy considerations.[116] This will be giving a wide latitude to such actions by any third State powerful enough to interfere and influence the course of a civil war to its own advantage. Even the Declaration on Principles does not support such a conclusion. Reference to the right of self-determination in the Declaration on Principles as representing 'the formulation of self-determination as a universal right, belonging to any people, colonial or non-colonial, constituting or not constituting a sovereign state' has been correctly qualified as reflecting *de lege ferenda*.[117] The principle of territorial integrity is still strong and vital to the interests of Third World States and, in the case of a clash with the right of self-determination, the former shall prevail. The practice of States is confirmed by the Declaration which supports the principle of territorial integrity and the prevalent attitude by clearly stating that the right of self-determination shall not 'be construed as authorizing or encouraging any action which would dismember or impair, totally or in part, the territorial integrity or political unity of sovereign and independent states'.[118]

Another, and in our case the most relevant, meaning attached to the principle of self-determination is that of 'internal' self-determination, however. The principle of 'internal' self-determination encompasses the right of each sovereign State freely to determine and pursue its economic, social, and cultural development without external interference. Whereas the Declaration on Principles formulates it as 'the right freely to determine, without external interference, their political status and to pursue their economic, social and cultural development, and every state has the duty to respect this right in accordance with the provisions of the Charter',[119] the *UNGA* Declaration on Non-Intervention (Res. 2131 (XX), 21 Dec. 1965) declares that 'every state has an alienable right to choose its political, economic, social and cultural systems, without interference in any form, by another state'.[120] Thus the interpretation of the principle of self-determination as a right to 'internal' self-determination shows it to be a complementary part of the principle of non-intervention.[121] Thus reference to the 'respect of the right of self-determination' in Art. II (*B*) 2 of the OIC Charter is neither a reference to the right of self-determination of colonial peoples nor to its application to 'all peoples' but is a direct reference to its formulation in the Declaration on Principles. The question of the applicability of the principle of self-determination to colonial countries and peoples has been endorsed in Art. II (*A*) 3 of the Charter which has as its objective the eradication of colonialism. The application of the right of self-determination to 'all peoples' and particularly, to 'Moslem peoples' is endorsed in Art. II (*A*) 6, although this right is circumscribed in the case of Member States by Art. II (*B*) 3. Thus the only possible explanation and interpretation of the right of self-determination in the context of Art. II (*B*) 2 is that which is given in conjunction with the principle of non-intervention. It is to be interpreted as the duty of every Member State to respect the political, economic, social, and cultural systems prevailing in other Member States.[122] While respect of the right of self-determination in the context of sub-paragraph 2 is a positive duty, the principle of 'non-interference in the domestic affairs of member States' is a negative injunction. Both principles, as embodied in Art. II (*B*) 2 of the OIC Charter, are two sides of the same coin.

The principle of non-intervention, as stipulated in Art. II (*B*) 2, is a corollary of the principles of sovereignty and independence.[123] By virtue of independence, which is a fundamental principle of international law,[124] each Member State has the right freely to regulate its internal affairs without outside interference. As far as the term 'domestic affairs' is concerned, it reflects the meaning of 'domestic jurisdiction' contained in Art. 2 (7) of the UN Charter. The latter concerns the prohibition of intervention on the part of the UN in matters which are essentially deemed to be within the domestic jurisdiction of any Member State.[125] The principle of non-intervention, if taken to mean armed intervention in its classical sense, is closely related with the prohibition of threat or use of force as enshrined in

Art. 2 (4) of the UN Charter. However, the principle concerning the duty not to intervene in matters within the domestic jurisdiction of any State, as elaborated by the Declaration on Principles, if read in conjunction with the exercise of the inalienable right of every State to choose its political, economic, social, and cultural systems, primarily involves the prohibition of use or the encouragement of the 'use of economic, political, or any other type of measures to coerce another state in order to obtain from it the subordination of the exercise of its sovereign rights and to secure from it advantages of any kind'.[126] Although the principle of non-intervention includes 'armed intervention' the drawing of a sharp line of difference between armed intervention and the definition of 'force' in Art. 2 (4) of the UN Charter has become difficult.[127] Some have set down five elements[128] closely modelled on the contents of the Declaration:

(*a*) acts of coercion involving the organizing of hostile expeditions;
(*b*) acts calculated to impair the authority of another sovereign;
(*c*) acts purposive of fomenting civil strife in another State;
(*d*) organizing rebellion in friendly States;
(*e*) activity of private individuals amounting to threat to security, as constituting salient features of the principle of non-intervention.

Others[129] hold the view that the principle of non-intervention includes prohibition of subversive activities but basically excludes the activities of private persons, including corporations.

Apart from subversive activities or direct military intervention, the principle of non-intervention prohibits coercive measures of an economic nature which may be taken by one or more States in order to coerce another State or States to act in a certain manner.[130] Although, in contrast to Eastern European, Latin American, and Afro-Asian States, the attitude of Western countries on the subject of economic coercion, as elaborated in the Declaration on Principles, was negative, their position changed dramatically in favour of this prohibition when confronted with the Arab Oil Embargo in 1973.[131] Thus Western countries, suddenly finding themselves in the shoes of another, were equally quick to complain when they pinched.

From the foregoing discussion of the parameters of the right of self-determination and the principle of non-intervention, we may conclude that 'respect of the right of self-determination' as stipulated in Art. II (*B*) 2 of the OIC Charter does not apply to the right of 'all peoples', including those ethnic groups and minorities inhabiting the territories of Member States, to secede from the political and territorial integrity of the existing national States. On the contrary, secession movements would be construed as falling within the ambit of the domestic affairs of the Member States, and any support, direct or indirect, political, military or otherwise, for the secessionists would be deemed to be an interference in the domestic affairs of the affected State and in violation of Art. II (*B*) 2.[132] Similarly, reliance by Member States of the OIC on such an interpretation severely restricts the furtherance of the objective stipulated in Art. II (*A*) 6, as the support of secessionist movements in non-Muslim States would constitute an interference in the domestic affairs of those States. By relying on a similar interpretation in their own case, they are estopped from embarking on contrary action. Furthermore, since every Member State is under a duty to respect the form of government and economic, social, and cultural systems prevailing in other Member States, the negative injunction implies that they are to refrain from undertaking any activities or use coercive measures in any form calculated to impair the authority or destabilize the government of another sovereign Member State.

3.2.2.4. *Principle of Sovereignty*

Art. II (*B*) 3 of the OIC Charter calls for 'respect of the sovereignty independence and territorial integrity of each member State'. The principle of sovereignty of States, together with that of equality, is one of the fundamental principles of international law. A fully sovereign State is said to be 'one which is not subordinate in its capacity for international action to any other legal entity',[133] whereby, the principle of independence is said to be a legal attribute of sovereignty.[134] The principle of sovereignty is endorsed by Art. 2 (1) of the UN Charter and Art. III (1) of the OAU Charter as the 'principle of sovereign equality'. We have already noted that the OIC Charter draws a distinction between the principles of sovereignty and equality by stating them separately. In its interpretation of the 'principle of sovereign equality' as contained in Art. 2 (1) of the UN Charter, the technical committee at the San Francisco Conference in 1945 noted the following four elements to be inherent in this principle:

(1) the states are juridically equal;
(2) that each state enjoys the rights inherent in full sovereignty;
(3) that the personality of the state is respected, as well as its territorial integrity and political independence;

(4) that the state should, under international order, comply faithfully with its international duties and obligations.[135]

During the deliberations in the UN Special Committee on Friendly Relations which finally produced the Declaration on Principles, there was a (unanimous) consensus of all States on the above-mentioned elements.[136] However, the Declaration does elaborate further upon these points by adding the following:

(1) the territorial integrity and political independence of the state are inviolable;
(2) each state has the right freely to choose and develop its political, social, economic, and cultural systems.[137]

Attempts on the part of Western countries to insert an additional interpretative clause in the Declaration to the effect that the principle of sovereignty is subject to the supremacy of international law was rejected by Soviet bloc States and 'uncommitted' countries which maintained 'that respect for state sovereignty was a basic condition for the maintenance of world peace and for co-operation . . . [it] was the foundation of contemporary international law, which reflected the voluntary agreement of states'.[138]

Thus the principle of sovereignty embodied in sub-paragraph 3 of Art. II (*B*) of the OIC Charter is not only reminiscent of Art. 2 (1) of the UN Charter, it also reflects the basic position taken by Latin American and Afro-Asian States on the relationship between the principle of sovereignty and international law. The emphasis laid by Member States of the OIC on the principle of sovereignty is an unequivocal and emphatic 'no' to supranationalism.[139] Following precedents of the OAS, OAU and the Pact of the Arab League, the OIC Charter underlines the dominant role of the principle of sovereignty, independence and territorial integrity in inter-Islamic relations. Jealously guarding their recently regained independence from colonial tutelage, laying stress on the exercise of sovereign control over their natural resources and economic activities, and upholding the principle of territorial integrity of Member States, the contents of Art. II (*B*) 3 of the OIC Charter sharply define and delimit the contours of 'Islamic solidarity'.

3.2.2.5. *Principle of Peaceful Settlement of Disputes*

Art. II (*B*) 4 of the OIC Charter is a corollary of the principle laid down in Art. II (*B*) 5 which calls for the 'abstention from the threat or use of force against the territorial integrity, national unity or political independence of any member State'. Both these stipulations reflect the essence of Art. 2 (3) and (4) of the UN Charter.[140]

Art. II (*B*) 4 stipulates the settlement of 'any conflict that may arise' by peaceful means. The essential content of sub-paragraph 4 is similar to Art. 2 (3) of the UN Charter which obliges Member States of the UN to settle their 'international disputes' by peaceful means. Art. 2 (3) does not specify the methods of peaceful settlement which are dealt with in Art. 33 and 37. Art. 33 (1) of the UN Charter specifies the methods as 'negotiation, enquiry, mediation, conciliation, arbitration, judicial settlement, resort to regional agencies or arrangements, or other peaceful means of their own choice'. Failing to achieve a settlement through these means, the parties to a dispute are to refer it, in accordance with Art. 37 (1) of the UN Charter, to the Security Council.

Art. II (*B*) 4 of the OIC Charter enumerates the means of peaceful settlement as 'negotiation, mediation, reconciliation or arbitration'. It is interesting to note that, except for a few omissions, sub-paragraph 4 retains on the whole the order listed in Art. 33 (1) of the UN Charter. The phrase 'first of all' occurring before the term 'negotiation' in paragraph 1 of Art. 33 tends to qualify the method of settling disputes through 'negotiations' as a primary means of pacific settlement with others following in a descending order. Thus 'negotiation' would be perceived, as appearing in the context of sub-paragraph 4 of the OIC Charter, to be a primary means of settling disputes among Member States of the OIC, failing which resort may be had to mediation, reconciliation, or arbitration. However, sub-paragraph 4 is conspicuous for its absence of the term 'judicial settlement' implying a negative attitude of Member States towards this particular method of pacific settlement.

This negative attitude, which is shared by other States, is reflected in the Declaration on Principles. Although the Declaration elaborates upon Art. 2 (3) of the UN Charter,[141] and repeats the formula of Art. 33 (1), emphasis is placed on the principle of sovereignty from which emanates the principle of free choice of means.[142] This is despite the fact that recourse to freely accepted judicial settlement of disputes is not a derogation of and incompatible with the principle of sovereignty, a point which is affirmed by the Declaration.[143] Socialist bloc countries and some Third World States consider direct negotiations to be the fundamental means of peaceful settlement.[144] The basic reason underlying the negative attitude of States toward third party adjudication in general, and the International Court of Justice in particular, is the conviction that judicial agencies are not suitable for resolution and settlement of all conflicts, the majority of which constitute disputes as to conflicts of interests based on claims for a change in the existing law.[145] Moreover, litigation, whether before the International Court of Justice or other regional agencies, is not considered by many States to be a friendly act;[146] as a result, many African and Asian States, including OIC Member States, prefer to settle their conflicts by negotiation, mediation, and conciliation. In Islam, methods of negotiation, mediation, and reconciliation have been given traditional preference and lent weight by the Prophet's advice that a direct arrangement between the parties at dispute is better than an arbitral or a judicial decision because a genuine peace and settlement can be achieved as a result of mutual concessions freely accepted by the parties and not imposed upon them by external authority.[147] Although the Islamic legal system provides legal machinery for judicial settlement, and we find in history several cases of political and legal arbitration during the Prophet's lifetime and afterwards,[148] the method of achieving settlement of disputes among Muslims through reconciliation (*sulh*) was considered permissible.[149] Thus in the spirit of Islamic legal tradition and practice Art. II (*B*) 4 lists various means of peaceful settlement in order of preference. Member States of the OIC are to seek peaceful settlement of conflicts, first by entering into negotiations. If this fails to achieve any results there may be efforts at mediation and reconciliation. Finally, if all other means have been exhausted without bringing about any settlement, resort may be had to arbitration. In showing preference for arbitration instead of judicial settlement, the OIC Charter confirms the attitude and practice prevailing in Member States,[150] which prefer arbitration because representatives of both parties to the dispute may take part in the judgment.

Art. II (*B*) 4 stipulates the settlement of conflicts by peaceful means but envisages no legal machinery to facilitate arbitration among Member States. Whereas other means of dispute settlement, such as negotiation, mediation, and reconciliation, may be launched through diplomatic channels and the good offices of third parties[151] or taken up for consideration by the Islamic Conference of Foreign Ministers in accordance with provisions of Art. V (2) *g*, the Charter fails to indicate any instrument or body within the framework of the OIC which could serve as an arbitral commission. This position may be contrasted with the OAU Commission of Mediation, Conciliation, and Arbitration established by virtue of Art. 19 of the OAU Charter.[152] Similarly, Art. 5 of the Pact of the League of Arab States empowers the Arab League Council to take decisions relating to arbitration and mediation by a majority vote,[153] or keeps the option open, as in Art. 19, for an amendment of the Pact to facilitate the creation of an Arab Court of Justice.[154] However, the inherent weakness of Art. 5 of the Arab League Pact, which excludes from arbitration all disputes over the independence, sovereignty, or territorial integrity of any State,[155] the rejection of compulsory jurisdiction by the Arab States, and the failure of arbitration before the Arab League Council,[156] may have acted as strong deterrents to any similar attempts being incorporated in the OIC Charter. Given the present mood of laying overemphasis on the principle of sovereignty, the negative attitude of many Member States of the OIC to compulsory jurisdiction in any form and before any court, and the loose character of the OIC as merely a forum of consultation and co-operation, the chances of reactivating the shelved plans of an Arab Court of Justice in the guise of an Islamic Court of Justice actively applying general principles of Islamic law in the development of international law between Islamic States seem, at present, to be limited.[157]

3.2.2.6. *Principle of Abstention from the Use of Force*

Art. II (*B*) 5 of the OIC Charter stipulates 'abstention from the threat or use of force against the territorial integrity, national unity or political independence of any member State'. Art. II (*B*) 5 seems to be a cardinal principle of the OIC Charter, the violation of which would make the contents of sub-paragraph 3 insignificant. The principle to respect the sovereignty, independence, and territorial integrity of each Member State would remain meaningless without any prohibition of resort to force. Thus in the context of Art. II, paragraph (*B*) as a whole, sub-paragraphs 3 and 5 are complementary in their meaning and application.

Apart from a slight change in wording and some omissions, Art. II (*B*) 5 of the OIC Charter could be considered to be a restatement of Art. 2 (4) of the UN Charter. The word 'refrain', as used in Art. 2 (4), has been replaced by the word 'abstention' in Art. II (*B*) 5 of the OIC Charter. Both words, however, are synonymous in their meanings, which is to withhold or forbear from committing some act. The principle of abstention from the threat or use of force, as embodied in Art. 2 (4) of the UN Charter, has become a fundamental principle of universal international law. It possesses not only the character of a contractual obligation embodied in a treaty binding on the members of the United Nations, but is said to be a general rule of customary international law having binding character for and even enforceable against non-Member States of the UN.[158]

Art. II (*B*) 5 of the OIC Charter calls upon Member States to abstain (or refrain) from the threat or use of force 'against the territorial integrity, national unity or political independence of any Member State'. Within the context of Art. 2 (4) of the UN Charter, the phrase 'against the territorial integrity or political independence' does not introduce any element of intent,[159] but epitomizes comprehensive legal rights against which the threat or use of force could be directed.[160] Analogously, the obligation to abstain from the threat or use of force in Art. II (*B*) 5 of the OIC Charter would be applicable to the totality of rights inherent in the concepts of political independence and territorial integrity. Furthermore, sub-paragraph 5 mentions the term 'national unity', which may be construed as an added emphasis on the prohibition of the use of force to break up the national unity of Member States; it would include the obligation to abstain from extending help to secessionist groups within the present territorial demarcations of Member States.

The term 'force', as used in Art. II (*B*) 5 of the OIC Charter and Art. 2 (4) of the UN Charter, and as understood for purposes of legal prohibition, primarily means the use of 'armed force'.[161] According to the Declaration on Principles, 'armed force' includes the regular armed forces of the state as well as 'irregular forces or armed bands, including mercenaries'.[162] It should, however, be noted that Art. II (*B*) 5 of the OIC Charter calls not only for abstention from the use of 'force' but also from the 'threat' of force. This constitutes an exception to the interpretation of 'force' as meaning 'armed force' and may be considered as an example of the use of 'non-physical force' coming within the definition of Art. II (*B*) 5 of the OIC Charter as well as Art. 2 (4) of the UN Charter.[163]

As far as the 'use' of force is concerned, it consists of direct and indirect use of force. The direct use of force includes all sorts of use by regular forces of a State directed towards the territory of another. It is immaterial whether these acts are intended to harm the territorial integrity or political independence of the affected State or not. All sorts of forceful actions carried out by regular forces, including acts of reprisal or retaliation involving the use of force, fall under the prohibition of the principle of abstention from the threat or use of force.[164] According to the elaborations contained in the Declaration on Principles, indirect use of force, in the form of 'armed force', consists of 'organizing or encouraging the organization of irregular forces or armed bands, including mercenaries, for incursion into the territory of another state'.[165] In addition, the Declaration elaborates upon another form of indirect force, distinct from the meaning of 'armed force'. Indirect non-military force consists of 'organizing, instigating, assisting or participating in acts of civil strife or terrorist acts in another state or acquiescing in organized activities within its territory directed towards the commission of such acts'.[166] It seems, therefore, that the prohibitionary regulation of subversive, terrorist, or armed activities involving indirect use of force falls within the ambit of the obligation to abstain (or refrain) from the 'use of force' in international relations, as embodied in Art. 2 (4) of the UN Charter and restated in Art. II (*B*) 5 of the OIC Charter, as well as the principle of non-intervention. Nevertheless, reference must be made to some objections made to the formulation contained in the Declaration to the effect that acts committed by guerrilla organizations and others with the object of liberating their lands from the yoke of colonialism or illegal occupation are to be excepted from the general rule of prohibiting indirect use of force.[167]

It is not clear from the wording of Art. II (*B*) 5 of the OIC Charter, however, whether the term 'force' is to be restricted to 'armed force', including regular and irregular forces, or may be construed as including 'other forms of pressure'[168]–the latter interpretation being favoured by Third World States (including Islamic States)[169] and Soviet bloc countries. The inclusion of 'other forms of pressure' within the technical meaning of the word 'force', as used in Art. II (*B*) 5 of the OIC Charter, seems to be problematical if Member States exercise the right of self-defence.

Although the OIC Charter does not mention any exceptions to the scope and application of Art. II (*B*) 5, it cannot be said to have impaired the inherent right of self-defence, the exercise of which is deemed as a lawful use of force.[170] Furthermore, Art. 51 of the UN Charter, which may be invoked by OIC Member States by virtue of their membership of the UN, and which provides for the use of force in cases of self-defence, unequivocally states that 'the inherent right of individual or collective self-defence' is to be exercised 'if an armed attack occurs'. This provision seems to restrict the exercise of the right of self-defence to causes in which an armed attack actually occurs.[171] Despite the clear wording of Art. 51 of the UN Charter, there seems to be some controversy about the phrase 'if an armed attack occurs'. It has been asserted that Art. 51 does not prohibit anticipatory self-defence which is a traditional right existing in relation to an 'imminent' attack.[172] Such an extensive interpretation would open up possibilities of justifying unlawful use of force under the mantle of anticipatory self-defence.[173] Whereas the criteria for deciding whether an armed attack is 'imminent' or not are left to the subjective discretion of the State claiming to have exercised the right of anticipatory self-defence, the conditioning clause of Art. 51 provides objectively verifiable criteria for the use of armed force in the exercise of the right of self-defence.[174]

Thus, if we were to include 'other forms of pressure', such as political and economic pressure threatening the territorial integrity or political independence of a State, within the meaning of the word 'force' used in Art. II (*B*) 5 of the OIC Charter, it would certainly inhibit the exercise of the right of self-defence under Art. 51 of the UN Charter by the affected State because the 'force' being directed towards it cannot be construed to mean 'an armed attack'.[175]

3.2.2.7. *Legal Character of the Principles*

From the foregoing discussion of principles contained in Art. II, paragraph (*B*) of the OIC Charter we may summarize the legal character of the principles as follows:

(i) the principles of sovereignty and equality are fundamental principles on which the whole edifice of international law rests;

(ii) the principle of abstention from the threat of force enjoys the status of being a principle of customary and universal international law;

(iii) the positive obligation to settle conflicts that may arise among Member States by peaceful means is a corollary of the prohibition of resorting to force, and, therefore, possesses the character of a rule of customary and universal international law;[176]

(iv) the principle of non-interference is primarily based upon the wider principles of sovereignty and total equality;

(v) finally, the right of self-determination has received recognition as a 'legal' right in the context of non-self-governing territories and peoples;[177] if applied in conjunction with the principle of non-interference, the right of self-determination elaborates upon the contents of the principles of sovereignty and political independence.

Thus we may conclude that the legal character of the principles embodied in the Islamic Charter, which accordingly represent the basis of inter-Islamic relations today, may be considered to be declaratory of existing general principles of international law and thus binding upon Member States by virtue of their being:

(*a*) treaty obligations incorporated in the OIC Charter. Even if the wording of Art. II (*B*) does not seem to create legal obligation in express terms, the principles constitute
(*b*) general principles embodied in universal legal instruments,
(*c*) and also reflect principles of customary international law.

3.2.3. Membership, Withdrawal, and Sanctions

The membership of the OIC is primarily composed of those States which participated in the first Summit Conference in Rabat and the subsequent Foreign Ministers' Conferences held in Jeddah and Karachi. Thus reference is made to these participatory States at the beginning of the Preamble as well as in Art. VIII. The condition of eligibility, as laid down by Art. VIII, refers to every 'Muslim State . . . expressing its desire and preparedness to adopt this Charter'.

The Charter does not define the term 'Muslim State' but it would probably include any State which feels itself bound by common ties of belief and the wish 'to promote Islamic solidarity'. This problem, however, caused considerable debate regarding the original draft text of the Charter which contained an appendix stipulating that those participatory States which 'owing to constitutional reasons have been unable to join the Conference as states of full membership, may participate in the Conference as participating states'.[178] The appendix caused strong objections on the grounds that it might create an artificial distinction between full members and half-members leaving the possibility open for States to claim participatory status only, thus gaining release from all obligations towards the Conference.[179] Moreover, the Charter contained no extraordinary obligations purporting to compel any State to apply the Islamic *Shariʿah* or take up arms for the sake of justice and right. Its duties and obligations were no different from any other international organization.[180] Finally, a compromise was achieved by deleting the appendix and adopting the Charter as it was; those States which had reservations were to submit them in writing.[181] Thus the preparedness of a State to adopt the Charter of the OIC does not imply the acceptance of the Islamic *Shariʿah* in any way.[182]

As far as withdrawal or the imposition of sanctions is concerned, any Member State may withdraw from the OIC by sending a written notification to the Secretariat which is to be communicated to all Member States (Art. X). The only obligation deemed binding upon the withdrawing State is the fulfilment of its financial commitments until the end of the fiscal year. Following precedents of the OAS and OAU Charters and the Pact of the Arab League, the Charter of the OIC does not contain any provisions dealing with the suspension or expulsion of Member States. The absence of any provision dealing with sanctions, however, did not deter the Member States of the OIC from declaring the membership of Egypt and Afghanistan suspended. Whereas the suspension of the membership of Afghanistan in the OIC still continues, that of Egypt seems to have been 'officially' removed in January 1984 because of its participation in the fourth Islamic Summit Conference held in Casablanca, Morocco.[183] In both cases, however, it may be argued that the imposition of such sanctions as the suspension of membership have no legal basis in the Charter.

As far as the suspension of the membership of Afghanistan is concerned, it may be interpreted as a collective act of non-recognition of the present Government of Afghanistan by the members of the OIC. As long as foreign armed forces 'occupy' the territory of Afghanistan, it would be difficult to accept the legitimacy of the Government of Afghanistan. Moreover, as a country tolerating and even encouraging continued Soviet military presence, Afghanistan cannot be said to be an 'independent' State in the proper sense of the term. It therefore cannot be said to be in a position to accept fully its obligations and enjoy rights ensuing from the OIC Charter. Hence the Conference of Kings and Heads of State and Government which is, by virtue of Art. IV, 'the supreme authority in the organisation', assembled for the third Summit Conference in Mecca in 1981 and unanimously decided to suspend the membership of Afghanistan. In this act of suspension the Summit Conference may be said to have acted in accordance with the objective set down in Art. II (*A*) 6 of the OIC Charter.

The suspension of Egypt's membership of the OIC was caused by

Egypt's participation in the Camp David Accords and the conclusion of a 'separate' peace treaty with Israel without achieving substantial concessions in favour of the Palestinians. Whether the substance of the Camp David Accords could serve the purpose of achieving peace in the Middle East and help the Palestinians regain their homeland or not is a matter of interpretation.[184] But the fact that Egypt acted alone, without any endorsement of its position and the act of recognition of Israel by other Arab and Islamic States, and has remained virtually isolated in its moves of conciliation with Israel, is an indicator of the general opinion about the value of these agreements. By its actions, Egypt has jeopardized the achievement of the objective outlined in Art. II (*A*) 5 of the OIC Charter which calls for the 'co-ordination of efforts for the safeguard of the Holy Places and support of the struggle of the people of Palestine'. Instead of co-ordinating with the efforts of the OIC, Egypt acted, in the opinion of Arab and Islamic States, in complete disharmony to undo what had already been consolidated. As a result Member States took a unanimous decision to suspend Egypt's membership of the OIC. Even the recent comeback of Egypt to the OIC forum does not invalidate the original objections to its participation in the Camp David Agreements. Only political events, such as the invasion of Lebanon by Israel and sectarian strife within the PLO, have facilitated Egypt's political comeback.

Nevertheless, it is appropriate to dwell on the question whether the imposition of such a sanction upon Egypt, even if it was of a temporary nature, has any legal basis in the OIC Charter, in treaty, or in customary international law. The OIC Charter does not contain any provisions on the imposition of sanctions. Therefore, the answer to the first part of the query is in the negative. However, the legal nature of the Charter and the legal consequences that may ensue from the violation of provisions contained therein necessitates the examination of the latter in some detail. The Charter of the OIC embodies the legal constitution and foundation of the Organization, which is in the nature of a contractual document (Charter) and as such duly signed and ratified by sovereign States. It is, therefore, a multilateral treaty establishing legal rights and obligations which the Member States are bound to carry out in good faith.[185] By acting alone and in complete disharmony with the general policy of the OIC Member States, Egypt has failed to fulfil its obligations under Art. II (*A*) 5 of the Charter. Since the Charter does not regulate situations concerning a breach of its provisions or failure of the parties to fulfil their obligations under it, we may look for the appropriate rule applicable in this particular situation to general principles of international law regulating termination of a treaty relationship on account of a breach of its provisions.

There is wide support for the proposition that a violation in the form of a 'material breach' of a treaty by one party entitles the other party or parties to terminate or suspend the operation of the treaty and to retaliate by means of peaceable reprisals.[186] The term 'material breach' has been defined in Art. 60 (3) *b* of the Vienna Convention on the Law of Treaties as 'the violation of a provision essential to the accomplishment of the object or purpose of the treaty'.[187] In the case of multilateral treaties, Art. 60 (2) of the Vienna Convention, *inter alia*, stipulates that a 'material breach' of a multilateral treaty by one of the parties entitles the others to suspend or terminate, by unanimous agreement, the operation of the treaty in whole or in part in the relations between themselves and the defaulting State. Furthermore, rules embodied in the Vienna Convention apply to a treaty which is the constituent instrument of an international organization without prejudice to any relevant rules of the organization (Art. 5).

Although the Vienna Convention on the Law of Treaties is in force[188] and, therefore, binding on the parties to the Convention, only a small number of OIC Member States have so far either signed, ratified, or acceded to the Convention.[189] States which have not become parties to a Convention cannot be held to have accepted its provisions as customary rules of international law if they happen to apply them as 'no general inference could justifiably be drawn that they believed themselves to be applying a mandatory rule of customary international law'.[190] It is, therefore, incumbent to show that the rules laid down by the Vienna Convention on the Law of Treaties concerning termination or suspension of a treaty on account of a breach may be considered to be a codification of the rules of customary law.

It has been asserted that the rule concerning the termination or suspension of a constituent instrument of an international organization as a consequence of its breach by one of its parties, as embodied in Art. 60 (2) *a* of the Vienna Convention, cannot be considered to have developed into a rule of customary international law.[191] Others have expressed the opinion that in case of violations of an obligation defined by the constituent instrument of an organization 'only the specially authorized organ of the organization will have the right to draw the conclusion from such an infringement'.[192] However, in the advisory opinion rendered on the Legal Consequences for States of the Continued Presence of South Africa in Namibia (South West Africa) Notwithstanding Security Council Resolution 276, the International Court of Justice expressed the learned opinion that: 'The rules laid down by the Vienna Convention on the Law of Treaties concerning termination of a treaty relationship on account of breach (adopted without a dissenting vote) may in many respects be considered as a codification of existing customary law on the subject.'[193]

Egypt's conclusion of a separate peace with and recognition of Israel is detrimental to the interests of the Palestinians as interpreted by the OIC Member States. It has driven a wedge in the concept of Islamic solidarity *vis-à-vis* the Palestine issue and weakened the purpose of Art. II (*A*) 5. And since the objective laid down in Art. II (*A*) 5 represents the basic purpose of the OIC Charter, violation of this provision by Egypt constitutes a 'material breach' of the treaty. Thus actions committed by Egypt justify the suspension of its membership of the OIC. In the light of the foregoing, and in accord with the opinion of the Court cited above, we may conclude that the unanimous decision of OIC Member States assembled for the third Summit Conference in Taif/Mecca (1981) to suspend Egypt's membership of the OIC is based upon rules codified in the Vienna Convention on the Law of Treaties which may be considered to be part of customary international law.[194]

3.3. ORGANIZATIONAL STRUCTURE

According to Art. III of the OIC Charter the Islamic Conference is composed of three main bodies, namely the Summit Conference of Kings and Heads of State and Government, the Conference of Foreign Ministers, and the General Secretariat and subsidiary organs.

3.3.1. Summit Conference

By virtue of Art. IV the Summit Conference 'is the supreme authority in the organization'. So far there have been three Summit Conferences, the first being held in Rabat (1969), the second in Lahore (1974) and the third in Taif/Mecca (1981). The irregular interval of time between the summits was a direct result of Art. IV which provides for them being held 'whenever the interest of Moslem nations warrants it to consider issues of vital concern to the Moslem world'. This was a vague and cumbersome provision which meant that in the absence of some spectacular event, such as in 1969, which aroused the Islamic States to unity or a rather pressing need felt by a majority of the States, a Summit Conference could not be convened. Furthermore, the phrase 'whenever the interest of Moslem nations warrants it' would normally require substantial diplomatic activity preceding the summit to achieve a consensus on 'the interest' warranting a Summit Conference. On the other hand, Art. V (1) *c* of the Charter bestows a 'right' on the Conference of Foreign Ministers 'to recommend the convening of a Conference'. Nevertheless, the recommendation had to be circulated to all Member States in the first place in order to obtain approval.

A resolution remedying this situation was passed by the third Summit Conference, thus regularizing the holding of summits every three years. This cannot be construed as an amendment of the Charter; it is the resolution of a procedural question which leaves the possibility of convening a summit in accordance with provisions of Art. IV open. However, the Charter says nothing as to the legal character of Summit Conference resolutions. We may, therefore, deduce from the Charter as a whole, and in particular by applying the provisions of Art. II, paragraph (*B*), that the rule of unanimity applies to resolutions of the Summit Conference. As far as procedural questions are concerned, resolutions of the Summit Conference probably have binding force on all organs and Member States of the Conference even if they are majority decisions. This is because of Art. IV which describes the legal character of the summit to be 'the supreme authority'. Resolutions dealing with substantive issues or policy decisions are binding on those who have voted for them. For, 'nations that vote for a particular statement of law cannot act quite as though they had not done so'.[195]

3.3.2. Conference of Foreign Ministers

The Conference of Foreign Ministers is by far the most important body of the OIC. By virtue of Art. V (1) *a* the Conference is to be convened once a year and when the need arises an extraordinary session may be convened at the request of any Member State or at the request of the Secretary-General if approved by two-thirds of the Member States.[196] Art. V (2) of the Charter sets out the functions and procedure of the Conference and thereby underlines its importance.

In its annual meetings the ICFM deliberates on all types of reports submitted by various commissions, committees and expert groups and takes appropriate decisions to implement the general policy of the Conference (Art. V (2) *a*). Decisions, resolutions, and recommendations of the Conference have to be adopted by a two-thirds majority (Art. V (3)). Thus, theoretically, a majority of the Member States supporting a decision taken at the ICFM would have (and should have) no objection to implementing it within their national territories. However, delays do occur in the implementation of decisions at the national level. Moreover, a decision of the ICFM does not have any binding force on those States which have voted against or abstained. It is also questionable whether a decision or resolution of the ICFM has binding force even on those who have voted for it as the Charter says nothing on this point. As we have argued in the case of resolutions issued by the Summit Conference (see 3.3.1) the same would probably apply in the case of ICFM resolutions and decisions dealing with substantive and policy issues. As far as procedural questions are concerned, the Conference of Foreign Ministers is empowered by virtue of Art. V (5) to decide the basic procedure it follows as well as the one to be followed by the Summit Conference. In matters of procedure a two-thirds majority decision would be binding. Only the General Secretariat is fully bound to comply with the substantive as well as the procedural decisions of the ICFM (Art. VI (3)).

In the implementation of the general policy of the OIC the ICFM is empowered to set up commissions, committees, and expert groups to study various matters or to create specialized agencies.[197] Another important function is to discuss the report of the Financial Committee and approve the budget of the Secretariat (Art. V (2) *d*). The first Islamic Conference of Foreign Ministers had already decided that all expenses incurred for the administration and the activities of the Secretariat were to be borne by the Member States.[198] This has been elaborated by Art. VII (1) of the Charter which adds the phrase 'according to their national incomes'. The Conference also stipulates rules of procedure in accordance with which the Secretariat administers its financial affairs (Art. VII (2)). The preparation and supervision of the annual budget is done by a Standing Financial Committee created by Art. VII (3), consisting of accredited representatives of the participating States, in conjunction with the Secretary-General. Thus the final word in financial matters lies with the ICFM which exercises detailed financial control through the

Standing Financial Committee.[199] The only type of obligation stipulated by the Charter is the fiscal obligation. According to provisions of Art. X (2) any State applying for withdrawal from the Islamic Conference 'shall be bound by its obligations until the end of the fiscal year during which the application of withdrawal is submitted'.

The ICFM also appoints the Secretary-General and four Assistants[200] to the Secretary-General on his recommendation, which is to give due consideration to their competence, integrity, dedication to the Charter's objectives and equitable geographical distribution (Art. V (*e*, 1, 2 and 3). In appointing the Secretary-General the ICFM takes care to distribute the post regionally so that it is held in turn by persons originating from Asia, Africa, and the Arab World. This is a rule which could be suspended if a consensus emerges regarding a particular candidate for the post.[201]

3.3.3. General Secretariat

The General Secretariat with its present headquarters in Jeddah is the main co-ordinating body of the Islamic Conference. It secures communications among Member States, offers facilities for consultations, and disseminates information having common significance to these States (Art. VI (4)). The main burden of work, such as the follow-up and implementation of resolutions and recommendations of the ICFM, rests on the General Secretariat (Art. VI (6)). In order to facilitate this task the General Secretariat is divided into a number of departments,[202] each headed by a director and aided by an assistant director, both appointed by the Secretary-General. Each department is responsible for preparing and supplying working papers and memoranda to the Member States through appropriate channels. This requires a certain amount of co-ordination between various standing and *ad hoc* committees set up in accordance with provisions of Art. VII (3), as well as subsidiary organs[203] and independent expert groups set up by resolutions of the ICFM.

The work carried out by the General Secretariat is supplemented by specialized commissions set up under the functionalist approach to Islamic solidarity. The Islamic Commission of Economic, Cultural, and Social Affairs, which is an independent and permanent commission,[204] studies proposals tabled by Member States and the General Secretariat and is also empowered to set up independent expert groups[205] reporting their findings directly to the Conference.

It seems that the strength and efficiency of the OIC will largely depend on two factors: the willingness of Member States to promote the role of the General Secretariat overriding the jealous claims of sovereignty, and the strength and organized capability of the General Secretariat itself. It is most probable, therefore, that appointments of well-known and widely respected personalities as Secretaries-General of the OIC have been crucial to the initial development of the General Secretariat. Since the burden of implementation of resolutions and follow-up of conferences largely rests upon the General Secretariat, the successful organization and realization of concrete projects in practice would depend on the active participation and promotion of these projects by the General Secretariat as well as the Member States concerned. In this respect the future role of the OIC would depend, in addition to the organizational capability of the General Secretariat as led by an active and efficient Secretary-General, primarily on the attitude of the Member States.[206]

3.4. AN ASSESSMENT OF THE CHARTER

Despite the heterogeneous character of the OIC, its Charter reflects some basic principles enjoying common consent not only amongst its Member States but also in the wider international community. Notwithstanding this fact, the OIC is unique in the sense that it is based on religion functioning as a cohesive element beyond regional commitments and national ideologies. The formal reiteration of Islam as constituting a strong factor for *rapprochement* and solidarity is kept within a general framework of mutual consultation and co-operation to achieve the objectives of the Charter. The resolution to preserve Islamic spiritual, ethical, social, and economic values does not reinforce any commitment on the part of the Member States to the *Shari*ʿ*ah*, nor does the Charter have as its objective the reinstatement of classical principles of the *Siyar*. Even the organizational structure, as embodied in the Charter, bears testimony to the loose and flexible character of the OIC. It is, perhaps, this very loose framework which hampers any effective implementation of common political and legal policies at the national level. Given the heterogeneous character of the Organization, however, and, as the Charter itself reiterates, the need for *rapprochement* and solidarity, it is probably desirable that the framework of co-operation among Islamic States remain loose and flexible, leaving ample room for intensified relations on the bilateral or other sub-regional and regional levels. Far from purporting to set up a 'supranational' entity or even laying the foundations of an economic community, the Charter establishes an interregional forum of consultation and co-operation among Islamic States.

Since the first Summit Conference in Rabat (1969) the agenda of the OIC has grown from primary concern with the Jerusalem Question to cover a wide range of issues. Practical co-operation among Member States, especially in the economic and financial fields, has grown steadily. The Palestine issue remains a central concern of the OIC, however. During a period of more than 10 years, the OIC has evolved a consistent policy with regard to Palestine which is jointly endorsed by all Member States of the OIC. As early as 1969, the Islamic States assembled at Rabat had given due weight to this problem and underlined their attitude towards the representation of the Palestinians by inviting Yasser Arafat of the PLO to this historic Conference. The consistency of this policy may be further noted in the unanimous agreement of all OIC Member States assembled at Taif/Mecca (Saudi Arabia) for the third Summit in 1981 to suspend the membership of Egypt because of its participation in the Camp David Agreements. This is a manifestation of one aspect of political solidarity.

The uniqueness of the Charter also lies in the fact that, as a formal body composed of Islamic States which are the successor States of the Islamic world extant during the medieval age, it has given due recognition to universally recognized principles of international law, which at the same time provide a basis for fruitful inter-Islamic co-operation in various other fields. The content and scope of the principles embodied in the OIC Charter reflect those enshrined in the UN Charter and further elaborated in the 'Declaration on Principles of International Law Concerning Friendly Relations and Co-operation Among States'. In the preceding examination of its contents, we have tried to show that the Charter may be interpreted in a manner generally recognized as permissible in the interpretation of the principles embodied in the UN Charter bearing in mind that interpretations attached by Islamic States to some principles are typical of the general attitude taken up by other Third World States toward the same issues. Such issues include the right of self-determination in the case of colonial peoples, the nature and scope of the principle of sovereignty, and the right of every State freely to determine and choose its political and economic systems without external interference. The OIC Charter has a declaratory effect. Herein lies its legal value and merit because it restates and confirms universally recognized principles of international law and deems them binding upon Islamic States. The Charter may also be seen as a formal recognition of the universality of some principles of international law which are compatible with general principles of the Islamic *Shariʿah* as reflected in the Koran and *Sunnah*. After all, the Islamic States participated fully during the centuries of interaction and conflict with European nations, the fruit of which may be perceived in the evolution of general principles of international law with universal binding quality.

It could nevertheless be argued that the OIC may, in future, take a more militant stand in its relations towards other non-Islamic States. A radical change of attitude towards the principles enshrined in the OIC Charter may be accelerated and supported by a steady radicalization of Islamic orders at a national level. This would, it may be argued, give an opportunity to radical elements in the Islamic world to pursue a militant course, and, perhaps, even translate it collectively, i.e., through the OIC, into action. The Islamic revolution in Iran conjures up the wildest fantasies of militant Islam on the march. It would, therefore, be appropriate to clarify these issues at this point and examine in detail the attitude of Iran toward certain fundamental rules of international law.

We have already expressed our views on Islamic legal concepts and their application to the external relations of Islam in Chapter 2. The gist of our argument is that the Koran and the *Sunnah* of the Prophet provide ample evidence to support peaceful relations with non-Islamic communities and political entities. We have also demonstrated the contents of the OIC Charter in the earlier sections of this chapter. It is true that the attitude taken by individual States in their foreign relations with other States is an internal matter of that State and may only be of relevance if it is either collectively endorsed by the OIC or carries special legal consequences for third States. However, the present situation in Iran has given rise to a great deal of invective and condemnation at an international level because of the attitude of its present Government to some fundamental issues and rules of international law. We submit that these acts need to be understood in a much wider perspective and may not be deemed to stem from the 'Islamic' nature of the regime in Iran nor be sanctioned by the Koran and *Sunnah*.

The radical and uncompromising stand taken by the Government of the Islamic Republic of Iran, following the 'Islamic' revolution and the overthrow of the Shah, has been marked by a fundamental change in its attitude to past policies. Some acts, such as the holding of US diplomatic and consular staff as hostages in Tehran, which were committed with the express or tacit knowledge and support of the Government of Iran, stand in diametric opposition to the contents of the reservation expressed by the former Government under the Shah at the time of adoption and signature of the OIC Charter.[207] Thus Iran has actually swung from one extreme of the pendulum to the other and seems to be stuck there without any hope of normalizing its foreign relations. The situation in Iran is complex and needs some differentiation, however. There is no doubt that the acts committed by Iran and referred to above represent a flagrant breach of the obligations owed by Iran under international conventions regulating diplomatic law and under long-established rules of general international law. On this point there was unanimous agreement among the Judges of the International Court of Justice.[208] And there is equally no doubt that these acts violate established rules of the *Shari'ah* and, particularly, the *Siyar*, concerning the practice of the Prophet in matters of the protection of diplomats.[209] As the Government of Iran asserted in two written communications to the ICJ, however, the basic issue involved not only the question of the hostages of the US Embassy but 'an overall problem, one such that it cannot be studied separately, and which involves, *inter alia*, more than 25 years of continual interference by the United States in the internal affairs of Iran, the shameless exploitation of [that] country, and numerous crimes perpetrated against the Iranian people, contrary to and in conflict with all international and humanitarian norms'.[210] Even if these allegations, if established, could not constitute a justification of Iran's conduct in the hostage case,[211] they do throw considerable light on the root cause of the injury,[212] and the incurrence of responsibility on the part of the US Government, 'by reason of its conduct both before and after the institution of proceedings'.[213]

This brings us to the fundamental problems posed by intervention by States in the internal affairs of other, mostly weaker, States. Some critical questions have been raised[214] concerning acts of intervention by a stronger State in the internal affairs of a weaker State and whether the only remedy, in the case of persons involved in espionage and even subversive activities under the cover of diplomatic protection, should continue to be the declaration of these persons as *personae non gratae* by the affected State. Even if we reject actions undertaken by the USA both before and after the institution of proceedings in the International Court of Justice as being irrelevant and immaterial to the case of the hostages, it should be noted that in the mutually acceptable solution achieved between Iran and the USA through the mediatory efforts of the Government of Algeria, the USA not only agreed to the return of Iranian assets and the withdrawal of claims arising out of the events but also pledged 'that it is and from now on will be the policy of the United States not to intervene, directly or indirectly, politically or militarily, in Iran's internal affairs'.[215] This is no vindication of the actions of Iran. But it does confirm the basic rule that any action prompts an equal and opposite reaction. Drastic illnesses require drastic remedies.

The hostile attitude of Arab countries towards Iran is unwarranted and unjustified. Hence the war waged by Iraq against Iran is equally to be condemned, if not more vigorously, on the grounds that it is an inter-Islamic war, totally in violation of the principles of the OIC Charter and the UN Charter. On the other hand, attempts by Iran to interfere in the internal affairs of Iraq are reminiscent of the tale of the oppressed turned oppressor. The OIC has failed to achieve any solution to the Iran-Iraq conflict and this is attributable not only to its structural and functional weaknesses but also to the intransigent attitude of Iran.

Nevertheless, it may be concluded that the Charter provides the basis of inter-Islamic co-operation and consultation in an elementary manner which could lead to further intensified co-operation in other fields. From its symbolic stance as the expression of a unified 'Ummah'–Islamic Community–the OIC is moving towards further economic, political, social, and cultural co-operation among Member States. In the subsequent sections of our examination, we shall focus our attention on various strategies and plans endorsed by the OIC to promote economic co-operation, and study in detail the legal framework of economic co-operation which has been set out in the General Agreement and the OIC Investment Agreement.

4

Islamic Economic Co-operation: Part I

4.1. ECONOMIC CO-OPERATION AMONG DEVELOPING COUNTRIES

THE call to establish a New International Economic Order not only involves new sets of relationships between developing and developed countries but also emphasizes the 'promotion of co-operation among developing countries'.[1] A key element of the strategy of 'collective self-reliance'[2] consists of economic co-operation among developing countries, a concept widely advocated by developing countries[3] and steadily gaining in importance. However, closer economic co-operation among developing countries does not imply autarky.[4] Following valuable expositions explaining the *dependencia* theory in the context of Latin American underdevelopment[5] the strategy of *dissociation* or *Abkoppelung* has been strongly recommended by others[6] in the wake of continued peripheral (unequal) development. However, a closer look at the strategy of 'dissociation' as an alternative strategy for developing countries suggests that the principal aim is not autarky but self-reliance and autocentric development with 'selective' co-operation in areas such as foreign trade.[7] In order to promote self-reliance among developing countries the permanent Committee on Economic Co-operation among Developing Countries set up within the framework of UNCTAD[8] has, in its very first resolution (1(I)), called upon its Secretary-General to give special priority to studies relating to

(i) a global scheme of trade preferences among developing countries,
(ii) co-operation among state trading organizations, and
(iii) the establishment of multinational marketing enterprises.[9]

The resolution also called for further intensification of on-going activities relating to, *inter alia*, the strengthening of sub-regional, regional, and interregional economic co-operation and integration.[10]

The predominant pattern of international trade, with developing-developed country orientation, is to be diverted towards expanding intra-developing country trade.[11] This requires preliminary studies to identify obstacles and seek solutions to remove structural barriers hampering trade between developing countries. Studies carried out under the auspices of the UNCTAD Secretariat on a global scheme of trade preferences (GSTP),[12] state trading organizations (STO),[13] and multinational marketing enterprises (MME)[14] have underlined three major areas of co-operation in trade which could become operational in the short and medium term implementation of ECDC.[15] Not only have African, Asian, and Latin American countries widely supported action plans relating to these priorities, they have unanimously emphasized that negotiations to establish a general system of trade preferences, taking into account manufactured goods as well as agricultural products, should only be conducted among those countries of the Group of 77 (consisting of developing countries) wishing to participate.[16] This, in essence, restricts the benefits of such a system to participant developing countries.

In addition to trade diversion of primary goods amongst themselves, developing countries are favouring a programme of accelerated industrialization[17] in order to export manufactured goods. The present outward-looking strategy, which is to replace the post-war strategy of import substitution,[18] is to be promoted within the framework of sub-regional, regional, and interregional economic co-operation. However, amidst deteriorating terms of trade and the increasing long-term debt burden of developing countries, which in turn are causing serious strains on the balance of payments, strong financial inputs would be necessary to get the programme of ECDC off the ground. Since the success of ECDC would not be possible without concomitant action on the part of developed countries, they have been urged to support and facilitate the programme of work of ECDC.[19] But confrontation between Group B (consisting of OECD countries) and the Group of 77 seemed inevitable in the first special session of the Committee on ECDC[20] held in Geneva from 23 June–2 July 1980. Whereas the Group of 77 wanted to retain complete autonomy over deliberations and implementation of ECDC measures, the developed market economy countries wished to participate in and influence the manner of determining and achieving the goals of ECDC.[21] Above all, the group of developed countries (Group B) insisted that the support and assistance which was to be made available to the developing countries 'must proceed on the basis of the participation of all States members of UNCTAD and their decision-making process'.[22]

Thus the primary objective of securing for the UNCTAD Secretariat a mandate from the Committee on ECDC to move from the phase of studies to that of implementation could not be achieved in its first special session. This failure, according to the spokesman for the Group of 77, was due to 'a consistently negative attitude shown by Group B even to the elementary consideration and endorsement of support measures for activities in favour of economic co-operation among developing countries'.[23]

We have tried in this general introduction to sketch out the contours of ECDC and the strategy of 'collective self-reliance' among developing countries. Since the programme of ECDC requires strong financial inputs and cannot be launched without concomitant action on the part of the developed States, the developed States are interested in using this leverage to secure a share in the benefits of the programme, in whatever form these might take, as well as some participation in the decision-making process. The developing States want to retain full autonomy over deliberations and implementation of ECDC measures, however. In such a conflict of interests and basic attitudes the programme is doomed to failure before it has even got off the ground. It can only be saved if the developing States are prepared to travel the path with or without support from the developed States. In that case any global programme of 'collective self-reliance' among developing countries would inevitably have to be transferred to regional and sub-regional levels for translation into action.

At regional levels we find numerous integration schemes, partly functioning and partly existing formally on paper, which could take an active part in the launching and intensification of ECDC measures. In the following section we shall briefly examine some plans and programmes of OIC Member States to achieve 'collective self-reliance' by intensifying economic co-operation among Islamic States. Once the contours have been outlined, the examination of the legal framework of such co-operation can be successfully understood and examined.

4.2. ECONOMIC CO-OPERATION AMONG ISLAMIC COUNTRIES

What was ceremoniously formulated and approved by a significant number of Heads of State and Government of Islamic countries as part of a solemn declaration, namely, the promotion of 'close co-operation and mutual assistance in the economic field',[24] came to be embodied as a principal objective of the Charter of the OIC[25] and was the focus of detailed deliberation at the third Islamic Summit Conference in Mecca (1981), which approved the 'Plan of Action to Strengthen Economic Co-operation Among Member States'.[26]

On the long and arduous path to achieve unity in the Islamic community (*Umma*), the long-term strategy of the Member States of the OIC is an integrated approach to development aiming 'at an economically developed Islamic community with the qualification, or at least the potential of an economic union'.[27] The efforts to achieve economic co-operation among developing countries on a global scale are being accompanied by similar efforts among Member States of the OIC in areas such as expanded intra-communal trade, bilateral and multilateral agreements allowing for mutual preferences and concessions, food and agriculture, joint ventures for an expanded and diversified industrial production, establishment of financial institutions and mechanisms, joint action towards integrated markets and economic unions, and increased co-operation in the field of energy, science, and technology, manpower, transport, tourism, population, and health.[28]

As regards resources, the Member States of the OIC are said to be well-placed to promote export-oriented economic development and regional integration through diversified production and joint ventures.[29] This fact has been further bolstered by the increase in financial resources possessed by oil-exporting Islamic States, which, if wisely and efficiently utilized, could help alleviate present financial constraints on economic development among Member States.[30] Apart from the transfer of financial resources by member countries of OPEC in the form of concessional assistance programmes and outright grants, the need for increased direct flow of non-concessional investment capital to developing countries has been emphasized on the grounds that this, while achieving a greater diversification in investment portfolios of capital-exporting OPEC countries, would enable capital-importing developing countries to obtain new sources of risk and loan capital for projects conforming to their own priorities.[31] In order to facilitate such transfers, OIC Member States have taken intitial steps to improve access to and promote intra-communal capital investments.[32]

The Member States of the OIC have a long and tedious path to travel before achieving their objective of self-sustaining growth. In the ever deteriorating world economic situation the Member States most affected are the least-developed countries, comprising a little less than half the total OIC membership.[33] For reasons of extreme vulnerability to external fluctuations, the development programmes of these seriously affected countries are bound to suffer unless a massive transfer of resources takes place. On the other hand, these countries would have to improve their terms of trade to procure resources to finance their development programmes. In the absence of suitable tradable goods,[34] however, efforts to increase bilateral and multilateral trade between OIC countries have so far yielded marginal fruits. Hence the long-term extensive strategy of industrialization in the OIC countries aims at shortening the duration of transition from primary producers to producers of capital goods by emphasizing co-operation in the production of some 'key' commodities, distributing vertically integrated production steps in different countries.[35] This would require a degree of co-ordination in industrial planning among OIC Member States and greater initial capital infusions to achieve infrastructural measures favourable to industrial production. Whereas an examination of the priorities in natural development plans of OIC Member States shows that development expenditures are weighted in favour of infrastructure and industry,[36] the level of institutional co-ordination of industrial planning and co-operation among Islamic countries remains to be improved.[37]

Economic co-operation, within the framework of free trade areas, customs unions, and common markets,[38] is being increasingly favoured by developing countries in general[39] and OIC Member States in particular.[40] Furthermore, the monetary (payments) arrangements[41] are a subsidiary scheme of co-operation which figure prominently as practical elements of trade expansion and payments issues. Being spread over an extensive geographical area, comprising sizeable portions of Asia and Africa, OIC Member States have initially opted for economic integration at the sub-regional and regional level before proceeding towards interregional economic co-operation.

In contrast to the promotion of sub-regional economic co-operation and integration in the three main geographical groups of the OIC, namely, in the African,[42] Asian,[43] and Middle Eastern (consisting of Arab countries)[44] Member States, the General Agreement for Economic, Technical and Commercial Co-operation is to be seen as a loose framework of interregional co-operation among Islamic countries. Preceding the efforts of the OIC, Latin American States, with considerable experience in the area of economic co-operation and integration at the sub-regional level,[45] have constructively moved towards interregional co-ordination and integration.[46] In a similar spirit, the Member States of the Organization of African Unity have committed themselves to setting up an African Economic Community by the year 2000.[47] It must be kept in mind, however, that in spite of some 20 years' experience in the area of integrative economic co-operation at sub-regional and regional levels, the record of performance and achievement of effective progress remains unimpressive.[48]

Since traditional integration concepts and theory have been revealed as limited, a serious in-depth examination of integration concepts, strategies, and mechanisms is required to give impetus to new and imaginative approaches necessary for translating integrative objectives into concrete acts of co-operation.[49] As integration is a long-term exercise, trade liberalization constitutes only an essential element in the economic integration process and must properly fit into the overall system of economic development planning[50] pursued by sub-regional and regional integrative economic groupings. Moreover, closer links among such groupings could facilitate the exchange of relevant information and experiences required for arriving at concrete interregional projects. Originally conceived as a forum of consultation and co-operation, the OIC could play a significant role in promoting and co-ordinating interregional economic co-operation among Islamic States.

4.3. LEGAL FRAMEWORK OF INTERREGIONAL ECONOMIC CO-OPERATION

In order to translate the various objectives and strategies of economic co-operation advocated by OIC countries into concrete acts, an institutional framework was essential to chalk out the main areas of co-operation and achieve a broad consensus on the subject. The General Agreement for Economic, Technical and Commercial Co-operation[51] lays down such a broad framework. We shall proceed first with an examination of the contents of the General Agreement and, secondly, give detailed treatment to the implementation of Art. 1 of the General Agreement which has led to the adoption of an Agreement for Promotion, Protection and Guarantee of Investments.[52] Both Agreements provide a general and particular legal framework of economic co-operation among Member States of the OIC.

4.3.1. The General Agreement for Economic, Technical and Commercial Co-operation

Prior to the approval of the General Agreement by the eighth Conference of Foreign Ministers in 1977, the seventh ICFM held in Istanbul from 12-15 May 1976 approved a draft convention on technical and trade co-operation among Member States of the OIC.[53] The General Secretariat submitted the draft convention to Member States for their remarks, whereupon the Islamic Commission of Economic, Cultural and Social Affairs was to introduce necessary amendments in the light of comments received from Member States. A final text of the General Agreement was prepared at a meeting of economic experts held in Tripoli (Libya) between 7-10 May 1977 and submitted to the eighth ICFM. Noting the recommendations of the Islamic Commission and reviewing the final text of the General Agreement, the eighth Conference of Foreign Ministers held in Tripoli from 16-22 May 1977 amended and approved the draft of the General Agreement and, in accordance with the provisions of Article 12, made it available to Member States for signature and ratification.[54] The General Agreement has come into force, in accordance with the provisions of Art. 13, after the deposition of instruments of ratification by twenty-three Member States.

Apart from the Preamble, the General Agreement contains four chapters, the first three dealing with provisions on economic, technical, and commercial co-operation respectively, and the fourth comprising the final provisions. Chapter IV of the Agreement provides for its implementation (Art. 11), signature, and ratification (Art. 12), entry into effect (Art. 13), and authentication in Arabic, English, and French. For our purpose we have used the English version of the Agreement. The implementation, review, and evaluation of the results of the implementation of the General Agreement are entrusted, by virtue of Art. 11, to the Islamic Commission for

Economic, Cultural and Social Affairs, which is to carry out this responsibility in co-operation with the General Secretariat.

In our interpretation of the General Agreement, the Preamble gains legal relevance[55] as it sets down the object and purpose of the treaty and aids in the comprehensive understanding of the provisions therein. While the general objective of the Agreement, as given expression in its Preamble, is the achievement of economic progress and development, the specific purpose of the treaty is to lay down a broad framework of co-operation in order to mobilize and exploit economic, human, and technical resources available in Member States. On the whole, the General Agreement aims at creating suitable and necessary 'circumstances' and 'conditions' to give impetus to economic, technical, and commercial co-operation among Member States. Thus the purpose of the Agreement, as may be understood from the Preamble of the treaty, is neither to establish an economic union nor to lay down general principles underlying such economic co-operation[56] among Member States of the OIC, but to achieve a broad consensual agreement as to the areas of co-operation and subsequent implementation of specific measures fostering closer co-operation in the economic, technical, and commercial fields through collective efforts or bilateral agreements. It is only in this sense that the General Agreement embodies a juridical framework of inter-regional co-operation among Islamic States.

4.3.2. Economic Co-operation

Chapter I of the General Agreement contains four Articles which outline some basic areas of economic co-operation. Article 1 stipulates that 'member States are to provide, where required, the necessary arrangements, guarantees and incentives to encourage the transfer of capital and investments among themselves'. It deals with one aspect of financial co-operation, namely the transfer of non-concessionary capital resources from the capital-surplus to the capital-deficit Islamic countries. Art. 1 deems the transfer of capital and investments among Member States of the OIC to be a suitable method of promoting economic development and achieving an optimal utilization of resources available within the Islamic world. Although the General Agreement does not define the terms 'capital' and 'investments', they are probably interrelated. 'Capital' embraces not only financial funds, the deployment of which yields profit or income, but also all kinds of 'assets', or property, as defined in Art. 1 (4) of the OIC Investment Agreement.[57] The term 'investment' would probably denote proprietary rights acquired by the act of laying out capital for profit.[58] In order to facilitate and expedite such transfers Member States are required to take certain steps and create certain conditions within their national territories. Art. 1 stipulates that Member States are to provide 'necessary arrangements, guarantees and incentives'. First, Member States are called upon to make 'necessary arrangements', where required, which are favourable to the transfer of capital and investments. These 'arrangements' usually have a legislative and administrative character with the function of regularizing the import of foreign capital for investment purposes. Secondly, these administrative measures are to be coupled with the provision of 'incentives' to foreign investors coming in from capital-exporting Member States, thus making investments more attractive in capital-importing Member States. Such 'incentives' usually consist of tax-exemptions and reductions during initial phases of investment and production, exemption from custom duties on imported goods belonging to the investor, privileges and other kinds of incentives.[59] Thirdly, Member States are to provide, where required, necessary 'guarantees' to encourage the transfer of capital and investments among themselves. The ordinary meaning of 'guarantee' is the giving of a surety or promise of responsibility; in the legal sense it means 'a collateral promise to answer for the debt, default or miscarriage of another, as distinguished from an original and direct contract for the promisor's own act'.[60] In the context of Art. 1 of the General Agreement, however, the term 'guarantee' refers to legal and political sureties to be given by the capital-importing Member State, which may play the role of collateral for its promise to forbear from doing certain acts detrimental to the interests of foreign investors. From the foreign investor's point of view, necessary 'guarantees' would mainly focus on the granting of legal protection to the investor's property, the freedom of transferring earnings and the invested capital, and the provision for compensation in case of expropriation or nationalization. These legal 'guarantees' may be provided either through legislative acts of the Member States or by concluding bilateral or multilateral agreements with other Member States[61] and may be differentiated from 'investment guarantee programmes' provided by capital-exporting countries for the benefit of their own nationals, covering insurance against risks of inconvertibility and transfer of earnings, war, revolution, and expropriation.[62] Art. 1 of the General Agreement recognizes the sovereign right of every Member State to plan, promote, and regulate the input of foreign private investments in accordance with its national needs and priorities. It also depends upon the discretion of the Member State concerned to implement those arrangements, guarantees, and incentives which it deems 'necessary' and compatible, in accordance with its domestic legal system. As a consequence, any 'guarantee' provided may be withdrawn by the promisor State if national objectives and public interest dictate such a course. In order to protect the interests of the investors, Art. 1 of the Agreement also calls upon Member States to provide international 'guarantees' by concluding bilateral or multilateral agreements among themselves. The OIC Investment Agreement is to be considered in this light.

Art. 2 of the General Agreement requires Member States of the OIC to encourage 'joint projects'. The vehicle of economic co-operation among Member States seems to be the launching of 'joint projects', or in other words, joint ventures. As a form of industrial co-operation suitable for foreign investments, the 'joint venture' or 'joint industrial production co-operation' is being increasingly preferred by capital-exporting as well as capital-importing States.[63] The term 'joint projects' underlines the character of the projects as being joint co-operation projects undertaken by two or more Member States. However, the wording of Art. 2 does not give rise to any reason for restricting the meaning of 'joint projects' to State or State-sponsored projects. It would, therefore, include 'joint projects' undertaken by nationals of Member States. The term nationals used here includes natural persons as well as juridical persons or corporate bodies. Art. 3 is related to the provisions of Art. 2 as the preparation of various studies to explore and identify the possibilities and opportunities of investing in joint projects, which could be technically seen as pre-feasibility studies, is a preliminary step towards realizing positive acts of co-operation in the form of meaningful and profitable 'joint projects'. By conducting such studies, Member States would be in a position to discern areas of investment which could reinforce economic complementarities in their territories. Investments in properly surveyed 'joint projects' are a prerequisite to achieve the projected OIC industrial strategy[64] of production of key commodities by distributing vertically integrated production steps in different Member States.

Art. 4 delineates another major area of economic co-operation, namely, the production of food within Islamic countries. The provisions of Art. 4 may be divided into two sets of objectives: first, a long-term agricultural strategy requiring investment in and improvement of food production techniques in Islamic countries; and secondly, the satisfaction of food requirements by importing foodstuffs from within the Islamic world. While the first objective provides for agricultural sectors to be regarded as additional and potential fields for intensive investments, the second objective poses some immediate problems as the present levels of food production in the Islamic world would need to be boosted considerably through increased inputs in order to achieve an intra-Islamic trade pattern in foodstuffs. A substantial number of OIC Member States, whose economic growth performance largely depends on agricultural production, have been affected by a decrease in domestic farm output and consequently, a reduction in per capita food availability.[65] Article 4 of the General Agreement takes cognizance of this problem and deems co-operation in the area of food production to be of as paramount importance as the promotion of inter-Islamic investments in the industrial sectors.[66] Thus Art. 4 calls upon Member States to diversify their investments and financial inputs by investing in industrial as well as agricultural sectors, and calls for diversion and reorientation of present trade patterns.[67]

4.3.3. Technical Co-operation

Chapter II of the General Agreement endorses some technical aspects of co-operation among Member States of the OIC. Due to shortage of skilled manpower in some countries of the OIC and the absence of technical facilities and other institutional capacities to absorb the available manpower in others, a common programme of use and exchange of available capacities could ameliorate some bottlenecks existing in this area. According to provisions of Art. 5 the exchange of experts and use of available technical facilities are to be coupled with further research activities and technical training with the aim of promoting specialization in various fields and supporting an exchange of scientific and technical information by means of conferences and seminars. In order to further scientific and technical research, Member States of the OIC agree in Art. 7 of the Agreement 'to establish an Islamic Foundation for Advanced Science and Technology'.

Art. 6 of the General Agreement has the objective of promoting interregional exchange of expertise and labour mobility. In the exchange of expertise and labour mobility priority is to be given to manpower from Member countries. However, the stipulations of 'priority' in Art. 6 is restricted by the phrase 'other things being equal'. The word 'things', as used in the context of Art. 6, would imply a state of affairs in general or within a specified sphere. The word 'equal' generally means identical in quantity or of the same value. Thus the phrase 'other things being equal' refers to the state of affairs or factors other than the exchange of manpower, which, when reviewed within the specified sphere, that is, within the context of national socio-economic policies pursued by Member States must be identical in value or proportionately significant. The stipulation of giving 'priority to manpower from Member countries' gains relevance if other factors figuring in socio-economic policies of Member States, are conducive to manpower exchange. It does not give rise to any 'rights' or claims to nationals from Member States to be given preferences above others. The stipulation of 'priority' is further conditioned by the consideration of bilateral and multilateral agreements already concluded by Member States, which set up legal and organizational frameworks dealing with equality of treatment meted out to foreign labour, regulation of manpower flows, and provision of social security benefits.[68] Some of the multilateral agreements covering manpower exchange and social security have been concluded on a regional and sub-regional basis between Member States of the OIC and other signatories.[69] In practice, these agreements would substantially restrict the application of the 'priority' stipulation of Art. 6 which is further conditioned by the requirement of 'conformity with national legislations'.

4.3.4. Commercial Co-operation

Arts. 8, 9, and 10 embodied in Chapter III of the General Agreement purport to promote and develop trade and commercial relations among Member States of the OIC.

While Arts. 9 and 10 deal with joint measures to be undertaken by Member States, such as the establishment of a trade centre and the organization, participation, and support of exhibitions and trade fairs, in order to promote and facilitate expanded trade exchanges between themselves, provisions of Art. 8 are concerned with substantive and policy issues of commercial co-operation among Member States of the OIC.

By virtue of Art. 8 (*a*) Member States will 'endeavour to apply equal and non-discriminatory commercial treatment towards one another with regard to foreign trade policies'. This provision is concerned with a general practice embodied in international bilateral and multilateral commercial agreements calling for the application of 'equal and non-discriminatory' treatment in international commercial relations.[70] For purposes of commercial co-operation the phrase 'equal and non-discriminatory' treatment, as provided in Art. 8 (*a*) of the General Agreement, is generally held to be a legal stipulation of equal and non-discriminatory commercial treatment, whereby any 'unequal treatment of equals either by the bestowal of favours or imposition of burdens'[71] may be said to be discriminatory. Although the rule, as far as international commercial relations are concerned, cannot be said to be part of customary international law,[72] it has, however, been embodied in bilateral and multilateral commercial treaties.[73] Both parts of the rule, that is the stipulations of 'equal' treatment as well as 'non-discriminatory' treatment, are positive and negative components of the same principle used either interchangeably and alternatively or in a concerted manner.[74]

Hence in the area of customs restrictions the positive aspect of the rule of 'equal and non-discriminatory' commercial treatment has been formulated as the 'most-favoured-nation Standard',[75] whereas the negative aspect of the rule calls for non-discriminatory treatment in the fixing of import quota restrictions.[76] The rule may be interpreted either strictly, in the sense that the stipulation applies to any kind of discriminatory commercial treatment, or it may imply the general prohibition of 'arbitrary discrimination' only, both depending upon the wording of the rule and its application in the particular case, taking note of all the relevant circumstances and the intention of the parties concerned.[77] Even within the scope of a 'strict' application of the rule one may discern three types of exceptions to it which have found expression in various trade agreements:[78] reservations have been expressed to the extent that the rule may be suspended in the case of customs unions and preferential or free trade areas which bestow favourable terms upon their own member States to the exclusion of non-members; discriminatory measures contrary to the rule may be enforced by a State for reasons of public health, safety, and security;[79] and finally the rule may be suspended in time of war or public emergency.[80]

In the light of what has been said, the rule of 'equal and non-discriminatory commercial treatment' embodied in Art. 8 (*a*) of the General Agreement may be understood as stipulating most-favoured-nation treatment and non-discriminatory treatment of Member States of the OIC by other Member States. However, this rule is to be applied keeping in view obligations already undertaken by reason of other Agreements. The reservation of 'obligations under Agreements already concluded by them' somewhat weakens the stipulation of 'equal and non-discriminatory' treatment within the context of interregional intra-Islamic commercial co-operation. Nevertheless, it does underline the fact that the General Agreement does not purport to override preferential commercial treatment granted by customs unions and free trade areas within the framework of regional and sub-regional commercial co-operation among Member States. In fact, paragraph (*b*) of Art. 8 encourages the removal of customs and other restrictions through bilateral and multilateral arrangements. We may, therefore, conclude that the provision of 'equal and non-discriminatory commercial treatment' as stipulated in Art. 8 (*a*) of the General Agreement, is to be regarded as reflecting a general commercial treaty-standard which Member States are to 'endeavour' to apply in their trade relations. The scope of its application may vary from a 'strict' interpretation of the rule prohibiting 'any' kind of discrimination to a general prohibition of 'arbitrary discrimination'.

In accordance with provisions of Art. 8 (*b*) of the General Agreement Member States of the OIC are to 'strive to enlarge and develop trade exchanges among themselves'. One of the favourite mechanisms employed for trade expansion and development between States, and which is also endorsed by Art. 8 (*b*), is that of 'trade liberalization'. The expansion and development of intra-Islamic trade exchanges is largely dependent on economic factors, such as the availability of suitable tradable goods in the Islamic world which could be exchanged to the mutual benefit of all Member States; it is, however, also faced with institutional barriers of State control, such as customs and other non-tariff barriers or restrictions, the reduction or removal of which could provide added incentives to the enlargement and extension of intra-Islamic trade exchanges.[81] Member States are to strive, in accordance with provisions of Art. 8 (*b*), to provide measures of trade liberalization 'by reducing or removing customs or other restrictions that are applied to export/import activities among them'. The measures of reduction or removal of trade barriers are to be carried out by Member States within the framework of bilateral and multilateral arrangements. Art. 8 takes note of the fact that obligations existing under such Agreements already concluded by Member States are binding and supersede provisions of the General Agreement. We may, therefore, conclude that the purpose of Art. 8 (*b*) is to encourage trade liberalization among Member States within the framework of regional and sub-regional commercial co-operation based on bilateral and multilateral arrangements. It also goes without saying that the rule of 'equal and non-discriminatory commercial treatment', as formulated by Art. 8 (*a*), finds no application in the case of customs unions which usually restrict favourable terms to their own members to the exclusion of non-members.[82] Art. 9 (*c*) of the General Agreement underlines the situation of least developed Member States as a 'special' case and calls upon Member States to 'give consideration to the special circumstances and situations of the least developed member states'. The purpose of Art. 9 (*c*) seems to be the bestowal of an exceptional status upon the least developed Member States, which are to receive preferential commercial treatment from other Member States in consideration of their 'special circumstances and situations'. Whereas provisions of Art. 8 (*c*) would seem to be contrary to the rule of 'equal and non-discriminatory commercial treatment' or specific tariff policies prevailing in regional and sub-regional customs unions, the idea of an exceptional status for an identifiable group of countries is not alien to international economic, financial, and commercial practice. The exceptional status of developing countries as a whole, as far as their 'infant-industry-argument', foreign currency restrictions, and non-reciprocal trade policies are concerned, has been recognized to some extent by developed countries within the framework of GATT, the IMF and the EEC.[83] Continuing violations of principles laid down by GATT and IMF by developing countries, which were usually met with waivers and later led to partial reforms 'legalizing' the violations and acceptance of practice already developed, and increasing preferential norms with specific regard to special needs of developing countries, are said to be indications of a growing international legal recognition of a 'double standard of morality' in favour of the Third World.[84] Preferential treatment of least developed countries is but a natural corollary of the overall development of general preferences in favour of developing countries. The UN Conference on Least Developed Countries held in Paris in 1981 also approved of granting extensive duty-free preferences to least developed countries, the reduction of tariff and non-tariff barriers against their products, and the guaranteeing of long-term supply contracts and overall market stability for exports of least developed countries.[85] Art. 8 (*c*) of the General Agreement creates the possibility of a 'double standard of morality' within the OIC by endorsing a 'special' status for least developed Member States with regard to extension of preferential commercial treatment in consideration of their special circumstances and situations.[86]

4.3.5. Implementation of the General Agreement

Having reviewed the contents of the General Agreement it would be appropriate to dwell briefly on the implementation of some of its provisions. According to Art. 11 of the General Agreement, the Islamic Commission for Economic, Cultural and Social Affairs, working in co-operation with the General Secretariat of the OIC, is 'responsible for following up the implementation of this Agreement, as well as for reviewing and evaluating the results of such implementation'. In the exercise of its mandate, the Islamic Commission submitted a report on the 'Status of the Signing, Ratification and Implementation of the General Agreement'[87] to the thirteenth Islamic Conference of Foreign Ministers (1982) which chalked out the following stages of implementation of the various chapters of the General Agreement.

(*a*) *Economic co-operation*

Efforts to implement provisions of Chapter I have led to the holding of two important conferences at the Ministerial level and the approval of a multilateral Investment Agreement. The first Ministerial Conference on Industrial Co-operation among Member States held in Islamabad in 1982 made several recommendations underlining specific measures supporting industrial co-operation in conformity with the provisions of the General Agreement. Similarly, the first Ministerial Conference on Food Security and Agricultural Development held in Ankara in 1981 made recommendations with a view to implement Art. 4 of the General Agreement. Both sets of recommendations, which are being followed up for implementation, show that measures taken so far are still in the preliminary stage and it is too early to comment on the concrete manner of implementation. However, measures to implement Art. 1 of the General Agreement have taken shape in the form of a multilateral 'Agreement for Promotion, Protection and Guarantee of Investments' which has been approved by the twelfth ICFM and is now open for signature and ratification by Member States.

(*b*) *Technical co-operation*

Provisions on technical co-operation embodied in Chapter II of the General Agreement were further elaborated upon by the 'Plan of Action to Strengthen Economic Co-operation' approved by the third Summit Conference. The Plan of Action provided eight specific recommendations,[88] *inter alia* dealing with improvement and development of information systems concerning the collection, processing, analysis, and dissemination of technical information available in Member States; identification of national potentialities; feasibility of a legal and administrative framework for effective and equitable technical co-operation; expansion of bilateral and multilateral arrangements; support of training activities of the OIC related institutions; and the provision to seek assistance from and conclude arrangements with the UNDP and other relevant agencies of the UN. A group of experts set up by the twelfth ICFM examined the provisions of the Plan of Action and recommended the establishment of a Multilateral Programme of Technical Assistance within the General Secretariat of the OIC.

OIC related institutions such as the Statistical, Economic, and Social Research and Training Centre for Islamic Countries (SESRTCIC) in Ankara and the Islamic Centre for Technical and Vocational Training and Research (ICTVTR) in Dhaka have been designated as focal points for the collection, processing, and dissemination of data and the launching of training programmes for Member States. A survey of existing services available in Member States has already been started by the Ankara Centre. As far as technical arrangements with other international organizations are concerned, a Memorandum of Understanding on Technical Co-operation with the UNDP has already been signed by the General Secretariat and other co-operation agreements have been initiated with the UNCTAD, GATT, UNIDO, FAO, WHO, and UNICEF. Finally, in fulfillment of the provisions of Art. 7 of the General Agreement, the Islamic Foundation for Science, Technology and Development has been established with headquarters in Jeddah.

(*c*) *Commercial co-operation*

In accordance with the provisions of Arts. 9 and 10 of the General Agreement an Islamic Centre for Development of Trade has been established in Casablanca,[89] and the Islamic Trade Fair has been institutionalized.[90] Whereas these measures are concerned with trade promotion activities, the Plan of Action called for an inventory of existing preferential schemes applied by various groups of Member States in order to strengthen and link them through a step-by-step approach, gradually reducing the tariff and non-tariff barriers with a view to achieving the ultimate aim of a free trade area.[91] The Islamic Centre for Development of Trade, the Islamic Chamber of Commerce, Industry, and Commodity Exchange in Karachi, and the Ankara Centre have been designated as focal points of implementing these provisions. The Islamic Development Bank is to function as the principal trade financing institution among the Member States.

4.3.6. An Assessment of the General Agreement

In assessing the value of the General Agreement as a juridical framework of interregional co-operation among Member States of the OIC one has to draw upon factors other than purely legal in order to reach an objective and fair conclusion. For, if we judge the value of the General Agreement from a purely legalistic point of view we may not be granting justice to the purpose of the treaty.

The General Agreement is basically a declaratory 'programme' document setting forth various areas of co-operation envisaged by Member States of the OIC as part of their objective of achieving 'Islamic solidarity'. The purpose of the treaty is to achieve a broad consensus among Member States as to the issues involved, the policies necessary for achieving economic, technical and commercial co-operation, and a basic agreement in principle on the willingness and intention of the Member States to follow up the implementation of the provisions set forth in the General Agreement. Notwithstanding specific legal provisions embodied in the treaty, their legal nature and effect, and their subsequent application, the General Agreement may be seen as an umbrella agreement laying the foundation of economic, technical and commercial co-operation among Member States. By signing and ratifying it Member States of the OIC have, first, given their consent to the fundamentals of the treaty and, secondly, expressed their willingness to participate in intra-Islamic economic, technical, and commercial co-operation. The implementation of specific provisions of the General Agreement would inevitably lead to several detailed legal instruments embodying precise rules in the field of inter-Islamic investments, industrial and agricultural co-operation, exchange of manpower, preferential trade arrangements, and the interregional link-up of regional and sub-regional customs unions and integrative units. Thus the General Agreement lays down a legal framework for further expanded and intensified bilateral and multilateral co-operation among Member States of the OIC.

Although it is not the purpose of the General Agreement to establish an economic union or to lay down general legal principles underlying such co-operation, the treaty endorses a step-by-step approach for achieving its ultimate aim–that is, the interregional economic link-up among regional groupings of the OIC. The cumulative effect of bilateral and multilateral arrangements among Member States of the OIC resulting from a detailed implementation of the General Agreement would be to create a network of agreements leading towards the achievement of this ultimate objective. The ultimate aim of the General Agreement may seem to be ambitious but its immediate law-making effect and binding quality is undoubtedly modest. In fact, its weak legal character has been prompted by the cautious attitude of OIC Member States towards traditional integration concepts which have already shown their limits. Furthermore, the heterogeneous political programmes and economic structures of OIC Member States act as natural brakes upon over-ambitious integration plans. A step-by-step, gradual approach to closer co-operation among Member States seems to be the only suitable and practical course for achieving some durable results in an atmosphere charged with political instability and economic uncertainty.

The signing and ratification of the General Agreement by over one half of the OIC Member States is no small achievement. For the first time in modern history a sizeable number of Islamic States have reached a basic consensus on the fundamental issue of co-operation and have exhibited considerable goodwill. The optimistic and positive start, however, must be followed up by concrete acts of implementation. The Agreement for Promotion, Protection and Guarantee of Investments, which is now open for signature and ratification by Member States, is one such result of the implementation of Art. 1 of the General Agreement. Whereas the OIC Agreement for Promotion, Protection and Guarantee of Investments may be taken as a hopeful indicator of implementation on the legal plane alone, its practical implementation and successful impact upon inter-Islamic investments could be a real cause for celebration and sustained optimism. Similarly, agreements in other fields must be concluded and put into effect before any evaluation of the General Agreement may be undertaken. At present, it is too early to discuss the impact or even partially evaluate the effect of the treaty as preliminary work and negotiations to implement the provisions of the Agreement are still going on. However, it goes without saying that the value of the General Agreement would depend largely on the concrete and successful implementation of its provisions on the legal, administrative, and practical planes.

5

Islamic Economic Co-operation: Part II, Promotion and Protection of Inter-Islamic Investments

As stipulated in Art. 1 of the General Agreement, the provision of 'necessary arrangements, guarantees and incentives to encourage the transfer of capital and investments' among Member States may be interpreted as calling for the provision of such measures collectively and singly. While every Member State signatory to the General Agreement is called upon to provide, where required, such measures as may be conducive for the promotion of inter-Islamic transfer of capital and investments on the national level, Art. 1 also requires the provision of 'guarantees' within the framework of the OIC which could be drawn up in a binding multilateral instrument.

Having considered a proposal made by the Economic Committee on the basis of a suggestion put forward by the delegation of the Kingdom of Saudi Arabia for the conclusion of an Agreement between Member States stipulating protection and guarantee of investments, the tenth Islamic Conference of Foreign Ministers (1970) held in Fez, Morocco, requested the General Secretariat of the OIC 'to draw up a draft agreement on the protection and guarantee and encouragement of investments in Member States' and empowered it to be guided in its task by 'the agreement concluded in this field between Arab States within the framework of the Arab League and by other similar Agreements'.[1] Following up its mandate the General Secretariat prepared a draft Agreement on the Protection and Guarantee of Investments in Member States which was scrutinized by an experts group, entrusted with the study of the draft, during its first meeting held in Jeddah in March 1980. Two other draft Agreements were submitted by the Kingdom of Saudi Arabia and the State of Kuwait respectively.

The eleventh Islamic Conference of Foreign Ministers meeting in Islamabad, Pakistan, in May 1980 requested the General Secretariat to circulate all three drafts together with the recommendations of the experts group to Member States in order to secure their observations.[2]

Furthermore, the General Secretariat was directed to convene a second meeting of experts with a view to drawing up a finalized Agreement and the Islamic Commission was requested by the Conference to revise the provisions of the draft Agreement preparatory to its approval by the third Islamic Summit Conference held in Mecca in 1981. The Summit Conference expressed the conviction 'that investment relations between Member States are among the major areas of economic co-operation between these States' and gave a clear mandate to the Secretary General 'to convene a high level meeting of representatives of Member States prior to the twelfth Islamic Conference of Foreign Ministers for the purpose of finalizing the text of the Agreement for adoption by the Conference or from authorized Ministers to a meeting for that purpose'.[3] A high-level meeting of the group of experts of Member States held in Jeddah from 14-16 March 1981 finalized the text of the draft Agreement on Promotion, Protection and Guarantee of Investments and submitted it to the twelfth ICFM held from 1-5 June 1981 in Baghdad, Iraq. The twelfth ICFM took note of the recommendations submitted by the Islamic Commission and decided to approve the draft Agreement and make it available to Member States for signature and ratification.[4]

5.1. ATTITUDE OF OIC MEMBER STATES TOWARDS THE ISSUE OF PRIVATE FOREIGN INVESTMENTS

The Agreement for Promotion, Protection and Guarantee of Investments has as its primary purpose the protection of private investments in Member States of the OIC by setting up a multilateral legal regime embodying normative statements and specific rules governing the subject. The protection of foreign private investments is itself a sensitive and controversial issue which has received its due share of attention in the field of public international law. Moreover, since the end of the Second World War the role played by foreign private investment in international business and economic 'activity' has steadily increased[5] despite efforts exerted by capital-importing states to gain national control of their economies,[6] either by excluding alien participation totally or by reducing it to a bearable minimum.[7] Developing countries in the Third World in general, and Islamic States in particular, have repeatedly asserted sovereignty and full control over their natural resources and economic activities.[8] The issue of foreign investment and its regulation, as perceived by developing countries, has received radical expression in Art. 2 (2)*c* of the Charter of Economic Rights and Duties of States,[9] which is conspicuous for its absence of any reference to international law or other formulas traditionally accepted.

On the other hand principal capital-exporting States have increasingly resorted to a wide variety of treaty arrangements[10] with capital-importing States aiming at securing adequate and effective protection of property invested abroad by their nationals. A number of Islamic States[11] are party to bilateral treaties concluded with the Federal Republic of Germany and the USA which, *inter alia*, embody some familiar treaty standards governing protection of foreign private investments.[12] This clearly indicates the ambivalent attitude of a substantial number of developing States, including OIC Member States, towards the issue of foreign private investments. On the one hand, they have challenged traditional rules of international law governing state responsibility for injuries to aliens by repeatedly condemning these rules as inequitable mechanisms designed to perpetuate exploitation of developing countries by developed States, and on the other, they have consented to abide by the same rules on the bilateral level with a view to promoting and attracting foreign private investment to boost up their national economies.

In fact, some developing States which have become major exporters of capital through accumulation of surplus financial resources have now adorned the traditional role of capital-exporting developed States by clinging to traditional rules governing expropriation and payment of compensation.[13] The attitude of some capital-exporting developing States towards protection of foreign private investments may be highlighted by a sampling from the regional Agreement on Investment and Free Movement of Arab Capital Among Arab Countries.[14]

At the time the Agreement was originally drawn up in 1970, Art. III stipulated that Member States of the Council of Arab Economic Unity and contracting parties to the Agreement were to determine 'in pursuance of the principle of each state's sovereignty over its own resources . . .' procedures, terms, and limits of control of Arab investments and designate the sectors earmarked for the same.[15] Furthermore, Art. VI read as follows: 'Admitting the inalienable right of the state recipient of the capital to nationalize, confiscate, and expropriate within the framework of public interest, the Arab investor shall be entitled in such cases to fair and effective compensation within a reasonable period of time.'[16] However, both the provisions of Arts. III and VI were later amended in 1973 by a Council Resolution[17] to the effect that host States are bound not to nationalize or expropriate Arab investments in the sectors earmarked thereof pursuant to the provisions of Art. III.[18] Thus the position of capital-exporting Arab States, as documented in the Arab Investment Agreement, may be summed up as follows:

(*a*) they are willing to accept the host State's sovereignty over its own resources;
(*b*) they are also willing to admit the inalienable right of the host State to nationalize, confiscate, and expropriate within the framework of public interest;
(*c*) although originally they were willing, in cases of expropriation, confiscation, or nationalization, to setttle for 'fair' and 'effective' compensation to be paid within a 'reasonable' period of time;
(*d*) they now prefer to invest in priorly designated areas where the host States are bound by a pledge not to nationalize.

Furthermore, a 'convention Establishing the Inter-Arab Investment Guarantee Corporation'[19] purports to minimize non-commercial risks by providing insurance coverage for Arab investors in the form of reasonable compensation.[20] Art. 18 of the Convention defines non-commercial risks as direct or indirect measures of the host country depriving the investor of his substantial rights with respect to his investment, and particularly confiscating measures, nationalization, sequestration, expropriation, compulsory seizure, deprivation of a creditor of his rights; any restrictions on transfer of the investor's capital and earnings including unreasonable delays and discriminatory exchange rates; and any military action emanating from a foreign source or from the host country directly affecting the tangible assets of the investor, and all public civil disturbances such as revolutions, *coups d'état*, insurrections, and acts of violence of a public character.[21] It is interesting to note that the legal regime established by Art. 6 of the Convention provides that in any particular case where the Convention and supplementary rules and regulations of the Council of the Corporation do not contain an applicable provision, it may be decided in accordance with 'legal principles common to the contracting countries and by the recognised principles of international law'.[22]

Thus the basic position of Arab capital-exporting States, as highlighted by regional agreements, is to secure maximum protection and guarantees for private investments of their nationals in other Arab States. This position is further reflected in provisions of the OIC Agreement for Promotion, Protection and Guarantee of Investments, which we have discussed below. The capital-importing Arab States have consented to grant protection to foreign investments in sectors priorly designated by them. Although they have pledged not to expropriate or nationalize Arab investments located in sectors earmarked for the purpose, this pledge may be withdrawn if national circumstances dictate such a course. For, nothing in an investment agreement can effectively prevent a State from committing a breach of the treaty by invoking its sovereign right to expropriate foreign property situated within its territorial jurisdiction if the measure is accompanied by payment of appropriate compensation.[23] In pursuance of the principle of sovereignty capital-importing Arab States may expropriate for reasons of public interest even if the contrary is pledged in a national or international legal instrument underlying the principle of *pacta sunt servanda*.[24] However, the principal deterrent to such measures does not lie in any provision of an investment agreement but in the promotion of joint ventures in which the host State shares the investment risks with foreign private investors. In the Arab States the model of 'public-private joint ventures' seems to be functioning as a viable vehicle of inter-Arab investment co-operation.[25]

5.2. GEOGRAPHICAL IMPLEMENTATION OF THE OIC INVESTMENT AGREEMENT

As we have already noted above, several Arab Member States of the Council of Arab Economic Unity are signatories to regional agreements covering the protection and guarantee of inter-Arab investments. The Agreement for Promotion, Protection and Guarantee of Investments among Member States of the OIC covers the same subject-matter as the regional Arab agreements. It is, therefore, doubtful whether capital-importing Member States of the Council of Arab Economic Unity would deem it necessary to accede to the OIC Agreement. In fact, if they do it would be a duplication of applicable measures already embodied in a regional instrument. The geographical function of the OIC Investment Agreement seems to be the broadening and extension of an already functioning regional legal network of provisions for the protection and guarantee of investments into an interregional multilateral instrument catering for other Asian and African Member States of the OIC. Thus the functional appeal of the OIC Investment Agreement would seem to be greater for capital-importing Member States not yet parties to existing regional or sub-regional investment agreements or similar arrangements. As for capital-exporting Member States of the OIC the Investment Agreement provides another framework of expanding and exporting capital and investments into other Member States of Africa and Asia. Hence what the Arab Investment Agreement purports to cover within a regional framework, the OIC Agreement tends to provide for in an interregional framework.

5.3. THE OIC AGREEMENT AS AN INSTRUMENT OF INVESTMENT PROMOTION

Apart from creating an institutional legal framework setting down substantive and procedural principles consolidating the position of investors from capital-exporting Member States, the title of the OIC Agreement itself suggests that its purpose is also to promote inter-Islamic investments. How far an investment agreement, whether bilateral or multilateral, may influence investors by creating a suitable investment climate in the contracting States is debatable. Previous experience with bilateral agreements of capital-exporting developed States covering the protection and guarantee of investments shows that they usually tend to 'record the existence of a favourable climate than create it'.[26] Some have questioned the value of the bilateral 'investment' agreement as a promotional instrument.[27] Such an Agreement cannot be conceived as an independent factor in the promotion of investments. For that matter, the 'Investment Promotion Agreement' (*Investitionsförderungsvertrag*) of the Federal Republic of Germany comprises only one part of a packet of measures designed to give incentives to nationals to invest abroad,[28] and may, at best, be described as an investment indicator.[29] The value of the OIC Investment Agreement as an instrument of investment promotion seems, therefore, to be limited. The Agreement's entry into force would most probably record the fact that a favourable climate of investment exists in the contracting parties and that the signatories are willing to abide by the provisions of the Agreement governing the protection of investments in order to attract such investments.

5.4. AGREEMENT FOR PROMOTION, PROTECTION AND GUARANTEE OF INVESTMENTS AMONG MEMBER STATES OF THE OIC

The Agreement for Promotion, Protection and Guarantee of Investments among Member States of the Organization of the Islamic Conference[30] contains, in addition to the Preamble, twenty-five Articles apportioned unevenly under the four chapters. As the title suggests, the provisions of the Agreement are concerned with measures and guidelines for inter-Islamic investment promotion as well as rules relating to the protection and guarantee of such investments. Chapter One deals exclusively with definitions of terms occurring in the Agreement; Chapter Two contains general rules governing promotion, protection, and guarantee of capitals and investments in the territories of the contracting States; Chapter Three is concerned with investment guarantees; and the treaty ends with General and Final Provisions. As the Agreement is drawn up in Arabic, English, and French, each version being equally authentic (Art. 25), we have referred to the English version for the purpose of our examination.

5.4.1. Entry into Force

In accordance with provisions of Art. 21, the Agreement comes into force 3 months from the date on which the instruments of ratification of ten Member States of the OIC are deposited. The Status Report on the Signature and Ratification of the Agreement submitted by the Islamic Commission to the thirteenth Islamic Conference of Foreign Ministers held between 22-6 August 1982 in Niamey, Niger, noted that 5 (five) Member States had so far signed the Agreement.[31] A resolution passed by the thirteenth ICFM expressed satisfaction that the number of signatories had risen to 6 (six) and other Member States were contemplating the necessary formalities to sign the Agreement.[32] It seems that far from being remote the possibility of its entry into force in the near future has become patently real.[33]

5.4.2. The Preamble

The Preamble of the Investment Agreement clearly mentions the objectives of the OIC Charter and Article 1 of the General Agreement in the implementation of which the present Agreement has been approved 'to provide and develop a favourable climate for investments'. The purpose of the Agreement, as set forth in the Preamble, is to create a 'legal' climate for investments because the provisions contained therein are to be considered 'as the minimum in dealing with the capitals and investments coming in from the Member States'. As to the value of the Agreement as an instrument of investment promotion, we have already dwelt upon it above; the legal value and scope of the provisions of the Agreement have been examined below. Seen within the perspective of the overall objective of OIC Member States to 'avail of the economic resources and potentialities available', the immediate subject-matter of the Agreement is the regulation of the field of investment which is 'one of the major areas of economic co-operation' among the Member States. Apart from emphasizing the purpose and object of the Agreement, the legal value of the Preamble seems to be limited. However, in cases of subsequent conflict and breach of treaty provisions by the signatories, their declared intention and 'complete readiness to put the Agreement into effect, in letter and in spirit', as the final paragraph of the Preamble states, may be drawn upon to interpret the provisions of the Agreement as providing absolute protection in favour of investors, the breach of which constitutes a breach of the contracting States' promise to 'put the Agreement into effect, in letter and in spirit'.

5.4.3. Chapter One: Definitions

Article 1 lays down definitions of certain terms used in the Agreement. For the purpose of the Agreement the terms are to be understood as defined in Art. 1, except where the context of any provision indicates a different meaning. Some of the terms defined in Art. 1 are of a general nature such as those set forth in paragraphs (1), (2), (8), (9), and (10). Others, however, require elaboration and discussion.

5.4.3.1. *Host State*

According to paragraph 3 of Art. 1, the host State is 'every contracting party in which the invested capital is present and to which it has come lawfully, or which permits the investor to employ the capital therein'. The Agreement draws a distinction between contracting parties, as defined in Art. 1 (2), and the host State defined in paragraph 3 above. Every contracting party may not necessarily qualify as a host State although every host State is by necessity a contracting party. Only those contracting parties may be deemed to qualify as host States which permit the investor to employ his capital therein. This capital must have come lawfully to the host State, i.e., it must have been admitted through the normal official channels of foreign exchange control or other authorizing bodies and must be recognized by the host State as constituting 'legal' earnings and funds, the admittance of which does not breach any financial regulations in force at the time of admittance and on which no back taxes are due. Moreover, it must have been admitted for the purposes stipulated in the Agreement, i.e., the investor employing his capital in the host State must have received the necessary permission from the official organs responsible for granting such permission. Only if both conditions are fulfilled, may a contracting party be considered as a host State falling within the definition of Art. 1 (3) and hence bound to abide by the provisions of the Agreement. Any contracting party which refuses to permit any investor to employ his capital within its territory, or which refuses to recognize as lawful, capital already located in its territory and owned by nationals of other contracting parties, cannot be deemed to have qualified as a host State under Art. 1 (3). Thus provisions of protection contained in the Agreement may be invoked on behalf of the investors by his national State against another contracting party only if the latter qualifies as a host State, recognizing:

(*a*) that the capital in question has come lawfully into its territory, and,
(*b*) that it has granted formal permission to the investor to employ his capital within its territorial jurisdiction.

5.4.3.2. *Capital*

For the purpose of the Agreement, Art. 1 (4) defines 'capital' as 'assets'. The ordinary meaning of 'assets' is the entire property belonging to a merchant or trading association. In the legal sense it is principally used to describe property available for the payment of debts but may be used in the commercial sense for capital used in business or trading.[34] Within the context of the Agreement, and especially Art. 1 (4), 'assets' means property of all sorts 'including every thing that can be evaluated in monetary terms'. Thus the term 'capital', as defined in paragraph 4 of Art. 1, may be equated with property of all kinds which can be evaluated in monetary terms and which is owned by a contracting party to the Agreement or by its nationals.[35] The property may be owned by a contracting party, i.e., a Member State of the OIC and signatory to this Agreement, or by its nationals, i.e., either a natural person or a corporate body.[36] The meaning of the term 'capital' is applicable to 'assets' located in the territories of another contracting party only. As such it makes no difference whether these 'assets' were transferred to it or earned in it; whether they consist of movables, e.g., personal property or goods, or immovables, such as land or real property;[37] whether they are in the form of ready money or in goods; and whether they are tangible, such as 'net profits accruing from such assets and the undivided shares', or intangible, such as good will, etc., pertaining to these capitals and investments or arising by way of a right, i.e., an interest recognized and protected by law,[38] or by way of a claim, i.e., the assertion of that right.[39]

The definition of 'capital' rendered in Art. 1 (4) of the Agreement may be equated with an all-embracing concept of property as used in connection with foreign investments.[40] In bilateral treaties, dealing, *inter alia*, with investments and protection of foreign property, concluded by capital-exporting developed States, the terms 'investment' or *Kapitalanlage* have been used to denote the same.[41] The concept of property, however, as defined in Art. 1 (4) for purposes of the Agreement, is conspicuous for its absence of two key words, namely 'direct' and 'indirect' ownership of capital. The OECD *Draft Convention on the Protection of Foreign Property* defined 'property' as 'rights and interests, whether held directly or indirectly',[42] thus using the term in its widest sense[43] by including investments directly owned by investors as well as portfolio investments.[44] In contrast Art. 1 (4) of the OIC Investment Agreement neither mentions 'property' nor any qualification of its being owned 'directly' or 'indirectly'. Nevertheless, the wording of the definition is clear as to the meaning of the term 'assets' and as to its ownership. The detailed mention of forms of 'assets' to which Art. 1 (4) applies as well as the stipulation of its ownership leaves hardly any room for further doubt; we may, therefore, safely assume that 'assets' means property, including all kinds of property that can be evaluated in monetary terms, and that it must be directly owned either by the contracting party or its nationals. Since the definition does not contain the word 'indirectly', it would be difficult to assume its implication in the ownership of 'assets'. Furthermore, every contracting State, which is a host State, determines and grants permission to the investor to employ his capital therein and, in the absence of express provisions in the Agreement, it lies solely in its discretion to admit direct or indirect investments in its territory. Nevertheless, this important omission could cause some problems in the interpretation of the definition of 'capital' which could have been avoided by a more express wording of the paragraph.[45]

5.4.3.3. *Investment*

In contrast to the term 'capital' the definition of the term 'investment' contained in Art. 1 (5) of the Agreement is a functional one within the meaning and purpose of the treaty. 'Investment' may either mean the 'employment of capital in one of the permissible fields in the territories of a contracting party with a view to achieving a profitable return' or it may mean 'the transfer of capital to a contracting party for the same purpose'. Thus the acts of transfer and employment of capital are 'investments' within the scope and meaning of Art. 1 (5). However, not every type of transfer or employment of capital may be deemed an 'investment'. Art. 1 (5) qualifies only that capital as 'investment' which is transferred or employed in the territory of a contracting party 'with a view to achieve a profitable return'. Thus transfer of capital and its employment for purposes other than profit, such as charitable institutions or non-profit public services, cannot be termed an 'investment' and, therefore, falls outside the scope of the Agreement. It is also questionable whether the transfer of capital and its employment in the territories of the contracting parties for the mere purpose of acquisition of property falls within the definition of 'property', although the acquired property may yield a profitable return. In such a case the classification used by the host State in accordance with its laws and regulations shall be useful in determining borderline cases.

5.4.3.4. *Investor*

Art. 1 (6) of the Agreement defines an 'investor' as 'the Government of any contracting party or natural corporate person, who is a national of a contracting party'. The definition extends the protective measures contained in the Agreement to governments of any contracting party which may be interested in playing the role of the investor. Thus the definition carries significant meaning for a majority of OIC Member States which mainly carry on trading and investment activities through State-trading organizations (STOs).[46] It is only recently that a number of OIC Member States have increasingly resorted to liberalization measures in the private sector of their economies, thus providing incentives to national private investors to play a more active role in fulfilling development goals.[47] Most of them, however, have mixed sectors in which private investors as well as State-trading-organizations or public corporations play a role. Thus Governments of contracting parties or their agencies investing in other contracting parties, either directly or through participation in joint ventures, may be deemed to be 'investors' within the definition of Art. 1 (6) of the Agreement. The purpose of the Agreement is, therefore, to promote inter-Islamic private as well as State-sponsored investments. This may be contrasted with the attitude of capital-exporting developed States, such as the United States and the Federal Republic of Germany, which are primarily and solely interested in promoting private investments on the bilateral level.[48]

Apart from the category of Government investors there are the nationals of any contracting party, who may be deemed to be 'investors' if they own the capital and invest it in the territory of another contacting party. The stipulatory condition conveyed by the word 'own' may be interpreted as direct ownership of the capital. This, in effect, clarifies to some extent the omission in Art. 1 (4) in connection with the definition of 'capital'. Thus an 'investor' within the scope of Art. 1 (6) is any Government of a contracting party or its nationals who 'owns' the capital it is investing in the territory of another contracting party. Employment of foreign capital not owned by the nationals of any contracting party may be said to be excluded from the definition.

According to Art. 1 (6) of the Agreement, nationality shall be determined, in the case of natural persons, in accordance with the provisions of the nationality law in force in a contracting party, and, in the case of a 'legal personality', the establishment of any entity 'in accordance with the laws in force in any contracting party and recognized by the law under which its legal personality is established'. As far as natural persons are concerned, their nationality may be determined by virtue of their passports or travel documents. In the case of 'legal' persons, or corporate bodies, however, the criteria for determining nationality are establishment and recognition by the laws in force, i.e., the entity must be established in any contracting party in accordance with the laws in force, and it must be recognized by the contracting party as such. The recognition is to be a juridical recognition in the form of registration or other requirement of the contracting party, which establishes the status of the entity. The words 'any entity' are wide enough to include any form of association or body provided it is recognized as possessing 'legal personality'.

The wording of Art. 1 (6) *b* leaves ample latitude for foreign corporate bodies or foreign-controlled companies and associations, which establish themselves and are recognized by any contracting party as possessing legal personality under its laws in force, to claim the nationality of such a contracting party.[49] Theoretically, contracting parties to the Agreement are bound to allow application of benefits of the OIC Investment Agreement to such bodies in accordance with the definition of Art. 1 (6) *b*. It is questionable whether this is compatible with the object and purpose of the Agreement as envisaged in the Preamble and in Art. 1 of the General Agreement. In practice, however, the rigour of the definition may be mitigated by the fact that most capital-exporting OIC Member States require some sort of national participation or controlling interest in corporate bodies or other entities established by foreign nationals in their territories.[50] Nevertheless, it is strange that no attempt was made to provide for the exclusion of foreign corporate bodies or foreign controlled entities which might slip in under the cover of 'nationals' of contracting parties, although the exclusion of such 'companies', whose ownership or direction is directly or indirectly controlled by nationals of third countries, is well established in some bilateral treaties concluded by the United States.[51]

5.4.3.5. *Investment Returns*

The term 'investment returns', as defined by Art. 1 (7) of the Agreement, is comparable in scope to the definition of 'capital' in paragraph 4. 'Investment returns' has been defined as the 'sums yielded by the investment or derived therefrom for a specified period'. The word 'sums' is further elaborated by the specific mention of 'profits, dividends, licence fees, royalties, leases, services and all the increases achieved on the capital assets and the utilization of intangible property rights'. This listing only elaborates upon the definition of 'investment returns' and in no way may be deemed to have an exclusive effect. Any sum which may accrue and be denoted by a name other than that listed above can, nevertheless, be considered as falling within the definition of 'sums yielded by the investment'. Although Art. 1 (4) defines 'assets' as including 'net profits' and 'undivided shares', paragraph 7 considers 'all increases achieved on the capital assets', including increases accruing from 'the utilization of intangible property rights', as falling within the definition of 'investment returns'. The function of both definitions seems to be to give the widest possible coverage to the terms 'capital', meaning property of all kinds, and 'investment returns', meaning increases of all kinds yielded by the investment.

5.4.4. Chapter Two: General Provisions regarding Promotion, Protection and Guarantee of the Capitals and Investments and the Rules Governing them in the Territories of the Contracting Parties

As the long and cumbersome title of Chapter Two suggests, its provisions deal with some general provisions in the form of rules governing inter-Islamic investments. In our treatment of the provisions, we have deviated from following the Articles numerically and have proceeded by discussing various provisions under several appropriate headings.

5.4.4.1. *Promotion of Investments*

Provisions concerning promotion and encouragement of investments are embodied in Arts. 3, 4, and 6 of the Agreement. The wording of these provisions, if contrasted with others governing normative statements, evidences the recommendatory character of these measures by using such phrases as 'shall endeavour', 'will endeavour' and 'shall encourage', whereby, 'endeavour' means to strive or to attempt to achieve some object. The language used contains no obligatory effect and the launching of an attempt to promote investments as well as the manner of striving remains within the discretion of the contracting party. The Agreement outlines some courses of action which are recommended to the contracting parties. Art. 3, for instance, calls upon contracting parties to 'endeavour to open up various fields and investment opportunities to the capital on the widest possible scale'. Contracting parties are to liberalize and open up their national economies in a manner favourable to the transfer of capital and promotion of investments. However, this is qualified by the fact that contracting parties are to promote investments 'in such a way that may suit their economic conditions . . . in a way that will foster the social and economic development of the host State in accordance with its set objectives and plans'. Here emphasis is placed on the national development plans and objectives of the host State. In the implementation of provisions of the Agreement, the host State is the sole and final authority to decide whether to permit the employment of capital and investment in its territory or not. If it is willing to permit transfer and employment of capital in its territory, it determines the fields in which the capital is to be invested in accordance with its 'set objectives and plans'. Once the host State permits the employment of capital and investment in its territory in accordance with its national plans and priorities, the basis of co-operation between the host State and the investor is to be one of 'mutual benefit', which, while contributing towards the execution of the national development targets of the host State, is, at the same time, to achieve 'a profitable investment return for the capital'. Herein may be seen the basic compromising formula between the protection of capital imported from other contracting parties and the right of sovereignty in taking national decisions in accordance with national interests. It is, in short, a quid pro quo. The capital-importing OIC States seem to be willing to grant protection to inter-Islamic investment provided it is limited to the areas of investment priorly designated by them. In these priorly designated areas they are willing to grant protection even on traditional lines i.e., the maximum amount of protection and guarantee of investments. However, this readiness cannot be said to be applicable for property in general, and any type of foreign owned property acquired in their territories.

Art. 4 calls upon contracting parties to 'offer various incentives and facilities for attracting capitals and encouraging its investment in their territories'. These are purely internal measures of the contracting party having a legislative and administrative character. The provision mentions such incentives as 'commercial, customs, financial, tax, and currency incentives' which the contracting parties are to grant in order to create a favourable and attractive climate of investment. Since the host State alone is empowered to decide which incentives to provide in accordance with its 'laws, regulations and priorities' the provision in Art. 4 remains of a purely recommendatory character. Thus the climate of investment in the contracting parties shall vary according to the political will and attitude of their governments toward liberalization measures and promotion of inter-Islamic investment. As such the stipulation on 'encouraging the local private sector to cooperate with and participate in investments in the contracting parties' in Art. 6 of the Agreement shall largely depend on the economic and social policies pursued by the contracting parties. Though recognizing the legitimate national interests and policies of the contracting parties, the Agreement calls upon them to encourage participation of the local private sector in inter-Islamic investments. Notwithstanding the binding quality of the OIC Investment Agreement as a multilateral instrument and the obligation of the contracting parties to carry out its provisions and implement them in good faith, the provisions on the promotion of inter-Islamic investments leaves them a wide latitude in the actual implementation of these measures.

5.4.4.2. *The Host State's Right to Regulate Transfer of Capital and Entry of Nationals of other Contracting Parties*

Article 2 of the Agreement stipulates, *inter alia*, that 'contracting parties shall permit the transfer of capitals among them and its utilization therein in the fields permitted for investment in accordance with their laws'. The promotion of investments and transfer of capital among the contracting parties is to be permitted in accordance with the national laws and regulations of each contracting party. Pursuant to the principle of sovereignty and in accordance with strictures on domestic jurisdiction, no State is under a duty to admit aliens into its territory or permit the acquisition of property by aliens therein unless it agrees to do otherwise.[52]

Article 2 gives effect to this rule by recognizing the fact that transfer of capitals may only take place in accordance with the prevailing laws in the territories of the contracting parties. This provision, nevertheless, underlines the duty of the contracting parties to permit the transfer of capitals and its utilization in the areas priorly determined and designated by them. The obligation to allow the transfer of capitals in designated areas of investment in the contracting parties stems from their promise to promote inter-Islamic transfer of capitals. By becoming signatories to the Investment Agreement the contracting parties have undertaken to permit such transfers for the purposes of the Agreement. However, the actual admission of investors into the territories of the contracting parties and their acquisition of property and utilization of transferred capital therein remains solely within the jurisdiction of the host State. No investor may claim, as of right, free entry into the territories of other contracting parties or the unimpeded acquisition of property therein. The stipulation that contracting parties 'shall permit' transfers 'in the fields permitted' in Art. 2 does not provide a right to the nationals of any contracting party to obtain admission or to acquire property in the territory of other parties. The inherent right of the contracting parties to control admission of investors and their acquisition of property and utilization of transferred capitals in their territories is clearly stated by the phrase 'in accordance with their laws'.

Similarly, the stipulation in Art. 5 to 'provide the necessary facilities and grant required permits for entry, exit, residence, and work for the investor and his family and for all those whose work is permanently or temporarily connected with the investment such as experts, administrators, technicians, and labourers in accordance with the laws and regulations of the host state' is only applicable to those transfers and employment of capitals which have received permission from the host State. Art. 5 does not set any absolute standards in connection with the right of the nationals of any contracting party to gain entry or permits of work and residence in the territory of the host State. It is within the discretion of the host State to decide in each individual case and in accordance with its laws and regulations. While this position is basically reflected in bilateral investment agreements concluded by the Federal Republic of Germany, the United States has purported to set up some basic standards regulating the entry of its nationals and their right to work, reside, or acquire property in the host State in its bilateral commercial treaties.[53]

Having established the right of the host State to regulate the transfer of capital, its employment and entry of investors from other contracting parties, the Agreement sets down in Art. 9 the obligations of the investor during his sojourn in the host State. The investor is 'bound by the laws and regulations in force in the host state' and is to 'refrain from all acts that may disturb public order or morals or that may be prejudicial to the public interest. He is also to refrain from exercising restrictive practices and from trying to achieve gains through unlawful means.' This is a general provision which puts the investor on the same footing as nationals of the host State as far as police and other security regulations are concerned. In the area of economic activities the investor is under a duty to respect the laws and regulations in force which lay out a general framework of reference. Exceptions in this area may, however, be granted by the host State on a preferential basis that permits deviations in favour of the investor.[54] But as a general rule investors do not enjoy any special status over and above the law of the host State. As a matter of fact the Agreement underlines the duty of the investor to refrain from acts that may be prejudicial to the public interests of the host State. These acts may consist of provoking a breach of the peace and thus disturbing public order, actively participating in political activities harmful to the interests of the host State, carrying on restrictive trade practices which are contrary to the public interest of the host State or pursuing commercial practices in order to achieve gains through unlawful means. Each individual investor is responsible for his personal actions in the territory of the host State and is liable for such acts in accordance with the laws and regulations in force therein. The provision governing obligations of the investor is the expression of a general reservation implicit in the grant of entry, work, and residence permits by the host State which is common in international treaty practice and appears in the form of a right of the contracting parties to take measures necessary for upholding public order.[55] However, the provision also tends to restrict the right of any contracting party to intervene diplomatically with the host State on behalf of its nationals in cases falling within the ambit of Art. 9 of the Agreement.

5.4.4.3. *The Standard of Adequate Protection and Security*

Whereas the first clause of Art. 2 recognizes the right of the host State to regulate transfer of capital and entry of investors, the second clause of the provision lays down the standard of 'adequate protection and security' which is to be enjoyed by the 'invested capital' and, as such, designed to safeguard investments after they have been made. Furthermore, the host State is to provide 'necessary facilities and incentives to the investors engaged in activities therein'.

Once the transfer of capital is permitted by the host State, the invested capital enjoys 'adequate protection and security'. The ordinary meaning of the word 'adequate' is sufficient. The words 'protection' and 'security' could be construed to mean legal protection and security. In that case, protection and security may be sought against interference or obstruction in the efficient functioning of the investment or acts committed by the host State, its agencies, or its nationals which are detrimental to the interests of the investor. The provision, therefore, obligates the host State to accord sufficient protection and security. Although the extent of adequateness or sufficiency of legal protection and security cannot be discerned from the context of the provision, it could be argued that the obligation of the host State to provide 'necessary facilities and incentives to the investors' denotes a treatment which goes beyond the mere duty of providing only 'legal' protection and security. The phrase suggests that the host State is to accord to the investor a friendly treatment facilitating instead of hampering, encouraging instead of discouraging his activities therein.

In contrast to the standard of 'adequate protection and security' embodied in Art. 2 of the OIC Investment Agreement, the standard most frequently occurring in other international treaties governing the protection of investments is that of 'most constant protection and security'.[56] The standard of 'most constant protection and security' has been interpreted to mean the obligation of the contracting State 'to exercise due diligence as regards actions by public authorities as well as others in relation to such property'.[57] This would, above all, constitute legal protection and security.[58] It has also been asserted that the phrase 'most constant protection and security' is an expression of the minimum standard of protection in international law.[59] The international minimum standard has usually been applied in concrete situations by tribunals and claims commissions, thus putting the propriety of governmental acts to the test in order to establish whether the State concerned has incurred responsibility or not. In the Neer Claim (1926) the General Claims Commission set up by Mexico and the United States stated that the treatment of an alien could constitute an international delinquency if such treatment could be said to 'amount to an outrage, to bad faith, to wilful neglect of duty, or to an insufficiency of governmental action, so far short of international standards that every reasonable and impartial man would readily recognize its insufficiency'.[60]

If we assume the above-mentioned to be a reasonable statement of the law,[61] the interpretation of the treaty standard of 'most constant protection and security' as an expression of the international minimum standard may be construed as nothing more than the obligation of the contracting State to provide legal protection and security to nationals belonging to other contracting parties which is reasonable in all circumstances of a given situation. In any case, the international minimum standard is said to be verifiable in a given situation by reference to municipal law[62] and to the International Covenant on Civil and Political Rights (1966).[63]

Article 2 of the OIC Investment Agreement deviates in its wording of the standard from that of 'most constant protection and security' by using the word 'adequate'. Since the content of both standards call for legal protection and security, which is to be exercised by the contracting State (host State) with diligence, the meaning of 'adequate protection and security' does not seem to differ substantially from that of 'most constant protection and security'. On the other hand, we have suggested above that the standard of 'adequate' protection, as embodied in the OIC Investment Agreement, goes beyond the mere provision of sufficient legal protection and could be considered to call for a treatment more preferential than normal standards would require.

5.4.4.4. *Most-Favoured-Nation Treatment*

Article 8 (1) of the Agreement stipulates that investors of any contracting party are to be granted by the host State 'a treatment not less favourable than the treatment accorded to investors belonging to another State not party to this Agreement'. This is, in essence, the formulation of a 'most-favoured-nation' clause appearing in bilateral treaties concluded by capital-exporting developed States and purporting to establish equally-favoured-treatment with third State nationals.[64] The most-favoured-nation clause also constitutes one of the standard forms used in international treaty practice to minimize and, if possible, eliminate discrimination of investors and their investments in the host States.[65] The standard of treatment laid down in Art. 8 (1) of the Agreement for investors from contracting parties is one of equality with investors from third States within the context of economic activity in which the former have employed their investments 'and in respect of rights and privileges accorded' to them. Thus Art. 8 (1) is a positive formulation of the 'most-favoured-nation' clause[66] stipulating the granting of 'rights and privileges' accorded to investors from third States. However, the measurement of favourable treatment accorded to third party States is qualified by the condition of 'like situations',[67] i.e., the treatment must be within the same context, for the same economic activity, and for the same purpose to qualify as a comparable situation. Thus general exceptions to the rule of 'most-favoured-nation-treatment', as embodied in Art. 8 (1) of the Agreement, have been further elaborated upon in paragraph 2.

Art. 8 (2) of the Agreement enumerates three exceptions to the application of 'most-favoured-nation-treatment'. The first case concerns any preferential arrangement concluded bilaterally between contracting parties to the Investment Agreement. Art. 8, paragraph (2) *a* refers to 'rights and privileges given to investors of one contracting party by another contracting party in accordance with an international agreement, law, or special preferential arrangement'. Thus preferential rights and privileges may be granted by virtue of an international agreement, in accordance with a national law, or by a special arrangement. The reference to contracting parties in the text of subparagraph (*a*) may be taken to be a reference to signatories of the OIC Investment Agreement. Yet this seems superfluous as the 'most-favoured-nation' clause in Art. 8 (1) is concerned with favourable treatment accorded to nationals of third States. Moreover, Art. 8 (2) is explicit to the extent that provisions of paragraph (1) 'shall not be applied to any better treatment given by a contracting party' to the cases mentioned. If we accept the meaning of 'contracting parties' as used in sub-paragraph (*a*) to mean Member States of the OIC, then we come to the conclusion that contracting parties cannot expect the same treatment for their nationals from the host State as it accords to other contracting parties by virtue of an international agreement, law, or preferential arrangement. If, however, we take the term 'contracting parties' to mean any contracting parties signatories to an international agreement and not specifically meaning OIC Member States signatory to the Investment Agreement, then we come to the conclusion that Art. 8 (2) *a* confirms as an exception to the 'most-favoured-nation-treatment' arrangements concluded between a contracting party and a third State on the basis of close historical, political, geographical, or economic ties. For such bilateral agreements have been described as presenting a general exception to the rule of 'most-favoured-nation' treatment.[68] This point seems to remain unclear and can be solved by way of interpretation only. Strictly speaking, however, the wording of the provision does not give any indication as to the meaning of 'contracting parties'. Only an absurd result presented by the wording which seems incompatible with Art. 9 (1) leads us to assume that 'contracting parties' is used in a general sense and not in accordance with the definition in Art. 1 (2) of the Agreement.

A second exception to the rule recognized by Art. 8 (2) (*b* of the Agreement concerns 'rights and privileges arising from an international agreement currently in force or to be concluded in the future and to which any contracting party may become a member and under which an economic union, customs union or mutual tax exemption arrangement is set up'. Thus preferential arrangements concluded between contracting parties and third States within the framework of sub-regional or regional economic integration and co-operation further limits the application of the 'most-favoured-nation' clause.[69]

The third type of exception, as stated in Art. 8 (2) *c*, concerns 'rights and privileges given by a contracting party for a specific project due to its special importance to that state'. This, in fact, includes such situations in which single investors, enjoying exceptionally favourable treatment granted by the host State within the framework of national plans and priorities, cannot be deemed as 'like situations'.[70]

Since the OIC Agreement does not contain any provisions stipulating 'national treatment' in favour of investors of contracting parties, a fundamental problem arises if national treatment is accorded to investors from third States. The relevant question is whether the host State must accord rights and privileges accorded to nationals of third States, and by virtue of the 'national treatment' standard, to investors from contracting parties. The formulation of Art. 8 (1) of the Agreement seems to extend the application of these privileges enjoyed by third State nationals, at least in principle, to investors of contracting parties.[71] On the other hand, the Agreement scrupulously avoids mentioning 'national treatment' for the benefit of nationals from contracting parties and is instead primarily concerned with 'most-favoured-nation' treatment. This omission is all the more difficult to grasp as the general tendency in other bilateral treaties dealing with the same subject is either to replace 'most-favoured-nation' clauses with 'national treatment' provisions or combine them both in a manner beneficial to the interests of the investor.[72] The standard of 'most-favoured-nation' in Art. 8 of the Agreement may be interpreted as the duty of the host State not to apply discriminatory treatment to investors of contracting parties solely on the basis of their nationality. In this sense the rule would be generally applicable as part of customary international law even without explicit treaty provisions.[73]

5.4.4.5. *Continued Validity of Provisions in Case of Withdrawal*

A significant provision seeking to secure effective long-term protection of investments made by nationals of contracting parties in the host State is embodied in Art. 7 of the Agreement. Its importance lies in the fact that any 'rights and obligations arising under the Agreement in the host state towards the investor' are valid even in the case of withdrawal of the host State from the Agreement. By virtue of Art. 7 contracting parties are bound, in their capacity as a host State, to respect the rights and obligations arising under the Agreement towards investors even in the case of their withdrawal if these rights and obligations 'have accrued before the receipt of the notice of withdrawal'. The scope of continued protection granted by Art. 7 to investors and their investments in the host State is very wide and without any time limitations as the wording of the provision states that the rights and obligations 'shall continue and shall not be affected by the withdrawal'.

Although this type of provision is not a novelty, as bilateral investment agreements concluded by the Federal Republic of Germany contain similar provisions,[74] its scope remains vague in the absence of a definite time limit applicable to investments made in the host State before the date of withdrawal from the Agreement. Experience with German investment agreements shows that capital-importing developing countries usually prefer negotiating a fixed period of time[75] during which protection provisions of the Agreement continue to apply to investments made before withdrawal. The failure of indicating a fixed period of time in Art. 7 of the Agreement may be an indication of the necessity of flexibility in this matter, in which case contracting parties would either have to declare their intentions and wishes concerning any time limits in relation to Art. 7 in the form of reservations at the time of signature or ratification, or they may resort to any additional protocols or other legal instruments. In the absence of such declarations Art. 7 could be construed as applicable for an unlimited period of time. This would run contrary to the right of a contracting party to withdraw from the Agreement if it deems it necessary to do so. In fact, withdrawal of a contracting party means that it is not willing to abide by the contents of the Agreement after the withdrawal has become effective. Even if the principle of non-retroactivity of law is applicable in the case of rights of an investor acquired prior to withdrawal, an unlimited period of application of protective measures originally granted under an Investment Agreement would tend to have a derogatory effect on the sovereignty of the host State. Under such circumstances, and in the absence of treaty provisions, any contracting party may exercise its sovereign rights and regulate foreign investments in accordance with its laws and within the limits imposed by international law and custom.

5.4.5. Chapter Three: Investment Guarantees

The Articles contained in Chapter Three of the Agreement embody the sum and substance of provisions covering the protection and guarantee of investments among Islamic States. The chapter deals with substantive principles as well as procedural points which are essential prerequisites for making the protection of investments effective and real. It covers such matters as expropriation, free transferability of capital and earnings, responsibility of the host State, access to courts, and rules on settlement of disputes. Subsequent sections examine the provision of Chapter Three in accordance with their subject-matter.

5.4.5.1. *General Undertaking by the Host State Guaranteeing Investments (Art. 10 (1))*

Chapter Three of the Agreement begins in Art. 10 (1) with a formal and general undertaking by the host State not to adopt measures affecting ownership of the investor's capital or investments. Art. 10 (1) seems to be a fundamental principle of the Agreement setting forth a basic guarantee or undertaking given by the host State. By virtue of Art. 10 (1) the host State undertakes 'not to adopt or permit the adoption of any measure' that 'may directly or indirectly affect the ownership of the investor's capital or investment'. The undertaking of the host State may be characterized as a strict one, in the sense that it is under an obligation not to adopt any measure or permit the adoption of any measure 'through one of its organs, institutions, or local authorities'. The type of measure which may directly or indirectly affect 'ownership' of the investor's capital or investment is further elaborated by Art. 10 (1). Any measure may be deemed as affecting the investor's ownership of his capital or investment if it deprives him 'totally or partially of his ownership'. The concept of 'ownership', as used in Art. 10 (1), includes basic rights of possession, enjoyment, and exercise thereof and is worded in a manner so as to include measures of expropriation and nationalization. Thus any measure which may deprive the investor 'of all or part of his basic rights or the exercise of his authority on the ownership, possession, or utilization of his capital, or of his actual control over the investment, its management, making use out of it, enjoying its utilities, the realization of its benefits or guaranteeing its development and growth' would be deemed a violation of Art. 10 (1) of the Agreement. Not only the active adoption but even the passive tolerance of such measures are proscribed, whether adopted by the host State's organs, institutions, or local authorities. Since the effect of such a measure may be 'direct' or 'indirect', both of which are explicitly included within the scope of Art. 10 (1), the aim of the provision seems to be the regulation of such cases where measures may either 'directly' affect ownership or 'indirectly' lead to some kind of 'creeping expropriation'.[76]

While the undertaking by the host State in Art. 10 (1) of the Agreement is instrinsically related to the standard of 'adequate protection and security' laid down in Art. 2, it seems that the effect and function of Art. 10 (1) is more of a 'guarantee' or undertaking not to adopt certain measures. In this sense it reinforces the declaratory character of Art. 2 as a general standard by explicitly underlining the obligatory character of the 'guarantee' given by the host State. Combinations of this type are rare in international treaty practice covering investments: whereas the bilateral treaties concluded by capital-exporting developed States do not contain a 'guarantee' provision,[77] and the OECD *Draft Convention* obligates each party to 'ensure the observance of undertakings given by it',[78] the 'Agreement on Investment and Free Movement of Arab Capital among Arab Countries' requires that Member States 'pledge not to nationalize or confiscate Arab investments',[79] which may be seen as a 'guarantee' provision similar to that contained in Art. 10 (1) of the OIC Investment Agreement. The practice of capital-exporting Islamic States, as reflected in the Arab and OIC Investment Agreements, seems to be the importation of 'guarantee' provisions or 'stabilization clauses' from the sphere of national investment codes of capital-importing States and concession contracts concluded by them into the sphere of international agreements. Embedded in the international agreement, the 'guarantee' provision seems to offer maximum security to investments in the host State and greatly curtails the freedom of the host State to exercise its sovereign rights; it is, however, qualified by Art. 10 (2) dealing with the permissibility of expropriation.

5.4.5.2. *Exceptions to the 'Guarantee' Provision in Art. 10 (1)*

Paragraph (2) of Art. 10 qualifies the provision of a 'guarantee' in paragraph (1) undertaken by the host State by laying down conditions under which the adoption of expropriation and preventive measures are permissible.

5.4.5.2.1. *Permissibility of Expropriationary Measures*

According to Art. 10 (2):

It will, however, be permissible to:

(*a*) Expropriate the investment in the public interest in accordance with the law, without discrimination and on prompt payment of adequate and effective compensation to the investor in accordance with the laws of the host state regulating such compensation, provided that the investor shall have the right to contest the measure of expropriation in the competent court of the host state.

Before we proceed to examine each condition in detail, a preliminary word about the term 'expropriate', as used in the context of Art. 10 (2) *a*, is essential. Expropriation may be generally understood to be a compulsory acquisition or 'taking' of property by the State.[80] Nationalization has also been defined as a compulsory transfer to the State of private property albeit 'dictated by economic motives and having as its purpose the continued essentially unaltered exploitation of the particular property'.[81] It must, however, be recognized that an interrelationship between the concepts of expropriation and nationalization does exist and that nationalization is a species of expropriation.[82] This interrelationship is demonstrated by the *UNGA* Resolution 1803 (XVII) of 14 December 1962, which categorically states that 'nationalization, expropriation, or requisitioning shall be based on grounds or reason of public utility'.[83] Thus rules governing expropriation of property have usually been applied to other types of 'taking', such as nationalizations or requisitioning of private property by the State. The Agreement itself does not contain any definition of the term expropriation or the phrase 'to expropriate'. We could, however, given the detailed elaboration of measures which may directly or indirectly affect the ownership of the investor's capital and as stipulated in Art. 10 (1), probably assume that the phrase 'to expropriate' would mean the 'taking' of capital and investment belonging to an investor of any contracting party by the host State, irrespective of the manner of 'taking' and the name by which it may be defined.

Art. 10 (2) implicitly recognizes the sovereign right of the host State to expropriate. This right is conditioned by certain limitations laid down in sub-paragraph (*a*) and we shall examine them in turn.

(*a*) '*in the public interest in accordance with the law*'

Article 10 (2), sub-paragraph (*a*) stipulates that it is permissible for the host State to expropriate in the public interest and in accordance with the law. This reflects a basic contention in public international law that foreign property cannot be 'taken' except for reasons of public utility[84] or, as the provision in Art. 10 (2)*a* states, 'in the public interest'. This condition, together with that of due process of law, frequently occurs in international agreements,[85] has figured in some international legal decisions,[86] and is to be found in domestic legal systems[87] or even in nationalization decrees.[88] However, the doctrine of public utility has also been challenged with the result that some have even doubted its usefulness as a 'rule'[89] of international law because of the scant support it has received in practice for obvious reasons. In fact, the principle of public utility has been held by a recent tribunal to be inapplicable to measures of nationalization as motives are indifferent to international law.[90] In such a changed international legal climate which looks with disfavour upon the doctrine of public utility or 'public interest', because of its vagueness as a legal rule,[91] one wonders at the continuous adherence to this principle in international agreements. A minimum function of the rule would most probably be the deterrence of expropriations which are manifestly in violation of the principle of public utility. In any concrete application of the rule, however, and especially in the context of Art. 10 (2) *a* of the OIC Agreement, to specific cases of expropriation of Islamic investments by the host State, it would be difficult to question the host State's measure of public interest in the 'taking' as well as its being in accordance with the law. At least the matter would not and cannot be resolved on the issue of public interest alone.

(*b*) '*without discrimination*'

Sub-paragraph (*a*) of Art. 10 (2) of the Agreement further requires that the measure of expropriation by the host State be 'without discrimination' in order to qualify as a permissible expropriation. We have already had occasion to discuss the rule of non-discriminatory treatment in the context of Art. 8 (*a*) of the General Agreement.[92] In the context of expropriation and nationalization the rule of non-discrimination seems to be an established rule of international law,[93] generally described as sound and resting on a fundamental principle of justice[94] and even said to constitute a 'newly emerged general norm . . . which seeks to forbid all generic differentiations among people . . . for reasons irrelevant to individual capabilities and contribution'.[95] The rule, however, is wide in its application, ranging from the objective legal wisdom contained in the statement 'equals must be treated equally' while 'different treatment of unequals is admissible'[96] to the concept of arbitrariness[97] encompassing cases involving violations of the most elementary rules of justice. The determination of the rule can only be made by reference to factual situations. This was, in fact, done in two recent Arbitration Awards,[98] each coming to a diametrically opposed conclusion according to the facts of the case. In the BP Award, the facts leading to the Libyan nationalization of British Petroleum's interests and assets in 1971 presented a 'blatant' case of discrimination,[99] whereas in the LIAMCO Award, the Sole Arbitrator, although upholding the rule of non-discrimination as 'clear and undisputed', acting as a test for the 'validity of a lawful nationalization', came to the conclusion that in the given case there was not sufficient proof to declare the act of the nationalizing State to be of a purely discriminatory character.[100]

In practice, the effective application of the rule of non-discrimination as a criterion for assessing the lawfulness of expropriation or nationalization measures would largely depend on the facts of the case. The conclusion put forward by Professor Weston, however, 'that foreign-wealth deprivation decisions (substantive and procedural) taken solely for reasons of racial, religious, cultural, ethnic, or nationality aversion or preference should and do constitute unlawful discriminations for being arbitrary'[101] could be safely endorsed. Thus violation of the rule of non-discrimination is itself a basis for taking issue and awarding some kind of reparations independent of the condition for compensatory payment for expropriation.

(*c*) '*on prompt payment of adequate and effective compensation in accordance with the laws of the host state*'

Article 10 (2) *a* further obligates the host State to make 'prompt payment of adequate and effective compensation' in cases of expropriation. The duty of the host State to pay compensation in cases of expropriation is established. This corresponds to the duty established under international law which requires the expropriating State to pay compensation to the owner,[102] which is also reflected in the nationalization decrees of several States,[103] and the *UNGA Res.* 1803 (XVII) of 1962.[104]

The formula used for the measure of compensation in subparagraph (*a*) of Art. 10 (2) may be termed a 'classical formula' which evolved during the nineteenth century and received precise contours in the note of 21 July 1938 sent by Secretary of State Cordell Hull to the Mexican ambassador in Washington.[105] This formula seems to have been retained in contemporary treaty practice.[106] The term 'prompt' has been understood as referring to time, in the sense that the payment of compensation should be made 'without undue delay';[107] the term 'adequate' has usually been substituted in some treaties for 'just' compensation, both being defined as corresponding to the full value of the property expropriated;[108] and finally the term 'effective' has been interpreted as the payment of compensation in a form which is of practical use to the person entitled, in the sense that it is convertible and transferable.[109]

In practice, however, not only have Third World States resisted attempts to interpret 'appropriate compensation' embodied in the *UNGA Res.* 1803 (XVII) 1962, as meaning 'prompt, adequate, and effective compensation',[110] others have recommended the classical formula as an 'expression of the desired aim rather than as a technical rule for the measurement of compensation',[111] and one which has been a standard of preference assumed for bargaining purposes than a rule of international law.[112] The evidence which supports the contention that expropriating countries have ultimately granted compensation 'in an amount and form not inconsistent with the "partial" compensation and valuation standards prevalent since World War II, and often with express reference to international law'[113] is overwhelming.[114] That the classical formula was not always accepted, neither in the inter-war period nor after the Second World War, has been confirmed in the LIAMCO Award, in which Sole Arbitrator Mahmassani came to the conclusion that 'adequate compensation as including loss of profits . . . was no more acceptable as an imperative general rule'.[115]

If expropriations in the host State take place and the Agreement is applied to the case it would be natural to assume that the formula of 'prompt, adequate and effective' compensation would apply irrespective of whether a generally established practice to the contrary exists. For the rule *pacta sunt servanda* applies and the Agreement is binding. Such an interpretation has been put forward in the case of West German bilateral agreements.[116] We submit, however, that such a conclusion would lead to absurd results in the case of the OIC Investment Agreement. Not only are the Member States of the OIC and, eventually, the contracting parties to the Agreement, actively vocal in supporting an alternative formula of compensation and principles governing expropriation in international forums, they have reflected some of their aspirations in the Agreement itself.

A closer look at the phrase 'prompt payment of adequate and effective compensation' would show that it is followed by the qualifying words 'in accordance with the laws of the host state regulating such compensation'. The wording sets up two different sets of propositions which seem irreconcilable at first. Either compensation is governed by the classical formula or it is to be decided in accordance with national laws. It cannot be both, i.e., follow an international standard explicitly set by the treaty and at the same time be entrusted to the discretion of national laws of the host State. A possible reason for incorporating two contradictory rules in one formula could be that one is to qualify the other, or one rule sets the maximum standard and the other a variable which is to orient around the maximum standard. For the phrase 'in accordance with the laws of the host state regulating such compensation' only sets a procedural rule which is to be governed by the substantive standard of 'prompt, adequate and effective'.

We have already shown above that international practice of States usually considers the classical formula to represent a maximum standard for claiming compensation in cases of expropriation and nationalization. This position may also be inferred from Art. 2 (2) *c* of the Charter of Economic Rights and Duties of States. The provision in sub-paragraph (*c*) of Art. 2 (2) of the Charter stipulates that in cases of nationalization, expropriation, or transfer of ownership of foreign property, 'appropriate compensation should be paid'. The phrase 'appropriate compensation should be paid' has been usually interpreted as concerned with the obligation to pay compensation. In this context the use of the precatory 'should' instead of the obligatory 'shall' has been pointed out as denying the obligation to pay compensation. If we further compare the wording of the provision where it stipulates that all controversies concerning compensation 'shall' be settled by the domestic tribunals of the nationalizing State, then indeed such an interpretation is warranted. We submit, however, that Art. 2 (2) *c* of the Charter does not necessarily concern itself solely with the obligation to pay compensation but with the measure of compensation. For, the obligation to compensate in cases of expropriation and nationalization has rarely been denied.[117] In fact, most States have provided for the payment of compensation either in their domestic legal systems or in the nationalization decrees. Thus it is submitted that the main controversy reflected in sub-paragraph (*c*) of Art. 2 (2) does not revolve around the obligation to pay but the measure of compensation. Third World States have generally preferred the formula of 'appropriate compensation' and resisted attempts to equate it with 'prompt, adequate and effective'. The failure to achieve a generally acceptable formula during the sessions of the working group set up to draft the Charter was mainly due to the fact that delegates from Third World States were intent on using a formula which would avoid equating 'appropriate' with 'prompt, adequate and effective'. If we, therefore, infer from the formula used in Art. 2 (2) *c* of the Charter as meaning the payment of compensation in accordance with the classical formula, i.e., 'appropriate compensation' being equated with 'prompt, adequate and effective', such compensation 'should' be paid, leaving the actual amount to be paid somewhere below the maximum standard, then the formulation embodied in sub-paragraph (*c*) reflects an accurate statement of present State practice.

It is the second part of sub-paragraph (*c*) of Art. 2 (2) of the Charter which is most interesting and relevant in the context of Art. 10 (2) *a* of the OIC Investment Agreement. The second part of sub-paragraph (*c*) of Art. 2 (2) of the Charter regulates the procedure for settling compensation questions in case the question gives rise to any controversy. The OIC Agreement incorporates the procedural rule set up by Art. 2 (2) *c* of the Charter by stipulating the payment of compensation 'in accordance with the laws of the host state regulating such compensation'. Here we perceive the same type of blending between a compensation formula and the Calvo clause as embodied in Art. 2 (2) *c* of the Charter. Thus the classical formula, as stipulated in Art. 10 (2) *a* of the OIC Agreement, would most probably remain a maximum guide to the measure of compensation due. The reference to national laws of the host State is an indication of the direction the Agreement is purporting to set. The similarity in content, if not in phraseology, between the relevant provisions of the Charter and the OIC Agreement is remarkable. If the formula 'prompt, adequate and effective' is to be interpreted in accordance with the national laws of the host State, it would certainly have to take, *inter alia*, note of the host State's capacity to pay. A disgruntled investor always retains his right to resort to arbitration in order to rectify the solution. On the other hand, any future guarantee system which might be set up in accordance with provisions of Art. 15 and under the auspices of the Islamic Development Bank would certainly demand some sort of contributions from the host State that may effectively deter the latter from embarking on adventures of expropriation.

Thus the complexity of the formula of compensation used in Art. 10 (2) *a* of the OIC Agreement is apparent. It purports to set a new trend in treaty standards which is applicable among developing States within an interregional framework, and may be clearly differentiated from other investment agreements concluded by capital-exporting developed States as far as the formula of compensation is concerned.

(*d*) '*the right to contest the measure of expropriation*'

The fourth and final condition on the right of the host State to expropriate investments protected by the Agreement is an express stipulation of the investor's 'right to contest the measure of expropriation in the competent court of the host state', embodied in Art. 10 (2) *a*. Such an express stipulation is also to be found in the West German bilateral treaty which has been interpreted as the right of the investor to challenge the measure of expropriation even if it has been adopted in the public interest.[118] The interpretation does not warrant such a provision to be denoted as an 'access to courts' clause; it is a basic right of the expropriated person to present his case and get a fair hearing. Such a provision inevitably tends to minimize 'denial of justice' although it seems clear that the investor cannot effect an abrogation of the decree of expropriation which must be given effect by all national courts. On the other hand, the investor has, in accordance with provisions of Art. 16 of the Agreement, a 'choice of court' clause by virtue of which he may raise any complaints either in the national courts of the host State or before an arbitral tribunal.

5.4.5.2.2. *Permissibility of Adopting Preventive and Judicial Execution Measures*

Article 10 (2) *b* of the Agreement provides for the adoption of 'preventive' and 'execution' measures. Preventive measures may be for reasons of national security, health, or the upholding of public order and morals.[119] Art. 9 of the Agreement, dealing with the obligations of the investor, acknowledges the applicability of such measures to the investor and his invested capital in the host State. The only specifying condition laid down in sub-paragraph (*b*) is that the measures be issued 'in accordance with an order from a competent legal authority'. Similarly, the host State has the right to enforce and execute decisions rendered by a 'competent judicial authority' within its territorial jurisdiction.

5.4.5.3. *Transferability and Convertibility*

Another substantial investment guarantee given by the host State is laid down in Art. 11 (1) of the Agreement, by virtue of which the host State undertakes 'to guarantee the free transfer to any contracting party of the capitals and its net proceeds in cash without the investor being subject to any discriminatory banking, administrative or legal restrictions and without any taxes or charges on the transfer'. The key words of the provision are 'guarantee', 'net proceeds', 'discriminatory', and 'taxes or charges on the transfer'. The extent of the 'guarantee' undertaken by the host State has been qualified to some extent by Art. 11 (4) which is dealt with below. The transfer of capitals originally imported by the investor into the host State is guaranteed by the host State. The income accruing to the investor from the investment may be transferred after it has been duly taxed by the host State, i.e., only the 'net proceeds' from the invested capital can be transferred by the investor to any contracting party. The stipulation 'discriminatory' would be understood to mean that the treatment given to investors of contracting parties must not be less favourable than that granted to other investors in a similar position, and not arbitrarily discriminatory on the basis of nationality. The stipulation on 'taxes' and 'charges' would mean that the host State is to refrain from putting any extra burdens or surcharges on remittances of the 'net proceeds' or the 'capitals' of the investor which lead to a depreciation or indirect interference with the general right of the investor to transfer such funds out of the host State. In short, the Agreement restricts the right of the host State to deduct any amounts from the remittance other than normal bank charges.

The substance of this provision would, to a great extent, determine and influence the decision of investors to invest in a host State. While the 'guarantee' provision not to adopt any measure affecting ownership or control of the invested capital, embodied in Art. 10 (1) of the Agreement constitutes a basic undertaking on the part of the host State, and the conditioning limitations on measures of expropriation build up a natural corollary striking a balance between the sovereign right of the host State to expropriate and the legitimate interests of the investor in the long term, the rules governing the free transfer of capitals invested and earnings gained therefrom constitute the decisive short-term 'guarantee', which is a prerequisite to any investment. Whereas free transfer and convertibility of funds is unproblematical in some capital surplus Member States of the OIC[120] demonstrating generous or virtually no foreign exchange controls and regulations, for a majority of the capital-importing Member States, it is a matter of most critical importance because of chronic shortages in foreign exchange earnings. In response to severe balance of payments problems developing countries, including OIC Member States, have intensified restrictive exchange practices.[121] In the area of current invisible transactions restrictions affecting remittances of incomes, profits, imports, and exports were intensified although the general trend affecting payments and proceeds for services performed by non-residents and transfers of income accruing to non-residents (such as profits, dividends, interest, royalties, and pensions) was one of liberalization.[122] Furthermore, the problem of external payments arrears, which usually occur when the authorities of a country are responsible for undue delays beyond those required by normal administrative procedures, has increased sharply.[123] Since payments restrictions on current and capital transactions are widely practised in a majority of OIC Member States[124] the 'guarantee' of free transferability and convertibility, if construed strictly, would be difficult to maintain in practice. Hence certain compromises achieved on this issue may be detected in the contents of Art. 11.

The repatriation of the original capital, for instance, is to be principally effected 5 years from the date of its transfer to the host State, or on the termination of the investment, whichever is earlier. Any realistic assessment, however, would underline the fact that direct foreign investments are medium- and long-term projects which may be difficult to realize within a minimum period of 5 years. Thus 5 years may be seen as a minimum period required by the enterprise to establish itself. On the other hand, the host State would be interested in maintaining some fixed periods of transfer stability in which huge amounts of capital funds may not be drained out of the country. Therefore, Art. 11 (1) seems to have the purpose of discouraging extremely short-term investors or speculators whose aim is to grab a speedy profit. Through its regulatory mechanisms the host State can assess any incoming investor's projects with regard to its developmental impact and the necessary period of initial establishment.

Furthermore, Art. 11 (2) and (3) set down some procedural rules and conditions on free convertibility, exchange rates with regard to the original incoming capital transferred to the host State, and the maximum periods of delay permitted in the transfer of funds.

Art. 11 (4) is important because any 'procedural measures instituted for exchange control in the host state for administrative purposes or to prevent the illegal transfer abroad of funds of its nationals' shall not be considered as a restriction within the meaning of Art. 11 (1) of the Agreement. This provision recognizes the justification for some procedural controls that may already be in existence in the host State, by virtue of which the host State may to some extent restrict the current or capital transactions of the investor. First, any procedural measures restricting the unauthorized transfer of the funds of its nationals cannot be considered to be a violation of Art. 11. Secondly, the host State may even stipulate that a certain amount, which is transferable from the 'salaries, wages, and rewards of the employees and investment experts', be deducted from such remittances. The Agreement only limits such deductions within the range of 50 per cent. This concession is clearly to the benefit of the host State which has an interest in the use or consumption of funds within its territory. Whereas no such compromise could be achieved on the 'net proceeds' of the capital invested, the absorption of some portions of the salaries and other payments to non-resident employees of the investor could be deemed to be in the interest of the host State if consumption on the local level may be promoted thereby.

It is, however, not clear from Art. 11 (4) whether the host State has a general freedom to impose restrictions affecting the current and capital transactions of the investor. Recent developments in Member States of the OIC indicate a general trend of liberalization with regard to capital transactions even though an intensification wave of restrictions and payments arrears in these States makes the substance of an absolute 'guarantee' of free transfers utopian. The phrase 'procedural measures for exchange control' seems to take the actual financial situation in Member States into consideration, by allowing a wide latitude to the host State to stipulate detailed rules in this matter. Even the phrase 'administrative purposes' leaves ample room to the host State for imposing general restrictions or procedural obstacles. In that case, the guarantee of transferability in Art. 11 (1) is certainly qualified by paragraph (4) and restricts its scope. This would generally be in conformity with the present practice of Members of the International Monetary Fund. According to Art. VI (3) of the Articles of Agreement of the IMF, the control or restriction of capital transfers is deemed to be exclusively within the monetary jurisdiction of the Member States of the IMF. Moreover, the effect of Art. VIII (2), which purports to promote an open multilateral system of payments by stipulating an obligation upon all Members of the IMF not to impose restrictions on current international transactions, is mitigated by provisions of Art. XIV (2), which allows members to avail themselves of transitional arrangements.[125] Thus most developing countries maintaining restrictions and currency practices inconsistent with Art. VIII of the IMF Agreement usually seek specific approval of the Fund or are generally authorized under the transitional provisions of Art. XIV to do so.

General exceptions on the guarantee of free transfer of funds may also be found in treaties concluded by capital-exporting industrial States. In US Commercial Treaties, the basic guarantee of transferability may be suspended if the contracting party imposing exchange restrictions takes such measures in order 'to prevent its monetary reserves from falling to a very low level or to effect a moderate increase in very low reserves'.[126] This indicates a subjective test for deciding what could be termed to be 'a very low level' in monetary reserves. In fact, it lies within the discretion of the contracting party imposing restrictions on financial transfers to apply any criteria for judging the situation as adequately qualifying for the imposition of such restrictions, thus permitting wide latitude and freedom of action to the host State.[127] In comparison to US Commercial Treaties, the wording of the provision covering transfer of capital and earnings in the Federal Republic of Germany investment agreements appears, at first, to be a strict one which does not allow for exceptions that are common in the international financial practice of States.[128] A closer examination, however, reveals that there are at least four types of variations concerning the provision on 'free' transferability, each according to the financial standing and monetary exchange politics of the capital-importing States, ranging from an absolute guarantee of 'free' transfers to a narrow commitment on the part of the contracting parties which, at the most, permits or authorizes the transfer of capital and the proceeds thereof.[129] In some agreements a compromise between the legitimate interests of the Federal Republic of Germany's investor and the wish of the host State to retain some flexibility in the matter has been achieved by the provision of minimum limits (in percentage) on the capital and net proceeds the transfer of which is 'guaranteed' by the host State, whereas in other agreements specific conditions under which the imposition of exchange restrictions by the host State are permissible have been incorporated.[130] In contrast to the Federal

Republic of Germany and US Treaties, the OECD Draft Convention contains a 'recommendation on transfers' only.[131]

5.4.5.4. *Freedom to Dispose of Invested Capital*

We have already noted that Art. 2 of the Agreement does not provide any 'right' of acquisition or entry into the territory of the host State for nationals of contracting parties. The Agreement does, however, provide a 'right' to the investor to dispose of the ownership of property acquired in the process of investment. In accordance with the provisions of Art. 12, the host State guarantees freedom of property and ownership rights that may accrue from the invested capital to the benefit of the investor. The investor has the freedom to dispose of ownership 'by selling it, wholly or partly, by liquidation, cession, or grant or by any other means'. In case the transfer of ownership is made to a national of one of the contracting parties, the capital continues to enjoy protection provided by the Agreement subject to the approval of the host State. Thus Art. 12 is curtailed in its application to the extent that the inherent right of the host State to control and regulate foreign investment, as clearly expressed in Art. 2 of the Agreement, supersedes the right of disposal in Art. 12 as far as the clearance of the new investor and owner by the authorities of the host State is concerned. Although the disposal of ownership to a new investor belonging to another contracting party does not create substantial change in the investment, Art. 2, nevertheless, confers upon the host State absolute authority to grant or refuse clearance to such investments as provided for in Art. 12. This may, in cases of arbitrary exercise of power by the host State, have the indirect effect of obliging the investor to sell to nationals of the host State.

5.4.5.5. *Responsibility of the Host State*

On the subject matter of State responsibility to be borne by the contracting parties for acts or omissions which may be detrimental to the interests of the investor, the Agreement is quite elaborate and sets down detailed provisions. By virtue of Art. 13 (1) of the Agreement, the investor is entitled to compensation 'or any damage resulting from any action of a contracting party or one of its public or local authorities or its institutions'. The phrase 'any action' is elaborated and applied in four sets of different cases in which violations of the obligations laid upon the host State may be incurred. Thus the host

State is responsible for actions causing damage to the investor, and which arise from Art. 13 (1):

(*a*) violation of any rights or guarantees accorded to the investor under this Agreement;
(*b*) breach of any of the international obligations or undertakings imposed on the contracting party and arising under the Agreement for the benefit of the investor or the non-performance of whatever is necessary for its execution whether the same is intentional or due to negligence;
(*c*) non-execution of a judicial decision requiring enforcement directly connected with the investment;
(*d*) causing, by other means or by an act or omission damage to the investor in violation of laws in force in the state where the investment exists.

Article 13 elaborates some major cases of violations which incur responsibility upon the host State. First, two sets of obligations arising from separate sources may be detected. These are:

(*a*) obligations arising under the Agreement, and
(*b*) obligations arising under national laws of the host state.

Obligations of the host State arising under (*a*), i.e., under the Agreement, may further be sub-divided into

(i) rights and guarantees accorded to the investor under the Agreement, and
(ii) international obligations or undertakings arising under the Agreement for the benefit of the investor.

Obligations arising under national laws of the host State, (*b*), may be further sub-divided into,

(i) the obligation to execute a judicial decision requiring enforcement and which is directly connected with the investment, and
(ii) obligation to exercise due diligence in its acts and bestowal of legal protection and security and the duty to refrain from acts or omissions which may cause damage to the investor.

Both sets of obligations undertaken by the host State toward investors are entrenched in the Agreement through the embodiment of various general standards or particular undertakings set down in the treaty. Hence the violation of these obligations entails a direct or indirect breach of the Agreement according to the facts of any given situation.

Under Art. 13 (1) the host State incurs responsibility if the violatory acts or omissions may be imputed to one of its public or local authorities.[132] Once the question of imputablity is settled, the host State is responsible for all acts or omissions including passive acts of 'non-performance' and 'non-execution', which constitute a violation of obligations embodied in Art. 13 (1) of the Agreement. In fact, the host State is strictly liable[133] for the breach of any international delegation or undertaking arising under the Agreement as sub-paragraph (b) of Art. 13 (1) explicitly declares 'whether the same is intentional or due to negligence'. The question whether 'injury' is an essential criterion[134] in assessing responsibility of the host State for acts or omissions constituting violations within the meaning and scope of Art. 13 may be answered by reference to the phrase 'any damage' stipulated in paragraph (1). Hence the investor is entitled to compensation only in the case that 'any damage' caused by such violations has been suffered by the investor.

Article 13 of the OIC Investment Agreement carries special significance for the investor. The provision is explicit on the question of reparation in lieu of any violations: it is not the contracting party but the investor who is 'entitled to compensation for any damage' caused by the host State. By virtue of the wording of the provision the investor seems to acquire directly rights under the Investment Agreement which may be considered to be uncommon on the international plane. In international law a State incurs responsibility for wrongful acts committed in its international relations with other States and entities. In the Chorzow Factory Case,[135] the Permanent Court stated the rule as follows: '(I)t is a principle of international law, and even a general conception of law, that any breach of an engagement involves an obligation to make reparation.'

Article 1 of the Draft Articles on State Responsibility prepared by the International Law Commission[136] restates this general principle as follows: 'Every internationally wrongful act of a State entails the international responsibility of that State'. It is common to consider the principle of responsibility in international law in relation to States as these are considered to be the 'normal' subjects of international law.[137] Disputes between private persons and a State are not considered to fall within the domain of international law unless the State, which is entitled to protect its subjects, takes up the case with the State deemed to have acted in contravention of international obligations. As was pointed out by the Permanent Court in the Mavrommatis Palestine

Concessions Case:[138] 'By taking up the case of one of its subjects and by resorting to diplomatic action or international judicial proceedings on his behalf (i.e. the individual), a State is in reality asserting its own rights–its right to ensure, in the person of its subjects, respect for the rules of international law.'

As a consequence what is regarded to be the 'right' of an injured State also lies within its sole discretion 'to decide whether its protection will be granted, to what extent it is granted, and when it will cease'.[139] If the rights of individuals, such as investors, emanate from a treaty, the breach of its obligations entails responsibility for the contracting party committing the breach. In that case the obligation to make reparation is owed to the injured State and not to the individual. Even the right to institute international judicial proceedings, for instance before the ICJ, can be exercised by the injured State and not by the individual concerned as Art. 34 (1) of the ICJ Statute stipulates that 'only States may be parties in cases before the Court'. In practice, bilateral investment agreements concluded by capital-exporting industrial States do not purport to grant an individual investor the procedural right to bring claims directly against the contracting parties.[140]

In exceptional cases, however, treaties have permitted individuals to bring claims against the contracting parties. In a memorandum prepared for the UN Secretariat in 1949, Sir Hersch Lauterpacht stated that procedural capacity of the individual to bring claims against a State was recognized

> not only in the provisions of the Treaty of Versailles relating to the jurisdiction of the Mixed Arbitral Tribunals, but also in other treaties such as the Polish-German Convention of 1922 relating to Upper Silesia in which–as was subsequently held by the Upper Silesian Mixed Tribunal–the independent procedural status of individuals as claimants before an international agency was recognised even as against the State of which they were nationals.[141]

Several other instances in which treaties have bestowed a procedural capacity on the individual in one form or other are the EEC Treaty of 1957 (Art. 173), the European Convention on Human Rights, 1950 (Art. 25, by virtue of which the European Commission of Human Rights may receive petitions from any person or group of individuals), and, the most relevant one in the case of investors, the Convention on the Settlement of Investment Disputes between States and Nationals of other States of 18 March 1965 (Articles 25-27), also commonly known as the World Bank Convention. Parties to the last-mentioned Convention may generally consent to the jurisdiction of the International Centre for Settlement of Investment Disputes (ICSID) and thereby acquiesce in the submission of investment disputes with foreign investors to the Centre.

Thus the far-reaching effect of Art. 13 of the OIC Investment Agreement, by virtue of which the investor seems to acquire directly 'rights' of a substantive and procedural kind bestowed by the treaty, is further enhanced by Art. 16, the provisions of which may be considered to be a procedural remedy for violations of substantive provisions enumerated in the Investment Agreement as a whole. This point has been further developed in the examination of clauses relating to 'access to courts' and the 'settlement of disputes' (Sections 5.4.5.8-5.4.5.9) below.

5.4.5.6. *Measure of Compensation for Breaches incurring Responsibility upon the Host State*

Article 13 (2) of the Agreement lays down rules governing the measure of compensation to which the investor is entitled for damage caused by the acts or omissions of the host State. According to Art. 13 (2) the compensation 'shall be equivalent to the damage suffered by the investor depending on the type of damage and its quantum'. This sets a basic guideline for tribunals or other bodies deliberating upon cases involving the award of such compensation. In the absence of further description or limitation of the 'type' of damage sustained which may be compensated, it may be assumed that the host State incurs responsibility for damages causing material as well as moral injuries to the investor.[142] Article 13 (3) makes provision for monetary compensation in case restoration of the investment to its state before the damage was sustained is not possible. The basic remedy laid down by Art. 13 (3) is restitution or specific performance. However, it does recognize the need for flexibility in cases where restitution is impossible. This recognition is also a basic rule of expediency in international law, which also accepts restitution as the fundamental form of making reparations for international wrongs, however conditioned by the possibility of performance.[143] Art. 3 (3) sets a time limit for the assessment and payment of compensation. Assessment is to be made within 6 months of the date when damage was suffered and payment is to follow within a year of assessment. Thus some grace is given in lieu of any financial difficulties which the host State might face.

5.4.5.7. *Compensation for Damage Caused due to Hostilities or other Civil Disturbances*

The provisions embodied in Art. 14 of the Agreement are concerned with any damage caused to 'physical assets of the investment' due to hostilities of an international nature, or due to civil disturbances or violent acts of a general nature. Art. 14 does not purport to assert any standard of liability of the host State but only sets up a 'national treatment' standard regarding compensation to its nationals or other investors. In such a case investors of contracting parties are to be 'accorded a treatment not less than that accorded by the host State to its national investors or others'.[144]

The provision must be evaluated in the context of any future investment guarantee programme that might be set up under provisions of Art. 15 of the Agreement. Such programmes set up by capital-exporting developed States or dealt with in the Convention establishing an Inter-Arab Investment Guarantee Corporation, provide insurance schemes to minimize non-commercial risks, such as wars, civil disturbances, or other acts of violence.[145]

5.4.5.8. *Access to Courts of the Host State*

A fundamental undertaking of the host State stipulated in Art. 16 of the Agreement is the investor's 'right to resort to its national judicial system'. The significance of Art. 16 would be apparent if we keep in mind that the investor, by virtue of Art. 10 (2) *a*, already enjoys a right to contest any measure of expropriation adopted by the host State. The right embodied in Art. 10 (2) *a* is independent of any general right of the investor to resort to local courts. As we have already seen above, such a right is also embodied in bilateral investment agreements concluded by some capital-exporting developed States.[146] But the OIC Agreement goes beyond the perfunctory right of an investor to receive a fair hearing. Art. 16 grants him a fundamental right to file complaints against the host State. In accordance with its provisions the host State undertakes to allow the investor to

(*a*) complain against a measure adopted by its authorities against him;
(*b*) contest the extent of its conformity with the provisions of the regulations and laws in force in its territory; and
(*c*) complain against the non-adoption by the host State of a certain measure which is in the interest of the investor, and which the host State should have adopted.

Thus Art. 16 provides procedural remedies for substantive violations of obligations undertaken by the host State under the Agreement. The provision in Art. 16 complements the provisions in Art. 13 by providing for procedural remedies in order to seek redress for any violations committed by the host State. These rights are far-reaching and have the character of constitutional rights which are to be granted to the investor. The investor may resort to local courts of the host State to complain of any acts or omissions on the part of the host State, 'irrespective of whether the complaint is related, or otherwise, to the implementation of the provisions of the Agreement to the relationship between the investor and the host State'. Since the rights of the investor accrue from the implementation of the Agreement, it would be acceptable to assume that the investor may only complain in connection with acts or omissions of the host State which ensue from direct or indirect violations of the Agreement. It seems, however, that Art. 16 goes beyond this general right by purporting to establish quasi-constitutional rights on behalf of the investor. He may not only complain against or contest measures, he can even seek an order of specific performance in case of the latter's refusal to adopt a measure beneficial to the investor, and which it should have adopted. The full import of Art. 13 becomes apparent as far as procedural aspects are concerned.

Article 16 is only effective and realistic, however, if the national judiciary of the host State is independent and strong enough to assert its role. Even if we take this for granted, national courts are bound to enforce that which is passed as law by the legislature or law-making authority of the host State. The national cannot question legislative acts having the aim of setting aside the rights of the investors. Thus in order to avoid the illusory effect of the basic procedural right granted to the investor in Art. 16, the provision stipulates a 'choice of court' clause in favour of the investor. He may choose either to resort to the national courts to complain of the measure, or to an arbitral tribunal, and having made his decision, he loses the right of recourse to the other.

Although we find no express provisions which allow the investor access to courts 'in all degrees of jurisdiction, both in pursuit or defense of their rights', as is the case in some commercial agreements of the United States,[147] we may assume that the right to resort to the national judicial system includes all degrees of jurisdiction. As far as the right to pursue ordinary litigation and the defence of one's interests are concerned, this right should fall under the standard of 'adequate protection and security' in Art. 2. It is also implied in the scope of Art. 16.

5.4.5.9. *Settlement of Disputes*

Article 17 covers methods and procedures relating to the settlement of disputes. An Organ is also envisaged for the settlement of disputes, but until the Organ is established disputes may be settled either through conciliation or arbitration. Art. 17 lays down detailed procedural rules relating to both methods of dispute settlement. It does not, however, stipulate that only contracting parties may take part in arbitral proceedings or conciliation efforts. Art. 17 refers to disputes that may arise under the Agreement and paragraph 1 refers to 'parties' to the disputes. But we have already noted that Art. 16 grants the investor a 'choice of court' clause and an arbitral tribunal is one of them. By analogy conciliation may also be included as it is not any kind of judicial proceeding but only an effort at arriving at an amicable settlement. Thus by virtue of provisions contained in Arts. 16 and 17 individual investors may take part in arbitral proceedings against the host State.

In case the parties to the dispute agree to conciliation, they shall choose a conciliator whose task would be 'confined to bringing the different view points closer which may lead to a solution that may be acceptable to the parties concerned' (Art. 17 (1) *b*). The report of the conciliator shall not have any legal authority before a court should the dispute be referred to it. Thus conciliation proceedings leave the option of resorting to a national court or arbitral tribunal open for both parties to the dispute.

If efforts at conciliation fail, each party to the dispute has a right, by virtue of Art. 17 (2)*a*, to resort to the Arbitration Tribunal for a final decision on the dispute. The procedures of setting up such a tribunal are laid down in Art. 17 (2)*b* and *c*. It is interesting to note that in accordance with the provisions of Art. 17 (2)*d*, the decisions of the Arbitral Tribunal are not only binding on the parties to the dispute but extend to all other contracting parties. This is clearly stated in the phrase 'no matter whether it be a party to the dispute or not and irrespective of whether the investor against whom the decision was passed is one of its nationals or residents or not, as if it were a final and enforceable decision of its national courts'. The uniform application of decisions rendered by Arbitration Tribunals and its enforcement in the territories of the contracting parties has the practical advantage of creating a body of legal precedents applicable to investment disputes. Even if few parties resort to arbitration the provisions of Art. 17 (2)*d* are wholly welcome as it aims at erecting a body of principles and decisions which are binding within a regional context and in the matter of investment disputes. Any other secondary matters which may be the subject of *obiter dicta* could also have an impact in unifying law in this field. If the Agreement is implemented in letter and spirit and is seen to be effectively functioning, then Art. 17 could give rise to an Islamic Community Law on Investment.

5.4.6. Islamic Institution for Guarantee of Investments

Though Art. 15 properly belongs to 'Investment Guarantees' provided under Chapter Three of the Agreement, we have treated it separately as it envisages the establishment of a subsidiary organ of the OIC. The Institution is to be set up with the purpose of taking charge of insuring property vested in the territories of the contracting parties. It is as yet too early to speculate about the principles and structure of such an institution, but one could assume that it would have the same function as guarantee programmes offered by capital-exporting developed States for the benefit of their nationals. Perhaps a model for the Institution could be perceived in the Convention establishing the Inter-Arab Investment Guarantee Corporation. The difference would most probably be the character of the Institution as a subsidiary organ of the OIC, while the Arab Investment Guarantee Corporation is a corporate body. It would, however, be interesting to observe the incorporation of *Shariʿah* principles within the framework of the guarantee schemes provided. Preliminary discussions on the compatibility or non-compatibility of Islamic *Shariʿah* principles with those of modern concepts relating to insurance have already been continuing for some time.[148] Art. 15 also stipulates 'conformity to the principles of Islamic Sharia'. A similar stipulation is contained in Art. 1 of the Articles of Agreement of the Islamic Development Bank. However, the latter has yet to develop and demonstrate a consistent and viable model of international trade financing based on *Shariʿah* principles.

5.4.7. General and Final Provisions

From a total of eight provisions constituting the final provisions of the Agreement, four are generally concerned with the entry of the

Agreement into force (Art. 21), the follow-up and implementation of the Agreement by the General Secretariat (Art. 20), the deposition of the text with signatures and instruments of ratification with the General Secretariat (Art. 24), and the authentication of the Agreement in Arabic, English, and French (Art. 25). The other four are considered below.

5.4.7.1. *Arrangements more Preferential than the Agreement*

According to Art. 18 of the Agreement, contracting parties may enter into an agreement between themselves which provides a treatment more preferential than that stipulated in this Agreement. This leaves the option open for some contracting parties to offer preferential and better treatment to some selective contracting parties either on a bilateral or a multilateral basis excluding others therefrom. The effect of Art. 18 is to permit different or unequal treatment even among contracting parties. This would basically reflect a similar exception to the general standard of 'most-favoured-nation' treatment, as envisaged in Art. 8 (*a*) of the Agreement. The optimal clause in Art. 18 is by necessity also applicable to any multilateral agreement currently in force within a regional or sub-regional framework or which might be concluded in the future among contracting parties. This exception, as embodied in Art. 8 (*b*) of the Agreement, also applies to the 'most-favoured-nation' clause.

5.4.7.2. *Validity of the Agreement in the Event of Disputes*

Article 19 provides that the Agreement 'shall continue to be in force in the event that disputes of any kind arise between the contracting parties and notwithstanding the existence or otherwise of diplomatic relations or any other type of representation between the states concerned'. This provision is of major significance as it aims at providing undisturbed and uninterrupted long-term protection measures and benefits of the Agreement to investors in the host State. Even in the event of 'disputes' arising between contracting parties, Art. 19 stipulates that the Agreement shall continue to be in force between them. The nature of 'disputes' may be of 'any kind', i.e., they could be investment disputes directly pertinent to the Agreement; political disputes; or any other kind of disputes. In all of these cases Art. 19 purports to protect and guarantee the investors' interests by stipulating the binding character of the Agreement even in the absence of diplomatic relations or other ties. Art. 19 may be seen as an alternative provision to Art. 7 which stipulates continued validity of Agreement provisions for the benefit of the investor's acquired rights in the case of withdrawal of the host State from the Agreement. Whereas in the event of political disputes or in the absence of diplomatic relations, when tempers are heated and arbitrary actions imminent, the host State may react harshly or take retaliatory action towards investors of the disputing contracting party or vice versa, Art. 19 would be applicable; in cases of withdrawal of the host State from the Agreement Art. 7 would cover the situation by providing the continued benefits and protection of the Agreement to investors in the host State.

5.4.7.3. *Amendments and Withdrawal*

The Agreement may be amended with the approval of four-fifths of the contracting parties (Art. 22). The request for an amendment must be endorsed by at least five States. Considering the minimum number, ten, of ratifications required in accordance with the provisions of Art. 21 in order to make the Agreement effective, and assuming that only the minimum number required accede to the treaty, the possibility of amendments, as perceived by Art. 22, seems quite remote. This is due to the fact that if ten Member States become parties to the Agreement, at least five would be capital-exporting countries, so that the balance as far as amendments are concerned is weighted in their favour. In practice, however, amendments could be achieved through the conclusion of additional protocols governing special problems.

The period of time during which the Agreement remains valid is unlimited. Art. 23 makes provision for withdrawal from the Agreement 5 years after its coming into force. Thus the Agreement, once effective, remains in force for the duration of 5 years at least, following which contracting parties may withdraw, if they wish to do so, by serving a written notice to the Secretary-General of the OIC, which becomes effective after the lapse of one year from the date of notification. For each new State that may accede to the Agreement, the initial 5 year rule applies. In fact, the first 5 years would probably be required to make a preliminary assessment of the impact of the Agreement on inter-Islamic promotion, protection, and guarantee of investments.

5.4.8. An Assessment of the Investment Agreement

We began our study by referring to the ambivalent attitude of developing countries in general, and Islamic countries in particular, to foreign investments and the issue of expropriation and posed the question whether the rules governing the inter-Islamic protection and guarantee of investments reflect traditionally established principles of international law, and, in the case of divergent norms, whether the basis of legal obligation is to be found in the *Shariʿah*.[149] From our preceding examination of the contents of the OIC Investment Agreement, it has become apparent that a substantial number of principles embodied in the Agreement are similar in content and phraseology to those incorporated in other bilateral and multilateral instruments governing the subject. In some provisions the OIC Agreement purports to set up wider and far-reaching measures of protection and in others embodies norms which reflect the attitude of capital-importing developing States as expressed in international forums. It is these norms which lend the Agreement a speciality of its own not to be found in investment agreements concluded by major capital-exporting developed States.

An objective legal assessment of the OIC Investment Agreement would by necessity have to take the present state of the law of expropriation into consideration. We have tried to show that expropriations and nationalizations are *per se* permissible because it would be extremely difficult to question the public utility criteria of such takings. Another approach has been highlighted by Judge Jiménez de Aréchaga who maintains that 'any measure of nationalization or expropriation constitutes the exercise of a sovereign right of the State and is consequently entirely lawful' because 'the right of every State to nationalize foreign-owned property, even if a predecessor State or a previous government engaged itself, by treaty or by a contract, not to do so' stems from 'the principle of permanent sovereignty of a State over all its wealth, natural resources and economic activities, as proclaimed in successive General Assembly Resolutions and particularly in Art. 2, paragraph 1 of Chapter II of the Charter'.[150] The particular innovation of this opinion, as Professor Brownlie has pointed out, is the proposal that treaty commitments given 'by previous governments become void by reason of the principle of permanent sovereignty'.[151]

Emerging in the 1950s and emanating from the *jus cogens* principle of self-determination,[152] the principle of permanent sovereignty over natural resources is now regarded as a fundamental principle of contemporary international law.[153] The present controversy involves primarily the status of the principle of permanent sovereignty as a peremptory norm (*jus cogens*) of general international law. Whereas the view taken by Judge Aréchaga emphasizes permanency of the right to sovereignty over natural resources indicating that 'the territorial state can never lose its legal capacity to change the destination or the method of exploitation of those resources, whatever the arrangements for their exploitation',[154] Brownlie expresses his reservations to the effect that the principle of permanent sovereignty can only be regarded as overriding all other considerations if it enjoys the status of *jus cogens*.[155] In fact, in the recent AMINOIL Award, the Tribunal rejected the contention that 'permanent sovereignty over natural resources has become an imperative rule of *jus cogens* prohibiting States from affording, by contract or by treaty, guarantees of any kind against the exercise of the public authority in regard to all matters relating to natural riches'.[156]

Even if we accept the argument that the principle of permanent sovereignty cannot be said to have become a peremptory norm (*jus cogens*), and therefore, cannot override treaty and contractual obligations which circumscribe the sovereignty of the promisor State, the fundamental issue is whether there are any legal consequences attached to treaty or contractual breaches committed by the expropriating State in the exercise of its sovereign rights, and, furthermore, whether these legal consequences provide effective remedies to compensate for the breaches. If we admit that the expropriation measure is legitimate because it is an exercise of sovereign rights or because it is in the public interest, then we cannot pretend to call it unlawful because it is in breach of treaty or contractual obligations. Such a construction would be contradictory and would create absurd results. If we assume that expropriationary measures in breach of treaty or contractual obligations give rise to a right to claim reparations independent of the right to claim compensation for the property taken, the immediate question would centre around the type of reparation to be awarded. The remedy of restitution or even specific performance, in case of expropriations and nationalizations, would be ineffective because of the impossibility of performance in the expropriating State. In fact, the duty of restitution of expropriated property would be tantamount to a denial of the right to nationalize.[157] In the case of contractual breaches and, especially, premature termination, it has been held that there is an obligation of indemnification.[158] In the case of a breach of treaty obligations, however, indemnification for the breach alone would be punitive and highly questionable. Thus the legal consequences attached to such breaches cannot provide effective reedies and may be considered to be practically without value. If we take a closer look at the State practice of offering bilateral or multilateral protection of investments through treaties, it will become apparent that a breach of such treaties by measures of expropriation only is virtually non-existent as expropriationary measures are permissible for a public purpose or utility. Thus it is the unsatisfactory state of affairs concerning the rights of sovereignty on the one hand and the principle of *pacta sunt servanda* on the other which facilitated the emergence of the doctrine of public utility as a conditioning clause on the State's right to expropriate in traditional international law. It also motivated drafters of investment agreements to include clauses on permissibility of expropriation conditioned by the public utility principle. Thus, we submit, every State has the right to expropriate or nationalize foreign-owned property even in breach of explicit treaty and contractual provisions to the contrary. In fact the concept of permanent sovereignty reinforces the public utility principle.[159] By inserting the public utility clause, the OIC Investment Agreement has basically accepted this position. Thus the public utility principle may be seen as a formalized formula of recognition of the State's right to expropriate when it deems necessary.

The obligation of the expropriating State to compensate for the taking remains, however. This obligation to compensate has not been denied by Third World States–the *travaux préparatoires* of the Charter bear testimony on this matter[160]–as the practice of States provides ample evidence to prove that the obligation has been complied with. It is a different matter if the classical formula of 'prompt, adequate and effective' compensation has been questioned.[161] The value of the OIC Agreement is greatly enhanced by the fact that the obligation of the expropriating host State to pay 'prompt, adequate and effective' compensation has been tempered by the qualification 'in accordance with the laws of the host State regulating such compensation'. This, in effect, incorporates the basic contentions of Art. 2 (2) *c* of the Charter of Economic Rights and Duties of States. Thus the provision on compensation reflects, on the one hand, an accurate statement of the present state of law by providing the classical formula of compensation as a maximum standard for the measurement of compensation, and, on the other, gives due recognition to the general consensus prevalent in the Third World that procedural questions of compensation should be entrusted to domestic tribunals except where otherwise mutually agreed upon solutions are indicated. Thus the apparently ambivalent attitude of Third World States towards foreign investments and the law of expropriation is greatly mitigated by the fact that most developing States are principally in favour of direct foreign investments (DFIs) and would welcome it by providing adequate and effective protection and guarantees on the domestic and international levels if these DFIs are coupled with beneficial forms of mutually intensified economic co-operation between the parties concerned.[162] The OIC Investment Agreement cannot be simply labelled as another 'classical' investment treaty being offered by capital-exporting Islamic States to their capital-importing fellow States; it must be evaluated within the broader perspective of interregional economic co-operation aimed at achieving benefits for all the Member States concerned.

As far as the rules of the *Shariʿah* governing protection of property and measures of expropriation are concerned, the OIC Investment Agreement, apart from stipulating conformity of insurance schemes for vested investments with the *Shariʿah* in Art. 15, refrains from expressly mentioning them in the substantive provisions of the treaty. This is not surprising as the treaty embodies standard formulations which frequently figure in international treaty practice covering protection of investments. Furthermore, specific mention of the *Shariʿah* is not required where the principles of international law correspond to similar principles contained in the *Shariʿah*. Similarity between principles of international law and the *Shariʿah*, as far as the protection of property and sanctity of contractual obligations are concerned, including the obligation to compensate in cases of expropriation or premature termination of contractual obligations, was amply demonstrated by Sole Arbitrator Dr Mahmassani in the LIAMCO Award.[163]

6

Conclusions

FINALLY, we may summarize our conclusions as follows:

1. The quest for regional international co-operation has led to the formation of an interregional forum of consultation and co-operation among Member States of the Islamic Conference.

2. Several universally recognized general principles of international law, as embodied in the Charter of the OIC, form the legal basis of inter-Islamic solidarity and co-operation today.

3. The acceptance of and adherence to general principles of international law by Islamic States is not contradictory to the legal basis of external relations in Islam. For the classical doctrine of 'Jihad' cannot be recognized as representing the only basis of external relations in Islam as it is neither warranted by any provisions contained in the Koran nor explicitly sanctioned as the 'sole' basis of conduct by the practice of the Holy Prophet. On the other hand, acceptance and application of general principles of international law by Islamic States in their external and inter-Islamic relations does not provide any evidence of their Europeanization, Westernization or secularization as similar general principles of law are common to Islam and other legal systems, religions, and philosophies.

4. The general legal framework of economic co-operation among Member States of the OIC consists of a broad consensus on the issues involved and the measures to be implemented as reflected in the General Agreement for Economic, Technical and Commercial Co-operation. The implementation of Art. 1 of the General Agreement has led to the provision of detailed legal principles governing protection of inter-Islamic investments in the Agreement for Promotion, Protection and Guarantee of Investments.

5. The particular legal framework of economic co-operation as provided in the OIC Investment Agreement adjusts the interests of capital-exporting and capital-importing Member States in a reasonable and fair manner by stipulating, on the one hand, adequate and effective protection and guarantee of inter-Islamic investments, and by giving, on the other hand, due recognition to the sovereign rights of the host State. The OIC Agreement incorporates principles governing expropriation and payment of compensation which are generally regarded as accurately reflecting the present state of the law on expropriation by a substantial number of Third World States. Thus the legal framework of investment promotion and protection provided by the OIC caters for the practical interests and needs of the Islamic States and may be considered as a positive contribution towards ascertaining and establishing the present state of the law of expropriation.

APPENDIX I[1]

In the name of God the Merciful
The Compassionate
Charter of the Islamic Conference

The Representatives of:

The Kingdom of Afghanistan, Algerian Democratic and Popular Republic, State of the United Arab Emirates, State of Bahrain, Republic of Chad, Arab Republic of Egypt, Republic of Guinea, Republic of Indonesia, Iran, Hashemite Kingdom of Jordan, State of Kuwait, Republic of Lebanon, Libyan Arab Republic, Malaysia, Republic of Mali, Islamic Republic of Mauritania, Kingdom of Morocco, Republic of Niger, Oman Sultanate, Islamic Republic of Pakistan, State of Qatar, Kingdom of Saudi Arabia, Republic of Senegal, Republic of Sierra Leone, Democratic Republic of Somalia, Democratic Republic of Sudan, Syrian Arab Republic, Republic of Tunisia, Republic of Turkey, Yemen Arab Republic, meeting in Jeddah from 14 to 18 Moharram, 1392 AH (29 February-4 March 1972).

REFERRING to the Conference of the Kings and Heads of State and Government of Islamic countries held in Rabat between 9 and 12 Rajab, 1389 (22-25 September 1969);

RECALLING the First Islamic Conference of Foreign Ministers held in Jeddah from 15 to 17 Moharram, 1390 (23-25 March, 1970), and the Second Islamic Conference of Foreign Ministers held in Karachi from 27 to 29 Shawal 1390 (26-28 December 1970);

CONVINCED that their common belief constitutes a strong factor for rapprochement and solidarity between Islamic people;

RESOLVED to preserve Islamic spiritual, ethical, social and economic values, which will remain one of the important factors of achieving progress for mankind;

REAFFIRMING their commitment to the UN Charter and fundamental Human Rights, the purposes and principles of which provide the basis for fruitful co-operation amongst all people;

DETERMINED to consolidate the bonds of the prevailing brotherly and

Sources: Organization of the Islamic Conference, Jeddah, Saudi Arabia, the text of the Charter as amended; see also *UNTS* 914, 111-16.

spiritual friendship among their people, and to protect their freedom and the common legacy of their civilization founded particularly on the principles of justice, toleration, and non-discrimination;

IN THEIR ENDEAVOUR to increase human well-being, progress and freedom everywhere and resolved to unite their efforts in order to secure universal peace which ensures security, freedom and justice for their people and all people throughout the world.

APPROVE the present Charter of the Islamic Conference:

Article I

The Islamic Conference:
The member States do hereby establish the Organization of 'The Islamic Conference'.

Article II

Objectives and Principles

(*A*) Objectives

The objectives of the Islamic Conference shall be:
1. to promote Islamic solidarity among member States;
2. to consolidate co-operation among member States in the economic, social, cultural, scientific and other vital fields of activities, and to carry out consultations among member States in international organizations;
3. to endeavour to eliminate racial segregation, discrimination and to eradicate colonialism in all its forms;
4. to take necessary measures to support international peace and security founded on justice;
5. to co-ordinate efforts for the safeguard of the Holy Places and support of the struggle of the people of Palestine, and help them to regain their rights and liberate their land;
6. to strengthen the struggle of all Moslem peoples with a view to safeguarding their dignity, independence, and national rights;
7. to create a suitable atmosphere for the promotion of co-operation and understanding among member States and other countries.

(*B*) Principles

The member States decide and undertake that, in order to realize the objectives mentioned in the previous paragraph, they shall be inspired and guided by the following principles:
1. total equality between member States;
2. respect of the right of self-determination, and non-interference in the domestic affairs of member States;

3. respect of the sovereignty, independence and territorial integrity of each member State;
4. settlement of any conflict that may arise by peaceful means such as negotiation, mediation, reconciliation or arbitration;
5. abstention from the threat or use of force against the territorial integrity, national unity or political independence of any member State.

Article III

Conference bodies

The Islamic Conference is composed of:

1. the conference of Kings and Heads of State and Government;
2. the conference of Foreign Ministers, and
3. the General Secretariat and subsidiary organs.

Article IV

Conference of Kings and Heads of State

The Conference of Kings and Heads of State and Government is the supreme authority in the organization and holds its meetings whenever the interest of Moslem nations warrants it to consider issues of vital concern to the Moslem world and to co-ordinate the policy of the organization accordingly.

Article V

Conference of Foreign Ministers

Conference sessions

1. (*a*) The Islamic Conference shall be convened once a year or when the need arises at the level of Ministers of Foreign Affairs or their officially accredited representatives. The sessions shall be held in any one of the member States;
   (*b*) An extraordinary session may be convened at the request of any member State or at the request of the Secretary-General, if approved by two-thirds of the member States. The request may be circulated to all member States in order to obtain the required approval; and
   (*c*) The Conference of Foreign Ministers has the right to recommend the convening of a Conference of the Heads of State or Heads of Government. The approval can be obtained for such a Conference by circulating the request to all member States.
2. The Islamic Conference of Foreign Ministers shall be held for the following purpose:

(*a*) To consider the means of implementing the general policy of the Conference;

(*b*) To preview the progress in the implementation of resolutions adopted at previous sessions;

(*c*) To adopt resolutions on matters of common interest in accordance with the aims and objectives of the Conference set forth in this Charter;

(*d*) To discuss the report of the Financial Committee and approve the budget of the Secretariat-General;

(*e*) 1. The Conference appoints the Secretary-General;

2. The Conference appoints four Assistants to the Secretary-General on recommendation of the Secretary-General; and

3. In recommending his Assistants, the Secretary-General shall take into due consideration their competence, integrity and dedication to the Charter's objectives as well as equitable geographical distribution.

(*f*) To fix the date and venue of the coming Conference of Foreign Ministers, and

(*g*) To consider any issue affecting one or more of the member States whenever a request to that effect is made with a view to taking appropriate measures in that respect.

3. Resolutions or recommendations of the Conference of Foreign Ministers shall be adopted by a two-thirds majority.

4. Two-thirds of the member States in any session of the Conference of Foreign Ministers shall form the quorum.

5. The Conference of Foreign Ministers decides the basic procedure which it follows and which could be followed for the Conference of Kings and Heads of State and Government, appoints a Chairman for each session. This procedure is also applied in subsidiary organs set up by the Conference of Kings and Heads of State and Government and also by the Conference of Foreign Ministers.

Article VI

The Secretariat-General

1. The General Secretariat shall be headed by the Secretary-General appointed by the Conference for a period of four years beginning from the date of his appointment.

2. The Secretary-General shall appoint the staff of the General Secretariat from among nations of member States, paying due regard to their competence and integrity, and in accordance with the principle of equitable geographical distribution.

3. In the performance of their duties, the Secretary-General, his Assistants, or the staff of the General Secretariat, shall not seek or receive instructions from any government or authority other than the Conference. They shall refrain from taking any action that may be detrimental to their position as international officials responsible only to the Conference. Member States undertake to respect this quality and the nature of their responsibilities, and shall not seek to influence them in any way in the discharge of their responsibilities.

4. The Secretariat-General shall secure communications among member States and offer facilities for consultations and exchange of views and the dissemination of information that have common significance to these States.
5. The headquarters of the Secretariat-General shall be in Jeddah pending the liberation of *Bait Ul Maqdis* (Jerusalem).
6. The General Secretariat shall follow up the implementation of the resolutions and recommendations of the Conference and report back to the Conference. It shall also directly supply the member States with the working papers and memoranda through appropriate channels, within the framework of the resolutions and recommendations of the Conference.
7. The General Secretariat shall prepare the meetings of the Conference through close collaboration with the host states on administrative and organizational matters.
8. In the light of the agreement on immunities and privileges to be approved by the Conference:

(*a*) The Conference shall enjoy, in the member States, such legal capacity, immunities and privileges as may be necessary for the exercise of its functions and the fulfilment of its objectives;

(*b*) Representatives of member States shall enjoy such immunities and privileges as may be necessary for the exercise of their functions related to the Conference; and

(*c*) The Staff of the Conference shall enjoy the immunities and privileges necessary for the performance of their duties as decided upon by the Conference.

Article VII

Finance

1. All expenses on the administration and activities of the Secretariat shall be borne by member States according to their national incomes.
2. The Secretariat shall administer its financial affairs according to the rules of procedure approved by the Conference of Foreign Ministers.
3. A Standing Financial Committee shall be formed by the Conference from the accredited representatives of the participating States, and shall meet at the Headquarters of the General Secretariat. This Committee shall in conjunction with the Secretary-General, prepare and supervise the budget of the General Secretariat according to the regulations approved by the Conference of Foreign Ministers.

Article VIII

Membership

The Organization of the Islamic Conference is composed of the States which participated in the Conference of Kings and Heads of State and Government held in Rabat and the Foreign Ministers' Conference held in Jeddah, Karachi and signatory to this Charter. Every Muslim State is eligible to join the Islamic Conference on submitting an application expressing its desire and preparedness to adopt this Charter. The application shall be deposited with the General Secretariat, to be brought before the Foreign Ministers' Conference at its first meeting after the submission of the application. Membership shall take effect as of the time of approval of the Conference by a two-thirds majority of the Conference members.

Article IX

Islamic Organizations

The General Secretariat shall act within the frame-work of the present Charter with the approval of the Conference to consolidate relations between the Islamic Conference and the Islamic Organizations of international character and to realize cooperation in the service of the Islamic objectives approved by this Charter.

Article X

Withdrawal

1. Any member State may withdraw from the Islamic Conference by sending a written notification to the Secretariat-General, to be communicated to all member States.
2. The State applying for withdrawal shall be bound by its obligations until the end of the fiscal year during which the application of withdrawal is submitted. It shall also settle any other financial obligation due to the Conference.

Article XI

Amendment

Amendment to this Charter shall be made, if approved and ratified by a two-thirds majority of the member States.

Article XII

Interpretation

Any dispute that may arise in the interpretation, application or implementation of any Article in the present Charter shall be settled peacefully, and in all cases through consultations, negotiations, reconciliation or arbitration.

Article XIII

Language

Languages of the Conference shall be Arabic, English and French.

Article XIV

Ratification

This Charter shall be approved or ratified by member States in the Organization of the Islamic Conference in accordance with the current procedure in their respective countries. This Charter goes into effect as of the date of deposition of the instruments of ratification with the General Secretariat by a simple majority of the States participating in the Third Islamic Conference of Foreign Ministers held in Jeddah from 14 to 18 Moharram 1392 (29 February-4 March 1970).

This Charter has been registered in conformity with Article 102 of the Charter of the UN on 1st February, 1974.

APPENDIX II

Doc. ICFM 8-77/ICES-9

General Agreement for Economic Technical and Commercial Cooperation among Member States of the Islamic Conference

Preamble

The Governments of the Member States of the Islamic Conference signatory to the present agreement;

IN KEEPING with the objectives contained in the Charter of the Organization of the Islamic Conference and in conformity with the resolutions of the Second Islamic Summit held in Lahore;

ANXIOUS to create the best possible circumstances and conditions for the economic progress and development of the Member States, and for raising the living standards of their peoples;

DESIROUS of strengthening the bonds between the Member States in all spheres, in order to achieve their common interests;

CONVINCED that economic, technical, and commercial cooperation among the Member States constitutes one of the principal means for consolidating the socio-economic development of the Islamic States;

ENDEAVOURING to utilise to the utmost the economic, human and technical energies and potentialities available in the Islamic world, in order to mobilise and exploit them in the best possible manner, within the context of a strong and systematic cooperation between the Member States, for the welfare and prosperity of their peoples;

HAVE APPROVED this agreement and have agreed to exert all their efforts, in the context of their economic and technical cooperation, to ensure its implementation with a view to achieving their objectives through collective efforts, or through bilateral and multilateral activities.

Chapter I. Economic Cooperation

Article 1

The Member States are to provide, where required, the necessary arrangements, guarantees and incentives to encourage the transfer of capital and investments among themselves, in conformity with the laws and regulations in force in each Member State, in order to promote the socio-economic development of all Islamic countries and to provide new avenues for the optimum utilisation of the economic resources available within the Islamic world.

Article 2

The Member States are to encourage joint projects which will realise broad economic benefits and advantages and will re-inforce and promote economic complementarities and the socio-economic structures of Member States.

Article 3

The Member States are to cooperate in preparing various studies to explore and identify the possibilities and opportunities of investing in joint projects.

Article 4

The Member States will encourage the maximum utilisation of the potential for food production within Islamic countries and will cooperate for the satisfaction of their food requirements from within the Islamic world.

Chapter II. Technical Cooperation

Article 5

Member States will endeavour to derive the utmost benefit from the expertise and technical capacities available to them, through exchange of experts, research, and scholarships for study, training and specialisation and the holding of various scientific and technical conferences and seminars.

Article 6

In order to meet their needs in the field of manpower and to derive advantage from the technical and administrative experience available, the Islamic States shall cooperate in the exchange of expertise in these fields and, other things being equal, give priority to manpower from Member countries taking into account the bilateral and multilateral agreements aready concluded and in conformity with national legislations in this respect.

Article 7

The Member States agree to take all necessary measures to establish an Islamic Foundation for Advanced Science and Technology.

Chapter III. Commercial Cooperation

Article 8

While keeping in view the obligations under other Agreements already concluded by them, the Member States will;

(*a*) endeavour to apply equal and non-discriminatory commercial treatment towards one another with regard to foreign trade policies;

(*b*) strive to enlarge and develop trade exchange among themselves, *inter alia* through trade liberalisation, by reducing or removing the customs or other restrictions that are applied to export/import activities among them through bilateral or multilateral trade arrangements; and

(*c*) give consideration to the special circumstances and situations of the least developed Member States.

Article 9

The Member States agree, in principle, to establish a centre for the development of trade among the Islamic States. Its main task will be to promote and develop trade exchanges amongst Member States.

Article 10

The Member States are to endeavour to organise exhibitions and fairs to exhibit and market their products in the Member States. They are also to endeavour, for the same end, to participate in international fairs and exhibitions held in other member countries, to make the products of the Member States known and to increase opportunities for developing trade exchanges amongst themselves. Each State is to provide suitable facilities to other Member States for this purpose, within the limits of its existing economic policies and systems.

Chapter IV. Final Provisions

Article 11

The Islamic Commission for Economic, Cultural and Social Affairs, with the cooperation of the General Secretariat of the Organisation of the Islamic Conference, will be responsible for following up the implementation of this agreement, as well as for reviewing and evaluating the results of such implementation.

Article 12

This Agreement is open for signature and ratification by the Member States of the Organisation of the Islamic Conference and the Instruments of Ratification are to be deposited with the General Secretariat of the Organisation of the Islamic Conference.

Article 13

This Agreement comes into effect as soon as Instruments of Ratification are submitted by more than half the Member States of the Organisation of the Islamic Conference.

Article 14

This Agreement has been done in three original versions–Arabic, English, and French–all three being equally authentic.

APPENDIX III

Doc. Annex–I to ICFM 12 81–E/D. 6.

Agreement for Promotion, Protection, and Guarantee of Investments among Member States of the Organisation of the Islamic Conference

Preamble

The Governments of the Member States of the Organisation of the Islamic Conference signatory to this Agreement,

IN KEEPING WITH the objectives of the Organisation of the Islamic Conference as stipulated in its Charter,

IN IMPLEMENTATION OF the provisions of the Agreement for Economic, Technical, and Commercial Cooperation among the Member States of the Organisation of the Islamic Conference and particularly the provisions of Article 1 of the said Agreement,

ENDEAVOURING TO AVAIL OF THE economic resources and potentialities available therein and to mobilize and utilize them in the best possible manner, within the framework of close cooperation among Member States,

CONVINCED that relations among the Islamic States in the field of investment are one of the major areas of economic cooperation among these States through which economic and social development therein can be fostered on the basis of common interest and mutual benefit,

ANXIOUS to provide and develop a favourable climate for investments, in which the economic resources of the Islamic countries could circulate between them so that optimum utilization could be made of these resources in a way that will serve their development and raise the standard of living of their peoples,

HAVE APPROVED this Agreement,

AND HAVE AGREED to consider the provisions contained therein as the minimum in dealing with the capitals and investments coming in from the Member States,

AND HAVE DECLARED their complete readiness to put the Agreement into effect, in letter and in spirit, and of their sincere wish to extend every effort towards realizing its aims and objectives.

Chapter One. Definitions

Article 1

The following terms which are used in the Agreement shall have the meanings assigned to each of them for the purpose of the Agreement unless the context indicates a different meaning:

1. THE AGREEMENT

The Agreement for the Promotion, Protection and Guarantee of Investments among the Member States of the Organisation of the Islamic Conference.

2. CONTRACTING PARTIES

The Member States of the Organisation of the Islamic Conference Signatories to the Agreement and in respect of which the Agreement has become effective.

3. HOST STATE

Every contracting party in which the invested capital is present and to which it has come lawfully, or which permits the investor to employ his capital therein.

4. CAPITAL

All assets (including every thing that can be evaluated in monetary terms) owned by a contracting party to this Agreement or by its nationals, whether a natural person or a corporate body and present in the territories of another contracting party whether these were transferred to or earned in it, and whether these be movable, immovable, in cash, in kind, tangible as well as every thing pertaining to these capitals and investments by way of rights or claims and shall include the net profits accruing from such assets and the undivided shares and intangible rights.

5. INVESTMENT

The employment of capital in one of the permissible fields in the territories of a contracting party with a view to achieving a profitable return, or the transfer of capital to a contracting party for the same purpose, in accordance with this Agreement.

6. INVESTOR

The Government of any contracting party or natural corporate person, who is a national of a contracting party and who owns the capital and invests it in the territory of another contracting party. Nationality shall be determined as follows:

(*a*) *Natural Person*:
Any individual enjoying the nationality of a contracting party according to the provisions of the nationality law in force therein.

(*b*) *Legal Personality*

Any entity established in accordance with the laws in force in any contracting party and recognized by the law under which its legal personality is established.

7. INVESTMENT RETURNS

The sums yielded by the investment or derived therefrom for a specified period which shall include, without limitation, the profits, dividends, licence fees, royalties, leases, services and all the increases achieved on the capital assets and the utilization of intangible property rights.

8. THE GENERAL SECRETARIAT

The General Secretariat of the Organisation of the Islamic Conference.

9. THE SECRETARY GENERAL

The Secretary General of the Organisation of the Islamic Conference.

10. THE ORGANISATION

The Organisation of the Islamic Conference.

Chapter Two. General Provisions Regarding Promotion, Protection and Guarantee of the Capitals and Investments and the Rules Governing them in the Territories of the Contracting Parties

Article 2

The contracting parties shall permit the transfer of capitals among them and its utilization therein in the fields permitted for investment in accordance with their laws. The invested capital shall enjoy adequate protection and security and the host State shall give the necessary facilities and incentives to the investors engaged in activities therein.

Article 3

The contracting parties shall endeavour to open up various fields and investment opportunities to the capital on the widest possible scale, in such a way that may suit their economic conditions and on the basis of achieving mutual benefits for the parties to the investment in a way that will foster the social and economic development of the host State in accordance with its set objectives and plans while, at the same time, achieving a profitable investment return for the capital.

Article 4

The contracting parties will endeavour to offer various incentives and facilities for attracting capitals and encouraging its investment in their territories such as commercial, customs, financial, tax and currency incentives, especially during the early years of the investment projects, in accordance with the laws, regulations, and priorities of the host State.

Article 5

The contracting parties shall provide the necessary facilities and grant required permits for entry, exit, residence and work for the investor and his family and for all those whose work is permanently or temporarily connected with the investment such as experts, administrators, technicians, and labourers in accordance with the laws and regulations of the host State.

Article 6

The host State shall–within the provisions of its regulations and its economic and social policies–encourage the local private sector to cooperate with and participate in investments in the contracting parties.

Article 7

In the case of withdrawal of a contracting party from the Agreement, the rights and obligations arising under the Agreement in the host State towards the investor, which have accrued before the receipt of the notice of withdrawal of the contracting party shall continue and shall not be affected by the withdrawal.

Article 8

1. The investors of any contracting party shall enjoy, within the context of economic activity in which they have employed their investments in the territories of another contracting party, a treatment not less favourable than the treatment accorded to investors belonging to another State not party to this Agreement, in the context of that activity and in respect of rights and privileges accorded to those investors.

2. Provisions of paragraph 1 above shall not be applied to any better treatment given by a contracting party in the following cases:

(*a*) Rights and privileges given to investors of one contracting party by another contracting party in accordance with an international agreement, law or special preferential arrangement.

(*b*) Rights and privileges arising from an international agreement currently in force or to be concluded in the future and to which any contracting party may become a member and under which an economic union, customs union or mutual tax exemption arrangement is set up.

(*c*) Rights and privileges given by a contracting party for a specific project due to its special importance to that State.

Article 9

The investor shall be bound by the laws and regulations in force in the host State and shall refrain from all acts that may disturb public order or morals or that may be prejudicial to the public interest. He is also to refrain from exercising restrictive practices and from trying to achieve gains through unlawful means.

Chapter Three. Investment Guarantees

Article 10

1. The host State shall undertake not to adopt or permit the adoption of any measure–itself or through one of its organs, institutions or local authorities–if such a measure may directly or indirectly affect the ownership of the investor's capital or investment by depriving him totally or partially of his ownership or of all or part of his basic rights or the exercise of his authority on the ownership, possession or utilization of his capital, or of his actual control over the investment, its management, making use out of it, enjoying its utilities, the realization of its benefits or guaranteeing its development and growth.

2. It will, however, be permissible to:

(*a*) Expropriate the investment in the public interest in accordance with the law, without discrimination and on prompt payment of adequate and effective compensation to the investor in accordance with the laws of the host State regulating such compensation, provided that the investor shall have the right to contest the measure of expropriation in the competent court of the host State.

(*b*) Adopt preventive measures issued in accordance with an order from a competent legal authority and the execution measures of the decision given by a competent judicial authority.

Article 11

1. The host State shall undertake to guarantee the free transfer to any contracting party of the capitals and its net proceeds in cash without the inestor being subject to any discriminatory banking, administrative, or legal restrictions and without any taxes or charges on the transfer. This shall not apply to the bank service charges. The repatriation of the original capital shall be effected on the termination of the investment according to its nature or after five years from the date of its transfer to the host State, whichever is earlier.

2. The transfer shall be effected in the currency in which the investment was made or in any other convertible currency, at the exchange rate fixed by the International Monetary Fund on the day when the transfer was made.

3. The transfer must be effected within the period normally required for the completion of bank procedures and without delay. In all cases this period shall not exceed 90 (ninety) days from the day in which a request for transfer fulfilling all the legal conditions was made.

4. It shall not be considered as a restriction the procedural measures instituted for exchange control in the host State for administrative purposes or to prevent the illegal transfer abroad of the funds of its nationals. Neither shall

the fixing of the percentage of transferable amounts of the salaries, wages, and rewards of the employees and investment experts within the range of 50% (fifty per cent) be considered a restriction.

Article 12

The host State shall guarantee for the investor the freedom to dispose of the ownership of the invested capital by selling it, wholly or partly, by liquidation, cession, or grant or by any other means. The capital shall continue to be treated in accordance with the provisions of this Agreement on condition that the transfer is made to an investor who is a subject of one of the contracting parties and subject to the approval of the host State.

Article 13

1. The investor shall be entitled to compensation for any damage resulting from any action of a contracting party or one of its public or local authorities or its institutions in the following cases:

(*a*) violation of any of the rights or guarantees accorded to the investor under this Agreement;

(*b*) breach of any of the international obligations or undertakings imposed on the contracting party and arising under the Agreement for the benefit of the investor or the non-performance of whatever is necessary for its execution whether the same is intentional or due to negligence;

(*c*) non-execution of a judicial decision requiring enforcement directly connected with the investment;

(*d*) causing, by other means or by an act or omission, damage to the investor in violation of laws in force in the State where the investment exists.

2. The compensation shall be equivalent to the damage suffered by the investor depending on the type of damage and its quantum.

3. The compensation shall be monetary if it is not possible to restore the investment to its state before the damage was sustained.

4. The assessment of monetary compensation shall be concluded within 6 (six) months from the date when the damage was sustained and shall be paid within a year from the date of agreement upon the amount of compensation or from the date when the assessment of the compensation has become final.

Article 14

The investor shall be accorded a treatment not less than that accorded by the host State to its national investors or others regarding the compensation of damage that may befall the physical assets of investment due to hostilities of international nature committed by any international body or due to civil disturbances or violent acts of general nature.

Article 15

The Organisation shall through the Islamic Development Bank, and in accordance with the provisions of its Agreement, establish as a subsidiary organ of the Organisation, an Islamic Institution for the Guarantee of Investments which is to take charge of the insurance of property invested in the territories of the contracting parties, in accordance with this Agreement and in conformity to the principles of Islamic Sharia.

Article 16

The host State undertakes to allow the investor the right to resort to its national judicial system to complain against a measure adopted by its authorities against him, or to contest the extent of its conformity with the provisions of the regulations and laws in force in its territory, or to complain against the non-adoption by the host State of a certain measure which is in the interest of the investor, and which the State should have adopted, irrespective of whether the complaint is related, or otherwise, to the implementation of the provisions of the Agreement to the relationship between the investor and the host state.

Provided that if the investor chooses to raise the complaint before the national courts or before an arbitral tribunal then having done so before one of the two quarters he loses the right of recourse to the other.

Article 17

Until an Organ for the settlement of disputes arising under the Agreement is established, disputes that may arise shall be settled through conciliation or arbitration in accordance with the following rules and procedures:

1. *Conciliation*

(*a*) In case the parties to the dispute agree on conciliation, the agreement shall include a description of the dispute, the claims of the parties to the dispute and the name of the conciliator whom they have chosen. The parties concerned may request the Secretary-General to choose the conciliator. The General Secretariat shall forward to the conciliator a copy of the conciliation agreement so that he may assume his duties.

(*b*) The task of the conciliator shall be confined to bringing the different view points closer and making proposals which may lead to a solution that may be acceptable to the parties concerned. The conciliator shall, within the period assigned for the completion of his task, submit a report thereon to be communicated to the parties concerned. This report shall have no legal authority before a court should the dispute be referred to it.

2. *Arbitration*

(*a*) If the two parties to the dispute do not reach an agreement as a result of their resort to conciliation, or if the conciliator is unable to issue his report within the prescribed period, or if the two parties do not accept the solutions proposed therein, then each party has the right to resort to the Arbitration Tribunal for a final decision on the dispute.

(*b*) The arbitration procedure begins with a notification by the party requesting the arbitration to the other party to the dispute, clearly explaining the nature of the dispute and the name of the arbitrator he has appointed. The other party must, within sixty days from the date on which such notification was given, inform the party requesting arbitration of the name of the arbitrator appointed by him. The two arbitrators are to choose, within sixty days from the date on which the last of them was appointed arbitrator, an umpire who shall have a casting vote in case of equality of votes. If the second party does not appoint an arbitrator, or if the two arbitrators do not agree on the appointment of an umpire within the prescribed time, either party may request the Secretary General to complete the composition of the Arbitration Tribunal.

(*c*) The Arbitration Tribunal shall hold its first meeting at the time and place specified by the Umpire. Thereafter the Tribunal will decide on the venue and time of its meetings as well as other matters pertaining to its functions.

(*d*) The decisions of the Arbitration Tribunal shall be final and cannot be contested. They are binding on both parties who must respect and implement them. They shall have the force of judicial decisions. The contracting parties are under an obligation to implement them in their territory, no matter whether it be a party to the dispute or not and irrespective of whether the investor against whom the decision was passed is one of its nationals or residents or not, as if it were a final and enforceable decision of its national courts.

General and Final Provisions

Article 18

Two or more contracting parties may enter into an agreement between them that may provide a treatment which is more preferential than that stipulated in this Agreement.

Article 19

The Agreement shall continue to be in force in the event that disputes of any kind arise between the contracting parties and notwithstanding the existence or otherwise of diplomatic relations or any other type of representation between the States concerned.

Article 20

The General Secretariat will follow up the implementation of this Agreement.

Article 21

The Agreement shall come into force after three months from the date on which the instruments of ratification of ten Member States of the Organisation of the Islamic Conference are deposited; and shall come into force, with regard to each new State that may join it, after three months from the date of depositing its instruments of ratification.

Article 22

The Agreement may be amended with the approval of four-fifths of the contracting parties and on the request of at least five States.

Article 23

The Agreement shall continue in force for an unlimited period and the contracting parties may withdraw from it, after five years from its coming into force with regard to the State concerned by notice in writing to the Secretary General provided that the withdrawal shall not become effective before the lapse of one year from the date of notification.

Article 24

The original text of the Agreement shall be deposited with the General Secretariat for signature. The General Secretariat shall receive the instruments of ratification. The General Secretariat shall notify all contracting parties of the signatures and ratifications of the Agreement.

Article 25

This Agreement is drawn up in Arabic, English, and French languages each version being equally authentic.

APPENDIX IV

A List of Member States of the OIC as per January 1986

Afghanistan (membership suspended)
Algeria
Bahrain
Bangladesh
Benin
Brunei
Cameroon
Chad
Comoros
Djibouti
Egypt
Gabon
Gambia
Guinea
Guinea-Bissau
Indonesia
Iran
Iraq
Jordan
Kuwait
Lebanon
Libyan Arab Jamahiriya
Malaysia
Maldives
Mali
Mauritania
Morocco
Niger
Nigeria
Oman
Pakistan
Palestine
Qatar
Saudi Arabia
Senegal
Sierra Leone
Somalia
Sudan
Syrian Arab Republic
Tunisia
Turkey
Uganda
United Arab Emirates
Upper Volta (presently called Burkina-Faso)
Yemen, Arab Republic
Yemen, People's Democratic Republic

Notes

Notes to Chapter 1

1. Such as H. Kruse, *Islamische Völkerrechtslehre* (2nd edn., 1979); M. Khadduri, *War and Peace in the Law of Islam* (1955), and id., *The Islamic Law of Nations: Shaybani's Siyar* (1966).
2. See H. Krüger, *Fetwa und Siyar* (1978), 24-5.
3. Such as M. Hamidullah, *Muslim Conduct of State* (7th edn., 1977); S. Mahmassani, 'The Principles of International Law in the Light of Islamic Doctrine', 117 *RdC* (1966), i. 201-328; M. T. Al-Ghunaimi, *The Muslim Conception of International Law and the Western Approach* (1968), to name just a few.
4. See R. Peters, *Islam and Colonialism: The Doctrine of Jihad in Modern History* (1979), 110-12, 140, 150.
5. For instance by Kruse, op. cit., p. vi; Krüger, op. cit., 27.
6. This was a general view held by many Muslim and non-Muslim 'experts' during the 1960s. See F. A. Sayegh, 'Islam and Neutralism', in J. H. Proctor (ed.), *Islam and International Relations* (1965), 92-3; M. Khadduri, 'The Islamic Theory of International Relations and its Contemporary Relevance', in Proctor, op. cit., 33-5.
7. See T. C. Young, 'Pan-Islamism in the Modern World: Solidarity and Conflict among Muslim Countries', in Proctor, op. cit., 200, 203.
8. This term has been used by B. Dodge, 'The Significance of Religion in Arab Nationalism', in Proctor, op. cit., 118, 119.
9. See Preamble of the OIC Charter in Appendix I.
10. W. Friedmann, *The Changing Structure of International Law* (1964), 60.
11. Ibid., 64.
12. Cf. D. W. Greig, *International Law* (2nd edn., 1976), 5; K. Ipsen, 'Entwicklung zur "collective economic security" im Rahmen der Vereinten Nationen?' in W. Kewenig (ed.), *Die Vereinten Nationen im Wandel* (1975), 26.
13. Since 1964 (the founding year of UNCTAD) an overwhelming number of publications have propagated the idea of regional integration among which the following are noteworthy: *Trade Expansion and Economic Co-operation among Developing Countries* (1966); *Trade Expansion and Economic Integration among Developing Countries: Report by the Secretariat* (New York, 1967); *Trade Expansion, Economic Co-operation and Regional Integration among Developing Countries*, TD/B/333, TD/BAK 10/6 (1970); *Current Problems*

of Economic Integration, TD/B/374 (1971); *Trade Expansion, Economic Co-operation, and Regional Integration among Developing Countries*, TD/110 (1972); *Current Problems of Economic Integration: The Distribution of Benefits and Costs of Integration among Developing Countries*, TD/B/394 (1974); *The Effects of Reverse Preference on Trade among Developing Countries*, TD/B/436 (1974); for further references and details of the activities of UNCTAD as well as the programme of ECDC see ch. 4.

14. A comparative survey of some main regional groupings has been carried out by E. U. Petersmann, *Wirtschaftsintegrationsrecht und Investitionsgesetzgebung der Entwicklungsländer* (1974). A few of these groupings are: Latin American Free Trade Association (LAFTA, 1960); Andean Common Market (Cartagena Agreement, 1969); Central American Common Market (CACM, 1960); Caribbean Free Trade Association (CARIFTA, 1965, 1968); East Caribbean Common Market (ECCM, 1968); East African Community (EAC, 1967); Economic Community of West Africa (ECOWAS, 1967); Arab Common Market (ACM, 1964); Regional Co-operation for Development (RCD, 1964); Association of South East Asian Nations (ASEAN, 1967). For further regional groupings, see ch. 4.
15. Cf. Petersmann, op. cit., 48; see also W. Röpke, 'Economic Order and International Law', 86 *RdC* (1954), ii. 211, 218.
16. For the text of the Charter of the OIC, see *UNTS* 914, 111-16, which is reproduced in Appendix I, as amended. The Charter came into force on 28 February 1973.
17. Doc. ICFM/8-77/ICESC-9 (Final), General Secretariat of the OIC, Jeddah, reproduced in Appendix II.
18. Doc. ICFM/12/81-E/D, 6, General Secretariat, OIC, reproduced in Appendix III.
19. See Second Annual Report (1976-7) at p. 4 of the Islamic Development Bank.
20. This is a term used by E. McWhinney, 'The "New" Countries and "New" International Law', 60 *AJIL* (1966), 30, to denote those 'new' States wishing to remain uninvolved in the cold war of the Super Powers.
21. For a typical example of this challenge, see G. Roy, 'Is the Law of Responsibility of States for Injuries to Aliens a Part of Universal International Law?', 55 *AJIL* (1961), 863 ff.; also cf. P. C. Jessup, 'Non-Universal International Law', 12 *COLJTL* (1973), 420-1.
22. Cf. P. C. Jessup, *A Modern Law of Nations* (repr. 1968), 96.
23. *UNGA Res.* 3201 (S-VI), 'Declaration on the Establishment of a New International Economic Order.'
24. See *UNGA Res.* 3281 (XXIX), 1974.
25. Such as the standard US 'Treaty of Friendship, Commerce, and Navigation', also known as 'Treaty of Amity and Economic Relations' and the German 'Vertrag über die Förderung und den gegenseitigen

Schutz von Kapitalanlagen'; other recent examples are: 'Treaty Concerning the Reciprocal Encouragement and Protection of Investments between Egypt and the United States', text reproduced in 21 *ILM* (1982), 927 ff.; 'Treaty Concerning the Treatment and Protection of Investments between Panama and the United States', in 21 *ILM* (1982), 1227 f.; 'Agreement for the Reciprocal Promotion and Protection of Investments between Sri Lanka and Switzerland', in 21 *ILM* (1982), 399 ff.; see also other agreements between Sri Lanka and the UK, in 19 *ILM* (1980), 886 ff.; between Sri Lanka and Japan, in 21 *ILM* (1982), 963 ff.; 'Agreement on the Mutual Protection of Investments between the People's Republic of China and Sweden', in 21 *ILM* (1982), 477 ff.

26. See O. Udokang, 'The Role of the New States in International Law', 15 *AdV* (1971/2), 170; see also Petersmann, *Wirtschaftsintegrationsrecht*, 15 n. 15; O. Schachter, *Sharing the World's Resources* (1977), 126; for a refutation of this opinion, see ch. 5.4.8.
27. Cf. A. Rahim, *Muhammadan Jurisprudence* (1911, repr. 1982), 50; G. M. Badr, 'Islamic Law: its relation to other Legal Systems', 26 *AJCL* (1978), 188.
28. Badr, op. cit., 189; see also Rahim, op. cit., 45-6.
29. A. Hasan, *The Early Development of Islamic Jurisprudence* (1970), 6-7.
30. See *Q* 5: 48 and 45: 18. In the citation of Koranic verses the first denotes the *Surah* (chapter) and the second the verse. The English translation of the Koran by M. Pickthall has been used. See also J. Penrice, *A Dictionary and Glossary of the Koran* (1873, repr. 1979), 76.
31. Hasan, *Islamic Jurisprudence*, 7.
32. Ibid., 6, 9.
33. A. A. A. Fyzee, *Outlines of Muhammadan Law* (1960), 21.
34. Cited by Hamidullah, *Muslim Conduct of State*, 4.
35. Hasan, *Islamic Jurisprudence*, 39; Rahim, op. cit., 20; J. Schacht, *An Introduction to Islamic Law* (1964), 60; M. Khadduri, *Islamic Jurisprudence: Shafiʿi's Risala* (1961), 78.
36. *Q* 7: 157.
37. M. M. Azami, *Studies in Hadith Methodology and Literature* (1977), 6-8. See also Khadduri, *Shafiʿi's Risala*, for Shafiʿi's brilliant contribution in determining and establishing the sources of legal knowledge and their relationship and status. 'The Sunna of the Apostle makes evident what God meant (in the text of His Book) indicating His general and particular (commands)', 112. See also pp. 109-122 for details.
38. Azami, *Studies in Hadith Methodology and Literature*, 3.
39. Ibid., 4.
40. J. Schacht, *Origins of Muhammadan Jurisprudence* (1950), 149, *Introduction to Islamic Law*, 34; A. Guillaume, *The Traditions of Islam* (1924), 19; M. Rodinson, *Islam and Capitalism* (repr. 1977), 12-13, 69. For the opinion of Rashid Rida see Azami, *Studies in Early Hadith Literature*, 24-5.

41. Azami, *Studies in Early Hadith Literature*, 18-27, 248-68; M. Hamidullah, *The earliest extant work on the Hadith: Sahifah Hammam Ibn Munabhih* (Paris, 10th rev. edn., 1979).
42. Hasan, *Islamic Jurisprudence*, 41-2.
43. Ibid., 55; A. Hasan, *The Doctrine of Ijma in Islam* (1976).
44. See, for example, M. Muslehuddin, *Philosophy of Islamic Law and the Orientalists* (no date; 1979?), 186-7.
45. A point well underlined by A. A. Maududi, 'Political Theory of Islam', in K. Ahmad (ed.), *Islam—Its Meaning and Message* (1976), 163.
46. M. U. Chapra, *The Economic System of Islam: A Discussion of its Goals and Nature* (1971); see also K. Ahmad (ed.), *Studies in Islamic Economics* (1980), which also contains a bibliography on Islamic economics prepared by M. N. Siddiqi (pp. 191-315); S. N. H. Naqvi, *Ethics and Economics: An Islamic Synthesis* (1981). Further writings on Islamic economics are also to be found in a bibliography prepared by V. Nienhaus, *Literature on Islamic Economics in English and German* (1982).
47. V. Nienhaus, *Islam und moderne Wirtschaft* (1982), 22-8.
48. During the Caliphate of Umar I (634-44) a dispute between the Caliph himself and a Jew came before the *Qadi* (judge), who on seeing the Caliph rose in his seat out of deference. Caliph Umar considered this to be such an unpardonable weakness on the judge's part that he dismissed him from office. This incident has been cited by Rahim, *Muhammadan Jurisprudence*, 17.
49. Khadduri, *War and Peace in the Law of Islam*, 147.
50. Rahim, op. cit., 47.
51. See Khadduri, *The Islamic Law of Nations*, 11; Krüger, *Fetwa und Siyar*, 34.
52. Khadduri, op. cit., 21; and Khadduri, *War and Peace in the Law of Islam*, 153-4.
53. A compromise solution proposed by the *Shafiʿi* jurist al-Mawardi (974-1058) advocated the recognition of subentities governed by self-appointed provincial rulers but stressed, at the same time, the ultimate authority of the Caliph. See Khadduri, *The Islamic Law of Nations*, 19-22, esp. p. 21; Hamidullah, *Muslim Conduct of State*, 86, 88.
54. Khadduri, *War and Peace in the Law of Islam*, 155-7; Hamidullah, op. cit., 87.
55. See e.g. the Preamble and Art. II *A*(1) of the Charter of the Islamic Conference in Appendix I.
56. 'Islamisch ist ein Land, in dem der Islam ausdrücklich oder auch andeutungsweise Staatsreligion ist.' A definition given by E. Gräf, 'Die Übertragbarkeit abendländischer Rechtsordnungen auf islamische Ländern', 10 *WINS* (1965/7), 131-63, esp. 137-41; also, cited by Krüger, op. cit., 21 n. 14.
57. See such a survey published under the title of *Dustur. A Survey of the Constitutions of the Arab and Muslim States* (1966); H. Reiners, *Die klassische*

islamische Staatsidee: Ihre moderne Interpretation und ihre Verwirklichung in den Verfassungsordnungen muslimischer Staaten (1968); M. Tworuschka, *Die Rolle des Islam in den arabischen Staatsverfassungen* (1976).

58. M. Kahf, 'International Trade Patterns of the Muslim Countries', in ICE (ed.), *The Muslim World and the Future Economic Order* (1979), 199-222.
59. N. Yalcintas, 'Trade and Co-operation among the Muslim Countries', in ICE, op. cit., 223.
60. A point which has not escaped the keen eye of observers in Socialist States, see e.g. R. Voigt and K. Höhne, 'Antwort auf Leserfragen: Organisation der islamischen Konferenz', 26 *Deutsche Außenpolitik* (1981), 120.
61. E. Hill, 'Comparative and Historical Study of Modern Middle Eastern Law', 26 *AJCL* (1978), 295.
62. R. H. Nolte, 'The Rule of Law in the Arab Middle East', 48 *MW* (1958), 295-307.
63. H. J. Liebesny, 'Religious Law and Westernization in the Moslem Near East', 2 *AJCL* (1953), 492-504; J. N. D. Anderson, 'The Significance of Islamic Law in the World Today', 9 *AJCL* (1960), 189. For constitutional developments on the modern pattern see J. A. M. Caldwell *et al.*, *Dustur: A Survey of the Constitutions of the Arab and Muslim States* (1966), 120-4.
64. W. M. Ballantyne, *Legal Development in Arabia: A Selection of Articles and Addresses on the Arabian Gulf* (1980), 109.
65. Liebesny, op. cit., 498; J. Schacht, 'Islamic Law in Contemporary States', 8 *AJCL* (1959), 133; Anderson, op. cit., 191.
66. Schacht, op. cit., 134-7; Anderson, op. cit., 197 n. 27. In Saudi Arabia many aspects of modern life not provided for in the *Shariʿah*, such as the regulation of complex commercial transactions, labour-management relations, and taxes, have been the subject of administrative pronouncements; see Hill, op. cit., 294.
67. Ballantyne, op. cit., 21; Anderson, op. cit., 191.
68. Liebesny, op. cit., 503; Anderson, op. cit., 189.
69. Ballantyne, op. cit., 25; see also 19, 110-11.
70. Liebesny, op. cit., 499; Anderson, op. cit., 195-6.
71. Ballantyne, op. cit., 86; Anderson, op. cit., 196, 198.
72. It should be kept in mind that for Pakistan 'Islam was the very raison d'être of the foundation of the State' and the first draft constitution abrogated by the military regime (1958) required 'all future legislation to conform to, and all existing legislation to be brought into conformity with the Quran and Sunnah', Anderson, op. cit., 197.
73. Ballantyne, op. cit., 86.
74. Ibid., 92.
75. The categories set down here have been borrowed from Hill, op. cit., 294.
76. For the embodiment of the *Shariʿah* in the constitutions of the Islamic States in the Arabian Gulf area see Ballantyne, op. cit.

77. Anderson, op. cit., 193.
78. Internationally Turkey is emerging as a leading Member State of the OIC. See 'Turks seek new role in Islamic world', in *Arabia. The Islamic World Review* (July 1982), p. 17.

Notes to Chapter 2

1. Hamidullah, *The Muslim Conduct of State*; id., 'The International Law in Islam', 39 *Isl. Rev.* (1951), no. 4, 8-11; id., 'Theorie und Praxis des Völkerrechts im frühen Islam', 5 *Kairos* (1963), 100-14; id., 'The Place of Islam in the History of Modern International Law', 2 *Hyderabad Acad. Stud.* (1940), 29-34; Kruse, *Islamische Völkerrechtslehre*; id., Die Begründung der islamischen Völkerrechtslehre–Muhammad aš-Šaibani–'Hugo Grotius der Moslimen', 5 *Saeculum* (1954), 221-41; id., 'The Foundation of Islamic International Jurisprudence', 3 *JPHS* (1955), 231-67; id., 'The Islamic Doctrine of International Treaties' 1 *ICLQ* (1954), 152-8; Khadduri, *War and Peace in the Law of Islam*; id., *The Islamic Law of Nations: Shaybani's Siyar*; id., 'The Islamic System: Its Competition and Co-existence with Western Systems', *Proc. ASIL* (1959), 49-52; id., 'The Islamic Theory of International Relations and its Contemporary Relevance'; al-Ghunaimi, *The Muslim Conception of International Law and the Western Approach*; Mahmassani, 'The Principles of International Law in the Light of Islamic Doctrine', 201-328; S. Akhtar, 'An Inquiry into the Nature, Origin, and Source of Islamic Law of Nations', 10 *Isl. Stud.* (1971), 23-37; Krüger, op. cit.; Peters, *Islam and Colonialism*.
2. For the definition of *Siyar* see Hamidullah, *Muslim Conduct of State*, 9-11; H. Kruse, 'The Notion of Siyar', 2 *JPHS* (1954), 16-25; Khadduri, *The Islamic Law of Nations*, 38-41; Krüger, op. cit., 31-4.
3. For the concept of *Dar al-Islam* see Hamidullah, *Muslim Conduct of State*, 131; Kruse, *Islamische Völkerrechtslehre*, 57-62; Khadduri, *War and Peace in the Law of Islam*, 155-61; al-Ghunaimi, op. cit., 155-8; D. B. Macdonald, 'Dar al-Islam', *HWI*, 89.
4. See Hamidullah, *Muslim Conduct of State*, showing 'acknowledgement of more Muslim States than one', 86-7; Khadduri, *Islamic Law of Nations*, 19-21; al-Ghunaimi, op. cit., 26-7.
5. Kruse, *Islamische Völkerrechtslehre*, 4-5; Krüger, op. cit., 34-6.
6. Hamidullah, *Muslim Conduct of State*, 8; in a similar strain al-Ghunaimi, op. cit., 96.
7. Cf. Hamidullah, *Muslim Conduct of State*, 22-3.
8. For instance, Caliph Umar's decision not to distribute conquered land amongst the Muslim army, but to leave it in the possession of the tillers and levy tax on it, was apparently contrary to the established custom of the Prophet but, nevertheless, a legally correct decision. For this and

several other examples see Hasan, *Early Development of Islamic Jurisprudence*, 119-21.

9. Cf. Hamidullah, *Muslim Conduct of State*, 23.
10. Khadduri, *Islamic Law of Nations*, 8.
11. Hamidullah, op. cit., 18, 32; Khadduri, op. cit., 142-57.
12. Hamidullah, op. cit., 18, 299-311; Khadduri, op. cit., 75-94.
13. Hamidullah, op. cit., 18, 23-8; Khadduri, op. cit., 8-9.
14. Hamidullah, op. cit., 153-6.
15. Ibid., 33.
16. Ibid., 34-7.
17. This has been contended by Khadduri in his *War and Peace in the Law of Islam*, 47-8, and *Islamic Law of Nations*, 9.
18. This formulation is used by Friedmann, *Changing Structure of International Law*, 188, in the following context: 'Three of the four sources enumerated in Article 38 are reasonably well defined: treaties, custom, and judicial decisions are in fact the three principal sources of legal authority in the international community.'
19. Cf. P. Guggenheim, *Traité de droit international public* (1953), i. 152, and G. I. Tunkin, 'Co-existence and International Law', *RdC* (1958), iii. 25-6.
20. See C. H. M. Waldock, 'General Course on Public International Law', 106 *RdC* (1962), ii. 54 ff.
21. For the view that the teachings of the most highly qualified publicists possess evident defects as a 'source', no matter how subsidiary, see P. C. Jessup, *Transnational Law* (1956), 11; C. Parry, *The Sources and Evidences of International Law* (1965), 103-5; also cf. 'The Spanish Zones of Morocco Claims' (1925), *UNRIAA* ii. 640.
22. As pointed out by K. Wolfke, *Custom in Present International Law* (1964), 79-80.
23. Cf. the discussion of the sources of the *Shariʿah* in ch. 1.3.2.
24. Khadduri, *War and Peace in the Law of Islam*, 48; *Islamic Law of Nations*, 9.
25. See Krüger, op. cit., 36-7.
26. Translated by Khadduri as *The Islamic Law of Nations: Shaybani's Siyar*.
27. This is also confirmed by Jessup in his foreword to Khadduri's *Islamic Law of Nations*, p. ix.
28. See ch. 3.0 below for a discussion of these principles embodied in the OIC Charter.
29. Sayegh, 'Islam and Neutralism', in Proctor, op. cit., 92; see also Khadduri, 'Islamic Theory of International Relations and its Contemporary Relevance', in Proctor, op. cit., 35.
30. Kruse, *Islamische Völkerrechtslehre*, p. vi. It is surprising that even as late as 1979, Kruse was not aware of the founding of the OIC; see also Krüger, op. cit., 27.
31. This appeal was made by C. W. Jenks, *The Common Law of Mankind*

(1958), who called upon international lawyers and scholars to 'draw upon a wider range of sources and legal systems in the future development of the law', 65-6.

32. Although formulated by Jenks in the late 1950s, this admonishment retains its validity today. See his *Common Law of Mankind*, 85.

33. Cf. Kruse, *Islamische Völkerrechtslehre*, 13-15, which is mainly based on al-Kāsānī's 'Kitāb badā'iʿ as-sanā'iʿ fi tartīb ash-sharā'iʿ' and the commentary by as-Sarakhsī (called 'Sharh as-Siyar al-Kabīr') on the legal compendium written by the Hanafi jurist as-Shaybani, 'as-Siyar al-Kabīr'; Khadduri, *War and Peace in the Law of Islam*, *Islamic Law of Nations*, *Islamic Jurisprudence*; Krüger, op. cit.; and a comprehensive survey by Peters, *Islam and Colonialism*, containing expositions of the classical doctrine of Jihad to be found in the prominent legal works of four Sunnite *Madhabs* (schools of law), the Zahirite sect, the Twelver Shiʿite and the Ismaʿilite persuasions.

34. See Kruse, Khadduri, Krüger, and Peters, op. cit. Following these authoritative Western scholars others have continued to reiterate some basic misconceptions about the doctrine of Jihad and the legal relevance of the classical conception of *Siyar*. See, e.g. Jenks, op. cit.; cf. Amerasinghe, *State Responsibility for Injuries to Aliens* (1967), 14; J. E. Dougherty and R. L. Pfaltzgraff, *Contending Theories of International Relations* (1971), 149.

35. According to Peters four basic approaches to the doctrine of Jihad can be discerned in the Muslim world:
    (*a*) the modernist approach of Sir Syed Ahmad Khan, Maulwi Cheragh Ali, Abu Said Husain, and Syed Ameer Ali appearing in India after 1857;
    (*b*) the modernist approach of Mohammad Abduh, Rashid Rida, Mahmud Shaltut, and Mohammad Abu-Zahra in the Arab world;
    (*c*) the fundamentalist approach supported by Maulana Maududi, Hassan al-Banna, and Sayid Qutb; and
    (*d*) the Ahmadiyah Movement (a sect) whose foremost exponents are Mohammad Ali and Zafarullah Khan.

    From amongst these approaches only the Ahmadiyah follow the position of group (*a*) which has been largely abandoned by others. See R. Peters, 'Djihad: War of Aggression or Defense', in *Akten des VII. Kongresses für Arabistik und Islam Wissenschaft* (1976), 282-9; see also Sir S. Ahmad, Review of Dr Hunter's *Indian Musalmans: Are they bound in conscience to rebel against the Queen?* (1872); J. N. S. Baljon, *The Reforms and Religious Ideas of Sir Sayyid Ahmad Khan* (1949); C. Ali, *A Critical Exposition of Popular Jihad* (1885); A. S. Husain, *A Treatise on Jihad* (trans. from Urdu, 1887); S. A. Ali, *The Spirit of Islam* (1922, 6th edn., 1965); A. Ahmad and G. E. von Grunebaum, *Muslim Self-statement in India and Pakistan 1857–1968* (1970); R. Peters, 'Jihad in Mediaeval and Modern Islam'. The

Chapter on Jihad from Averroes's legal handbook 'Bidayat al-Mudjtahid' and the treatise 'Koran and fighting' by the late Sheikh al-Azhar, M. Shaltut (1977); M. Abu-Zahra, *Begriff des Krieges im Islam* (trans. 1961); id., 'International Relations in Islam', in *The First Conference of the Academy of Islamic Research* (Cairo, 1964), 187-236; M. Ali, *The Religion of Islam* (1936); Z. Khan, 'Islam and International Relations', 10 *Int. Spectator* (1956), 308-22. However, in our opinion it is necessary to underline the fact that none of the modernist authors has challenged the 'universal' validity of Islam as a religion; rather they have objected to the violent and aggressive method of promoting and achieving Islamic rule which is alien to the Islamic spirit.

36. See al-Ghunaimi, op. cit., 192.
37. On the reconsideration of the classical doctrine of Jihad cf. also al-Ghunaimi, op. cit., 162-91; S. S. Pirzada, 'Islam and International Law', in A. Gauhar (ed.), *The Challenge of Islam* (London, 1978), 204; M. Akbar, 'The Ailing World Made Better', *Isl. Lit.* (1949), 39; A. Subhan, 'Jihad and Islam', *Isl. Lit.* (1951), 5; A. Latif, 'The Will of God: The Law of the World', *Isl. Lit.* (1952), 15.
38. Cf. Hamidullah, *Muslim Conduct of State*; Mahmassani, op. cit., 201-328; al-Ghunaimi, op. cit., 193; N. O. Madani, 'The Islamic Content of the Foreign Policy of Saudi Arabia' (1977), 7-11.
39. e.g. Peters, *Islam and Colonialism*, 110-12, 140, 150; id., 'Djihad: War of Aggression or Defense'.
40. Peters, *Islam and Colonialism*, 137, 140, 142.
41. We have already dealt with this point; see ch. 1.3.2.
42. Badr, 'Islamic Law', 189. It is only in this sense that Islamic law has been called a jurist's or lawyer's law. The writings of early Muslim jurists, who developed the law in abstract terms and by discussing hypothetical cases, belonged to various schools which were not formal educational institutions or officially sanctioned law-making bodies. They were rather groups of jurists each following a certain doctrine that can be traced back to a prominent pioneer of the second century of the Muslim era whose name the school carries. This is a situation unprecedented in other legal systems. Badr, op. cit.
43. Khadduri, *Islamic Law of Nations*, 19.
44. Al-Ghunaimi, op. cit., 184; in a similar vein Kruse citing Juynboll opines the same about the development of the 'aggressiveness' of the Jihad doctrine. See his *Islamische Völkerrechtslehre*, 45 and n. 173.
45. Madani, op. cit., 14.
46. Sufyan al-Thawri (d. AH 161/AD 778) was a famous traditionist and lawyer. A school founded on his doctrines existed for several centuries.
47. A. H. Abu-Suliman, 'Islamic Theory of International Relations in the Contemporary World' (1970), 1-12; also cited by Madani, op. cit., 21, and Peters, *Islam and Colonialism*, 15.

48. Al-Awzaʿi (d. AH 157/AD 774), famous lawyer. Like the school of al-Thawri, his school was superseded after a few centuries.
49. Malik Ibn Anas (d. *c.* AH 179/AD 796), well-known traditionist and founder of the still extant Maliki school (*madhab*) of Islamic law.
50. Khadduri, *Islamic Law of Nations*, 58.
51. See Khadduri, 'Islamic Jurisprudence', 84.
52. Cf. Khadduri, *Islamic Law of Nations*, 58 n. 132.
53. Ibid., 58 n. 134.
54. See Kruse, *Islamische Völkerrechtslehre*, 14, 32; Peters, *Islam and Colonialism*, 15 n. 15; al-Ghunaimi, op. cit., 74.
55. Cited by Khadduri, *Islamic Law of Nations*, 58 n. 135.
56. Ibn Taymiya (d. AH 728/AD 1328), 'one of Islam's most forceful theologians who, as a member of the pietist school founded by Ibn Hanbal, sought the return of Islamic religion to its sources: the Quran and the Sunnah'. *Encyclopaedia Britannica*, v. 272.
57. See Khadduri, *Islamic Law of Nations*, 59 n. 137 and n. 138; for a commentary on the Koranic injunction see M. Asad, *The Message of the Quran* (1980), 57-8 n. 249.
58. Cf. E. W. Lane, *An Arabic–English Lexicon* (1865, repr. 1968), book 1, part 2, 473; Penrice, op. cit., 30; *Encyclopaedia of Islam* (1965), ii. article on 'Djihad', 538; commentary by A. H. Siddiqi on Muslim's 'Kitab al Jihad waʿl Siyar' (The Book on Jihad and Expedition), in *Sahih Muslim* (trans. A. H. Siddiqi) (1973), iii. 938; al-Ghunaimi, op. cit., 135-6; Madani, op. cit., 20.
59. Lane, op. cit.; Madani, op. cit.
60. Penrice, op. cit.; Lane, op. cit.
61. Cf. Q 4:95 (see English translation by A. Y. Ali); Sahih Muslim, op. cit.
62. See Sahih Muslim, op. cit.; it is only in this sense that the Jihad means an effort which could be directed:

    (*a*) against a visible enemy;
    (*b*) against the devil;
    (*c*) against one's self (*nafs*), meaning the lower passions.

    See *Encyclopaedia of Islam*, op. cit.; Lane, op. cit.
63. Cf. Latif, op. cit., 15.
64. See al-Ghunaimi, op. cit., 136.
65. Khadduri, *War and Peace in the Law of Islam*, 59; on the obligatory nature of the Jihad for Muslims, see his *Islamic Jurisprudence*, 84-6.
66. *Encyclopaedia of Islam*, 539; al-Ghunaimi, op. cit., 138 n. 1.
67. On the classical implications and methodological treatment of this doctrine see Khadduri, *Islamic Jurisprudence*, 123-45. In modern times the doctrine of abrogation has been rejected by a wide number of Muslim scholars. We have dealt with this point in ch. 2.4.3.1.

68. According to Sarakhsi, the periods were as follows:

    (i) a period of trust, forgiveness and withdrawal (*Q* 15: 94);
    (ii) a period of summoning them (the non-believers) to Islam (*Q* 16: 126);
    (iii) a third period of fighting in self-defence (*Q* 31: 40);
    (iv) a fourth period of aggressive fighting at certain times (*Q* 2: 187);
    (v) a fifth period of aggressive fighting in general or absolute terms (*Q* 9: 5; 2: 216).

    See al-Ghunaimi, op. cit., 74; and Kruse, *Islamische Völkerrechtslehre*, 46-9.
69. Al-Ghunaimi, op. cit., 165.
70. Other verses mentioning abrogation are 16: 101 and 13: 39.
71. A. Y. Ali, *The Holy Quran, Text, Translation and Commentary* (1968), 46 n. 107; M. Ali, *The Holy Quran: Translation and Commentary* (1928), 20-1 n. 2; M. Asad, *The Message of the Quran* (1980), 22 n. 87; Hasan, *Early Development of Islamic Jurisprudence*, 70-2.
72. Hasan, op. cit., 67; M. Ali, op. cit., Introduction, p. xxi.
73. Hasan, op. cit., 48.
74. The word 'incongruity' has been translated by M. Ali and A. Y. Ali as 'discrepancy' on pp. 93 and 205 respectively and by Asad as 'inner contradiction', op. cit., 120. All three, however, refer to the same.
75. See M. Ali, op. cit., 20-1 n. 2.
76. Hasan, *Early Development of Islamic Jurisprudence*, 69.
77. Using R. Bell's translation of the Koran (Edinburgh, 1939) Peters replaces the Arabic word *fitna* meaning 'persecution' in verse 193 with 'dissension' which is all the more misleading. See his *Islam and Colonialism*, 10 n. 6.
78. Another reading is: 'but do not commit aggression', see Asad, op. cit., 41 n. 167.
79. For details of Meccan persecution of the Holy Prophet and his Companions, see H. G. Sarwar, *Muhammad, the Holy Prophet* (repr. 1974), 70-151; al-Ghunaimi, op. cit., 166.
80. Verse 190 of *Surah al-Baqara* is said to be the earliest revelation regarding the permission to fight, and in the whole body of the Koran, wherever the Muslims are told to carry on war against non-Muslims, it is subject to the limitation imposed upon them. See M. Ali, op. cit., 33 n. 1, see also Asad, op. cit., 41 n. 167, who supports this view and adduces evidence from Tabari and Ibn Kathir; Hamidullah, *Muslim Conduct of State*, 165-6. For a further commentary on these verses see also al-Ghunaimi, op. cit., 166-7; also cf. *Q* 8: 61.
81. It should be noted that a *hadith* of the Prophet reads thus: 'Do not desire an encounter with the enemy; but when you encounter them, be firm.' See Muslim, op. cit., iii. 945.

82. See commentary by Asad, op. cit., 41 n. 170; al-Ghunaimi, op. cit., 167.
83. See ch. 2.4.1 above. The *Encyclopaedia of Islam* also quotes al-Thawri's opinion as an isolated one although it conforms to the general spirit of the Koranic message. See entry on 'Djihad', ii. 538.
84. As faithfully restated by Peters relying on classical Islamic sources. See *Islam and Colonialism*, 15.
85. Which reads: 'Slay the idolators wherever ye find them.'
86. For a detailed contextual interpretation of *Q*. 9: 5 see al-Ghunaimi, op. cit., 168-70; Asad, op. cit., 256 n. 9.
87. For rules of interpretation see Rahim, op. cit., 78-110; Asad, op. cit., 66 n. 5; M. Ali, 'Interpretation' in *The Holy Quran*, pp. xvii-xix; al-Ghunaimi, op. cit., 165.
88. See Khadduri, *War and Peace in the Law of Islam*, 59 and n. 15, who cites Taj al-Din al-Subki's *Kitab Muʿid al-Niʿām wa Mubid al-Niqam*, ed. D. W. Myhrman (London, 1908), 27, the Koranic injunction in *Surah* 9: 5, and a *hadith* of the Prophet in support of this contention. Although Khadduri himself admits (in n. 16, p. 59) that the idea of Islam ultimately replacing other religions *is not stated in the Koran*, he accepts it as implicit in the objective of the Jihad and clearly stated in a *hadith* in which the Prophet is reported to have said: 'I am ordered to fight polytheists until they say: "there is no god but Allah".' This is all the more contradictory because Khadduri in an earlier passage (on p. 57) on the meaning of Jihad cites (in n. 8, p. 57) Ibn Hazm, *Kitab al-Fasl fi al-Milal wa'l—Ahwa' wa'l-Nihal* (Cairo, AH 1321), ii. 135, as distinguishing 'between the jihad by the tongue and the jihad by ra'y and tadbir (i.e., reason)' and maintains 'that the Prophet Mohammad showed preference for reason over the sword'. In his *Islamic Law of Nations*, 58, Khadduri points out that 'early Hanafi jurists seem to have stressed that tolerance should be shown unbelievers . . . and advised the Imam to prosecute war only when the inhabitants of the dar al-harb came into conflict with Islam'.
89. See *Dialogues of Plato, Laws*, i. trans. B. Jowett, in R. M. Hutchins (ed.), *Great Books of the Western World* (1978), 7. 641, para. 626 (hereinafter cited as *Great Books*).
90. Ibn Khaldun, *Al-Muqqadima*, Engl. trans. F. Rosenthal (1958), ii. 73 ff.; also cited by Khadduri, *War and Peace in the Laws of Islam*, 70.
91. See *The Works of Aristotle, Politics*, i. ch. 8, trans. B. Jowett, *Great Books*, 9. 450, para. 1256*b*, no. 25.
92. Cf. J. von Elbe, 'The Evolution of the Concept of the Just War in International Law', 33 *AJIL* (1939), 665 ff.; Cicero, *De Republica*, p. xxiii; W. Ballis, *The Legal Position of War* (1937), 27 ff.; C. Phillipson, *The International Law and Custom of Ancient Greece and Rome* (1911), ii. 180.
93. See St Augustine, *The City of God*, xix. ch. 7; also cf. Book IV, chs. 14-15, trans. M. Dods, in *Great Books*, 18. 515, 196-7.

94. See St Thomas Aquinas, *The Summa Theologica*, Part I of the Second Part, 'Treatise on Law', Question 105, Art. 103, in *Great Books*, 20. 317.
95. *Summa Theologica*, Part II of the Second Part, 'Treatise on Faith, Hope and Charity', Question 40, Art. 1, in *Great Books*, op. cit., 578.
96. See J. L. Kunz, 'Bellum Justum and Bellum Legale', 45 *AJIL* (1951), 531; D. W. Bowett, *Self-Defence in International Law* (1958), 6-7 points out that 'since self-defence is only one aspect of the larger concept of bellum justum, little distinction is drawn between self-defence and the use of force for securing redress or inflicting punishment' which also come under the criteria of a just war. Hence, a just war has been characterized as 'defensive' or 'offensive' without making any distinction between self-defence and other forms of self-help.
97. Whereas J. Locke, *Concerning Civil Government*, Second Essay, ch. 3, in *Great Books*, 35. 28, supports the reasonable and just 'right to destroy that which threatens me with destruction' on the principle of self-preservation, Montesquieu, *The Spirit of Laws*, Book X, 'Of Laws in the Relation they Bear to Offensive Force', ch. 2, in *Great Books*, 38. 62, maintains that the 'right of war . . . is derived from necessity and strict justice'; also cf. Kunz, 'Bellum Justum and Bellum Legale', 530; Bowett, *Self-Defence*, 4-5; H. Kelsen and R. Tucker, *Principles of International Law* (2nd edn., 1966), 30; I. Brownlie, *International Law and the Use of Force by States* (1963), 7-13; H.-G. Mähler, 'Die völkerrechtliche Bedeutung des Kriegs- und Gewaltverbots' (Diss. Munich, 1965), 9-10.
98. Cf. Khadduri, *War and Peace in the Law of Islam*, 62, 69.
99. Ibn Khaldun, *Al-Muqqadima*, ii. 73-88, also cited by Khadduri, *War and Peace in the Law of Islam*, 71, and *Islamic Law of Nations*, 16 n. 33.
100. W. E. Hall, *International Law* (8th edn.), ed. A. P. Higgins (1924), 82; also cited by I. Brierly, 'International Law and Resort to Armed Force', 4 *Cambridge Law Journal* (1932), 308.
101. Cf. Brownlie, *International Law and the Use of Force*, 20-1, 47, 49.
102. See L. Oppenheim and H. Lauterpacht, 'International Law' (7th edn. 1952), ii. 178; Kelsen and Tucker, 29; Brownlie, op. cit.
103. Kelsen and Tucker, 29.
104. On the regulation of force by the Covenant, see Oppenheim and Lauterpacht, ii. 180; Kunz, op. cit., 'Bellum Justum and Bellum Legale', 532; M. S. McDougal and F. P. Feliciano, *Law and Minimum World Public Order* (1961), 138-40; Kelsen and Tucker, op. cit., 34-6; Brownlie, *Use of Force*, 56-65; M. Bothe, 'Das Gewaltverbot im allgemeinen', in W. Schaumann (ed.), *Völkerrechtliches Gewaltverbot und Friedenssicherung* (1971), 13-14; E. Menzel and K. Ipsen, *Völkerrecht* (1979), 446.
105. For the text of the Treaty, see *League of Nations Treaty Series*, 94. 57 ff.; at the outbreak of the Second World War in 1939 sixty-three States were parties to the Treaty, and, at present, it still remains in force with the number of parties reaching sixty-five.

106. For the legal effect of the Kellogg Pact, see Oppenheim and Lauterpacht, op. cit., ii. 182-93; Bowett, *Self-Defence*, 132-8; McDougal and Feliciano, op. cit., 141-2; Brownlie, *Use of Force*, 74-92; Kelsen and Tucker, op. cit., 37-9; Mähler, 'Die völkerrechtliche Bedeutung des Kriegs- und Gewaltverbots durch Kellogg-Pakt und UN Satzung'; Menzel and Ipsen, op. cit., 447; the parties to the Saavedra-Lamas Pact, which contained provisions similar to those of the Kellogg Pact, were Bolivia, El Salvador, Uruguay, and Argentina: see M. O. Hudson, *International Legislation*, vi. 448; it must, however, be noted that San Marino, Yemen, and Nepal became parties to none of these pacts.
107. Brownlie, *Use of Force*, 110.
108. Cf. Preamble of the Charter and Art. 1 (1); also see Oppenheim and Lauterpacht, op. cit., ii. 153; H. Kelsen, *The Law of the United Nations* (1951), 13-15, 708; Kelsen and Tucker, op. cit., 40-1; Bowett, *Self-Defence*, 146; Brownlie, *Use of Force*, 113; for a detailed consideration of the provision see ch. 3.2.2.6.
109. See Brownlie, *Use of Force*, 112-13, and *Principles of Public International Law* (1979), 513; R. L. Bobrov, 'Basic Principles of Present-Day International Law', in G. I. Tunkin (ed.), *Contemporary International Law Collection of Articles* (1969), 36-58, 46; R. M. Derpa, *Das Gewaltverbot der Satzung der Vereinten Nationen* (1970), 16; Kelsen, *Law of the United Nations*, 708-9; B. zu Dohna, *Die Grundprinzipien des Völkerrechts* (1973), 52-4; R. Falk, 'The New States and International Legal Order', 118 *RdC* (1966), ii. 47; Jessup, 'Non-Universal International Law', 426; Bothe, 'Das Gewaltverbot im allgemeinen', 15; W. Kewenig, 'Gewaltverbot und noch zulässige Machteinwirkung und Interventionsmittel', in Schaumann, op. cit., 177; G. Dahm, *Völkerrecht* (1958), i. 200; A. D. McNair, *Law of Treaties* (1961), 217; K. Skubiszewski, 'Use of Force by States. Collective Security. Law of War and Neutrality', in M. Sørensen (ed.), *Manual of Public International Law* (1968), 745; R. Rosenstock, 'The Declaration of Principles of International Law Concerning Friendly Relations: A Survey', 65 *AJIL* (1971), 717; Menzel and Ipsen, op. cit., 449; also see ch. 3.2.2.6 n. 158 below for statements made by delegates of various countries in the UN Special Committee on Friendly Relations.
110. See Kelsen and Tucker, op. cit., 59-61; Brownlie, *Use of Force*, 274.
111. See Oppenheim and Lauterpacht, op. cit., ii. 154-5; Kelsen and Tucker, op. cit., 61; for a discussion of NATO as an instrument of regional collective self-defence based on Art. 51 of the UN Charter, see K. Ipsen, *Rechtsgrundlagen und Institutionalisierung der atlantisch-westeuropäischen Verteidigung* (1967), 27-32.
112. Cf. Art. 39.
113. For supporting and opposing views on the issues of restrictive interpretation of Art. 51 and the lawfulness of armed intervention for

humanitarian reasons, see J. L. Kunz, 'Individual and Collective Self-Defense in Art. 51 of the Charter of the United Nations', 41 *AJIL* (1947), 872-9, 878; Oppenheim and Lauterpacht, op. cit., ii. 156; Jessup, *Modern Law of Nations*, 166; Kelsen, *Law of the United Nations* 797, 914; Q. W right, 'The Goa Incident', 56 *AJIL* (1962), 621, and 'The Cuban Quarantine', 57 *AJIL* (1963), 560; Brownlie, *Use of Force*, 251-308, 430, 433-6; Henkin, 'International Law and the Behaviour of Nations', 114 *RdC* (1965), i. 171, 262-6; J. de Aréchaga, 'Réglement pacifique des Différens', 111 *RdC* (1964), i. 423, 503-8; Kelsen and Tucker, op. cit., 64-73; Skubiszewski, op. cit., 765-8, 778; M. Akehurst, *A Modern Introduction to International Law* (1970), 315 ff.; Derpa, op. cit., 115 f.; Bothe, op. cit., 16, 21, 22-3; P. Wittig, 'Der Aggressionsbegriff im internationalen Sprachgebrauch', in Schaumann, op. cit., 51-2, 62-3; Kewenig, 'Gewaltverbot und noch zulässige Machteinwirkung und Interventionsmittel', 193-213; L. Wildhaber, 'Gewaltverbot und Selbstverteidigung', in Schaumann, op. cit., 150-60, with a detailed note on the views expressed over the interpretation of Art. 51; T. M. Franck, 'Who killed Article 2 (4)? Or: Changing Norms Governing the Use of Force by States', 64 *AJIL* (1970), 821 ff.; zu Dohna, op. cit., 90; Dahm, *Völkerrecht*, ii. 413-16, 424-5; Friedmann, op. cit., 260; R. Higgins, *The Development of International Law through the Political Organs of the United Nations* (1963), 176, 189, 199-200; W. Wengler, *Das völkerrechtliche Gewaltverbot* (1967), 4-7, 13-14, 17-18; J. E. S. Fawcett, 'Intervention in International Law', 103 *RdC* (1961), ii. 344, 391-409; Bowett, *Self-Defence*, 187-9, see also pp. 22-5, 29-115, 146-54, 184-97, 270-1; C. G. Fenwick, 'The Quarantine against Cuba: Legal or Illegal', 57 *AJIL* (1963), 592, and 'The Dominican Republic: Intervention or Collective Self-Defense', 60 *AJIL* (1966), 64; H. G. Franzke, 'Die militärische Abwehr von Angriffen auf Staatsangehörige im Ausland–insbesondere ihre Zulässigkeit nach der Satzung der Vereinten Nationen', 16 *ÖZöR* (1966), 128-75; McDougal and Feliciano, *Law and Minimum World Public Order*, 233-41; McDougal, 'The Soviet-Cuban Quarantine and Self-Defense', 57 *AJIL* (1963), 597-604; J. Stone, *Legal Controls of International Conflict* (1959), 244 and n. 8, and *Aggression and World Order* (1958), 92-103; Brierly, *Law of Nations*, 417-20; C. H. M. Waldock, 'The Control of the Use of Force by Individual States in International Law', 81 *RdC* (1952), ii. 498; D. P. O'Connell, *International Law* (2nd edn., 1970), 316-17, 304; S. M. Schwebel, 'Aggression, Intervention and Self-Defence', 136 *RdC* (1972), ii. 481; Rosenstock, op. cit., 723; L. C. Green, 'Armed Conflict, War and Self-Defence', 6 *AdV* (1956/7), 387, 430-5; Menzel and Ipsen, op. cit., 453-4; for an interpretation of the provision of Art. 51 in connection with the interpretation of Art. II (B) 5 of the OIC Charter, see ch. 3.2.2.6 below; on reprisals involving recourse to armed force, see D. W. Bowett, 'Reprisals Involving Recourse to Armed Force', 66 *AJIL* (1972), 1 ff.; Harib Fort Incident, SCOR, 19th year, 1106th-1111th Meetings, 2-8 April

1964; the Caroline Case, R. Y. Jennings, 'The Caroline and McLeod Cases', 32 *AJIL* (1938), 82 ff; the Cuban Quarantine, C. R. Christol and C. R. Davis, 'Maritime Quarantine; The Naval Interdiction of Offensive Weapons and Associated Material to Cuba, 1962', 57 *AJIL* (1963), 525, 530, Q. Wright, 'The Cuban Quarantine', 57 *AJIL* (1963), 546; L. C. Meeker, 'Defensive Quarantine and the Law', 57 *AJIL* (1963), 515 ff.; the Anglo-French Invasion of the Suez (1956), Q. Wright, 'Intervention, 1956', 51 *AJIL* (1957), 257, Hansard, House of Lords, vol. 199. cols. 1348-59, 1 November 1956, and SCOR, 11th year, 749th Meeting; the Entebbe Raid, 15 *ILM* (1976), 1224; the Mayaguez Affair (1975), *Digest of US Practice in International Law* (1975), 776.

114. For a general documentation of this fact, see Peters, *Islam and Colonialism*, who covers most of these Jihad movements during the colonial period.

115. Cf. *UN Yearbook* (1960), 48-9, (1966), 905-6, and (1967), 740, 745; for Third World views in general, see R. P. Anand, *New States and International Law* (1972), 57-8; for Socialist (Soviet) views, see F. C. Schröder, 'Die Rechtmaßigkeit des Krieges nach westlicher und sowjetischer Völkerrechtsauffassung', in R. Maurach and B. Meißner (eds.), *Völkerrecht in Ost und West* (1967), 178-218.

116. See McWhinney, 'The "New" Countries', 12; Jessup, 'Non-Universal International Law', 423-6; Udokang, 'The Role of the New States', 182-7; Wright, 'The Goa Incident', 620; Menzel and Ipsen, op. cit., 456-7; Bothe, 'Das Gewaltverbot', 24; Wildhaber, 'Gewaltverbot', 158; Kewenig, 'Gewaltverbot', 208-9.

117. See Anand, *New States*, 57-8, who points out that such a declaration was made by Heads of State of Non-Aligned Countries assembled in Cairo in 1964; also cf. the 'Declaration on Principles of International Law Concerning Friendly Relations and Co-operation among States' (Res. 2625 (xxv), 24 Oct. 1970), in Brownlie (ed.), *Basic Documents* (1983), and 65 *AJIL* (1971), 246.

118. See Udokang, op. cit., 185, who asserts that only the Security Council is empowered, by virtue of Art. 39, UN Charter, to determine whether a situation constitutes 'any threat to the peace, breach of the peace, or act of aggression'.

119. See Anand, 'Attitude of the Asian-African States Towards Certain Problems of International Law', 15 *ICLQ* (1966), 65.

120. See Namibia (South West Africa), Advisory Opinion, *ICJ Rep.* (1971), 31 ff.; Western Sahara, Advisory Opinion, *ICJ Rep.* (1975), 31-2.

121. *ICJ Rep.* (1971), para. 119, p. 54.

122. *ICJ Rep.* (1971), para. 120, p. 55.

123. Cf. al-Ghunaimi, op. cit., 28; A. Nussbaum, *A Concise History of the Law of Nations* (rev. edn., 1964), 45 ff., 51 ff.

124. See Hamidullah, *Muslim Conduct of State*, 60, where he has dealt with these topics in some detail.
125. Cf. al-Ghunaimi, op. cit., 33-44. He bases his contention on the fact that the Prophet concluded a treaty or covenant with a delegation representing some Medinan tribes in AD 622 even before his emigration. The unique position of the Pope in modern international law may be cited as an exceptional case of recognition of the individual as possessing international personality, cf. Kunz, 'The Status of the Holy See in International Law', 46 *AJIL* (1952), 308-14; O'Connell, *International Law*, i. 289; Menzel and Ipsen, op. cit., 98, 134 ff.
126. On the emigration and constitutional acts subsequently see M. Hamidullah, *The First Written Constitution of the World* (3rd edn., 1976); al-Ghunaimi, op. cit., 36-9; M. Watt, *Muhammad at Medina* (1962); Muhammad Ibn Ishak, *Sirat Rasul Allah (The Life of Muhammad)* trans. A. Guillaume (1955), 201-6, 221-35.
127. 'When the Meccans knew that the Prophet had settled in Medina they addressed a letter to ʿAbdullah ibn Ubayy asking him to deport Muhammad from the city, failing which they would come with a mighty force and slaughter the males and enslave the females', al-Ghunaimi, op. cit., 39. ʿAbdullah ibn Ubayy was a man of incontestible authority among his people in Medina and they wanted 'to crown him their king' when the Prophet arrived in Medina; see Guillaume, op. cit., 277-8.
128. For the text of the Treaty, see Hamidullah, *Muslim Conduct of State*, 271 ff.
129. Al-Ghunaimi, op. cit., 42, 55.
130. For details see Guillaume, op. cit., 540-1.
131. Cf. M. Bukhari, *Sahih al-Bukhari*, trans. M. M. Khan (1971), 4. 160; Muslim, op. cit., iii. 943, 946; B. Lewis, *Islam from the Prophet Muhammad to the Capture of Constantinople: A Documentary History* (1974), i. *Politics and War*, 'Abu Bakr on the Rules of War', 213; Hamidullah, *Muslim Conduct of State*, 205-8, 300-2.
132. The translation rendered by A. Y. Ali, op. cit., has been used here; see also Hamidullah, op. cit., 287.
133. Here we have reverted to the translation by M. Pickthall. A. Y. Ali variates the last sentence as 'for God loveth the righteous', op. cit., 439.
134. See Hamidullah, *Muslim Conduct of State*, 290-1 for details of these treaties; for the Prophet's covenant with the Jews and their subsequent breach of its provisions, see al-Ghunaimi, op. cit., 36-9, 54-61; see also Guillaume, op. cit., 363 where Ibn Ishak relates that the Banu Qaynuqāʿ 'were the first of the Jews to break their agreement with the apostle (Prophet) and to go to war'.
135. Al-Ghunaimi citing Abdul Rahman Arabi (*L'Islam et la guerre à l'époque du Prophète Mahomet* (Ambilly, 1954), 17), op. cit., 42; see also A. L. Tibawi, 'Christians under Muhammad and his First Two Caliphs', in his *Arabic*

and Islamic Themes (1976), 57, a reprint of an article originally published in the *IQ*.

136. See Guillaume, op. cit., 607.

137. Tibawi, 'Christians under Muhammad', 57; for a short treatment of the *dhimmis* as subjects of the Islamic State see 2.6.2 below.

138. For instance, Khalid ibn al-Walid, the Commander of Muslim forces, stipulated in a pact made with Sulāba ibn Nastūnā and his people in the year AH 12/AD 633 that 'You have protection (*Dhimma*) and defence. If we defend you, the *jizya* is due to us; if we do not, it is not, until we do defend you.' See Lewis, *Islam*, 234-5. Similarly, when the Muslims retreated, prior to the decisive battle of Yarmuk with the Byzantines in AD 636, all towns with which agreements for Jizya had been signed 'received back the amounts they had paid to the Muslims, who were not, according to the terms of the compact, able to protect them'. See Tibawi, who cites A. Ysuf, *Kitab al-Kharaj*, 81, on this matter, op. cit., 60-1.

139. According to Hamidullah, the earliest extant work on *Fiqh* (law) is that of Zaid Ibn Ali (d. AH 20/AD 742), titled, 'Al-Majmuʿ fi-'l Fiqh', *Muslim Conduct of State* 61, 76.

140. Hamidullah, op. cit.; al-Ghunaimi, op. cit., 34.

141. Hamidullah, op. cit., 62; Kruse, 'Die Begründung der islamischen Völkerrechtslehre', 221-41; Khadduri, *Islamic Law of Nations*.

142. This is one of the conclusions drawn by Krüger, op. cit., 153.

143. Cf. Shaybani's 'Abwab al-Siyar fi Ard al-Harb', trans. Khadduri, *Islamic Law of Nations*, which is in the form of questions put to the teacher Abu Hanifah on hypothetical legal issues that may have been reflected in daily life, and Abu Hanifah's answers to these bolstered by legal arguments in support of his opinion.

144. Bergsträsser distinguished three broad categories of adherence to the *Shariʿah*:

(1) in matters of ritual, family, and inheritance law which adhered closest to the *Shariʿah*;
(2) constitutional, criminal, and fiscal law which diverged farthest and, in some cases completely, from the *Shariʿah* (in this category *Siyar* could also be included);
(3) commercial law, which lies between the above extremes.

Cf. J. Schacht (ed.), *G. Bergsträsser: Gründzüge des Islamischen Rechts* (1935), 119-22; J. Schacht, 'The Schools of Law and Later Developments of Jurisprudence', in M. Khadduri and H. J. Liebesny (eds.), *Law in the Middle East* (1955), i. 77. For the development of some Islamic commercial legal concepts, see A. L. Udovitch, *Partnership and Profit in Medieval Islam* (1970).

145. Cf. P. K. Hitti, *History of the Arabs* (5th edn., 1953), 298, who cites Eginhard (*Vie de Charlemagne*) as his source; al-Ghunaimi, op. cit., 46-7.

146. As early as AD 658-9 Muʿāwiyah, the then Governor of Syria and later founder of the Umayyad dynasty, concluded a truce with the Byzantine Emperor Constans II at the price of a yearly tribute. See Hitti, op. cit., 199; al-Ghunaimi, op. cit., 43-4. Although the Umayyads resumed hostilities with the Byzantines as soon as they thought themselves strong enough, their coveted goal of capturing Constantinople remained unfulfilled and the practice of the Islamic State of paying tribute to Byzantium was a common occurrence under them. It was only under the Abbasid Caliph al-Mahdi (AD 775-802) that a Muslim army commanded by his son Harun (who later became the Caliph al-Rashid) inflicted defeat upon the Byzantines and forced the Empress Irene (797-805) to sign a humiliating treaty imposing a heavy tribute. However, it must be kept in mind that relations between Byzantine and the Islamic State did not only encompass incessant warfare but consisted of 'a long succession of war and peace, ruin and creation, enmity and friendship'. A. A. Vasiliev, 'Byzantium and Islam', in *Byzantium: An Introduction to the East Roman Civilisation* (1961), 311-12, cited by al-Ghunaimi, op. cit., 44-5.
147. Thus Charlemagne, a 'natural ally' of the Abbasids, was even invited by an Arab confederacy in Spain in 778 to fight the first Umayyad Emir of Spain Abd al-Rahman I (756-78). But the army despatched by Charlemagne failed to achieve its objective and suffered heavy losses. See Hitti, op. cit., 507; al-Ghunaimi, op. cit., 46.
148. Thus according to B. Lewis, 'Politics and War', in J. Schacht and C. E. Bosworth (eds.), *The Legacy of Islam* (1974), 176: 'a widening gap appeared between legal doctrine and political fact which the politicians ignored and jurists did their best to conceal.'
149. See W. B. Stevenson, *The Crusaders in the East* (1907), 143-5; Hitti, op. cit., 645; U. and M. C. Lyons and J. S. C. Riley-Smith (eds.), *Ayyubids, Mamlukes and Crusaders: Selections from the Tarikh al-Duwal wa'l-Muluk of Ibn al-Furat* (1971), ii. translation, 1 ff.; H. A. R. Gibb, *The Life of Saladin* (1973); K. M. Setton (ed.), *A History of the Crusades*, i. *The First Hundred Years*, ii. *The Later Crusades 1189–1311* (2nd edn., 1969); S. Runciman, *A History of the Crusaders* (1951-4), i-iii; A. S. Atiya, *The Crusade in the Later Middle Ages* (1938, repr. 1965), and *Crusade, Commerce, and Culture* (1962); R. A. Newhall, *The Crusades* (rev. edn., 1963); H. E. Mayer, *Geschichte der Kreuzzüge* (1965); al-Ghunaimi, op. cit., 48-50.
150. Though the Ottomans were forced, because of military weakness and incapacity, to turn to peace-making, they nevertheless glossed up the realities of the Treaty of Carlowitz and perceived it to be a 'temporary peace' being 'equivalent in meaning to the Jihad/holy war'. See R. A. Abou-El-Haj, 'Ottoman Attitudes Toward Peace Making: The Karlowitz Case', 51 *Der Islam* (1974), 136; even during the negotiations preceding the conclusion of the treaty the Ottomans maintained the role and stance which they had held in the past; see Abou-El-Haj, op. cit.,

134. For a detailed discussion and assessment of the Ottoman negotiations of 1698-9 and the immediate implications and ideological significance of the closure of the Ottoman frontier with Europe, see R. A. Abou-El-Haj, 'Ottoman Diplomacy at Karlowitz', 87 *JAOS* (1967), 498-512. After Carlowitz, the Ottoman Empire steadily retreated in the face of rising European Imperialism. According to Kruse, *Islamische Völkerrechtslehre*, 165, 'vom Jahre 1669 bis zum Pariser Frieden von 1856 hatte die Hohe Pforte gegenüber den europäischen Mächten nur ständiges Zurückweichen gekannt und keinen Friedensvertrag mehr ohne erhebliche Gebietsabtretungen erlangen können'.

151. According to J. Wansborough, the earliest documentary evidence for commercial privileges granted to Europeans dates from the 6th century AH/12th century AD. See *Encyclopaedia of Islam* (n. edn.), iii. 1178; cf. also J. Wansborough, 'The Safe-Conduct in Muslim Chancery Practice', 34 *BSOAS* (1971), 20-35; H. Inalcik, 'Imtiyazat', *EI*, iii. 1182, cites the case of Seldjuk Sultans of Anatolia granting commercial privileges to the Kingdom of Cyprus and the Venetians as early as AH 603/AD 1207; however, W. Heffening, *Das islamische Fremdenrecht bis zu den islamisch-fräkischen Staatsverträgen* (1925, repr. 1975), lists thirty-three so-called 'islamisch-fränkische Staatsverträge' dealing with capitulations which were concluded by Islamic rulers with Christian European States between AD 1149-1290. See op. cit., p. xvi.

152. For details of this legal concept see 2.6.5 below.

153. J. Wansborough, 'A Mamluk Commercial Treaty Concluded with the Republic of Florence, 894/1498', in S. M. Stern (ed.), *Documents from Islamic Chanceries: Oriental Studies III* (1965), 39-79. However, M. A. Boisard, 'On the Probable Influence of Islam on Western Public and International Law', 11 *IJMES* (1980), 433, points out that the 'treaty appears rather as a decree from the Sultan to his administration in Egypt and the Syrian Levant than as a bilateral and reciprocal international instrument binding the two parties'.

154. See Inalcik, op. cit., 1179. Even in pre-Ottoman times Muslim rulers endeavoured to mention the *Sharīʿah* and specific prescriptions thereof in the document (*ʿahdname*) granting the capitulation. Thus Boisard, op. cit., 433, points out that the treaty of 1489 with the Republic of Florence refers to the *Sharia* (Arts. 8 and 6) and to the *huquq sharʿiyya* (Arts. 18 and 20).

155. Inalcik, op. cit., 1182; J. C. Hurewitz (ed.), *The Middle East and North Africa in World Politics: A Documentary Record*, i. *European Expansion, 1535–1914* (2nd edn., 1975), 1.

156. See al-Ghunaimi, op. cit., 51; *EB*, 6. 1086*b–c*; for the text of the draft treaty see Hurewitz, *The Middle East and North Africa in World Politics*, 2-5; Inalcik points out that this form of 'treaty' concluded between equal parties is a solitary example among the 'capitulations', *EI*, iii. 1183. This

opinion, we submit, cannot be fully supported as the Ottomans concluded peace treaties with European States in the eighteenth century which also included capitulatory clauses. See notes 163-8 below.

157. See Hurewitz, op. cit., 2.
158. See Asylum Case, *ICJ Rep.* (1950), 266; Right of Passage Case, *ICJ Rep.* (1960), 6 ff.
159. See Asylum Case, *ICJ Rep.* (1950); also cf. The Lotus Case, *PCIJ Rep.* (1927), Ser. A, no. 10, 28; Anglo-Norwegian Fisheries Case. *ICJ Rep.* (1951), 116; North Sea Continental Shelf Cases, *ICJ Rep.* (1969), 3 ff., paras. 70 ff. esp. 77 and 78.
160. For example, the Russian-Ottoman Treaty for the Partition of Persia's Northwest Provinces, 1724; Treaty of Peace (Belgrade), 1739; Treaty of Peace signed at Kücük Kaynarca in 1774; Treaty of Peace (Jassy), 1792; Treaty of Peace (Bucharest), 1812; for texts of these treaties, see Hurewitz, op. cit., 66-9, 72-4, 93-101, 106-9, and 194-7 respectively.
161. See al-Ghunaimi, op. cit., 53, who mentions the Peace of Passarovitz in 1718 and the Treaty of Sistova in 1791.
162. See Hurewitz, op. cit., in note 160 above.
163. In this and the following annotations only a brief number of treaties and grants of capitulatory privileges have been cited. Following the Draft Treaty of Amity and Commerce, 1536, with France, Sultan Süleyman I gave in 1553 a Grant of Trading Privileges to Anthony Jenkinson (an English merchant); other agreements are, Treaty of Commerce with England, 1580; Final Treaty of Capitulations with England, 1675; Treaty of Peace (Kücük Kaynarca) with Russia, 1774, which promised to give Russians the most-favoured-nation treatment in trade with the Ottoman Empire; Ottoman Grant of Privileges in the Black Sea to British Merchant Vessels, 1799; Treaty of Peace, Commerce, and Secret Alliance (Dardanelles) with Great Britain, 1809, reaffirming the capitulations agreed upon in 1675; Treaty of Commerce and Navigation with the United States, 1830, being the only non-European Western power to receive a capitulation. For texts see Hurewitz, *The Middle East and North Africa*, 5, 8, 34, 92, 140, 189, and 245 respectively.
164. Grant of Commercial Privileges to the (English) Muscovy Company by the Shah Tahmasp of Persia, 1566-8; Promise by Shah ʿAbbas of Extraterritorial Privileges to Europeans, 1600; Grant of Capitulations to the Netherlands by Shah ʿAbbas, 1623; Grant of Capitulations to England by Shah Safi, 1629; in 1631 a Dutch agent of Shah Safi succeeded in obtaining a Grant of Extraterritorial Privileges to Persian Merchants in the Netherlands–this promise of reciprocal capitulations failed to materialize, however, as the Persian merchants rarely established branches in Europe; Grant of Capitulations by Shah Sulṭan Husayn to France, 1708; Treaty of Friendship and Commerce with France, 1715; Treaty of Peace, Amity, and Commerce with Russia, 1732; Grant of

Special Privileges at Bushire to the (British) East India Company, 1763; Treaties of Alliance and Commerce with British India, 1801; Treaties of Peace and Commerce (Turkmanchay) with Russia, 1828; and the Treaty of Friendship and Commerce with the United States in 1856. For texts see Hurewitz, op. cit., 7, 15, 17, 22, 24, 49, 56, 69, 84, 117, 231, and 337 respectively.

165. Treaty of Peace and Commerce and Coral Fishery Concession concluded between France and the Garrison of Algiers, 1628; Treaty of Peace and Commerce with Great Britain, 1682; Treaty of Peace and Amity with the United States, 1795; Treaty of Peace with the United States, 1815; Treaties of Peace with Great Britain and the Netherlands, 1816. See Hurewitz, op. cit., 19, 44, 109, 203, and 209.

166. Treaty of Peace and Commerce with France, 1682; Treaty of Peace and Commerce with Great Britain, 1721; Treaty of Peace, Amity, and Commerce with France, 1767; Treaty of Peace, Friendship, and Ship-Signals with the United States, 1786; Treaty of Peace, Friendship, Navigation, Commerce, and Fishing with Spain, 1799; Treaty of Peace with Great Britain, 1801. See Hurewitz, op. cit., 42, 63, 87, 101, 134, and 149 respectively.

167. Treaty of Peace and Commerce, and Commercial Concession concluded between the Garrison of Tunis and France, 1665-6; Treaty of Peace and Capitulations with France, 1742; Treaty of Peace and Commerce with Great Britain, 1751; Treaty of Peace and Renewal of Capitulations with France, 1824. For texts see Hurewitz, op. cit., 29, 75, 80, and 222 respectively.

168. Napoleon's Egyptian campaign in 1798 led the English to seek an agreement with the Imam of Musqat as a defensive measure. (East India Company's Agreement with the Imam of Masqat Excluding the French from his Territories, 1798); Treaty of Amity and Commerce with the United States, 1833. See Hurewitz, op. cit., 124 and 255.

169. With the objective of displacing the dominant position granted to France by virtue of the Treaty of 1536 which required English merchants to conduct business under the French flag, England launched efforts in 1577 to procure capitulatory privileges for England equal to those of France. See text of the Treaty of Commerce of 1580 between the Ottoman Empire and England in Hurewitz, op. cit., 8-10; see also Inalcik, op. cit., 1184; n. 163 above mentioning the Treaty of 1774 with Russia.

170. See Inalcik, op. cit. 1187.

171. Cf. C. V. Findley, 'The Foundation of the Ottoman Foreign Ministry', 3 *IJMES* (1972), 395. See also his other article, 'The Legacy of Tradition to Reform: Origins of the Ottoman Foreign Ministry', 1 *IJMES* (1970), 334-57; Naff, 'Reform and the Conduct of Ottoman Diplomacy in the Reign of Selim III, 1789-1807', 83 *JAOS* (1963), 295-315; B. Lewis, *The Emergence of Modern Turkey* (1961), 59-61.

172. See K. H. Karpat, 'The Transformation of the Ottoman State, 1789-1908', 3 *IJMES* (1972), 243-81, who convincingly argues this point.
173. Cf. J. C. Hurewitz, 'The Europeanization of Ottoman Diplomacy: The Conversion from Unilateralism to Reciprocity in the Nineteenth Century', 25 *Belleten* (1961), 455-66; see also his other article, 'Ottoman Diplomacy and the European State System', 15 *MEJ* (1961), 141-52.
174. See H. M. Wood, 'The Treaty of Paris and Turkey's Status in International Law', 37 *AJIL* (1913), 262-74; T. Schieder, 'Pariser Friede von 1856', in *WVR*, ii. 737-9; R. Rie, 'Europäisches Konzert', in *WVR*, i. 491-3; for the text of the Treaty see Hurewitz, *The Middle East and North Africa*, 319-21; for the text of the Convention (London) 1840, op. cit., 271.
175. It should be noted that during the Mughal period in India and even subsequently, 'European powers and the several East India Companies dealt with Asian rulers on footing of equality on the basis of a universalist law of nations.' Jenks, op. cit., 69; C. H. Alexandrowicz, 'Mogul Sovereignty and the Law of Nations', 4 *IYIA* (1955), 316-24; M. K. Nawaz, 'Some Legal Aspects of Anglo-Mogul Relations', 5 *IYIA* (1956), 70-83; K. K. Pillay, 'Relations between the East Indian Company and Bengal', 5 *IYIA* (1956), 350-7.
176. The exclusive 'European' character of the family of nations evolved subsequent to the Congress of Vienna in 1815. See Jenks, op. cit., 69. See also Kruse's assessment of the Treaty of Paris 1856:

> Damit hatte einerseits das europäische Völkerrecht seinen christlichen Geltungsbereich überschritten, andererseits die Hauptmacht des Islam offiziell auf die Befolgung der Regeln des fiqh für ihre Beziehungen zum ungläubigen Abendland verzichtet und sich stattdessen einer fremden Völkerrechtsordnung unterworfen. (*Islamische Völkerrechtslehre*, 164.)

This is only partly correct. For the Ottoman Empire and the Mughals in India had, long before 1856, consented to conclude treaties with European powers on the basis of equality and reciprocity.

177. Cf. Menzel and Ipsen, op. cit., 22; Oppenheim and Lauterpacht, op. cit., 6, called it 'essentially a product of Christian civilization'; see also Greig, op. cit., 2; however, there were others such as E. Nys, *Les origines du droit international* (1894), T. A. Walker, *A History of the Law of Nations* (1889), i, and Baron M. de Taube, 'Etudes sur le developpement historique de droit international dans l'Europe orientale' (esp. ch. 2: 'Le monde de l'Islam et son influence sur l'Europe orientale'), 11 *RdC* (1926), i, who recognized the influence of Islam on modern international law.
178. A. K. Pavithran, *Substance of Public International Law, Western and Eastern* (1965), 34; also cf. R. P. Anand (ed.), *Asian States and the Development of Universal International Law* (1972), p. xxi.
179. Hamidullah, *Muslim Conduct of State*, 66-72; al-Ghunaimi, op. cit., 82-4.
180. Peters, *Islam and Colonialism*, 139.
181. Walker, *History of the Law of Nations*, 89; also cf. Atiya, *Kreuzfahrer und*

Kaufleute, 19, which is a translation of the author's *Crusade, Commerce and Culture*.

182. See *EB*, 13. 783*c–d*.
183. Cf. W. M. Watt and P. Cachia, *A History of Islamic Spain* (1965), 169-75.
184. Cf. A. Ahmad, *A History of Islamic Sicily* (1975), 88-104.
185. On contacts between Islam and Christendom and the transmission of ancient knowledge as well as other subject-matters fashionable in those times, see J. B. Trend, 'Spain and Portugal', in T. Arnold and A. Guillaume (eds.), *The Legacy of Islam* (1931), 1-39; F. Gabrieli, 'Islam in the Mediterranean World', in Schacht and Bosworth, op. cit., 63-103; J. Schacht, 'Islamic Religious Law', in Schacht and Bosworth (eds.), The Legacy of Islam (1974), 392-403; D. de Santillana, 'Law and Society', in Schacht and Bosworth, op. cit., 284-310; F. Gabrieli, 'The Transmission of Learning and Literary Influences to Western Europe', in P. M. Holt, A. K. S. Lambton, and B. Lewis (eds.), *The Cambridge History of Islam* (1970), ii. 851-89; M. Watt, *The Influence of Islam on Medieval Europe* (1972); N. Daniel, *The Arabs and Medieval Europe* (1975); K. I. Semaan (ed.), *Islam and the Medieval West: Aspects of Inter-Cultural Relations* (1980); A. Chejne, in Semaan, op. cit., 110 ff.; C. Cahen, 'Commercial Relations between the Near East and Western Europe from the VIIth to the XIth Century', in Semaan, op. cit., 1. ff.
186. 'Law and Society', in Schacht and Bosworth, op. cit., 309-10.
187. M. A. Boisard, 'On the Probable Influence of Islam on Western and Public International Law', 429-50.
188. T Landscheit, 'Der Einfluß des Islam auf die Entwicklung der Temperamenta Belli im europäischen Völkerrecht' (Diss. Göttingen, 1955).
189. See Boisard, op. cit., 444-5.
190. Cf. Grotius's *De Jure Belli*, x. §3, v, cited by Hamidullah, *Muslim Conduct of State*, 70; also cited by Boisard, op. cit., 446. Postliminium, originally a doctrine of Roman law, holds 'that persons captured by the enemy were, on their return, deemed to revert to their original status, on the fiction that no capture had occurred. The doctrine has been adopted by international law as the rule by which persons, property, and territory tend to revert to their former condition on the withdrawal of enemy control.' J. Burke, *Osborn's Concise Law Dictionary* (6th edn., 1976), 257.
191. Landscheidt, op. cit., 33, citing E. Nys, ('Les *Siete Partidas* et le droit de la guerre', in *Revue de droit international et de législation comparée*, xv (1883), 478 ff.) notes that the *Siete Partidas* is said to have been written under the patronage of King Alphonse X between 1256 and 1265 by the Castilian jurists Ruiz, Martinez, and Roldan; Boisard, op. cit., 435, however, contrary to Landscheidt and the *Encyclopaedia Britannica*, 17. 410*g–h*, mentions Alphonse IX most probably adhering to the edition of *Las Siete Partidas des Sabio Rey Don Alonso el IX* by G. Lopez (Madrid, 1829).
192. As Boisard, op. cit., 436, points out several examples in this context.

193. According to Landscheidt, op. cit., 32-3:

> Die katholische Kirche, die im Mittelalter das öffentliche Leben im Abendland beherrschte, kannte keine Toleranz. Augustin hatte das Wort aus dem Lukasevangelium: 'Exi in vias . . . et compelle intrare, ut impleatur domus' dahin ausgelegt, daß der christliche Glaube mit Gewalt ausgebreitet werden dürfe.

For the relevance of Landscheidt's arguments and for the sake of contrast between the then prevalent Christian view and what the *Siete Partidas* introduced, see also pp. 52-3; also cf. G. Höffner, *Christentum und Menschenwürde: Das Anliegen der spanischen Kolonialethik im Goldenen Zeitalter* (Trier, 1947), 40; C. Hernández, 'Spanien und der Islam', 3 *Saeculum* (1952), 362.

194. The *Arbre des Bataille* was most probably written in 1387. Cf. Landscheidt, op. cit., 56. After comparing it with the preceding *Siete Partidas* Landscheidt comes to the conclusion that:

> Vergleicht man die Abschnitte des Arbre des Batailles, die es verbieten, einen Ungläubigen zum Glauben zu zwingen und außer im Kampf auf dem Schlachtfeld einen Menschen zu töten, mit den entsprechenden Stellen der Siete Partidas, so fällt abgesehen von der Übereinstimmung in sachlicher Hinsicht die Ähnlichkeit der Formulierung auf. Berücksichtigt man weiter, daß Bonet darauf hinweist, daß sich seine Darstellung nach geschriebenem Recht richte ('. . . selon droit escript'), und daß seiner Darstellung entsprechende Regeln als geschriebenes Recht seinerzeit nur in den Siete Partidas niedergelegt waren, so drängt sich der Schluß auf, daß Honoré Bonet bei der Abfassung seines Arbre des Batailles von den Siete Partidas beeinflußt wurde. (Op. cit., 58.)

195. See Landscheidt, op. cit., 59, 67-84; he notes that even as far back as the time of Sultan Saladin (AD 1186-93) certain Islamic Laws of War incorporated provisions similar to modern stipulations in the Geneva Conventions. Citing F. Groh, *Das Recht der Kriegsgefangenen und Zivilpersonen nach der Genfer Konvention vom 12.8.1949* (Hamburg, 1952), 4, Landscheidt argues,

> daß auf muslimischer Seite der Sultan Saladin in einem Kriegsgesetz 'schon fast die gleichen Grundsätze wie die Genfer Verwundetenkonvention' aufstellte und in einem Gesetz den Johanniter-Rittern unter anderem 'sogar Zugang in das von ihm eroberte Jerusalem gewährte, damit sie ihren verwundeten Brüdern Hilfe und Trost bringen konnten'. (Op. cit., 25-6.)

196. See Jenks, op. cit., 69; C. H. Alexandrowicz, 'Treaty and Diplomatic Relations between European and South Asian Powers in the 17th and 18th Centuries', 100 *RdC* (1960), ii. 207 ff.; also his *Introduction to the History of the Law of Nations in the East Indies, 16th, 17th, and 18th Centuries* (1967); see also n. 175 above.

197. For a detailed treatment of the 'universal' conceptions of these authors, see Jenks, op. cit., 66-8.

198. J. T. Abdy, *Kent's Commentary on International Law* (2nd edn., 1878);

H. Wheaton, *Elements of International Law by Dana* (8th edn., 1866); R. J. Phillimore, *Commentaries Upon International Law* (3rd edn., 1879); W. E. Hall, *A Treatise on International Law by P. Higgins* (8th edn., 1924); J. Westlake, *International Law, Part I: Peace* (1910); Oppenheim and Lauterpacht, op. cit.; other European authorities on international law such as Anzilotti, Fauchille, Holtzendorf, Nys, Bello, Rivier, and Frederic de Martens are cited by Jenks, op. cit., 71-3.

199. P. C. Jessup, 'Diversity and Uniformity in the Law of Nations', 58 *AJIL* (1964), 342.

200. Hamidullah, *Muslim Conduct of State*, 3. It is this view which has been criticized by Peters, *Islam and Colonialism*, 137 and 140, as the inclination of Muslim scholars to retain classical definitions of the *Siyar*, thus reiterating its unilateral character and on the other hand deviating from its contents.

201. Cf. 20 *ILM* (1981), 37 and Mahmassani, op. cit., 201-326, 235, and sections 2.1-2.2 above; also cf. the AMINOIL Award, in 21 *ILM* (1982), 1000, in which the Arbitral Tribunal refers to the point that the Government of Kuwait 'has been at pains to stress that "established public international law is necessarily a part of the law of Kuwait"' (*GCM*, para. 3.97 (5)).

202. Cf. LIAMCO Award, 20 *ILM* (1981), 36; Arts. 36, 37, 43-5 of the Ottoman Majallah Code; S. Mahmassani, *The Philosophy of Jurisprudence in Islam*, Engl. trans. F. Ziadeh (Leyden, 1961), 132-3.

203. See Mahmassani, 'The Principles of International Law', 268.

204. For a commentary on these verses see A. A. Maududi, *The Meaning of the Quran* (1976), vi. 96 and nn. 90-1; Asad, op. cit., 410 n. 110; A. Y. Ali, op. cit., 681 n. 2128 and 2131; also cf. Kruse, *Islamische Völkerrechtslehre*, 81; Mahmassani, op. cit., 268 ff.; al-Ghunaimi, op. cit., 91, 96-103.

205. See ARAMCO Arbitration, 27 *ILR* (1958), 163; also cf. LIAMCO Award, 20 *ILM* (1981), 54-5.

206. Cf. A. Y. Ali, op. cit., 434 n. 1241; Asad, op. cit., 252 n. 81; Mahmassani, op. cit., 268.

207. See commentary by Asad, op. cit., 249, n. 61 and 62; and Mahmassani, op. cit., 268.

208. Both express and implied consent create legal obligations in Islamic law, see Hamidullah, *Muslim Conduct of State*, 4. The Holy Prophet usually adhered to pre-Islamic customs and practices which were not repugnant to the Islamic spirit, see Hasan, *The Early Development of Islamic Jurisprudence*, 88.

209. Cf. Greig, op. cit., 52; Menzel and Ipsen, op. cit., 51-2.

210. Cf. Menzel and Ipsen, op. cit., 42-3, who point out that the effect of the *Selbstverpflichtungslehre* has been mitigated by the *Vereinbarungslehre* to the extent that unilateral abrogation of consent already given by a State is not recognized any more.

211. Kelsen and Tucker, op. cit., 446; also cf. P. Guggenheim, *Traité de droit*

international public (2nd edn., 1967) i. 39 ff.; A. Verdross, 'Zum Problem der völkerrechtlichen Grundnorm', in *Festschrift Wehberg* (1956), 385-94; Menzel and Ipsen, op. cit., 45-6.

212. See U. Scheuner, 'Naturrechtliche Strömungen im heutigen Völkerrecht', *ZaöRV* (1950/1), 556-614; A. Verdross, *Statisches und dynamisches Naturrecht* (1971); Menzel and Ipsen, op. cit., 46.

213. Cf. C. de Visscher, *Théories et réalités en droit international public* (4th edn., 1970), 122-3; L. Duguit, *L'état, le droit objectif, et la loi positive* (1901); S. Hoffmann, 'International Systems and International Law', in R. Falk and S. H. Mendlovitz (eds.), *The Strategy of World Order* (1966), ii. 134-66, 162; M. McDougal, 'International Law, Power and Policy: A Contemporary Conception', *RdC* (1953), i. 133 ff., 157-60; see also B. Simma, 'Völkerrechtswissenschaft und Lehre von den internationalen Beziehungen: Erste Überlegungen zur Interdependenz zweier Disziplinen', *ÖzöR* (1972), 293-324; and O. Kimminich, 'Völkerrecht und internationale Beziehungen', *AdV* (1974), 129-49.

214. For a criticism of various theories see the following: for *the classical theory of consent*, M. Sørensen, *Les sources du droit international* (1946) 16; G. Fitzmaurice, 'The General Principles of International Law', *RdC* (1957), ii. 1-227; Menzel and Ipsen, op. cit., 45; for *the normative theory*, J. J. Lador-Lederer, 'Some Observations on the Vienna School in International Law', 17 *NILR* (1970), 126-50; Dahm, *Völkerrecht*, i. 16 ff.; O'Connell, *International Law*, i. 40-1; Menzel and Ipsen, op. cit., 45-6; for the *natural law theory*, Dahm, op. cit., i. 11; Friedmann, *The Changing Structure*, 77-8; Menzel and Ipsen, op. cit., 47; J. L. Kunz, 'Natural Law Thinking in the Modern Science of International Law', 55 *AJIL* (1961), 951-8; for *the objectivist theories*, Dahm, i. 12; Menzel and Ipsen, op. cit., 48.

215. As Menzel and Ipsen, op. cit., 48, have pointed out. The valuable service that positivism has rendered to intrnational law may not be underestimated. See also J. L. Brierly, *The Law of Nations* (1963), 54.

216. Cf. Friedmann, , 86; J. L. Brierly, *The Outlook for International Law* (1944), 4-5; P. C. Jessup, 'The Reality of International Law', 18 *Foreign Affairs* (1940), 244; G. Fitzmaurice, 'Foundations of the Authority of International Law and the Problem of Enforcement', 19 *MLR* (1956), 1 ff.; Menzel and Ipsen, op. cit., 48; Brownlie, *Principles* (1979), does not even mention it.

217. The Lotus Case, *PCIJ* (1927), Ser. A, no. 10, 18.

218. See G. I. Tunkin, *Völkerrechtstheorie* (1972), 153-63, 167, 243; and his article in *RdC* (1958), iii. 25-6.

219. See e.g. S. P. Sinha, *New Nations and the Law of Nations* (1967), 145; R. P. Anand, 'Role of "New" Asian-African Countries in the Present International Legal Order', 56 *AJIL* (1962), 383-406 and 'Attitudes of the Asian-African States Towards Certain Problems of International Law', 15 *ICLQ* (1966), 55-75; I. Shihata, 'The Attitude of the New States

towards the International Court of Justice', 19 *IQ* (1965), 213; H. Ghanem, 'The Asian-African Legal Consultative Committee: 1958', 14 *Rev. Egypt*. (1958), 63-73; Roy, op. cit., 863 ff.

220. See L. C. Green, 'New States, Regionalism, and International Law', 5 *CYIL* (1967), 120; Udokang, op. cit., 152.
221. Roy, op. cit., 863; Anand, 'Role of "New" Asian-African Countries in the Present International Legal Order', 383 ff., and 'Attitude of the Asian-African States Towards Certain Problems of International Law', 55 ff.; Shihata, op. cit., 213; Ghanem, op. cit., 63 ff.
222. See Oppenheim and Lauterpacht, op. cit., i. 19; D. P. O'Connell, 'Independence and Problems of State Succession', in W. V. O'Brian (ed.), *The New Nations in International Law and Diplomacy* (1965), 12.
223. See J. J. G. Syatauw, 'The Relationship between the Newness of States and Their Practices of International Law', in Anand, *Asian States and the Development of Universal International Law*, 13.
224. The 'new' States are only averse to a system which does not provide adequate room for change prompted by new conditions. See Syatauw, op. cit., 14; Anand, op. cit., p. xiv; Jessup, 'Diversity and Uniformity in the Law of Nations', 343.
225. *International Law*, i. 17.
226. For general criticisms, see Brierly, *The Law of Nations*, 51-2; Kelsen and Tucker, *Principles of International Law*, 444 ff.
227. Oppenheim and Lauterpacht, op. cit., i. 19.
228. 'Some Problems Regarding the Formal Sources of International Law', in *Symbolae Verzijl* (1958), 153.
229. As Sir Gerald Fitzmaurice points out on another occasion, 'The General Principles of International Law', 1 ff. 40.
230. See Oppenheim and Lauterpacht, op. cit., i. 800-1; see also T. O. Elias, *The Modern Law of Treaties* (1974), 40 ff.
231. *The Law of Nations*, 53.
232. Cf. LIAMCO Award, 20 *ILM* (1981), 54.
233. J. L. Brierly, *The Basis of Obligation in International Law* (repr. 1977), 10; and *The Law of Nations*, 53.
234. As Brierly, *The Law of Nations*, 54, asserts.
235. Ibid., 56.
236. Brierly, *The Basis of Obligation*, 65.
237. Cf. *Q* 67: 1; 3: 26; Maududi, 'Political Theory of Islam', 160; Muslehuddin, *Philosophy of Islamic Law and the Orientalists*, 56; Hamidullah, *Muslim Conduct of State*, 86.
238. Cf. *Q* 2: 30; Maududi, op. cit., 168; an extreme consequence of this concept would be that an elected legislature in an Islamic State could not presume to be a fully sovereign body. This view has been criticized by F. Rahman, 'Implementation of the Islamic Concept of State in the Pakistani Milieu', 6 *Isl. Stud.* (1967), 205-44, who argues that 'the Muslim

legislature is the supreme body unencumbered by any limitations except such as are accepted by the Muslim community. God neither acts as political sovereign nor as a law-maker. The Muslim people themselves are the sovereign and the law-maker' at p. 209. D. Khalid, 'Theocracy and the Location of Sovereignty', 11 *Isl. Stud.* (1972), 187-209, goes to the other extreme and declares the Islamic State to be a secular one. The question is, however, one of location of sovereignty and this could be vested in different legal persons or bodies at different times. Nevertheless, it must be kept in mnd that in an Islamic State the Sovereign body is not considered to be absolutely supreme because it cannot legislate to do away with the Koran and *Sunnah*.

239. See al-Ghunaimi, op. cit., 93.
240. Cf. Khadduri, *War and Peace in the Law of Islam*, 12.
241. Cf. *Q* 42: 38; and also M. C. Hudson, 'Islam and Political Development', in J. L. Esposito (ed.), *Islam and Development* (1980), 4.
242. See al-Ghunaimi, op. cit., 93; Schacht, 'Islamic Law in Contemporary States', 144-5.
243. Cf. Khadduri, *War and Peace in the Law of Islam*. Opinions among classical Islamic jurists diverge considerably on this matter. See also Hamidullah, *Muslim Conduct of State*, 185-6.
244. Khadduri, op. cit.
245. This statement, which was made by Hamidullah, op. cit., 4, has misled some to interpret Muslim international law as wholly internal and unilateral, see Peters, *Islam and Colonialism*, 137, which is not correct as historically Islamic States did conclude treaties with non-Islamic States on the basis of reciprocity. See sections 2.4.5 and 2.4.6 above.
246. See 2.4.8 above.
247. On this point cf. Hamidullah, *Muslim Conduct of State*, 32.
248. Cf. Menzel and Ipsen, op. cit., 42, on the *Selbstverpflichtungslehre* developed by Bergbohm, Jellinek, Zorn, Wenzel, and others on the Hegelian concept of *äußeren Staatsrecht*. See also Greig, *International Law*, 4.
249. See Muslehuddin, *Philosophy of Islamic Law*, 180-8; see also his 'Islamic Jurisprudence and the Rule of Necessity and Need', 12 *Isl. Stud.* (1973), 37-52.
250. Cf. *Q* 2: 173; 5: 3; 6: 120, 146; 16: 115.
251. The theory of *al-masalihu'al-mursalah* may be traced back to the notion that *Shari'ah* is for social utility, and its function is to promote benefit and prevent evil. Malik, the founder of the Malikite school of Islamic jurisprudence, is said to have approved of the idea of public interest as one of the sources of the *Shari'ah* and named it *al-masalihu'al-mursalah*. See Muslehuddin, *Philosophy of Islamic Law*, 156-79.
252. Cf. Rahim, *Muhammadan Jurisprudence*, 206; Schacht, *An Introduction to Islamic Law*, 134 ff.

253. See Rahim, op. cit., 207, esp. Ch. 6 on 'Ownership'.
254. Ibid., 208.
255. See ibid., 208; Schacht, op. cit.; Hamidullah, *Muslim Conduct of State*, 93 ff.
256. Classical Islamic law and legal practice has worked out eight different groups of people eligible as recipients of *Zakah*; see Z. Ahmad, 'Zakat and Economic Well-Being', 20 *Isl. Stud.* (1981), 23-46.
257. See M. A. al-Araby, 'Eight Islamic Rules Governing Private Ownership of Property: The Report to the Arab League in 1952 on the question of *Zakah* and the meaning of property: Part III', 55 *Isl. Rev.* (July 1967), 30.
258. Al-Araby, op. cit., 30-2.
259. M. N. Siddiqui, 'Muslim Economic Thinking: A Survey of Contemporary Literature', in K. Ahmad (ed.), *Studies in Islamic Economics* (1980), 196-200 which gives a broad survey of the opinions held by various Muslim scholars.
260. See among others M. U. Chapra, 'Objectives of the Islamic Order', K. Ahmad (ed.), *Islam—its Meaning and Message* (1976), 191-2; 'The Islamic Welfare State and its Role in the Economy', in Ahmad, *Studies in Islamic Economics*, 216; Naqvi, op. cit., 52-3, etc.
261. Cf. a series of articles by M. A. al-Araby on the subject; 'Private Ownership of Property: The Ethical and Moral Injunctions of Islam: Part I' (*Isl. Rev.*, July-August 1966); 'Part II: Governmental Injunctions' (*Isl. Rev.*, June 1967); 'Part III: Eight Islamic Rules Governing Private Ownership of Property' (*Isl. Rev.*, July 1967).
262. For details see Rahim, op. cit., 206-22; Schacht, *An Introduction to Islamic Law*, 134-43.
263. These points have been surveyed by Siddiqui, op. cit., 197 ff.
264. Cf. A. A. Maududi, *Maʿāshiyāt-e-Islām* (Economics of Islam), in Urdu (1969); I. al-Tahawi, *al-iqtisad al-islami madhaban wa nizaman wa dirasah muqaranah* (Islamic Economics–a School of Thought and a System, a Comparative Study), in Arabic (1974); S. Qutb, *Social Justice in Islam* (1970); Chapra, 'Objectives of the Islamic Economic Order'; Schacht, 'Islamic Law in Contemporary States', 140.
265. G. A. Parwez, *Quranic Economics* (nd); N. A. Sheikh, *Some Aspects of the Constitution and the Economics of Islam* (1967); Naqvi, op. cit.
266. M. B. al-Sadr, *Iqtisaduna* (Our Economics), in Arabic (1968); M. N. Siddiqi, *Some Aspects of the Islamic Economy* (1970).
267. See e.g. Schacht, 'Islamic Law in the Contemporary States', 141-2; A. al-Qadir Audah, *al-Māl wa'l-hukm fi'l-Islām* (Property and Government in Islam), in Arabic (1971).
268. Cf. Siddiqi, 'Muslim Economic Thinking', 199.
269. See e.g. A. al-Qadir Audah, op. cit., 49; Jama ʿat-e-Islami Pakistan, *Manshūr barā'ē intikhābāt 1970* (Manifesto for 1970 Elections), in Urdu (20 Dec. 1959); A. F. Abu Sunnah, *Tahdīd al-Mīlkiyah fi'l-Islām* (Ceiling on

Property in Islam), in al-Azhar (Cairo), 24 (3) Nov. 1952, 300-63 (in Arabic).

270. *Q* 4: 29.

271. For example: 'Whatever a Muslim possesses is unlawful for another Muslim, his wealth and property and his life', quoted by U. Chapra, 'The Islamic Welfare State', in K. Ahmad (ed.), *Studies in Islamic Economics* (1980), 205; see also A. Kannun, 'Private Property in Islam', 58 *Isl. Rev.* (1970), 22-5, 34.

272. Al-Sadr, op. cit.; M. al-Mubarak, *Nizām al-Islām al-iqtisād, mabādī wa gawā'id ʿāmma* (Islamic System: The Economy, Elements and General Principles), in Arabic (1972); A. Ali, *Political Economy of the Islamic State* (1970); F. Rahman, 'Economic Principles of Islam', 8 *Isl. Stud.* (1969), 1-8; Chapra, *The Economic System of Islam*; M. N. Siddiqi, *Islam ka nazariya-e-milkiyat* (Islam's Theory of Property), in Urdu (1968); K. Ahmad and N. Siddiqi, *Maujudah iqtisadi buhran aur Islami hikmat-e-maʿishat* (Contemporary Economic Crisis and the Economic Policy of Islam), in Urdu (1970).

273. A. A. al-Kader, 'Land Property and Land Tenure in Islam', 5 *IQ* (Apr.-July 1959), 11, notes that the economic philosophy of Islam 'did not change the ordinary juristic attitude to the practical relations of people and property'; some examples have also been cited by Rodinson, *Islam and Capitalism*.

274. Siddiqi, 'Muslim Economic Thinking', 211; increase of social controls and intervention of the State in Western industrialized economies has also led to modifications in the concept of absolute ownership of property.

275. Cf. Hamidullah, *Muslim Conduct of State*, 111-14; Khadduri, *War and Peace in the Law of Islam*, 175-201 and *The Islamic Law of Nations*, 143 ff.; see also Tibawi, 'Christians under Muhammad and His First Two Caliphs', 60-1 and n. 137-38 above.

276. See Khadduri, *War and Peace in the Law of Islam*, 177-82, who describes the covenants with the *dhimmis* as constitutional charters.

277. Grant of *amān* to natural persons was the rule and to artificial persons such as companies rare. An exception is the Grant of Privileges to the (English) Muscovy Company by Shah Tahmasp of Persia in 1566 and 1568. For texts of these documents see Hurewitz, *The Middle East and North Africa in World Politics*, i. 7-8.

278. For a thorough treatment of the concept see Heffening, op. cit., 15-86; J. Hatschek, *Der Musta'min: Ein Beitrag zum internationalen Privat-und Völkerrecht des islamischen Gesetzes* (1919), 5-50; J. Schacht, 'Amān', in *EI*, i. 429 ff.; M. Hartmann, 'Die islamisch-fränkischen Staatsverträge', 11 *Zeitschrift für Politik* (1919), 1-64; Hamidullah, *Muslim Conduct of State*, 131-5, 209-11; Kruse, *Islamische Völkerrechtslehre*, 74-85; Khadduri, *War and*

Peace in the Law of Islam, 162-9 and *The Law of Nations*, 158-94; Krüger, op. cit., 136-9; *amān* may be granted during war as well as in periods of truce. Peaceful relations were regulated by treaties.

279. Khadduri points out that the Hanbalis permit giving *amān* for as long a period as 10 years. See his *War and Peace in the Law of Islam*, 163 n. 3.
280. Kruse has given detailed treatment to the concept of State treaties (*muwadaʿa*) in his *Islamische Völkerrechtslehre*, 85-149. For further references see Hamidullah, op. cit., 202; Khadduri, op. cit., 203 ff.
281. *State Bank of India* v. *The Custodian of Evacuee Property*, West Pakistan, PLD (1969), Lahore, 1050; also cited by Krüger, op. cit., 17-20 to prove that the principles of *Siyar* are still considered to be relevant and applicable in modern times.
282. Cited by Krüger, op. cit., 17.
283. In accordance with the provisions of Section 83 (1) Civil Procedure Code (Pakistan) only alien enemies residing in Pakistan with the permission of the Central Government may sue in the courts.
284. PLD (1969), Lahore, 1062-4.
285. As Krüger, op. cit., 20-1, points out.
286. According to traditional rules of international law the deprivation of enemy aliens of their property may only be of a temporary nature (*ILR* (1955), 142) and cannot be considered to be a measure of expropriation but, on the contrary, must be treated as trust property administered temporarily by the confiscating state. Cf. W. Veith and K. H. Bockstiegel, *Der Schutz von ausländischem Vermögen im Völkerrecht* (1962), 194 ff.; I. Seidl-Hohenveldern, *Investitionen in Entwicklungsländern und das Völkerrecht mit einer Bibliographie über Staatseingriffe in ausländisches Privateigentum* (1963), 32; J. Alenfeld, *Die Investitionsfürderungsverträge der Bundesrepublik Deutschland* (1971), 44-5; however, Katzarov, *The Theory of Nationalization* (1964), 375 ff., is of the opinion that traditional rules have been modified by state practice. See also Jessup, 'Enemy Property', 49 *AJIL* (1955), 57, who held that confiscation of enemy alien property is contrary to international law.
287. The translation used here is that by Pickthall; also cf. Ali, *The Holy Quran*, 75 n. 201: Asad, *The Message of the Quran* 40 n. 163-4; the LIAMCO Award, 20 *ILM* (1981), 47.
288. The translation used here is taken from that used by the Sole Arbitrator Mahmassani in the LIAMCO Award, 20 *ILM* (1981), 47.
289. See Art. 26 of the Ottoman Majallah Code; the LIAMCO Award, 20 *ILM* (1981), 47; S. Mahmassani, *The General Theory of Obligations and Contracts under Islamic Law*, in Arabic (Beirut, 1948), i. 93 and *Philosophy of Jurisprudence in Islam*, Engl. trans. (1961), 157; al-Araby, 'Private Ownership of Property: Governmental Injunctions', 30, and 'Eight Islamic Rules Governing Private Property', 30.

290. al-Araby, ibid.; also cf. Hamidullah, *Muslim Conduct of State*, 101, §179, who cites an identical principle in a different context.
291. See Schacht, 'Islamic Law in Contemporary States', 142.
292. See Chapra, 'The Islamic Welfare State', 159; al-Araby, 'Eight Islamic Rules Governing Private Property', 30.
293. See Hamidullah, *Muslim Conduct of State*, 93.
294. Cf. Rahim, *Muhammadan Jurisprudence*, 210-11.
295. Ibid., 221-2
296. Since the Prophet is reported to have said: 'Every land has its appurtenance forbidden (to other than the proprietors)', see A. Yusuf, *Kitab al-Kharaj*, 57, also cited by Hamidullah, *Muslim Conduct of State*, 97, §171 and n. 12; it is therefore difficult to assume that the State can usurp private property rights by laying claim to natural resources to be found on its premises. It is obliged to buy that land by paying a fair price in order to exploit those resources for the entire community.
297. Cf. Ibn Juzay, *Al-Qawaneen al-Fikhiyyah* (The Legal Rules) (Fez, 1935), 102; Ibn Hazm, *Al-Muhalla* (Cairo, 1347-52), 6. 111; 8. 238; also cited by Sole Arbitrator Mahmassani in the LIAMCO Award as examples of Maliki opinion on the subject, 20 *ILM* (1981), 48; see further, A. H. A. Sulaiman, 'The Theory of the Economics of Islam: The Economics of Tawhid and Brotherhood; Philosophy, Concept, and Suggestions', in *Contemporary Aspects of Economic and Social Thinking in Islam* (Gary, Indiana, 1973), 26 ff., 69-70; Siddiqi, 'Muslim Economic Thinking: A Survey of Contemporary Literature', 197-8; also cf. n. 266 above.
298. *Saudi Arabia* v. *Arabian American Oil Company*, 27 *ILR* (1958), 117 ff.
299. 27 *ILR*, 170.
300. 27 *ILR*, 171.
301. *British Petroleum Exploration Company (Libya)* v. *Government of the Libyan Arab Republic*, 53 *ILR*, (1973), Merits 297 ff.
302. 53 *ILR*, 355; according to Art. 1 (1) of the Libyan Petroleum Law of 1955: 'All Petroleum in Libya in its natural state in strata is the property of the Libyan State.' Cited in 53 *ILR*, 321.
303. (1977) 20 *ILM* (1981), 53 and 61.
304. Cf. Ibn Abdessalaam, *Qawa'ed al-Ahkam* (Cairo, 1934), 1. 172; Mahmassani, *The General Theory of Obligations and Contracts*, i. 10; Rahim, *Muhammadan Jurisprudence*, 249-50; LIAMCO Award, 20 *ILM* (1981), 53.
305. 27 *ILR*, 164; see also the LIAMCO Award, 20 *ILM* (1981), 30, which also confirms the contractual nature of concessions; see also 'Arbitration between the Government of the State of Kuwait and the American Independent Oil Company' (AMINOIL Award), in 21 *ILM* (1982), 1001, in which the Tribunal considers the Concession Agreement to be a contract entailing contractual obligations.
306. As was asserted to be the case under Libyan law; see opinion rendered by

Professor M. A. Omar of Cairo University and submitted by BP (Claimant) to the Tribunal in the BP Arbitration, 53 *ILR*, 324.

307. See the LIAMCO Award, 20 *ILM* (1981), 55, 61; BP Award, 53 *ILR*, 324.
308. Chapra, 'The Islamic Welfare State', 159; Schacht, 'Islamic Law in Contemporary States', 142.
309. Audah, *Property and Government in Islam* (Arabic), 48-9, also cited by Siddiqi, 'Muslim Economic Thinking', 198.
310. I. al-Tahawi, *Islamic Economics—A School of Thought and a System: A Comparative Study* (in Arabic), i. 217.
311. Cf. the LIAMCO Award, 20 *ILM* (1981), 68, in which Sole Arbitrator Mahmassani cites Imam Malik's *Al-Mudawwana al-Kubra* (in Arabic) (Cairo, AH 1323), 14. 62-5 and his own work, *General Theory of Obligations*, i. 161-2.
312. Provisions of compensation were made in the Iranian Law Regulating Nationalization of the Oil Industry in 1951 (see A. Ford, *The Anglo-Iranian Oil Dispute* (1954), 268-9); in the Egyptian Presidential Decree on the Nationalization of the Suez Canal in 1956 (see T. T. F. Huang, 'Some International and Legal Aspects of the Suez Canal Question', 51 *AJIL* (1957), 303-4); in Art. 3 of the Iraqi Law No. 69 of 1972 Nationalizing the Operations of the Iraq Petroleum Co. Ltd. (see 11 *ILM* (1972), 847); in Art. 5 of the Libyan Law Nationalizing British Petroleum Exploration Co. (11 *ILM* (1972), 380-2) and for further Libyan decrees see 13 *ILM* (1974), 58-9 and 60-3; for Kuwaiti decrees see AMINOIL Award, 21 *ILM* (1982), 976 ff.
313. Cf. B. A. Wortley, *Expropriation in Public International Law* (1959), 38 ff.; G. White, *Nationalisation of Foreign Property* (1961), 3, 43; Amerasinghe, *State Responsibility for Injuries to Aliens*, 123; Brownlie, *Principles of Public International Law*, 532.
314. For the clarification of an interrelationship between various concepts of 'taking', see ch. 5.4.5.2.1.
315. *PCIJ* (1926), Ser. A, no. 7, 22.
316. *PCIJ* (1928), Ser. A, no. 7, 46, 47-8; also cf. 'Certain German Interests in Polish Upper Silesia Case', *PCIJ*, Ser. A, no. 17, in which the Court held that the Polish act was in violation of the Geneva Convention of 1922.
317. Cf. Wortley, op. cit., 24-5; White, op. cit., 5 ff.
318. Cf. D.-C. Dicke, *Die Intervention mit wirtschaftlichen Mitteln im Völkerrecht* (1978), 127.
319. Cf. arguments submitted by the United Kingdom in the Anglo-Iranian Oil Company Case (1952) in which she did not dispute the sovereign right of Iran to nationalize, *ICJ Pleadings*, 100; for the US attitude to Mexican nationalizations and Dutch reactions to Indonesian measures, see H. W. Baade, 'Indonesian Nationalization Measures Before Foreign Courts–A Reply', 54 *AJIL* (1960), 827 ff.; R. Higgins, *Conflict of Interests*

(1965), 55-6; Z. Kronfol, *Protection of Foreign Investment* (1972), 22 ff.; Statement made by the British Minister of State for Foreign Affairs in reply to a question in the House of Commons, cited in the BP Award, 53 *ILR*, 316.

320. See Baade, 'Indonesian Nationalization', 801 ff.; Petersmann, *Wirtschaftsintegrationsrecht und Investitionsgesetzgebung der Entwicklungsländer*, 138; Greig, *International Law*, 576, 579; Dicke, op. cit., 127; J. de Aréchaga, 'International Law in the Past Third of a Century', 159 *RdC* (1978), i. 297; Brownlie, *Principles of Public International Law*, 538; Menzel and Ipsen, op. cit., 177; E. Liemen, 'Érdöl Produktionsverträge des Iran' (1981), 193; also cf. UNGA Res. 1803 (XVII), 1962 and Res. 3281 (XXIX), 1974, commonly known as 'Charter of Economic Rights and Duties of States'.

321. Cf. the Hull Note to the Mexican Government dated 22 Oct. 1938, reproduced in *AJIL* (1938), Suppl. 193; Art. 10 of the 'Harvard Draft Convention on the International Responsibility of States for Injuries to Aliens', 1961, in 55 *AJIL* (1961), 548 ff.; BP Award, 53 *ILR*, 317; Brownlie, *Principles of Public International Law*, 544; Menzel and Ipsen, op. cit., 178.

322. See Report of the Chairman, Mr Castaneda, of the Working Group set up to draft the 'Charter of Economic Rights and Duties of States', submitted to the second committee of the General Assembly, *UNGAOR*, 29th Session, 2nd Committee, 1638th Meeting, p. 384; also cf. de Aréchaga, op. cit., i. 297; Brownlie, *Principles of International Law*, 544; E. F. Müller, 'Der Völkerrechtliche Eigentumsschutz' (Diss. Marburg, 1981), 349 ff.

323. *UNGA* Res. 1803 (XVII) of 14 Dec. 1962, para. 4.

324. According to Sole Arbitrator Dupuy in the Arbitral Award of *Texaco* v. *Libyan Arab Republic*, 53 *ILR*, 492, Res. 1803 (XVII) 'seems to this Tribunal to reflect the state of customary law existing in this field'; also cf. Brownlie, *Principles of Public International Law*, 543.

325. Cf. S. Friedman, *Expropriation in International Law* (1953), 140-2; G. White, op. cit., 146-50; Amerasinghe, op. cit., 137; H. W. Baade, 'Permanent Sovereignty over Natural Wealth and Resources', in R. Miller and R. Stanger (eds.), *Essays on Expropriation* (1967), 3 ff., 23; B. Weston, 'The Charter of Economic Rights and Duties of States and the Deprivation of Foreign-Owned Wealth', 75 *AJIL* (1981), 439-40; LIAMCO Award, 20 *ILM* (1981), 58; also cf. ch. 5.4.5.2.1.

326. Cf. Brownlie, *Principles of Public International Law*, 543-4, and 'Legal Status of Natural Resources in International Law (Some Aspects)', 162 *RdC* (1979), i. 269; on the rule of non-discrimination see further ch. 4.5.5.2.1.

327. Cf. G. Dawson and B. Weston, '"Prompt, Adequate and Effective": A Universal Standard of Compensation?', 30 *Fordham Law Review* (1962), 751-3; O. Weigel and B. Weston, 'Valuation upon the Deprivation of Foreign Enterprise: A Policy Oriented Approach to the Problem of Compensation under International Law', in R. B. Lillich (ed.), *The*

Valuation of Nationalized Property in International Law (1972), i. 6 ff.; Greig, *International Law*, 579; R. Dolzer, 'New Foundations of the Law of Expropriation of Alien Property', 75 *AJIL* (1981), 557 ff.; also cf. ch. 5.4.5.2.1 n. 112-14.

Notes to Chapter 3

1. As of Jan. 1986, see List of Member States in Appendix IV. At present, only the membership of Afghanistan remains in a state of suspension as the suspension of Egypt's membership was officially withdrawn at the summit in Casablanca, Jan. 1984.
2. See *UNTS*, 914 (1974), 111.
3. Preamble of the Charter of the OIC, para. 3.
4. According to UN terminology this includes Less and Least Developed Countries as well as Most Seriously Affected Countries (LDCs, LLDCs, MSACs).
5. In Islamic terms all Muslims, regardless of their state of origin, are considered to be 'one nation' (*Ummah*). Hence, in the spirit of the Pan-Islamic Movement, which began in the late nineteenth century with the aim of reinstating Islamic unity and solidarity among all Muslim States following colonial encroachment, modern authors have called for Islamic unity and the formation of a Commonwealth of Muslim Countries and also suggested various modes of economic co-operation. See contributions made by L. A. Sherwani, Moulana R. Ahsan, C. N. A. Khan, and I. Khan, in World Muslim Congress (ed.), *Studies on Commonwealth of Muslim Countries* (Karachi, nd, 1964?); C. N. A. Khan, 'Commonwealth of Muslim States', 12 and 13 *Voice of Islam* (1963-5); S. A. A. Maududi, *Unity of the Muslim World* (1967, repr. 1979); M. Hamidullah, 'A Suggestion for an Interest-Free Islamic Monetary Fund', 43 *The Islamic Review* (June 1955), 11-12; M. Uzair, 'Foreign Trade in an Interestless Economy', 7 *Voice of Islam* (1958), 90-104; A. Ali, 'A plea for Greater Trade among Muslim Countries', 4 *The Criterion* (1969), 17-19; S. A. Hasan, 'Islamic Unity and World Co-operation', in M. A. Khan (ed.), *International Islamic Conference* (1970), i. 12-23; M. Muslehuddin, 'Two Needs of Islamic World: 1. A Commonwealth of Islamic Countries; 2. A Muslim "World Bank"', 58 *The Islamic Review & Arab Affairs* (Dec. 1970), 25-32; M. A. Mannan, 'A Muslim World Bank–Urgent Need', 6 *The Criterion* (1971), 15-20; K. A. Faruki, 'Approaches to Muslim Unity', 7 *The Criterion* (1972), 21-33; M. Ahmad, 'Umma–The Idea of a Universal Community', 14 *Islamic Studies* (1975), 27-54; K. Siddiqui, *Beyond the Muslim Nation-States* (1980).
6. See World Muslim League Magazine (Singapore), 1. no. 1 (1963/4), 22, also cited by Hans Kruse, 'The Politics of the Islamic Call, 1962-66', in his *Islamische Völkerrechtslehre*, 204-5.

7. Cf. Madani, 'The Islamic Content of the Foreign Policy of Saudi Arabia', 88 ff.
8. Ibid., 88-9.
9. See M. Kerr, *The Arab Cold War 1958–1967: A Study of Ideology in Politics* (1967); G. Lenczowski, 'Arab Bloc Realignments', 53 *Current History* (Dec. 1967), 346, also cited by Madani, op. cit., 64.
10. See Kruse, *Islamische Völkerrechtslehre*, 213; Madani, op. cit., 89.
11. Madani, op. cit., 91; Kruse, *Islamische Völkerrechtslehre*, 215-16; 'King Faisal visits Tehran', *The Times* (London, 9 Dec. 1965), 9; 'Persian Gulf Pact Signed', *The Times* (15 Dec. 1965), 8. The visit to Iran by King Faisal was followed by other visits to Jordan (Jan. 1966), Sudan (Mar. 1966), Pakistan (Apr. 1966), Turkey (Aug. 1966), Morocco, Guinea, Mali, and Tunisia (Sept. 1966).
12. Kruse, *Islamische Völkerrechtslehre*, 217-18, points out that the Islamic Alliance was initially defined by the former British Minister of State, Anthony Nutting, in an article published in the New York *Herald Tribune* in 1957, which advocated the establishment of a regional alliance consisting of Arab countries and including Turkey, Iran, and Pakistan, on the basis of Muslim solidarity, which could come to an understanding with the West and eventually eliminate the Middle Eastern 'vacuum' and possibly even accommodate Israel. For views of the Shah and King Faisal, see 'Muslim Summit Proposals', *The Times* (16 Dec. 1965), 8, and *The Times* (11 Feb. 1966), 9.
13. Madani, op. cit., 78; Madani also assesses the intentions of Faisal, 92-6 and cites Kerr, op. cit., 146 in support.
14. 'Islamic Pact Opposed by President Nasser', *The Times* (7 Feb. 1966), 9; Kruse, *Islamische Völkerrechtslehre*, 218 ff.; Madani, op. cit., 90-1.
15. King Faisal's Call for Islamic Solidarity, on the one hand, had renewed the struggle for leadership in the Arab world between President Nasser, the Ba'athists (Syria and Iraq), and Faisal, and, on the other hand, was seen as a threat to 'revolutionary' Arab nationalism. See Madani, op. cit., 78-9; Kruse, *Islamische Völkerrichtslehre*, 224.
16. Kruse, op. cit., 232.
17. Cf. Madani, op. cit., 79. It is ironical that Arab nationalism was pitted against the idea of Islamic unity. For throughout the 1960s modern Arabs were 'increasingly emphasizing their association with Islam . . . it (was) difficult to sustain the idea of Arab nationalism without at the same time sustaining the Islamic ideal. Arab nationalism finds its intellectual stimulus in the great Arab-Islamic culture of the past–a culture which was made possible by Islam.' E. Salem, 'Nationalism and Islam', 52 *MW* (1962), 282. In a similar strain B. Dodge was more categorical: '(N)o Muslim can dissociate the regaining of Arab dignity from the revival of Islam. He knows intuitively that the Arabs have never been great except when Islam was great, just as Islam itself has

depended upon the Arabs for its vitality', 'The Significance of Religion in Arab Nationalism', 112.

18. 'Fire in Jerusalem Mosque arouses Arab World', *The Times* (22 Aug. 1969), 4; 'Spannung in Jerusalem nach Brand der El Aqsa Moschee', *FAZ* (22 Aug. 1969); 'King Hussain Calls for Summit Meeting', *The Times*, op. cit.
19. 'Islamic Summit Opens in Rabat', *The Times* (23 Sept. 1969), 7.
20. 'Nasser Backs Plan for Summit', *The Times* (28 Aug. 1969), 3.
21. 'Islamic Summit', *The Times* (23 Sept. 1969), 7.
22. See 'Declaration of the Rabat Islamic Summit Conference', in *Resolutions on Economic, Social and Cultural Affairs: Conferences of the OIC 1969–1979*, prepared by the General Secretariat and cited hereinafter as *Resolutions*, 3-5.
23. 'Joint Communiqué of the First Islamic Conference of Foreign Ministers', in *Resolutions*, 9-12.
24. Ibid., 12; the Conference decided to request Malaysia to nominate a Secretary-General to head the Secretariat. Malaysia nominated its former Prime Minister, Mr Tunku Abdur Rahman as Secretary-General, who was confirmed by the Second ICFM held in Karachi, see *Resolutions*, 15.
25. See 'Joint Communiqué of the Second ICFM', in *Resolutions*, 20.
26. 'Joint Communiqué', op. cit., and Madani, op. cit., 149.
27. For a detailed report of the discussion and changes made in the draft Charter, see Madani, op. cit., 149-58.
28. However, one must note the reservations formulated by Chad, Indonesia, Lebanon, and Turkey on the occasion of the adoption of the Charter because of the secular nature of their respective constitutions and the application of any Charter provisions in case conflicts or contradictions arise. See *UNTS*, 914, 123-8.
29. See reservation expressed by the Indonesian delegate, *UNTS*, 914, 124.
30. See Art. 1 of the Charter of the OIC.
31. The Preamble of the Charter states that the Member States of the OIC are 'resolved to preserve Islamic spiritual, ethical, social, and economic values which will remain one of the important factors of achieving progress for mankind'.
32. The basic criteria distinguishing between an 'international' and a 'supranational' organization are those of structure and competence. Whereas an 'international' organization in the 'classical' sense usually means an inter-governmental body with the purpose of promoting co-operation among its Member States and generally having competence to issue recommendations or declarations with virtually no legal binding effect, the 'supranational' organization possesses competence to issue regulations which are deemed legally binding not only on its Member States but also on their nationals. Cf. Menzel and Ipsen, op. cit., 205, 208.

33. For a legal appraisal of the suspension of Egypt's membership of the OIC, see ch. 3.2.3.
34. See e.g. Polish Postal Service in Danzig (1925) *PCIJ*, Ser. B, no. 11, 37-9; Eastern Greenland Case (1933), *PCIJ*, Ser. A/B, no. 53, 49; Admissions Case (Second) *ICJ Rep.* (1950), 8; 'Anglo-Iranian Oil Company Case', *ICJ Rep.* (1952), 105, 142: 'US Nationals in Morocco', *ICJ Rep.* (1952), 183-4, 195-8; for a discussion of some early pronouncements on treaty interpretation in the International Court of Justice, see G. Fitzmaurice, 'The Law and Procedure of the International Court of Justice: Treaty Interpretation and Certain Other Treaty Points', 28 *BYIL* (1951), 1 ff., and 33 *BYIL* (1957), 203 ff.; also cf. G. Haraszti, 'Some Fundamental Problems of the Law of Treaties' (1973), 209-12; T. O. Elias, *The Modern Law of Treaties* (1974), 71-87.
35. For statements made by various Governments endorsing general rules of interpretation, see 'Sixth Report of the Special Rapporteur of the International Law Commission, Sir Humphrey Waldock', *Yearbook of the ILC* (1966), ii. 51-103; also cf. R. G. Wetzel and D. Rauschning, 'The Vienna Convention on the Law of Treaties', *Travaux Préparatoires* (1978), 239-49; for the assessment of general 'methods' of interpretation from a Socialist point of view, see Haraszti, 'Some Fundamental Problems', 79-195, 210.
36. The Vienna Convention entered into force on 27 Jan. 1980, see 17 *UN Chronicle* (1980), no. 2, 91. In the final voting during the Conference on Arts. 31 and 32 of the Convention no negative votes or abstentions were rendered, a fact which testifies to the wide recognition and endorsement of these principles. Cf. Wetzel and Rauschning, 'The Vienna Convention', 256; Elias, *The Modern Law of Treaties*, 87; nevertheless, it is essential to note that among Member States of the OIC only the following have either signed, ratified, or acceded, to the Convention: Afghanistan, Egypt, Iran, Kuwait, Morocco, Niger, Pakistan, Sudan, Syria, and Tunisia. See 'Multilateral Treaties', UN Doc. ST/LEG/SER E/2 (1983), 651.
37. For a discussion of various theories of treaty interpretation, such as the textual, teleological, and intentions approach, see Fitzmaurice, 28 *BYIL*, 4-9 and 33 *BYIL*, 207-12; Haraszti, 'Some Fundamental Problems', 79-195; Brownlie, *Principles of Public International Law*, 624-30.
38. Unfortunately, the interpretation of provisions embodied in the OIC Charter have been attempted without any direct recourse to the *travaux préparatoires* of the Charter as the author had no access to these. Hence, any reference to debates preceding the adoption of the Charter should be deemed to be a reference culled from sources other than documents relating to preparatory work of the treaty.
39. See Madani, op. cit., 153.
40. According to Madani, op. cit., 153, the Saudi Arabian 'representative explained his position by stating that it was not necessary to include this

provision in the Islamic Charter, which had nothing to do with the United Nations. Besides, there was no precedent for such a provision in the Arab League or the African Unity Organization Charters. "Why then do we always fear as Muslims as if we fear the word Charter or the term Islamic Charter? After all, what has the United Nations offered to the world so that we say that we must not infringe on the members' obligations toward it?" '

41. Iran remained dissatisfied with the deletion and expressed its reservation to the Charter as follows:

 1. Charter of the Islamic Conference

 (a) In view of the deletion of article XII designed to establish in clear terms that there shall exist no conflict between the present Charter and the Charter of the United Nations, and basing itself on the provision of Art. 103 of the Charter of the United Nations, the Government of Iran wishes to confirm that any obligation that it might assume as a result of the ratification of the Charter of the Islamic Conference shall be subject to, and not in variance with its rights and obligations under the Charter of the United Nations. In the case of a conflict between the Charter of the Islamic Conference and the Charter of the UN, its obligations under the latter shall prevail.

 For the text of the reservation, see *UNTS*, 914, 126; a brief mention is made by Madani, op. cit., 154 n. 126. However, it should be noted that this attitude was representative under the Government of the former Shah of Iran. The present attitude of the Government of the Islamic Republic of Iran towards various issues of international law have been discussed in ch. 3.4.

42. See the Preamble of the OAU Charter, *UNTS*, 479, 70; also reproduced by I. Brownlie (ed.), *Basic Documents in International Law* (1983), 76; also cf. F. C. Okoye, *International Law and the African States* (1972), 121 ff.
43. Art. 1 (2) of the OAU Charter reads: 'The Organization shall include the Continental African States, Madagascar, and other Islands surrounding Africa.' *UNTS*, 479, 72.
44. On the problem of defining a 'Muslim State' and the application of the provisions of Art. VIII to new Member States in practice, see ch. 3.2.3.
45. See Art. II (1) *e* of the OAU Charter, *UNTS*, 479, 72; reference to the Universal Declaration on Human Rights is obviously to the UNGA Res. adopted on 10 Dec. 1948 (UN Doc. A/811).
46. See ch. 3.2.2 for a discussion of the contents of Art. II (*B*).
47. In his interpretation of the term 'principles of justice' as used in Art. 1 (1) of the UN Charter, Kelsen, *The Law of the United Nations*, 18, citing the President of Commission I at the San Francisco Conference (UNCIO, Doc. 1006, I/6, 2) maintains: 'If justice is identical with international law,

one of the two terms is superfluous.' See also P. E. Corbett, *Law and Society in the Relations of States* (1951), 268, who states: 'If we may judge by the wording of Article I, paragraph I of the Charter, the "principles of justice" are something distinct from "international law" '; according to H. Cattan, *Palestine and International Law* (1976), 72: 'The concept of justice introduces into the international sphere a gauge of moral and ethical values which are not conspicuous in the field of international law in its strict sense.'

48. In drawing a distinction between the obligations of a State towards the international community as a whole and those arising *vis-à-vis* another State, the Court expressed the view that the former are obligations *erga omnes*, and are, *inter alia*, derived 'from the principles and rules concerning the basic rights of the human person, including protection from slavery and racial discrimination'. See *ICJ Rep*. (1970), 3, 32, paras. 33-4; in the South West Africa Cases, *ICJ Rep.* (1966), 293, Judge Tanaka, in his dissenting opinion, expressed the view that 'the norm of non-discrimination or non-separation on the basis of race has become a rule of customary international law'; also cf. dissenting opinion of Judge Padillo Nervo, South West Africa Cases, op. cit., 455 ff. and 464, who was sympathetic towards this view. However, in 1966, this view was rejected outright by Judge *ad hoc* van Wyck, South West Africa Cases, op. cit., 168-72, and an alternative view that no such 'legal principle' exists but that international practice only reflects such a standard as an aid to interpretation was expressed by Judge Jessup in his dissenting opinion, South West Africa Cases, op. cit., 432-3, 441; see also Brownlie, *Principles*, 596-7; for a discussion of the principle of non-discrimination in the context of expropriation, see ch. 5.4.5.2.1.
49. For the text of the Convention, see *UNTS*, 660, 212 ff.; the Convention, which has been in force since 4 Jan. 1969, does 'not apply to distinctions, exclusions, restrictions or preferences made by a State party to this Convention between citizens and non-citizens' (Art. 1 (2)); see also the 'Convention on the Suppression and Punishment of the Crime of Apartheid' (1973), text in 13 *ILM* (1974), 51 ff.; see also Brownlie, *Principles* (1979), 597-8.
50. For a discussion of the parameters of the principle of self-determination, see ch. 3.2.2.3.
51. See Brownlie, *Principles*, 595; also cf. Waldock, 'General Course', 33; Judge Moreno Quintano, *ICJ Rep.* (1960), 95-6.
52. For text of the Declaration on Principles see 65 *AJIL* (1971), 249; also cf. Brownlie, *Basic Documents in International Law*, 42.
53. See e.g. 'Namibia (South West Africa) case, Advisory Opinion', *ICJ Rep.* (1970), 31 ff.; 'Western Sahara Case, Advisory Opinion', *ICJ Rep.* (1975), 12, 31-3, paras. 54-9; also cf. separate opinion of Judge Dillard in the Western Sahara Case, *ICJ Rep.* (1975), 121.

54. Cf. Art. II (1) *e* and the Preamble of the OAU Charter which declare the determination of African States 'to fight against neo-colonialism in all its forms', *UNTS*, 479, 72 and 70.
55. One of these variations, which could emerge in the connection of exploring and exploiting natural resources of the seabed and subsoil and which should be avoided, has been mentioned by Menzel and Ipsen, op. cit., 19.
56. For a discussion of the objectives, principles, and structure of the OAU, cf. T. O. Elias, 'The Charter of the OAU', 59 *AJIL* (1965), 243-67; B. Boutros-Ghali, 'The Addis Ababa Charter', *International Conciliation* (Jan. 1964), no. 546; M. Hess, 'Die Organisation der afrikanischen Einheit' (Diss. Marburg, 1967); Z. Cervenka, *The Organisation of African Unity and its Charter* (1968); Okoye, op. cit., esp. ch. IV, 121-74; M. N. Akwensioge, 'Die Organisation für afrikanische Einheit' (Diss. Tübingen, 1974).
57. For a discussion of the Pact of the Arab League including its objectives, principles, and structure, see M. Khadduri, 'The Arab League as a Regional Arrangement', 40 *AJIL* (1946), 756-77; M. F. Anabtawi, *Arab Unity in Terms of Law* (1963); E. Foda, *The Projected Arab Court of Justice* (1957); B. Boutros-Ghali, 'The Arab League (1945-1970)', 25 *Rev. Egypt.* (1969), 67-118, and 'La Ligue des états arabes', 137 *RdC* (1972), iii. 11-81.
58. See Art. II (1) *a* of the Charter, *UNTS*, 479, 72.
59. Art. 2 of the Pact *UNTS*, 70, 252.
60. According to I. Goldziher, 'Djamal al-Din al-Afghani' in *EI* (new edn. 1965, repr. 1970), 416-19, al-Afghani is known as 'the founder of modern Muslim anticolonialism' whose 'ultimate object was to unite Muslim states (including Shi'i Persia) into a single Caliphate, able to repulse European interference and recreate the glory of Islam', 416, 417; also cf. E. G. Browne, *The Persian Revolution of 1905–1909* (1910, repr. 1966), 1-29; C. C. Adams, *Islam and Modernism in Egypt: A Study of the Modern Reform Movement inaugurated by Muhammad Abduh* (1933), 4-17; H. A. R. Gibb, *Mohammadenism* (1957), 175; A. M. Ahmad, 'Die Auseinandersetzung zwischen al-Azhar und der modernistischen Bewegung in Ägypten von Muhammad Abduh bis zur Gegenwart' (Diss. Hamburg, 1963), 4-7: Young, 'Pan-Islamism in the modern World', 195-7; Dodge, 'The Significance of Religion in Arab Nationalism', 103; N. R. Keddie, *Sayyid Jamal ad-Din 'al-Afghani'. A Political Biography* (1972), tries to prove some contradictions and inconsistencies in al-Afghani's thought and statements.
61. Despite the disappearance of classical conceptions of Islamic religious and political unity and the advent of nationalism, Islam is still held by some to be a strong 'integrating' force. Cf. H. A. R. Gibb, 'Politics and Prospects in the Arab Middle East', in D. Grant (ed.), *The Islamic Near East* (1960), 175; I. R. A. al-Faruqi, *On Arabism, Urubah and Religion* (1962),

173; E. I. J. Rosenthal, *Islam and the Modern National State* (1965), p. xiii; W. M. Watt, 'Thoughts on Islamic Unity', 3 *IQ* (1956), 193-4; Hasan, 'Islamic Unity and World Co-operation', 15, 18-19; also cf. n. 5 above.

62. An examination of the legal aspects of these multilateral treaties is the subject-matter of ch. 4.3 and 5.4.

63. *ICJ Rep.* (1971), 31; see also 'Western Sahara Case', *ICJ Rep.* (1975), 31.

64. For conflicting claims laid by Israel, Jordan, and the Palestinians to the City of Jerusalem, see L. Kletter, 'The Sovereignty of Jerusalem in International Law', 20 *COLJTL* (1981), 319-63.

65. Cattan, op. cit., 112; Z. Hashem, 'Some International Law Aspects of the Palestine Question', 23 *Rev. Egypt.* (1967), 63-107; W. T. Mallison, 'An International Law Appraisal of the Juridical Characteristics of the Resistance of the People of Palestine', 28 *Rev. Egypt.* (1972), 1-19; the Pact of the Arab League contains a special 'Annex on Palestine' dealing with the question of sovereignty and independence of Palestine as follows:

> At the end of the last Great war, Palestine, together with the other Arab States, was separated from the Ottoman Empire. She became independent, not belonging to any other state.
>
> The Treaty of Lausanne proclaimed that her fate should be decided by the parties concerned in Palestine.
>
> Even though Palestine was not able to control her own destiny, it was on the basis of the recognition of her independence that the Covenant of the League of Nations determined a system of government for her. Her existence and her independence among the nations can, therefore, no more be questioned *de jure* than the independence of any of the other Arab States.

See *UNTS*, 70, 260; by virtue of Art. 16 of the Treaty of Lausanne Turkey renounced all rights and title whatsoever over territories detached from it (including Palestine) but the future of these territories was to be decided or 'settled by the parties concerned'. See Cattan, op. cit., 114.

66. In a memorandum dated 3 Feb. 1919 addressed to the Supreme Council of the Allied Powers at the Paris Peace Conference in 1919, the Zionist Organization advanced its claim to an historic title to Palestine. For a refutation of this Zionist claim which lacks any juridical basis see Cattan, op. cit., 47-50.

67. In the Balfour Declaration, which was in the form of a writen communication from the British Foreign Minister, Arthur James Balfour, addressed to Lord Rothschild (dated 2 Nov. 1917) the British Government viewed with favour 'the establishment . . . of a national home for the Jewish people' in a country where the Arabs made up 'well over 90 per cent of the population' and where the identity of the majority was 'concealed under the phrase "non-Jewish communities" and nothing was said about their national rights, since the declaration guaranteed for them only "civil and religious rights"'. A. L. Tibawi, *A Modern History of Syria including Lebanon and Palestine* (1969), 252. On the political developments in Palestine at the close of the First World War, the Balfour

Declaration and the British role in the denial of self-determination to the Palestinians, see the following publications by A. L. Tibawi, *Anglo-Arab Relations and the Question of Palestine 1914–1921* (2nd edn., 1978); 'Denial of Self-Determination to the Palestine Arabs. The British Responsibility', in *Arabic and Islamic Themes*, 331-40; 'Palestine in an Anglo-Zionist Conspiracy–From the McMahon Pledge to the Peace Conference', in *Arabic and Islamic Themes*, 324-30; 'T. E. Lawrence, Faisal and Weizmann', in *Arabic and Islamic Themes*, 315-23.

68. The League of Nations' Mandate for Palestine dated 24 July 1922 explicitly states that 'the Mandatory should be responsible for putting into effect the declaration originally made on November 2nd, 1917, by the Government of His Britannic Majesty' and goes so far as to give recognition to the so-called 'historical connexion of the Jewish people with Palestine and to the grounds for reconstituting their national home in that country'. See Preamble of the Mandate cited by Cattan, op. cit., Appendix II, 260.

69. For legal grounds justifying the invalidity of the mandate over Palestine, see Cattan, op. cit., 65-8. According to Cattan, 'The invalidity of the Palestine mandate carries two legal consequences. On the one hand, the mandate could not, at least in theory, impair or destroy the rights of the original inhabitants. In fact, its implementation gravely injured their rights and status. On the other hand, the mandate could not confer on the Jews who emigrated to Palestine during the period of the mandate national rights that conflicted with the fundamental rights of the original inhabitants.' 68.

70. Art. 22 of the Covenant of the League of Nations categorically states the case as follows: 'Certain communities formerly belonging to the Turkish Empire have reached a stage of development where their existence as independent nations can be provisionally recognized subject to the rendering of administrative advice and assistance by a Mandatory until such time as they are able to stand alone.' See Appendix I, Cattan, op. cit., 259, containing the full text of Art. 22; also cf. H. D. Hall, *Mandates, Dependencies and Trusteeships* (1948), 80, who states: 'Underlying Art. 22 was the assumption of independent national sovereignty for mandates. The drafters of the Covenant took as their starting point the general notions of "no-annexation" and "self-determination" '; with regard to the mandate for South West Africa, the ICJ has confirmed this principle as follows: 'The terms of this Mandate, as well as the provisions of Article 22 of the Covenant and the principles embodied therein, show that the creation of this new international institution did not involve any cession of territory or transfer of sovereignty to the Union of South Africa.' See Advisory Opinion of the International Court of Justice regarding the status of South West Africa, *ICJ Reports* (1950), 132; Cattan, op. cit., 112-21.

71. Unable to master the growing explosive situation in Palestine the British Government decided in 1947 to refer to the UN the question of the future government of Palestine. The Special Committee appointed by the General Assembly and known as UNSCOP submitted to the UNGA on 3 Sept. 1947 two plans; a majority plan which proposed the termination of the mandate and the partition of Palestine, creating an Arab and a Jewish State with economic union between them, and a *corpus separatum* for the City of Jerusalem which was to be subjected to an international regime to be administered by the UN; and a minority plan which also proposed the termination of the mandate but proposed the establishment of a federal state comprising of an Arab and a Jewish State. Cf. UN Doc. A/364, of 3 Sept. 1947 two plans: a majority plan which proposed the termination of issues affecting the Palestine Question and the legal question regarding the competence of the UNGA to recommend or enforce any partition plan to the ICJ for an advisory opinion, and its formulation in a resolution outlined by Sub-Committee 2 to the Ad Hoc Committee on the Palestine Question, the General Assembly denied these requests. See UN Doc. A/AC, 14/21, 14 Oct. 1947; A/AC, 14/24, 16 Oct. 1947; A/AC, 14/25, 16 Oct. 1947; and A/AC, 14/32, 11 Nov. 1947. The UN Doc. of 11 Nov. 1947 (A/AC, 14/32) endorses the draft resolution of the Sub-Committee 2, 299-301. Thus *UNGA Res.* 181 (II) adopted on 29 Nov. 1947 recommended the majority plan of partition with economic union in Palestine. For text of this Resolution see Cattan, op. cit., Appendix III, 265 ff.; for legal grounds of invalidity of the *UNGA Res.* calling for partition of Palestine, see Cattan, op. cit., 75-89; P. B. Potter, 'The Palestine Problem Before the United Nations', 42 *AJIL* (1948), 860; Q. Wright', 'The Middle East Problem', 64 *AJIL* (1970), 277; Brownlie, *Principles of Public International Law*, 175-6; Kelsen, *The Law of the United Nations*, 97; it is important to note, apart from the legal incompetence of the UNGA to dispose with sovereignty over Palestine which it did not possess, the *UNGA Res.* 181 (II) of 29 Nov. 1947 was not only rejected by the Arabs of Palestine and by the Arab States, who all decided to oppose its execution, but even the British Government refused to enforce it and announced its intention to terminate the mandate and withdraw British forces and administration by the middle of May 1948. See Tibawi, *A Modern History of Syria including Lebanon and Palestine*, 381.
72. The Report of the Sub-Committee 2 to the Ad Hoc Committee on the Palestine Question reasoned that since Art. 22 of the Covenant stipulated for the emergence of Palestine as a fully independent nation on the termination of the mandate, and contrary to specific provisions of the mandate for Palestine and in direct violation of the principles and objectives of the Covenant, the proposal of partition also contravened Art. 1 of the UN Charter by virtue of which the UN was bound to act 'in conformity with the principles of justice and international law' and to respect

'the principle of equal rights and self-determination of peoples'. Under Art. 73 of the UN Charter the UN undertook to 'take due account of the political aspirations of the peoples' living in non-self-governing territories and mandated areas. Thus the *UNGA Res.* 181 (II) of 29 Nov. 1947 violated the Covenant of the League of Nations and the Charter of the UN. See *UNGAOR*, Doc. A/AC, 14/32, 278-9, also cited by Cattan, op. cit., 78-9.

73. See Peters, *Islam and Colonialism*, 100, and esp. the chapter on 'Religious Opposition in Palestine'.
74. Outbreaks of violence and public disturbances occurred regularly in 1920, 1921, 1929, and 1933 and between 1936-9 they grew to the proportions of open revolt.
75. Peters, *Islam and Colonialism*, 101-2.
76. See Madani, op. cit., 150, who adds that 'the suggested amendment was supported by Guinea on the ground that if the war waged by the Palestinians ends tomorrow then para. 5 will no longer have its raison d'être.'
77. See Madani, op. cit.; according to Tibawi, *A Modern History of Syria*, 252-3, the uniqueness of the Palestine issue in political history and international law lies in the fact that the Balfour Declaration and subsequent international acts 'deliberately and persistently denied political rights to the vast Arab majority, the indigenous inhabitants of Palestine, in order to promote those of a small Jewish minority which was to be created largely from alien immigrants'. On the uniqueness of the Palestine situation see also Sir John Glubb, *The Middle East Crisis* (1967), 41; Cattan, op. cit., 213. Since an exhaustive examination of the Palestinian problem is beyond the scope of our subject-matter, it suffices here to mention that in contrast to 1947-8, an overwhelming majority of States have given due recognition to the rights of the Palestinians and since 1969 the UNGA has given due recognition to 'the inalienable rights of the people of Palestine' (see *UNGA Res.* 2535 (XXIV) *B*, of 10 Dec. 1969) 'including (*a*) The right to self-determination without external interference; (*b*) The right to national independence and sovereignty' (see *UNGA Res.* 3236 (XXIX) of 22 Nov. 1974) and invited the PLO in 1974 to participate in the sessions and the work of the General Assembly in the capacity of observer (*UNGA Res.* 3237 (XXIX) of 22 Nov. 1974). However, the basic problem involves the support of the right of the Palestinians to recover their homeland on the one hand, and, on the other, Israel's right to exist. The problem is further compounded by the increasing violence in the Middle East and, above all, by the following:

    (*a*) Israel's continued intransigence to the question of extending recognition to or negotiating, directly or indirectly, with the PLO, which it does not recognize as the sole representative of the

Palestinian people despite the fact that an overwhelming majority of States and international organizations have done so;

(*b*) its continuing aggressive military actions towards its Arab neighbours, as exemplified by its aerial bombardment of the Iraqi nuclear reactor and its military operations in Lebanon, which are in violation of Resolutions of the Security Council and the General Assembly as well as general principles of international law;

(*c*) its defiance of other resolutions calling upon it to refrain from effecting changes in the status of Jerusalem or in enforcing administrative measures, forcibly and illegally, in the occupied Arab territories with the objective of bringing about demographic changes;

(*d*) its adamant resolution to conclude separate peace treaties with its Arab neighbours, dealing only with the withdrawal of Israeli forces from occupied Arab territories in exchange for non-aggression pacts, embodying so-called 'secure' border delineations and the recognition of the State of Israel without any reciprocal recognition of Palestinian rights by Israel.

Following the example of the Camp David Agreements with Egypt, similar proposals have been made to Lebanon and Jordan. All this is being pursued by Israel with the sole objective of totally effacing the Palestinian issue and reducing the Palestinians to a factual non-entity. Even if we ignore the legal issues involved and acquiesce in the *fait accompli* and accept the contention put forward by some States, that regardless of the circumstances in which Israel was created, it has a right to exist, does this contention involve the right of Israel to exist within the geographical boundaries envisaged by the *UNGA Res.* 181 (II) of 29 Nov. 1947? Or does it claim legitimacy for a State enlarged by territorial conquest and subsequent annexations since 1948–annexations which were coupled with the forcible and illegal ejection of sizeable segments of the indigenous Arab population inhabiting those territories? (See Cattan, op. cit., who has raised these questions, 214-15.) Whatever contentions or plans, political, legal, or otherwise, may be advanced in favour of Israel, it is worth noting that any attempt at achieving a peaceful solution 'in the Middle East without the Palestinians is like attempting to celebrate a wedding without the bride' (Cattan, op. cit., 233).

78. See Madani, op. cit., 150-1. This sub-paragraph has gained pertinence because of the recent Soviet invasion of and continuing military presence in Afghanistan. Whereas the objective calls for the safeguarding of independence, in the case of Afghanistan, it would imply the 'regaining' of political independence from Soviet tutelage and military occupation.

79. According to *Osborn's Concise Law Dictionary*, the term 'Dignity' is an incorporeal hereditament (p. 119), having the character of an intangible

object (p. 163), such as an easement which confers no proprietary rights on its owner but is a privilege without a profit and is capable of existing as a legal interest (at p. 127).

80. See *UNTS*, 479, 74.
81. See Kelsen, *The Law of the United Nations*, 9.
82. The OIC Charter could also be considered a 'law-making' treaty if it lays down general norms formulated as legal propositions governing the future conduct of all parties. See e.g. A. D. McNair, *Law of Treaties* (1961), 5, 124, 749-52; and also Brownlie, *Principles*, 12-13.
83. For a treatment of the OAS and OAU Charters and the Pact of the Arab League of States, see G. Kutzner, *Die Organisation der amerikanischen Staaten OAS* (1970), 114-22, 169-76; Okoye, *International Law and the New African States*, 131; Anabtawi, *Arab Unity in Terms of Law*, 89 ff., respectively.
84. Hereinafter cited as Declaration on Principles or simply Declaration.
85. Cf. Kelsen, op. cit., 87 ff.; L. M. Goodrich, E. Hambro, and A. P. Simons, *Charter of the United Nations* (1969), 36-40.
86. See ch. 3.2.2.7.
87. Since the author did not have any access to the preparatory work of the OIC Charter and since there are reasons to believe that no prolonged discussion on the principles took place during the debates concerning the articles of the draft Charter (see Madani, op. cit., which contains some extensive reports on the discussions which did take place), reference is made to the UN Charter and the Declaration on Principles which reflect some basic attitudes of the Islamic States on the principles concerned.
88. As Menzel and Ipsen, op. cit., 449, have done by stating that the Declaration cannot be considered to be a source of international law.
89. The debate on the binding force of General Assembly Resolutions has been long and therefore only a brief mention of some contributions on the subject may be mentioned here: F. B. Sloan, 'The Binding Force of a "Recommendation" of the General Assembly of the United Nations', 25 *BYIL* (1948), 1-33; D. H. N. Johnson, 'The Effect of Resolutions of the General Assembly of the United Nations', 32 *BYIL* (1955/6), 97-122; O. Y. Asamoah, *Legal Significance of the Declarations of the United Nations General Assembly* (1966); R. Falk, 'On the Quasi-Legislative Competence of the General Assembly', 60 *AJIL* (1966), 782-91; A. Verdross, 'Kann die Generalversammlung der Vereinten Nationen das Völkerrecht weiter bilden?', 26 *ZaöRV* (1966), 690-7; J. Castaneda, *Legal Effects of United Nations' Resolutions* (1967); R. Khan, 'The Legal Status of the Resolutions of the UN General Assembly', 19 *IJIL* (1979), 552-9.
90. Brownlie, *Basic Documents*, 35; Brownlie states that the Declaration was adopted without vote, while G. Arangio-Ruiz, 'The Normative Role of

the General Assembly of the United Nations', 137 *RdC* (1972), iii. 437 reports that the Declaration was adopted by 108 votes to none!

91. Cf. Rosenstock, 'The Declaration of Principles of International Law Concerning Friendly Relations', 714 ff.; zu Dohna, 'Die Grundprinzipien des Völkerrechts über die freundschaftlichen Beziehungen und die Zusammenarbeit zwischen Staaten', 249-54.
92. Arangio-Ruiz, op. cit., 607.
93. Cf. zu Dohna, op. cit., 242, who reproduces statements of delegates Engo (Cameroon), Njenga (Kenya), Krishnan (India), Hamilton (Chile), Molina Landaeta (Venezuela), Critescu (Romania) expressed at the final session of the UN Special Committee. Cf. UN Doc. A/AC, 125/SR, 114, 49, 59, 68, 30, 34, 37 ff.; also cf. Rosenstock, op. cit., 714, who cites delegates of Hungary and Iraq in n. 4.
94. Cf. zu Dohna, op. cit., 244; Rosenstock, op. cit., 714-15. Since the Declaration cannot be considered to be an amendment of the UN Charter (see, e.g., Brownlie, *Basic Documents*, 35) Rosenstock believes that the effect of the Declaration on the state of international law is limited by the San Francisco Conference interpretations which 'limit to some extent the efficacy of efforts at interpretation other than through the amendment route'. Such an opinion tends to defeat the very purpose of progressive codification. For a contrary view see M. Sahovic, 'Codification of the Legal Principles of Co-Existence and Development of Contemporary International Law', in M. Sahovic (ed.), *Principles of International Law Concerning Friendly Relations* (1972), 9-50, at 45 ff.
95. See UN Doc. A/AC, 125/SR, 114, at 46, also cited by zu Dohna, op. cit., 244, who endorses the view expressed by the Italian delegate (257); since UNGA Resolutions may be regarded as law-making if they are declaratory of existing principles of general international law (see Brownlie, *Principles of Public International Law*, 696 and 15) the Declaration may be held to have law-making propensity.
96. See Verdross, op. cit., 690-7, who stipulates this condition; also cf. M. Bohn, 'Die Kodifikation des Völkerrechts durch die General Versammlung der Vereinten Nationem' (1972), 137-9: Castaneda, op. cit., 168 ff.; E. Schwelb, 'Neue Etappen der Fortentwicklung des Völkerrechts durch die Vereinten Nationen', 13 *AdV* (1966/7), 51; Johnson, op. cit., 121 ff.
97. See Goodrich, Hambro, and Simons, op. cit., 37; the OAU Charter reaffirms the principle in Art. III (1), see *UNTS*, 479, 74.
98. See Kelsen, op. cit., 52-3, the Declaration reaffirms the principle of sovereign equality as enshrined in Art. 2 (1) of the UN Charter and includes the following additional elements: 'i) the territorial integrity and political independence of the state are inviolable; ii) each state has the right freely to choose and develop its political, social, economic, and

cultural systems'. For texts, see Brownlie, *Basic Documents*, 43; the text of the document is reprinted in 65 *AJIL* (1971), 243 ff.

99. Cf. Menzel and Ipsen, op. cit., 202; O'Connell, *International Law*, i. 320.
100. See Brownlie, op. cit., 43; 65 *AJIL* (1971), 243-51.
101. See H. Weinschel, 'The Doctrine of Equality of States and its Recent Modifications', 45 *AJIL* (1951), 417-42; O'Connell, op. cit., i. 320-1; B. Broms, *The Doctrine of Equality of States as Applied in International Organizations* (1959); B. Boutros-Ghali, 'Le Principe d'égalité des états et les organisations internationales', 98 *RdC* (1960), ii. 1-73.
102. One of the purposes of the UN Charter, as laid down in Art. 1(2) of the UN Charter, is 'to develop friendly relations among nations based on the respect for the principle of equal rights and self-determination of peoples'.
103. Art. 1 of both the International Covenant on Economic, Social, and Cultural Rights as well as the International Covenant on Civil and Political Rights state in identical words the following: 'All peoples have the right of self-determination. By virtue of that right they freely determine their political status and freely pursue their economic, social, and cultural development.' See Brownlie, *Basic Document,* 259, 271.
104. *UNGA Res.* 1514 declares in para. 2 'All peoples have the right to self-determination'; and the rest of the passage is identical with that cited in note 103 above. It shows that with very few minor changes the wording contained in para. 2 of the 'Declaration on Independence' was taken over by the Covenants.
105. See Brownlie, op. cit., 41-3; 65 *AJIL* (1971), 249-500.
106. See R. Emerson, 'Self-Determination', 65 *AJIL* (1971), 459-75, 463.
107. Cf. Hall, op. cit., 80.
108. See Higgins, *The Development of International Law Through the Political* Organs of the United Nations, 101-5; H. S. Johnson, *Self-Determination within the Community of Nations* (1967), 54; A. Shukri, *The Concept of Self-Determination in the United Nations* (1965), 338-50; O'Connell, *International Law*, i. 312-13; even U. O. Umozurike, *Self-Determination in International Law* (1972), 203, who tends to recognize the right as a fundamental human right enjoyed by 'all peoples, regardless of race, religion, or sex . . . free from internal or external domination' finally admits that the legal recognition of the principle has come about 'principally in the context of decolonization', at p. 272; for further references on similar qualifications, see A. R. Sureda, *The Evolution of the Right of Self-Determination: A Study of United Nations Practice* (1973), 355; Menzel and Ipsen, op. cit., 126; Goodrich, Hambro, and Simons, op. cit., 33; C. J. Dugard, 'The Organisation of African Unity and Colonialism: An Inquiry into the Plea of Self-Defence as a Justification for the Use of Force in the Eradication of Colonialism', 16 *ICLQ* (1967), 157-90; Z. Mustafa, 'The Principle of Self-Determination in International Law',

5 *International Lawyer* (1971), 479-87; Anand, *New States and International Law*, 57-8; G. B. Starushenko, 'Abolition of Colonialism and International Law', in G. Tunkin (ed.), *Contemporary International Law Collection of Articles* (1969), 77-96.

109. See Brownlie, *Basic Documents*, 42; 65 *AJIL* (1971), 249; for a brief survey of different views expressed by Third World, Western, and Soviet bloc countries, see McWhinney, 'The "New" Countries', 1-33; P. Houben, 'Principles of International Law Concerning Friendly Relations', 61 *AJIL* (1967), 703-36; on the application of the Declaration to colonial situations and explicit legal implications of the principle of self-determination in the context of wars of liberation, see G. Abi-Saab, 'Wars of National Liberation in the Geneva Conventions and Protocols', 165 *RdC* (1979), iv. 353 ff., 370-2.

110. See Emerson, op. cit., 470, who notes that the Special Committee of 24 set up by *UNGA Res.* 1654 (XVI) to put *UNGA Res.* 1514 of 1960 into effect tended to equate the proper exercise of the right of self-determination with a decision for independence; see also para. 4 of *Res.* 1514 which emphasizes the right of dependent peoples to complete independence, in Brownlie, *Basic Documents*, 300; see also Johnson, *Self-Determination*, 40 ff.

111. Brownlie, *Basic Documents*, 42; 65 *AJIL* (1971), 249; for evidence of this paragraph being applicable to colonial peoples, see Emerson, op. cit., 470; Rosenstock, op. cit., 731-3; it is, therefore, incomprehensible and rather misleading that Menzel and Ipsen, op. cit., 127, interpret this right as being applicable to 'all peoples'. Furthermore, the modes of implementing the principle refer to colonial peoples and situations and cannot be applied in a general context. Such an interpretation runs contrary to the intention of the paragraph as it appears in the context of the Declaration.

112. See Johnson, *Self-Determination*, 54-7; for the widely held view that the right of self-determination is a fundamental principle of international law, see Umozurike, op. cit., 178-80, 272, who cites the views of various publicists; see also Brownlie, *Principles*, 595.

113. See statement made by the former UN Secretary-General U Thant (in 7 *UN Monthly Chronicle*, Feb. 1970, 36) who succinctly answered the question of secession as follows: 'So far as the question of secession of a particular section of a Member State is concerned, the United Nations' attitude is unequivocable. As an international organization, the United Nations has never accepted and does not accept and I do not believe it will ever accept the principle of secession of a part of its Member State'; also cited by Emerson, op. cit., 464; and V. P. Nanda, 'Self-Determination in International Law', 66 *AJIL* (1972), 321-36, at 327.

114. On the support of the principle of territorial integrity in the case of Nigeria by the OAU, see Umozurike, op. cit., 186-7; Okoye, op. cit., 99; Nanda, op. cit., 326-7.

115. Cf. Nanda, op. cit., 321-36; K. P. Misra, *The Role of the United Nations in the Indo-Pakistani Conflict* (1971), 135-40; S. R. Chowdhury, *The Genesis of Bangladesh: A Study of International Legal Norms and Permissive Conscience* (1972), 192-202.
116. The question of aid by Indian armed forces was raised by Jessup, 'Non-Universal International Law', 426; see also T. M. Franck and N. S. Rodley, 'After Bangladesh: The Law of Humanitarian Intervention by Military Force', 67 *AJIL* (1973), 275-305, who hold the unilateral use of armed force by India as, *inter alia*, justified on human rights grounds; in a similar strain, E. Suzuki, 'Self-Determination and World Public Order: Community Response to Territorial Separatism', 16 *VJIL* (1975/6), 779-862, esp. 805-11. For the contrary view that Indian armed intervention was designed to dismember Pakistan see G. W. Choudhury, *The Last Days of United Pakistan* (1974), 202-27.
117. Arangio-Ruiz, op. cit., 571, 620; for African views on territorial integrity and the denial of self-determination, cf. Okoye, *International Law and the New African States*, 99, who points out that the fundamental issue between the principle of territorial integrity and the application of the principle of self-determination has led to a contradiction which 'involves the active furtherance of the freedom of subjugated peoples (meaning colonial peoples as referred to in *UNGA Res.* 1514, para. 1) by the OAU and the complete refusal to apply the principle of self-determination between independent African states'.
118. Brownlie, *Basic Documents*, 43; 65 *AJIL* (1971), 250; see also O'Connell, *International Law*, i. 313 who endorses this view.
119. Brownlie, op. cit., 42; 65 *AJIL* (1971), 249; the *UNGA Res.* 1514 of 1960 as well as the International Covenants make the same point; see also Brownlie, *Principles*, 595.
120. For text of the Resolution see 60 *AJIL* (1966), 662.
121. See McWhinney, 'The "New" Countries', 23; Emersen, op. cit., 466; for a short survey of the concept of non-intervention in international law and its extended form, taking into account the views of German, Anglo-American, French, Soviet, and other publicists, see Dicke, op. cit., 177 ff.; also cf. Menzel and Ipsen, op. cit., 197, who perceive the *UNGA Res.* 2131 (XX) of 1966 to be an extension of the classical concept of non-intervention.
122. A similar conclusion may be drawn from the contents of Art. 2 of the *Grundvertrag* concluded between the Federal Republic of Germany and the German Democratic Republic (21 Dec. 1972). See *BGBl.*, ii. 423.
123. Menzel and Ipsen, op. cit., 195; Brownlie, *Principles of Public International Law*, 291-3; Dicke, op. cit., 143 ff.
124. See Eastern Carelia Case, *PCIJ* Series B, no. 5 (1923), 27; O'Connell, *International Law* OR op. cit., i. 298.

125. See Kelsen, op. cit., 769-70; Goodrich, Hambro, and Simons, op. cit., 60-72; O'Connell, op. cit., i. 308-12.
126. Brownlie, *Basic Documents*, 40; 65 *AJIL* (1971), 248. The US view, put forward in the UN Special Committee on Friendly Relations, that the only principle of non-intervention is Art. 2 (7) of the UN Charter received no support from the East European, Latin American, and Afro-Asian States. See Rosenstock, op. cit., 726; the phrase 'subordination of the exercise of its sovereign rights' is reminiscent of the arguments advanced on behalf of Third World countries in the Anglo-Iranian Oil Company affair and in the Suez Affair. In the latter case the question of armed intervention by Great Britain, France, and Israel would be a suitable example of the violation of the principle as well as Art. 2 (4) of the UN Charter.
127. Cf. Menzel and Ipsen, op. cit., 197-8.
128. Cf. O'Connell, *International Law* OR op. cit., i. 299-306; see also R. Vincent, *Non-Intervention and International Order* (1974), on subversive activities as constituting 'illegal' intervention. All five categories of interventionary acts are applicable in several critical situations prevailing at present in the Central and Latin American regions.
129. Menzel and Ipsen, op. cit., 197, 198, are of the opinion that, in principle only States and international organizations are in a position to violate the rule of non-intervention. Activities of private persons and especially of transnational corporations may constitute an intervention only if such 'activities' are incited and promoted by their home States. Would this justify labelling the activities of transnational and US corporations in Chile prior to the overthrow of President Allende as falling outside the ambit of the rule of non-intervention, although it appears that direct CIA intervention in Chile was launched at the instigation of these corporations?
130. See Derpa, op. cit., 58; zu Dohna, op. cit., 103 ff.; D. W. Bowett, 'International Law and Economic Coercion', 16 *VJIL* (1975/6), 245-59; B. Lindemeyer, *Schiffsembargo und Handelsembargo* (1975), 139-42; Dicke, op. cit., 143-63; Menzel and Ipsen, op. cit., 199.
131. See Menzel and Ipsen, op. cit., 200; whereas I. Shihata, 'Destination Embargo of Arab Oil: Its Legality under International Law', 68 *AJIL* (1974), 591-627 argues that Arab oil measures were legal and were similar to those used by other States to further their foreign policies, R. B. Lillich, *Economic Coercion and the International Legal Order*, 51 *Int. Aff.* (1975), 358-71 and his second contribution 'Economic Coercion and the "New International Economic Order": A Second Look at Some First Impressions', 16 *VJIL* (1975/6), 233-44, argues that certain acts, which are of a unilateral nature and which may cause severe economic disruption on a world scale, may violate international norms. J. J. Paust and

A. P. Blaustein, 'The Arab Oil Weapon–A Threat to International Peace', 68 *AJIL* (1974), 410-39 go a bit too far by applying a wide interpretation to Art. 2 (4) and its use of the word 'force', which they include to mean force other than military or armed force. Hence they hold the Oil Embargo to be in violation of Art. 2 (4). For a refutation of such a claim see Bowett, 'International Law and Economic Coercion', 245. As to the effectiveness and success of the Oil Embargo as a measure of coercion in the cause of furthering foreign policy measures, Dicke, op. cit., 216-18, holds, contrary to Shihata, 'Destination Embargo of Arab Oil', 627, that the Oil Embargo was not a success. It is true that the Oil Embargo did not achieve any substantial change in the attitude of the US Government towards the Palestinian Question. However, success must be measured in relative terms as none of the Arab States were convinced that the Embargo could create dramatic results. The success lay in the fact that the Palestinian cause received tremendous publicity as well as increased recognition after the October War of 1973 and the Arab Oil Embargo. See also Lindemeyer, op. cit., 283-98. Measures of economic coercion have rarely achieved any political success, see M. P. Doxey, *Economic Sanctions and International Enforcement* (1971), 139.

132. It remains, however, to be seen whether some secessionist movements in the Islamic world may be taken to be legitimate cases of the exercise of the right of self-determination. Such a case is claimed by the Algerian support of the Polisario (see Suzuki, op. cit., 779-80). The question concerning the legality of armed intervention on humanitarian grounds is far from settled; although it has been rejected by some (see Menzel and Ipsen, op. cit., 458) and supported in the case of Bangladesh by others (Franck and Rodley, op. cit., 303-5, Suzuki, op. cit., 807), arguments in support of armed intervention on humanitarian grounds opens up new areas of conflict. One must draw a distinction between the right of self-determination of colonial peoples, in the exercise of which, it has been held by Third World States, they may 'legitimately' resort to armed force by invoking the right of self-defence under Art. 51 of the UN Charter, and armed intervention by a third State in favour and support of the group claiming the right of self-determination, as in the case of Indian armed intervention in Bangladesh.
133. O'Connell, op. cit., i. 284; see also Brownlie, *Principles*, 287-90.
134. Menzel and Ipsen, op. cit., 102, 195; see also Eastern Carelia Case, *PCIJ*, Ser. B, no. 5 (1923), 27; O'Connell, op. cit., 298; Dicke, op. cit., 59 ff.
135. Cf. 6 *UNCIO* Docs. 457; for a commentary on this interpretation see Kelsen, op. cit., 52-3; Goodrich, Hambro, and Simons, op. cit., 36-40.
136. Cf. McWhinney, 'The "New" Countries', 25-6.
137. See Brownlie, *Basic Documents*, 43; 65 *AJIL* (1971), 250.
138. McWhinney, 'The "New" Countries', 28-9; see also Rosenstock, op. cit., 713-35; Houben, op. cit., 703-36; zu Dohna, op. cit., 158-78.

139. See Arangio-Ruiz, op. cit., 599, who states that in his view this is not a wise policy; also cf. Udokang, op. cit., 152-3.
140. On the interrelationship between Art. 2 (3) and (4) of the UN Charter see Goodrich, Hambro, and Simons, op. cit., 41-55; Menzel and Ipsen, op. cit., 477; in the deliberations of the UN Special Committee on Friendly Relations, the principle of peaceful settlement of disputes was accepted as being a logical corollary of the prohibition of resort to force, see McWhinney, 'The "New" Countries', 17; Rosenstock, op. cit., 725; in effect the Declaration on Principles confirms the full purport of Art. 2 (3) of the UN Charter, see zu Dohna, op. cit., 134-58.
141. Art. 2 (3) has been held to be a positive duty, i.e. States must actively seek to solve international disputes by peaceful means, see Menzel and Ipsen, op. cit., 478; Continental Shelf Case, *ICJ Rep.* (1969), 47; zu Dohna, op. cit., 156 ff.
142. See Brownlie, *Basic Documents*, 40; 65 *AJIL* (1971), 247.
143. Rosenstock, op. cit., 725-6 considers it to be the only positive achievement of the UN Special Committee.
144. McWhinney, 'The "New" Countries', 18; Rosenstock, op. cit.
145. See R. P. Anand, *Compulsory Jurisdiction of the International Court of Justice* (1961), 79, 84-5, 87, 252, 253; see also his article, 'Role of "New" Asian-African Countries in the Present International Legal Order', 393-402; Shihata, 'The Attitude of the New States', 203-22; according to Lord McNair, *The Development of International Justice* (1956), 32, 'The more serious disputes between states can only be solved by changes in the rights of states, while it is the business of a court of law to give effect to existing rights', also cited by Anand, *Compulsory Jurisdiction*, 89. The view expressed by Lord McNair sums up the still widely held distinction between legal and political disputes, which was reiterated in the deliberations of the UN Special Committee on Friendly Relation; see E. McWhinney, 'The "New" Countries', 18. However, there seems to be some belated change in the attitude of the Third World States towards the ICJ. According to E. McWhinney, *The World Court and the Contemporary International Law-Making Process* (1979), 6, the new Third World majority has 'begun to discover the potentialities of the ICJ as an international law-making, policy-making arena. These countries have in a conscious way (after the politically controversial 8 to 7 majority decision of the Court in the South West Africa Case in 1966) tried to use their voting power in the General Assembly to elect judges who might be expected to be disposed to create new law, as distinct from logically developing or re-stating the old. This process can only be said to have begun as yet; this if developed would be a significant differentiation and departure of Third World attitudes to the Court from both Soviet and Western based approaches'.
146. See Anand, 'Role of "New" Asian-African Countries', 406.

147. See Foda, op. cit., 52.
148. See Hamidullah, *Muslim Conduct of State*, 153-6; Khadduri, *War and Peace in the Law of Islam*, 234 ff.; Foda, op. cit., 50-2.
149. See Foda, op. cit., 53.
150. Islamic States have usually resorted to arbitration in cases of commercial disputes with foreign companies, see *Petroleum Development Ltd.* v. *Sheikh of Abu Dhabi*, 18 *ILR* (1951), 144-61; *Petroleum Development (Qatar) Ltd.* v. *Ruler of Qatar*, 18 *ILR* (1951), 161-4; *Ruler of Qatar* v. *International Marine Oil Co.*, 20 *ILR* (1953), 534-47; Aramco Arbitration', 27 *ILR* (1958), 117-233; so far Pakistan submitted its boundary dispute in the Kutch-Sind area with India to arbitration, see M. G. Untawale, 'The Kutch-Sind Dispute: A Case Study in International Arbitration', 23 *ICLQ* (1974), 818-39; also compare Art. 64 of the Articles of Agreement of the Islamic Development Bank which stipulates that: 'If a disagreement should arise between the Bank and a country which has ceased to be a member, or between the Bank and any member, after adoption of a resolution to terminate the operations of the Bank, such disagreement shall be submitted to arbitration by a tribunal of three (3) arbitrators.'
151. See Menzel and Ipsen, op. cit., 479-81.
152. Art. 19 of the OAU Charter calls for a separate Protocol to establish the Commission, see *UNTS*, 479, 80, which was signed on 21 July 1964 by thirty-two Member States. For a survey of the constitution, functions and awards or conciliations achieved by the Commission, see V. D. Degan, 'The Commission of Mediation, Conciliation, and Arbitration of the OAU', 20 *Rev. Egypt.* (1964), 53-80; T. O. Elias, 'The Commission of Mediation, Conciliation, and Arbitration of the OAU', 40 *BYIL* (1964), 336-54; Okoye, op. cit., 138-54.
153. For the text of Art. 5 of the Pact see *UNTS*, 70, 254.
154. *UNTS*, 70, 258; a Draft Statute of the Arab Court of Justice was prepared by a three man Commission appointed by the Council of the Arab League at its 12th Ordinary Session, 13 Apr. 1950. For the text of the Draft Statute see Foda, op. cit., Appendix B, 226-36.
155. Foda, op. cit., who examines the legal implications of Art. 5 (pp. 22-42) and comes to the conclusion that 'A survey of the arbitration treaties initiated by Saudi Arabia and agreed between the Arab States between 1931-1937 gives striking proof that (reservations expressed in Art. 5 of) the Arab League Pact of 1945 was a step backward in the field of the settlement of disputes by arbitration', 32.
156. Ibid., 17-20, 42-9; according to T. O. Elias, *New Horizons in International Law* (1979, 1980), 27, 'The League of Arab States is no doubt a political organ primarily, but the importance of certain of its declarations and resolutions on international issues is that they connote legal consequences.'
157. Recently, there have been some calls for setting up an International

Islamic Court of Justice, see 8 *Journal of the Muslim World League* (Jan. 1981), 27.

158. See statements made by delegates Schwebel (USA), Doc. A/AC, 119/SR, 3, 12, and Bierzanek (Poland), Doc. A/AC, 119/SR, 9, 6, in the UN Special Committee on Friendly Relations on the legal effect of this principle; for support of this proposition among international law publicists, see R. L. Bobrov, 'Basic Principles of Present-Day International Law', in G. Tunkin (ed.), *Contemporary International Law Collection of Articles* (Moscow, 1969), 36-58; Brownlie, *International Law and the Use of Force by States*, 113, and *Principles of Public International Law*, 513; zu Dohna, op. cit., 52-4; R. Falk, 'The New States and International Legal Order', 118 *RdC* (1966), ii. 1-103; Jessup, 'Non-Universal International Law', 426; Kewenig, 'Gewaltverbot und noch zulässige Machteinwirkung und Interventionsmittel', 175-217; Menzel and Ipsen, op. cit., 449; Rosenstock, op. cit., 713-35, 717; Skubiszewski, 'Use of Force by States', 739-855, 745.

159. As asserted by Bowett, *Self-Defence in International Law*, 150-2, who interprets the principle of refraining from the threat or use of force as embodying an element of intent, whereby any threat or use of force is in contravention of Art. 2 (4), 'only where intended to jeopardize the political independence or territorial integrity of another state'.

160. As pointed out by Brownlie, *International Law and the Use of Force by States*, 268; also cf. zu Dohna, op. cit., 69-72.

161. See McWhinney, 'The "New" Countries', 8; Houben, op. cit., 703-36; Rosenstock, op. cit., 717 ff.; zu Dohna, op. cit., 56-103; Menzel and Ipsen, op. cit., 449; also cf. Bowett, *Self-Defence*, 148, and 'International Law', 245-59; G. Dahm, 'Das Verbot der Gewaltanwendung nach Art. 2 (4) der UNO Charta und die Selbsthilfe gegenüber Völkerrechtsverletzungen, die keinen bewaffneten Angriff enthalten', *JIR* (1962), 48-72; Derpa, op. cit.; H. G. Mähler, 'Die völkerrechtliche Bedeutung des Kriegs- und Gewaltverbots' (Diss. Munich, 1965); Skubiszewski, op. cit., 739 ff.; C. H. M. Waldock, 'The Regulation of the Use of Force', 81 *RdC* (1952), ii. 451-517; Kewenig, 'Gewaltverbot', 190 ff.; G. Schwarzenberger, *International Law as Applied by International Courts and Tribunals* (1968), ii. 51.

162. See Brownlie, *Basic Documents*, 38; 65 *AJIL* (1971), 246.

163. See Menzel and Ipsen, op. cit., 450; another form of 'non-physical force' coming under the ambit of Art. 2 (4) of the UN Charter is war propaganda, cf. the Declaration on Principles, Brownlie, *Basic Documents*, 38; 65 *AJIL* (1971), 246.

164. See Declaration on Principles, Brownlie, *Basic Documents*, 38; also cf. Corfu Channel Case, *ICJ Rep.* (1949), 4; zu Dohna, op. cit., 63-4; Kewenig, 'Gewaltverbot', 184; G. Schwarzenberger, *A Manual of International Law* (1967), 185; R. Falk, 'The Beirut Raid and the International Law of Retaliation', 63 *AJIL* (1969), 442; Waldock, op. cit., 217. On the

other hand, Bowett, 'Reprisals involving recourse to armed force', 66 *AJIL* (1972), 3, 21 ff., 26, argues that the law of reprisals is degenerating to a point where the Security Council has abstained from condemning an otherwise unlawful reprisal.

165. Brownlie, *Basic Documents*, 38; 65 *AJIL* (1971), 246.
166. Brownlie, *Basic Documents*, 39; 65 *AJIL* (1971), 246.
167. See statement made by the Syrian delegate Allaf in the UN Special Committee on Friendly Relations, UN Doc. A/AC, 125/SR, 114, 64; also cf. zu Dohna, op. cit., 60, who rejects these objections on the grounds that an objective interpretation of the prohibition warrants no such exceptions.
168. See McWhinney, 'The "New" Countries', 9; Houben, op. cit.; zu Dohna, op. cit., 54-8; Menzel and Ipsen, op. cit., 449; Bowett, 'International Law', 245 ff.; Goodrich, Hambro, and Simons, op. cit., 49, reject various forms of economic and political coercion as necessarily coming under the prohibition of Art. 2 (4).
169. It is interesting to note that even in the context of Art. 52 of the Vienna Convention on the Law of Treaties, the phrase 'threat or use of force' has been interpreted as extending to 'the employment of economic, political, military and psychological coercion and to all types of coercion'. See declaration made by the Syrian Arab Republic on its accession to the convention, in: 'Multilateral Treaties deposited with the Secretary-General', UN Doc. ST/LEG/SER, E/2 (1983), 653.
170. See comments on Art. 2 (4) UN Charter in the reports of Commission 1, 6 *UNCIO*, 459, which said 'the use of arms in legitimate self-defence remains admitted and unimpaired'; also cf. Bowett, *Self-Defence*, 185.
171. See Kelsen, op. cit., 914; zu Dohna, op. cit., 89; on the other hand, Bowett, *Self-Defence*, 185, maintains: 'It is . . . fallacious to assume that members (of the UN) have only those rights which the Charter accords to them; on the contrary they have those rights which general international law accords to them except in so far as they have surrendered them under the Charter. . . .'
172. See Bowett, *Self-Defence*, 187-93, and 'Reprisals Involving Recourse to Armed Force', 66 *AJIL* (1972), 1 ff.; in similar terms Waldock asserts a similar right from the interpretation of Art. 51, see op. cit., 498; also cf. Brierly, *The Law of Nations* (1963), 420; O'Connell, *International Law*, i. 317; Rosenstock, op. cit., 723.
173. Thus Menzel and Ipsen, op. cit., 454 in accord with S. M. Schwebel, 'Aggression, Intervention and Self-Defence', 136 *RdC* (1972), ii. 481, cite the launching of armed attacks on Arab territories by Israel in 1967 as a significant example of anticipatory ('preventive') self-defence.
174. See M. Akehurst, *A Modern Introduction to International Law* (1970), 315 ff.; Derpa, *Das Gewaltverbot* (1970), 115 ff.; zu Dohna, op. cit., 90; T. M. Franck, 'Who Killed Art. 2 (4)? or: Norms Governing the Use

of Force by States', 64 *AJIL* (1970), 809–37, 821 f.; Jessup, *A Modern Law of Nations*, 166; Kelsen, op. cit., 797; Kunz, 'Individual and Collective Self-Defence in Art. 51 of the Charter', 872 ff., 878; Skubiszewski, op. cit., 778.

175. The interpretation of the right of self-defence as being permissible in cases where vital interests of a state are at stake has been rejected for being too wide and thus falling outside the ambit of Art. 51, see Fawcett, op. cit., 391-409; Menzel and Ipsen, op. cit., 453.

176. Although there is a free choice of means, the duty is to actively seek a peaceful settlement of disputes, see 'North Sea Continental Shelf Cases', *ICJ Rep.* (1969), 47; zu Dohna, op. cit., 156 ff.

177. This has been confirmed in the Advisory Opinions of the ICJ in the Namibia (South West Africa), 1971, 31, and the Western Sahara (1975), 31-3.

178. Cf. Madani, op. cit., 154-5 who cites this draft appendix in full. The States which insisted on the inclusion of such an appendix in the Drafting Committee were Indonesia, Turkey, Lebanon, Chad, and Syria.

179. Objections raised by Mauritania were seconded by Saudi Arabia, see Madani, op. cit., 155-6.

180. As pointed out by the Mauritanian Delegate, see Madani, op. cit.

181. Cf. Madani, op. cit., 157; for the text of reservations expressed by Chad, Indonesia, Lebanon, and Turkey, see *UNTS*, 914, 123-8.

182. This has facilitated the membership of some African States with a Muslim population of less than 40 per cent and having weak, if not remote, historical connections with Islam.

183. See A. Abdullah, 'OIC Summit–Egypt's Casablanca Comeback', in 31 *Arabia* (London, March 1984), 14.

184. See S. El-Gebali, 'Die OAPEC als Organisation zur Interessenvertretung der arabischen Ölländer in den internationalen wirtschaftlichen Beziehungen' (Diss. Kiel, 1981), 64 ff., who argues in favour of Egypt.

185. See Oppenheim and Lauterpacht, op. cit., 800-87; J. L. Kunz, 'The Meaning and Range of the Norm Pacta Sunt Servanda', 39 *AJIL* (1945), 180; also cf. Okoye, op. cit., 126, on the legal character of the OAU Charter; for a definition of the term 'treaty', see Art. 2 (1) *a* of the Vienna Convention on the Law of Treaties.

186. Cf. Commentary on Art. 57 in the ILC Final Draft in *Yearbook of the International Law Commission* (1966), ii. 253-5, also cited by R. G. Wetzel and D. Rauschning, 'The Vienna Convention on the Law of Treaties', *Travaux Préparatoires* (1978), 412; Dissenting Opinion of Judge Anzilotti in the Diversion of Water from the Meuse, PCIJ (1937), Ser. A/B, no. 70, 50; Tacna Arica Arbitration, *UNRIAA*, ii. 929, 943-4; Namibia (South West Africa) Advisory Opinion, *ICJ Rep.* (1971), 47, para. 96; A. D. McNair, *The Law of Treaties* (1961), 539 ff.; S. P. Sinha, *Unilateral Denunciation of Treaty Because of Prior Violations of Obligations by Other Party*

(1966), 84-8; I. Detter, *Essays on the Law of Treaties* (1967), 89-93, G. Schwarzenberger, *Manual of International Law* (1967), 168-9; B. Simma, 'Reflections on Article 60 of the Vienna Convention', *ÖZöR* (1970), 5 ff., 28-31; G. Haraszti, *Some Fundamental Problems of the Law of Treaties* (1973), 310 ff., 322; T. O. Elias, *The Modern Law of Treaties* (1974), 114 ff.; Brownlie, *Principles of Public International Law*, 615; Menzel and Ipsen, op. cit., 330-1; also cf. Art. 60 (1) and (2) of the Vienna Convention on the Law of Treaties.

187. For the text of the Vienna Convention, see 63 *AJIL* (1969), 875 ff.
188. The Convention entered into force on 27 Jan. 1980, see 17 *UN Monthly Chronicle* (1980), no. 2, 91, and Multilateral Treaties Deposited with the Secretary-General. Status as at 31 Dec. 1982, UN Doc. ST/LEG/SER, E/2 (1983), 651.
189. These are Afghanistan (signature only), Egypt (accession), Iran (signature), Kuwait (accession), Morocco (ratification), Niger (accession), Pakistan (signature), Sudan (signature), Syria (accession), and Tunisia (accession), as on 31 Dec. 1982.
190. 'North Sea Continental Shelf Cases', *ICJ Rep.* (1969), 3 ff., para. 76.
191. Cf. Menzel and Ipsen, op. cit., 330.
192. See G. Haraszti, 'Some Fundamental Problems of the Law of Treaties' (1973), 318.
193. *ICJ Rep.* (1971), 47, para. 94.
194. In his examination of the suspension of Egypt's membership of OAPEC, El-Gebali, op. cit., 52-66 comes to the conclusion that the act lacks any legal basis because Egypt did not commit any 'material breach' of OAPEC treaty provisions. It must, however, be noted that the suspension could be construed as a permissible act of reprisal, cf. Menzel and Ipsen, op. cit., 331; B. Simma, 'Reflections on Article 60 of the Vienna Convention', *ÖZöR* (1970), 5-83.
195. See L. Henkin, *How Nations Behave* (1968), 168 ff.
196. Such an extraordinary session was convened in Jan. 1980 in Islamabad to discuss the Soviet invasion of Afghanistan.
197. For example, the third ICFM held at Jeddah decided to establish an International Islamic News Agency, see *Resolutions*, 26-7; the fourth ICFM meeting in Benghazi, Libya, decided to set up a Permanent Economic Experts Committee within the Secretariat, see *Resolutions*, 33; other examples are the 'Resolution on the Establishment of a Statistical, Economic and Social Research Centre' (7 ICFM, Istanbul, 1976), *Resolutions*, 79; 'Resolution on the Establishment of an Islamic Historical, Art and Cultural Research Centre in Istanbul' (7 ICFM), *Resolutions*, 81; 'Resolution on the Establishment of an Islamic Centre for Technical and Vocational Training in Dacca' (8 ICFM, Tripoli, 1977), *Resolutions*, 124; 'Decision to establish an Islamic Centre for Development of Trade in Tangiers' (Summit Conference, 1981), see 2 *JECIC* (1981), no. 3, 7, etc.

198. See 'Joint Communiqué', in *Resolutions*, 12.
199. The provisions of Art. VII (1) could in practice give leverage to States with substantial financial contributions and thus create factual inequality in the voting power of members in contravention of Art. II (*B*) 1.
200. Art. V (2) *e*. 2 stipulating 'three assistants' has been amended to read 'four assistants', three of them representing the regional groupings of the OIC and the fourth for Jerusalem.
201. So far there have been four Secretaries-General of the OIC, the first from Malaysia, the second from Egypt, the third from Senegal, the fourth from Tunisia, and the fifth and present one, H. E. Syed S. Pirzada, from Pakistan. By virtue of Art. VI (1) as amended, the Secretary-General holds office for a term of four years only.
202. Such as the Political, Economic, and Legal Affairs departments.
203. So far several subsidiary organs of the General Secretariat have been set up. The most prominent ones are the Islamic Chamber of Commerce, Industry, and Commodity Exchange (Karachi); the Islamic Centre for Development of Trade (Tangiers); the Statistical, Economic, and Social Research and Training Centre for Islamic Countries (Ankara); and the Islamic Centre for Technical and Vocational Training and Research (Dacca).
204. Initially set up as a Committee of Representatives and Experts to deliberate on Economic Matters by the second Islamic Summit Conference held in 1974, the seventh Islamic Conference of Foreign Ministers held in 1976 in Istanbul resolved to expand its original membership of eight countries to eighteen and rename it the 'Islamic Commission of Economic, Cultural, and Social Affairs'. It is patterned on the UN ECOSOC and acts as a review and implementing body, meeting at the ambassadorial level.
205. So far there have been expert groups on Shipping, Civil Aviation, Telecommunications, Meteorology, and Joint Ventures.
206. Some renowned experts and scholars on Islamic affairs in Western countries have come to perceive the OIC as a kind of Saudi-Pakistani joint venture, see D. Khalid *et al.*, 'Reislamisierung und Entwicklungspolitik: Forschungsberichte des Bundesministeriums für wirtschaftliche Zusammenarbeit' (1982), 30. 106, whereas others from the Socialist bloc seem to observe a perpetual tussle going on between pro-imperialist, reactionary forces on the one side and revolutionary-progressive states on the other, see R. Voigtländer and K. Höhne, 'Organisation der Islamischen Konferenz', 26 *Deutsche Außenpolitik* (1981), 120. The latter view is also held to some extent by Khalid, op. cit.; it is further claimed by Khalid, op. cit., that Saudi Arabia uses the OIC to extend its religious and financial influence by supporting conservative forces in the Islamic world. Given the loose constitutional character of the OIC, every Member State is sovereign in its decisions to implement any joint policy

decided upon by the OIC. And we have come to the conclusion that the principle of sovereignty gives the right to every Member State to decide what to implement, when and where. That Islamic and Arab States, after years of bitter squabbling, have come to sit at one table to consult is an achievement in itself. Furthermore, the General Secretariat does develop independent positions and proposals which are not acceptable to financial bodies of Member States, see 3 *JECIC* (1982), 53.

207. See ch. 3.2 above and also n. 41 for the text of the reservation expressed by the former Government of Iran.
208. See Case Concerning United States Diplomatic and Consular Staff in Tehran, *ICJ Rep.* (1980), 44-5.
209. See M. C. Bassiouni, 'Protection of Diplomats under Islamic Law', 74 *AJIL* (1980), 609-33; also cf. the brief summary given by Judge Tarazi in his dissenting opinion, *ICJ Rep.* (1980), 59-60.
210. Cited in *ICJ Rep.* (1980), 8.
211. As the majority of the Court reasoned, *ICJ Rep.* (1980), 38.
212. See dissenting opinion of Judge Tarazi, *ICJ Rep.* (1980), 58-65.
213. Ibid., 65; see also dissenting opinion of J. Mozorov, *ICJ Rep.* (1980), 51-7.
214. By R. Falk, 'The Iran Hostage Crisis: Easy Answers and Hard Questions', 74 *AJIL* (1980), 412 ff.; see also B. V. A. Röling, 'Aspects of the Case Concerning US Diplomatic and Consular Staff in Tehran', 11 *NYIL* (1980), 152-3.
215. See Point I: Non-Intervention in Iranian Affairs in the 'Declaration of the Government of the Democratic and Popular Republic of Algeria', reproduced in 75 *AJIL* (1981), 418, 419-32. On the legal aspects of the holding of hostages in Tehran Embassy, see L. Gross, 'The Case Concerning United States Diplomatic and Consular Staff in Tehran', 74 *AJIL* (1980), 315-410; L. C. Green, 'The Tehran Embassy Incident', 19 *AdV* (1980/1), 1-22; K. Grzybowski, 'The Regime of Diplomacy and the Tehran Hostages', 30 *ICLQ* (1981), 42-58; A. Jeffery, 'The American Hostages in Tehran', 30 *ICLQ* (1981), 717-29, also dealing with the legality of the (US) rescue mission.

Notes to Chapter 4

1. See 'Declaration on the Establishment of a New International Economic Order', *UNGA Res.* 3201 (S-VI), 1 May 1974 and 'Programme of Action on the Establishment of a New International Economic Order', *UNGA Res.* 3202 (S-VI), 1 May 1974, ch. vii; also cf. the Report by the UNCTAD Secretary-General at the fifth session in Manila, entitled 'Restructuring the international economic framework', Doc. TD/221, also reproduced in *Proceedings* of UNCTAD, fifth session, vol. iii, Basic Documentation (1981), hereinafter cited as *Proceedings*.

2. In the Report of UNCTAD Secretary-General to the 1976 Nairobi Conference the concept of 'collective self-reliance' was presented as an additive rather than a substitutive relationship. See 'New Directions and New Structures for Trade and Development', Doc. TD/183/Rev. 1, cited in Doc. TD/B/C, 7/14 (1978), 2, para. 4; see also Report of the UNCTAD Secretary-General to the fifth session in Manila, in *Proceedings*, 11-12.
3. Since 1976 a good deal of attention has been given to the problem, a lot of action groups being set up, which in turn have adopted a variety of action programmes. Meetings have generally been held at the Ministerial and Heads of State level, such as the third Ministerial Meeting of the Group of 77 held at Manila in 1976, the fifth Conference of Heads of State or Government of Non-Aligned Countries in Colombo, 1976, and in Havana, 1979, the Conference on Economic Co-operation among Developing Countries in Mexico City, 1976, and in Caracas, 1981, to mention just a few. See also statement by Mr Gamani Corea, Secretary-General of UNCTAD at the Preparatory Meeting of Governmental Experts of Developing Countries on ECDC, Doc. TD/B/C, 7/39 (1980), Annex, 1, para. 4.
4. The official position of UNCTAD is that 'collective self-reliance is not inimical to global co-operation', Doc. TD/183, cited in Doc. TD/B/C, 7/14 (1978), 3; see also 'Economic Co-operation among Developing Countries: Priority Areas for Action-Issues and Approaches', Report by the UNCTAD Secretariat, Doc. TD/244, in *Proceedings*, 444.
5. See e.g. A. G. Frank, *Latin America: Underdevelopment or Revolution* (1969); S. Bodenheimer, 'Dependency and Imperialism: The Roots of Latin American Underdevelopment', in 4 *North American Congress for Latin America (NACLA) Newsletter*, no. 3 (1970), 18-27; S. J. Stein and B. H. Stein, *The Colonial Heritage of Latin America: Essays on Economic Dependence in Perspective* (1970); D. Senghaas (ed.), *Imperialismus und strukturelle Gewalt: Analysen über abhängige Reproduktion* (1978); T. T. Evers and P. von Wogau, ' "dependencia": lateinamerikanische Beiträge zur Theorie der Unterentwicklung', 79 *Das Argument* (1973), no. 4-6, 404-54.
6. See e.g. S. Amin, *Accumulation on a World Scale. A Critique of the Theory of Underdevelopment* (1974), i-ii; id., *Unequal Development: An Essay on the Social Formations of Peripheral Capitalism* (1976); id., 'Zur Theorie von Akkumulation und Entwicklung in der gegenwärtigen Weltgesellschaft', in D. Senghaas (ed.), *Peripherer Kapitalismus: Analysen über Abhängigkeit und Unterentwicklung* (1977), 71-97; D. Senghaas, *Weltwirtschaftsordnung und Entwicklungspolitik: Plädoyer für Dissoziation* (1978).
7. For a critique of the 'Dissociation' strategy, as developed by Amin and Senghaas, see G. Simonis, 'Autozentrierte Entwicklung und kapitalistisches Weltsystem–Zur Kritik der Theorie der abhängigen Reproduktion', 5/6 *Peripherie* (1981), 32-48.

8. At the fourth session of UNCTAD in Nairobi, 1976, authority was given to establish a Committee on ECDC as part of the permanent machinery of UNCTAD. The Committee, which was set up by a consensual decision of the Trade and Development Board (decision 142 (XVI) of 23 Oct. 1976) held its first session in May 1977. The Committee encompasses the full membership of UNCTAD comprising the developed countries, the Socialist countries, and the Group of 77 (developing countries).
9. Cf. Report of the Committee on ECDC in its first session, Doc. TD/B/652 (1977) cited in 'Measures of Support by the UNCTAD Secretariat in the Field of ECDC', Progress Report by UNCTAD Secretariat, Doc. TD/B/C, 7/11 (1978), 2.
10. Other areas include the establishment of export credit and export credit guarantee schemes; co-operation in the transfer and development of technology; the transit and transportation problems of developing land-locked and island countries; insurance and reinsurance schemes among developing countries; promotion of capital flows and the establishment of multinational production enterprises; see Doc. TD/B/C, 7/11, op. cit.
11. See e.g. UNCTAD, 'Steps to be taken to facilitate the carrying out of UNCTAD's programme of work on ECDC', Doc. TD/B/C, 7/14 (1978), 3-6.
12. 'Preferential trade measures within the integration and co-operation schemes of the ESCAP and ECWA regions', study prepared at the request of UNCTAD Secretariat by F. Uddin, Doc. TD/B/C, 7/19; 'Measures and arrangements for the promotion of trade in commodities and other agricultural products within a global system of trade preferences among developing countries', study prepared by J. B. Kelegama, Doc. TD/B/C, 7/20 and Add. 1; 'Experience to date with preferential measures in the context of Latin American integration schemes: Review aimed at deriving suggestions for a global system of trade preferences', by F. Pena, Doc. TD/B/C, 7/22 and Add. 1; 'Monetary and Financial Co-operation in support of the programme of trade preferences', report prepared by R. L. Martinez, Doc. TD/B/C, 7/27; 'Trade preferences of the African economic co-operation and integration groupings', study prepared at the request of UNCTAD Secretariat by M. Yadi, Doc. TD/B/C, 7/32; 'Rules of Origin within a global system of trade preferences, with special reference to provisions ensuring that preferential measures benefit national development, Part I: Main approaches and concepts, Part II: Review of origin systems within existing preference schemes and their compatibility with the origin rules of a global system of trade preferences' study prepared by G. Valenzuela, Doc. TD/B/C, 7/33; 'Special, differential and non-reciprocal measures in favour of least developed countries within a global system of trade

preferences among developing countries', report by UNCTAD Secretariat, Doc. TD/B/C, 7/35 and Add. 1; 'Issues for consideration in preparing for GSTP negotiations', Doc. TD/B/C, 7/42; Measures to counterbalance the loss of customs and fiscal revenues that might ensue for least developed countries from the introduction of GSTP', Doc. TD/B/C, 7/46; 'Review of the preferential arrangements established under the GATT Protocol relating to Trade Negotiations among Developing Countries', study prepared by M. A. Hamza, Doc. TD/B/C, 7/49.

13. 'Co-operation among State trading organizations in Latin America', study prepared by Sanchez and E. Ostoloza, Doc. TD/B/C, 7/16; 'Co-operation among State trading organizations of Asian developing countries', report prepared by B. R. Bhandari, Doc. TD/B/C, 7/17; 'Co-operation among State trading organizations of sub-Saharan African developing countries', Doc. TD/B/C, 7/18, and 'Co-operation among developing countries in English-speaking Africa', Doc., op. cit., Add. 1, and 'Co-operation among State marketing companies in French-speaking Africa south of Sahara', Doc., op. cit., Add. 2; 'Co-operation among State trading organizations of Arab countries', report prepared by M. K. Anous, Doc. TD/B/C, 7/37; 'Possibilities for co-operation among STOs in fertilizer trade', Doc. TD/B/C, 7/52; 'International trade in tin and copper', Doc. TD/B/C, 7/53; 'International trade in the field of Sugar', Doc. TD/B/C, 7/54.
14. This concept is not to be confused with transnational corporations. It is a multinational States' enterprise with multinational capital, multinational decision-making power, and multinational economic co-operation objectives. See 'Juridical aspects of the establishment of multinational marketing enterprises among developing countries', Doc. TD/B/C, 7/28 (1978), 3, para. 11; 'Juridical regimes for the establishment of multinational enterprises among developing countries organized in integration and economic co-operation groupings', Doc. TD/B/C, 7/30 and Add. 1; 'Report of the Round Table on the Role of Transnational Enterprises in the Latin American Integration Process', Doc. TD/B/C, 7/29; 'Some Aspects of Multinational Marketing Enterprises in Africa: report prepared at the request of UNCTAD Secretariat by F. Liondjo, Doc. TD/B/C, 7/34; 'Latin American Multinational Enterprises: An analytical compendium', Doc. TD/B/C, 7/50.
15. See Doc. TD/B/C, 7/41 (1980), 5, para. 14, action-oriented proposals relating to UNCTAD's work programme on ECDC based on the Arusha Programme.
16. See 'Report of the Preparatory Meeting of Governmental Experts of Developing Countries on Economic Co-operation among Developing Countries', Doc. TD/B/C, 7/39 (1980), 3-5, 14-17.
17. As promoted by the UNCTAD Secretariat, see 'Steps to be taken to

facilitate the carrying out of UNCTAD's Programme of Work on ECDC', Doc. TD/B/C, 7/14 (1978), 5-6, paras. 19-21; also emphasized during the fifth session of UNCTAD in Manila, see 'Evaluation of the world trade and economic situation and consideration of issues, policies, and appropriate measures to facilitate structural changes in the international economy', Doc. TD/224, and Add. 1 reproduced in *Proceedings*, 25, para. 36; see also 'Comprehensive measures required to expand and diversify the export trade of developing countries in manufactures and semi-manufactures', Doc. TD/230, reproduced in *Proceedings*, 139-57.

18. For supporters of the inward-looking strategy see I. Sachs, 'Outward-Looking Strategies: A Dangerous Illusion?', in P. Streeten (ed.), *Trade Strategies for Development* (1973), 51-61; O. Aboyade, 'Advancing Tropical African Development: A Defence of Inward-Looking Strategy', in Streeten, op. cit., 62-75; N. Islam, 'National Import Substitution and Inward-Looking Strategies: Policies of Less Developed Countries', in Streeten, op. cit., 76-92. A possible forerunner stressing the combination of outward-looking trade with a revision of existing development strategies and formulating an alternative as recommended by UNCTAD for the 1980s could have been M. ul Haq, 'Industrialisation and Trade Policies in the 1970s: Developing Country Alternatives', in Streeten, op. cit., 93-102, esp. 101.
19. Both the developed market economy countries and the Socialist countries of Eastern Europe have been called upon to lend support to the work programme of ECDC. See Doc. TD/B/C, 7/14 (1978), 8, para. 28 ff.
20. See 'Report of the Committee on ECDC', Doc. TD/B/C, 7/44, reproduced as Doc. TD/B/818, Supplement 4 (1981).
21. Cf. the statement made by the spokesman of Group B at the special session of the ECDC Committee, Doc. TD/B/818, op. cit., 4, para. 16.
22. Doc. TD/B/818 (1981), op. cit., 10, para. 49.
23. Doc. TD/B/818, op. cit., 9, para. 45. Group D (consisting of the Socialist bloc) welcomed the efforts of the developing countries to launch ECDC and expressed the hope that ECDC would not lead 'to any form of isolation of developing countries from the results of the international division of labour, or to discrimination against Socialist countries in their relations with developing countries'. See p. 9, para. 47. The representative of China stated that his delegation understood the position of the Group of 77 and supported the willingness of that group to pursue co-operation among developing countries. See Doc., op. cit., 10, para. 50.
24. Cf. 'Declaration of the Rabat Islamic Summit Conference' (1969), reproduced in *Resolutions*, 4.
25. Art. II (*A*), 2 reads 'to consolidate co-operation among Member States in the economic, social, cultural, scientific and other vital fields of activities'.

26. The plan of action was drawn up at a high-level meeting of Member States held in Ankara from 4-6 Nov. 1980 to examine the economic prospects of the Islamic countries during the Third Development Decade. For text see Resolution no. 1/3-E (1981) on the 'Plan of Action to Strengthen Economic Co-operation Among Member States', reproduced in 2 *Journal of Economic Co-operation Among Islamic Countries* (April 1981), no. 3, 9-14, published by the Statistical, Economic, and Social Research and Training Centre for Islamic Countries (SESRTCIC) in Ankara, and hereinafter cited as *JECIC.*
27. See 'A Long-Term Strategy for Development and Co-operative Communal Action for the Members of the Islamic Conference', 1 *JECIC* (Jan. 1980),no. 2, 15. The idea of co-ordination of economic policies among Islamic countries has been advocated by Muslim scholars for some time. See e.g. A. K. Katanani, 'Co-ordination of Economic Policy Among Muslim Countries', in Association of Muslim Social Scientists (ed.), *Outlines of Islamic Economics* (1977), 57-65; A. A. Quraishi, 'Problems and Prospects of Co-ordinating Common Economic Policies among Muslim Countries', in AMSS (ed.), op. cit., 66-74; H. M. Nazer, 'The Goal and Strategy of Economic Development for the Muslim World', in Islamic Council of Europe (ed.), *The Muslim World and the Future Economic Order* (1979), 165-73; E. Rashid, 'Development Strategy for the Muslim World', in ICE, op. cit., 194-8; S. Husain, 'Financial and Economic Co-operation among Muslim Countries', in ICE, op. cit., 316-35.
28. See 'A Long-term Strategy for Development', op. cit., 16; 'Plan of Action', op. cit., 10-13; 'Joint Ventures and Islamic Economic Co-operation: Concepts and Issues', 1 *JECIC* (July 1980), no. 4, 9-13; 'Foreign Trade of Islamic Countries: The Present State and Problems', 2 *JECIC* (Oct. 1980), no. 1, 5-10; 'Multilateral Clearing Arrangements, Economic Co-operation and Promotion of Trade Among Developing Countries', 2 *JECIC* (Oct. 1980), no. 1, 37-49; 'Technical Co-operation Among Member States of the Islamic Conference', 2 *JECIC* (Jan. 1981), no. 2, 5-19; 'The Exchange of Manpower and Social Security Systems in Islamic Countries', 2 *JECIC* (July 1981), no. 4, 3-17; A. N. M. A. Rahman, 'Co-operation between Financial Institutions in Member Countries to Finance Trade and to Support Local Islamic Banks: the Role of the Islamic Development Bank', 3 *JECIC* (Jan. 1982), no. 2, 3-5; 'Industrial Co-operation Among OIC Member Countries', 3 *JECIC* (July 1980), no. 4, 11-17.
29. Cf. Islamic Development Bank, 'Sixth Annual Report', 1401 H, corresponding to Nov. 1980-Oct. 1981 (1982), 28; 'A Long-term Strategy for Development', op. cit., 14; A. M. El Banna, 'Economic and Financial Resources in the Muslim World and their Effective Utilisation', in ICE, op. cit., 155-64; A. S. Heiba, 'Agricultural Resources in the Muslim World–Capacity and Future Growth', in ICE, op. cit., 296-315; M. K.

Hussain, 'Efficient and Productive Utilization of Economic and Financial Resources in the Muslim World and Prospects of Trade among Muslim Countries', in Islamic Economics Research Bureau (ed.), *Thoughts on Islamic Economics* (1980), 182-200; A. F. M. A. Rahman, 'The Resources of the Muslim World and its Effective Utilisation', in IERB, op. cit., 201-7; M. Y. Ali, 'Optimal Utilisation of Resources and Maximisation of Production in Islam', in IERB, op. cit., 218-27.

30. Despite a steady decline and increasing chances of deficits in current-account surpluses, a majority of OPEC member countries have continued providing aid and investment in other developing countries through national aid institutions such as Abu Dhabi Fund for Arab Economic Development (ADFAED)l Iraq Fund for External Development (IFED), Kuwait Fund for Arab Economic Development (KFAED), and the Saudi Fund for Development (SFD), and through multilateral institutions such as the OPEC Special Fund, Arab Fund for Economic and Social Development (AFESD), Arab Bank for Economic Development in Africa (BADEA), etc. For details see 'Financial Solidarity for Development: Efforts and Institutions of the Members of OPEC, 1973-1976 Review', UNCTAD Doc. TD/B/C, 7/31, (1979), i. 4-5.
31. Cf. Doc. TD/B/C, 7/31, op. cit., 5.
32. Outlines of such co-operation have been set out in the 'Plan of Action', 2 *JECIC* (April 1981), no. 3, 11; on the role of the Islamic Development Bank, see A. M. Ali, 'The Role of the Islamic Development Bank in the Future', in ICE, op. cit., 336-42; A. N. M. A. Rahman, 'Co-operation between Financial Institutions', in 3 *JECIC* (Jan. 1982), no. 2; IDB, 'Sixth Annual Report', op. cit., 30-1; and the 'Agreement for Promotion, Protection and Guarantee of Investments in Member Countries', the provisions of which are discussed in detail, see ch. 5.4.
33. Out of forty-one member countries of the IDB, sixteen are least developed countries; nine are OPEC members, and the remainder in the middle-income range. See IDB,'Sixth Annual Report', op. cit., 18; see also 'The World Economy in 1981 with special reference to Islamic countries', 3 *JECIC* (Apr. 1982), no. 3, 3-14.
34. Nienhaus, *Islam und moderne Wirtschaft*, 167-8; IDB, 'Sixth Annual Report', op. cit., 23-8; 'Foreign Trade of Islamic Countries', 2 *JECIC* (Oct. 1980), no. 1, 5-10; being producers of primary goods, the dominant trade pattern is developing-developed country orientation.
35. See 'Industrial Co-operation Among the OIC Member Countries', 3 *JECIC* (July 1982), no. 4, 13-17.
36. See 'An Examination of Priorities in National Development Plans of Islamic Countries', 4 *JECIC* (Oct. 1982), no. 1, 25-33, tables at 44-51.
37. See 'Industrial Co-operation', op. cit., 16-17.
38. Generally speaking a free trade area implies the abolition of tariffs only among the members, a customs union is characterized by the existence of

a common tariff policy towards third parties and a common market is an intensive form of integration, permitting free flow of commodities and factors of production.

39. Economic integration schemes among developing countries were first initiated in Latin America in the 1960s. Cf. 'Economic Co-operation and Integration Among Developing Countries: A Review of Recent Developments in subregional, regional, and interregional organizations and arrangements', report by the UNCTAD Secretariat, vol. i, Latin America Doc. TD/B/C, 7/51, Part I (1982); for similar developments in Africa, see Doc., op. cit., vol. ii, Africa (1982), Part II.
40. For a brief survey of some selected arrangements among OIC Member States see 'Multilateral Clearing Arrangements, Economic Co-operation and Promotion of Trade Among Developing Countries', 2 *JECIC* (Oct. 1980), no. 1, 37-49.
41. Multilateral monetary (payments) arrangements have been basically classified as (i) clearing arrangements, consisting of payment mechanisms simplifying and facilitating foreign trade transactions; (ii) credit arrangements, providing substantive amounts of credit as balance of payments support to members; and (iii) monetary unions, involving a complete pooling of monetary reserves and substantial integration of financial markets and national monetary policies. This classification has been borrowed from R. F. Khan *et al.*, 'The Contribution of Payments Arrangements to Trade Expansion', in P. Robson (ed.), *International Economic Integration* (1972), also cited in 'Clearing Arrangements', op. cit., 41-3.
42. Notable integrative schemes with OIC Member States' participation are: Common Afro-Mauritian Organization (OCAM); West African Economic Community (CEAO); Economic Community of West African States (ECOWAS); Mano River Union (MRU); Council of the Entente States; West African Monetary Union (UMOA); Central African Customs and Economic Union (UDEAC); Eastern and Southern African Preferential Trade Area (ESAPTA); for details see UNCTAD Doc. TD/B/C, 7/51 Part II (1982), op. cit.
43. For instance, Bangladesh, Indonesia, Iran, Malaysia, Pakistan, and Turkey are participating in the following sub-regional arrangements: Regional Co-operation for Development (RCD, Turkey, Iran, and Pakistan); Association of South East Asian Nations (ASEAN, Malaysia and Indonesia); Bangkok Agreement (Bangladesh); Asian Clearing Union (ACU, Bangladesh, Iran, Pakistan).
44. Among Arab States the following sub-regional schemes are noteworthy: Council of Arab Economic Unity (CAEU); Arab Common Market (ACM); Permanent Consultative Committee of the Maghreb (CPCM); Gulf Co-operation Council (GCC); Arab Monetary Fund (AMF); and the Arab Fund for Economic and Social Development (AFESD).

45. For example the Latin American Free Trade Association (LAFTA); Central American Common Market (CACM); Caribbean Development and Co-operation Committee (CDCC); Caribbean Community (CARICOM); East Caribbean Common Market (ECCM); Andean Common Market (ACM); Treaty for Amazonian Co-operation (TAC); for details of these sub-regional integration schemes and other financial institutions, see UNCTAD Doc. TD/B/C, 7/51 (Part I), Latin America, op. cit.
46. There are two interregional organizations in Latin America: the first one is the Latin American Economic System (SELA) which is envisaged as an advisory body dealing with co-operation, consultation, and inter-regional co-ordination. The constituent agreement establishing SELA entered into force in June 1976; the second one is the Latin American Integration Association (LAIA), established in March 1981 and which replaces the Latin American Free Trade Association (LAFTA) established by the 1960 Treaty of Montevideo. The LAFTA agreement continues to apply to signatory States which have not yet ratified the LAIA treaty. While LAFTA's membership consisted of the countries of South America and Mexico, LAIA is open to all Latin American States. The short-term objective of LAIA is the establishment of an economic preference area, whereas the long-term objective is the establishment of a Latin American Common Market. Cf. UNCTAD Doc. TD/B/C, 7/51, op. cit., 3-28.
47. The Final Act of Lagos and the Lagos Plan of Action, adopted by the OAU Assembly of Heads of State and Government in Apr. 1980, envisage the establishment of new regional structures and the strengthening of existing structures in order to set up an African Common Market as a first step towards the creation of an African Economic Community by the year 2000. See UNCTAD Doc. TD/B/C, 7/51, Part II (1982), 3, paras. 16 and 17.
48. See 'Report of the Working Party on Trade Expansion and Regional Economic Integration Among Developing Countries' second session, 28 June-2 July 1982, Geneva, Doc. TD/B/C, 7/55 (1982), 16.
49. 'Report', op. cit., 16, 6.
50. This is one of the conclusions drawn by the Working Party on Trade Expansion and Regional Economic Integration, see 'Report', op. cit., 10. Other conclusions were the need for flexible trade preferential schemes taking into account disparities in the level of development of participating countries, the need for an appropriate flow of information, the crucial importance of telecommunications and fiscal infrastructures, and the need to co-ordinate monetary and exchange rate policies among participating countries.
51. Hereinafter cited as the General Agreement. For text of the treaty see Appendix II.

52. Hereinafter cited as Investment Agreement. For text see Appendix III.
53. See Resolution no. 9/7, E reproduced in *Resolutions*, 88.
54. See Resolution no. 1/8, E on the General Agreement, reproduced in *Resolutions*, 107, with annexed text of the Agreement, at 110-13. The General Agreement came into effect by June 1981 (see Resolution, no. 19, E of the twelfth ICFM held in Baghdad). By Aug. 1982, thirty-six Member States had signed the General Agreement of which the following twenty-four Member States had also ratified it: Bahrain, Bangladesh, Comoro Islands, Egypt, Guinea, Indonesia, Iraq, Jordan, Kuwait, Libyan Jamahiriya, Malaysia, Mali, Mauritania, Morocco, Niger, Oman, Pakistan, Palestine, Qatar, Saudi Arabia, Senegal, Syria, Tunisia, and United Arab Emirates. See 'Status of the Signing, Ratification and Implementation of the General Agreement', Doc. ICFM/13-82/EC/D, 24, 361, hereinafter cited as Status Report of the General Agreement (1982).
55. Cf. provisions of Art. 31 (2) of the Vienna Convention on the Law of Treaties which underlines the importance of taking the Preamble into consideration for the purpose of interpretation; also cf. Menzel and Ipsen, op. cit., 318; Fitzmaurice, 'The Law and the Procedure of the International Court of Justice 1951-1954', 229; L. Dischler, 'Präambel', in *WVR*, ii. 790-1.
56. This position may be contrasted with the Agreement on Arab Economic Unity (1957) which purported to establish 'a complete economic unity'. For translated text of the Agreement see UN Doc. TD/B/609/Add. 1, v. 8-14.
57. See *Osborn's Concise Law Dictionary* (1976), 63; H. Frick, *Bilateraler Investitionsschutz in Entwicklungsländern* (1975), 113, for the term 'capital' as used in the US Treaties of Friendship, Commerce and Navigation; also cf. ch. 5.4.3.2.
58. Cf. Art. 1 (5) of the OIC Investment Agreement, also discussed in ch. 5.4.3.3; see Frick, op. cit., 113-14 and 178 ff.; H. Walker, 'Treaties for the Encouragement and Protection of Foreign Investment: Present US Practice', 5 *AJCL* (1956), 292; Alenfeld, *Die Investitionsverträge der Bundesrepublik Deutschland*, 28-35; H. Jüttner, *Förderung und Schutz deutscher Direktinvestitionen* (1975), 245-8; S. Beyer, *Der diplomatische Schutz der Aktionäre im Völkerrecht* (1977), 164-6, 174-80.
59. Cf. M. Brandon, 'Legal Deterrents and Incentives to Private Foreign Investments', 43 *Trans. Grot. S.* (1957), 39-60; J. Baumann, 'Neuere Tendenzen in der Investitionsgesetzgebung der Entwicklungsländer', 5 *AWD* (1959), 237-40; W. Friedmann and R. C. Pugh (eds.), *Legal Aspects of Foreign Investment* (1959), 741 ff.; H. Goltz, 'Voraussetzungen, Vorteile und Hindernisse privater Kapitalanlagen in Entwicklungsländer', *Der Betrieb*, Beilage no. 20/65 zu Heft 46 (19 Nov. 1965); E. I. Nwoguga, *The Legal Problems of Foreign Investments in Developing Countries* (1965), 34 ff.; Frick, op. cit., 39-40; Jüttner, op. cit., 74-9 and 124-8.

60. See *Osborn's Concise Law Dictionary*, 159.
61. Capital-importing States have usually provided legislative 'guarantees' and concluded bilateral investment agreements with capital-exporting countries, see Frick, op. cit., 34-5, 56; Jüttner, op. cit., 124 ff., and 222 ff., 257; Alenfeld, op. cit., 21-6; see also provisions of the Investment Agreement of the OIC which is described in ch. 4.5. The Member States of the Council of Arab Economic Unity have concluded a multilateral Agreement on Investment and Free Movement of Arab Capital among Arab Countries, see UNCTAD, Doc. TD/B/609, Add. 1, v. 15-20.
62. Cf. M. von Neumann-Whitman, *The US Investment Guaranty Program and Private Foreign Investment* (1959); R. Seymour, The Investment Guaranty Programme of the United States', *Proc. ASIL* (1962), 77 ff.; Philipps, 'Insurance of Overseas Investment–the Australian Scheme', in G. Starke (ed.), *The Protection and Encouragement of Private Foreign Investment* (1966), 119 ff.; Higgins, *Conflict of Interests*, 66 ff.; Alenfeld, op. cit., 27 ff.; Frick, op. cit., 53-9; Jüttner, op. cit., 105 ff.; Greig, *International Law*, 567; A. A. Akinsanya, *The Expropriation of Multinational Property in the Third World* (1980), 329-31; for a discussion of international guarantee schemes, see A. Broches, 'International Investment Guarantees', *Proc. ASIL* (1962), 81 ff.; W. C. Brewer, 'The Proposal for Investment Guarantees by an International Agency', 58 *AJIL* (1964), 62 ff.; W. Schulz-Thurmann, 'Internationaler Guarantiefonds', *Der Volkswirt* (1961), 2078 ff.; D.-M. Polter, *Auslandsenteignungen und Investitionsschutz* (1975), 161 ff.
63. Cf. W. Friedmann and G. Kalamanoff (eds.), *Joint International Business Ventures* (1961); W. Friedmann and J. P. Beguin, *Joint International Business Ventures in Developing Countries: Case Studies and Analysis of Recent Trends* (1971); C. Uhlig, 'Industrial Production Co-operation as Instrument of Development Policy', in K. Hottes and C. Uhlig (eds.), *Joint Ventures in Asien* (1983), 1-16; D. Ahn, 'Indigenisierungstendenzen und Joint Venture Praxis in ASEAN-Ländern', in Hottes and Uhlig, op. cit., 277-306, see also his other publication, *Gemeinschaftsunternehmen in* Entwicklungsländern: Joint Ventures als Entwicklungsinstrument in den ASEAN-Staaten (1981); C. Uhlig and M. Lange, *Internationale Produktionskooperation im Vorderen Orient: Joint Ventures und andere Formen der unternehmerischen Zusammenarbeit* (1983); DEG (ed.), *Investitionen in Entwicklungsländern* (1980), 6 ff.; DEG, *Geschäftsbericht 1981* (1982), 18-25; see also 'Joint Ventures and Islamic Economic Co-operation: Concepts and Issues', 1 *JECIC* (July 1980), 9-13.
64. See ch. 4.2.
65. Among the seriously affected Member States with decreased agricultural output due to severe weather conditions, such as drought and floods, are Chad, Niger, Upper Volta, Mali, Mauritania, Senegal, Gambia, Somalia, and Bangladesh. See IDB, 'Sixth Annual Report', 1401 H (1980-1), 19.

66. This view has been endorsed by the third Summit Conference held in Mecca in 1981. See 'Plan of Action To Strengthen Economic Co-operation Among Member States', reproduced in 2 *JECIC* (Apr. 1981), no. 3, 10-14, which calls for a 'balanced development of the agricultural and industrial sectors of the economies of Member States' at p. 10.
67. The essential nature of constant reorientation in international trade patterns cannot be over-emphasized; bilateral agreements strengthening economic ties concluded between Morocco and Kuwait show that by importing Morocco's vegetables, meat, and citrus fruits, Kuwait has to some extent replaced the European customers Morocco lost with the admission of Spain and Greece, two citrus fruit growing and exporting countries, to the EEC. See report in 1 *JECIC* (Oct. 1979), no. 1, 13.
68. Here mention may be made of bilateral agreements between Mauritania and Senegal, Libyan Arab Jamahiriya and Mauritania, Morocco and Tunisia, Algeria and Tunisia, Libyan Arab Jamahiriya and Turkey, Libyan Arab Jamahiriya and Tunisia, and Jordan and Pakistan. Among multilateral agreements mention may be made of the Agreement on the Mobility of Labour within Member Countries of the Council of Arab Economic Unity, the OCAM Convention of 1971, and the Communal Convention for Social Security adopted by the UDEAC. See 'The Exchange of Manpower and Social Security Systems in Islamic Countries', 2 *JECIC* (July 1981), no. 4, 3-17.
69. For example the OCAM and UDEAC Conventions concluded between regional and sub-regional African States which consist of Member and non-Member States of the OIC. For the Council of Arab Economic Unity, which consists of Member States of the OIC, there would not be any basic impediment of implementing the priority stipulation of Art. 6 of the General Agreement. However, priority would most probably be given to nationals of Member States of the Council. Cf. 'Agreement on the Mobility of Labour within the Council Member Countries', UNCTAD, Doc. TD/B/609/Add. 1, v. 21-4, which provides in Art. IV that 'contracting parties shall pledge to give priority in work to Arab workers in conformity with each party's requirements'.
70. See W. Kewenig, *Der Grundsatz der Nichtdiskriminierung. Band I: Der Begriff der Diskriminierung* (1972), 25.
71. Cf. K. Hyder, *Equality of Treatment and Trade Discrimination in International Law* (1968), 14; H. Mosler, 'Zur Anwendung der Grundsatzartikel des Vertrages über die Europäische Gemeinschaft für Kohle und Stahl', 17 *ZaöRV* (1956-7), 418; H. Kipp, 'Das Verbot der Diskriminierung im modernen Völkerrecht', 9 *AdV* (1961-2), 141-2; Kewenig, op. cit., 196.
72. See Kewenig, op. cit., 32, 45, 50-1; Hyder, op. cit., 30; G. Jaenicke, Stichwort 'Diskriminierung' und 'Gleichbehandlung' in *WVR*, i. 391, 691; V. A. S. Muhammad, *The Legal Framework of World Trade* (1958), 126; G. Schwarzenberger, 'The Most-Favoured-Nation Standard in British

State Practice', 22 *BYIL* (1945), 103; H. Steinberger, *Gatt und regionale Wirtschaftszusammenschlüsse* (1963), 2-3.

73. See 'Treaty of Friendship, Commerce, and Navigation between the United States of America and the Federal Republic of Germany' (1954), Arts. XIV and XVI, text *BGBl* (1956), ii. 487 ff., also reproduced by R. R. Wilson, *United States Commercial Treaties and International Law* (1960), 335-55; see also the GATT, *UNTS* 55, 194 ff.; also cf. Kewenig, op. cit., 52.
74. See G. Jaenicke, *Der Begriff der Diskriminierung im modernen Völkerrecht* (1940), 32 ff., 37 and also in *WVR*, i. 390, 690; Kewenig, op. cit., 51-2, 60; Hyder, op. cit., 15; I. Bode, *Die Diskriminierungsverbote im EWG-Vertrag* (1968), 6; Kipp, op. cit., 143; E. Steindorff, *Der Gleichheitssatz im Wirtschaftsrecht des Gemeinsamen Marktes* (1965), 1; H. Zerr, 'Der Begriff der Diskriminierung im Vertrag über die Europäische Gemeinschaft für Kohle und Stahl' (Diss. Heidelberg, 1961), 3; E. Zimmermann, *Die Preisdiskriminierung im Recht der Europäischen Gemeinschaft für Kohle und Stahl* (1962), 51.
75. See Schwarzenberger, op. cit., 96 ff.; G. Jaenicke, Stichwort 'Meistbegünstigungsklausel', in *WVR*, ii. 497 ff.; P. Roesner, 'Die Meistbegünstigungsklausel in den bilateralen Handelsverträgen der Bundesrepublik Deutschland' (Diss. Heidelberg 1964); Kewenig, *Der Grundsatz*, 56.
76. Cf. Kewenig, op. cit., 56-60 who points out that 'Die Nichtdiskriminierungsklausel wurde im Gegensatz zur Meistbegünstigungs-oder Inländerklausel erst mit der zu Beginn der dreißiger Jahre um sich greifenden Praxis mengenmäßiger Außenhandelsbeschränkungen regelmäßiger Bestandteil der Handelsverträge, und zwar wurde sie verwendet, um deutlich zu machen, daß der Charakter des bekämpften Handelshindernisses einen anderen Mechanismus der Gleichbehandlung erforderte, als ihn traditionsgemäß die Meistbegünstigungsklausel zur Verfügung stellt', 59-60.
77. Ibid., 197-8.
78. Ibid., 70-2.
79. Cf. Arts. 20 and 21 of GATT, *UNTS*, 55, 194 ff., which provide for 'General Exceptions' and 'Security Exceptions' respectively.
80. Cf. Art. 19, GATT; Art. 15 (1) of the European Convention on Human Rights, reproduced by Brownlie, *Basic Documents*, 212.
81. See 'Foreign Trade of Islamic Countries: The Present State and Problems', 2 *JECIC* (Oct. 1980), no. 1, 8-10.
82. This falls under one of the exceptions to the rule of equal and non-discriminatory treatment mentioned above.
83. See Petersmann, *Wirtschaftsintegrationsrecht und Investitionsgesetzgebung der Entwicklungsländer*, 25; violations of principles laid down by the IMF have

led to reforms in order to accommodate the practice prevailing; see E. U. Petersmann, 'Völkerrechtliche Fragen der Weltwährungsreform', 34 *ZaöRV* (1974), 491 ff.; H. J. Hahn, 'Elemente einer neuen Weltwährungsordnung', in W. Kewenig (ed.), *Völkerrecht und internationale wirtschaftliche Zusammenarbeit* (1978), 215-40; also cf. J. Gold, 'Developments in the International Monetary System', 174 *RdC* (1982), i. 107 ff.

84. Cf. Petersmann, *Wirtschaftsintegrationsrecht*, 24, 17-19; Hahn, op. cit., 219 ff., 240.
85. Cf. C. Baysan, S. Karim and I. Ugurel, 'An Evaluation of the United Nations' Conference on Least Developed Countries', 3 *JECIC* (Oct. 1981), no. 1, 5-9.
86. The Plan of Action to Strengthen Economic Co-operation among Member States approved by the third Islamic Summit Conference in 1981 endorses this position by calling upon Member States to give 'special treatment . . . in favour of products of export interests to least developed Member States'. See 2 *JECIC* (Apr. 1981), no. 3, 11.
87. Doc. ICFM/13-82/EC/D, 24, 361-3, hereinafter cited as Status Report of the General Agreement (1982) and from which information on implementation of the General Agreement has been drawn.
88. See the text of the Plan of Action reproduced in 2 *JECIC* (Apr. 1981), no. 3, 13.
89. A subsidiary organ of the OIC, the Trade Centre was originally planned to be located in Tangiers. However, the Status Report of the General Agreement, 363, mentions its location as Casablanca.
90. According to the Status Report of the General Agreement, 363, the first Islamic Trade Fair was held in Istanbul in 1979, the second in Libya in 1983, and the third in the kingdom of Morocco in 1984-5.
91. See Plan of Action, 2 *JECIC* (1981), 11.

Notes to Chapter 5

1. Cf. Resolution no. 18/10 *E*, 'Agreement on Protection and Guarantee of Investments in Member States of the Islamic Conference', 10 ICFM, 8-12 May 1979, in *Resolutions*, 211.
2. See Resolution no. 7/11-*E*, 'Draft Agreement on the Protection and Guarantee of Investments in Member States', 11 ICFM, 17-22 May 1980.
3. Resolution no. 3/3-*E* (IS), third Islamic Summit, 25-8 Jan. 1981; see also 2 *JECIC* (1981), 8.
4. Cf. Resolution no. 7/12-*E*, 'Agreement on Promotion, Protection, and Guarantee of Investments', 12 ICFM, 1-5 June 1981.
5. Cf. G. Modelski (ed.), *Multinational Corporations and World Order* (1972), 9 n. 4; also cf. A. A. Said and L. R. Simmons (eds.), *The New Sovereigns: Multinational Corporations as World Powers* (1975); V. Bethke and

G. Koopmann, *Multinale Unternehmen und Entwicklungsländer* (1975); W. Schneider, *Direktinvestitionen und die Politik der Entwicklungsländer* (1974).

6. For various motives of expropriation in developing States, see Akinsanya, *The Expropriation of Multinational Property in the Third World*, 77-114.
7. Whereas total exclusion of alien economic participation may be achieved by measures of expropriation and nationalization, a systematic reduction of participation ranges from stipulating national majority participation by the host State to measures of 'indigenization'–i.e., limiting participation in a particular industry or sector of the economy to its nationals. See Akinsanya, op. cit., 4-7; for nationalizations and participation measures in OAPEC countries, see El-Gebali, op. cit., 112-18; on 'indigenization' measures carried out in African States see D. A. Ijalaye, 'Indigenization Measures and Multinational Corporations in Africa', 171 *RdC* (1981), ii. 11-79.
8. Cf. *UNGA Resolutions*, 523 (VI), 1952; 626 (VII), 1952; 837 (IX), 1954; 1314 (XIII), 1958; 1720 (XVI), 1961; 1803 (XVII), 1962; 2158 (XXI), 1966; 2386 (XXIII), 1968; 2692 (XXV), 1970; 3016 (XXVII), 1972; 3171 (XXVIII), 1973; and finally the assertion of sovereignty over natural resources climaxed in *UNGA Res.* 3201 (*S*-VI), 1974 and the Charter of Economic Rights and Duties of States, *Res.* 3281 (XXIX), 1974. A brief survey of the contents of these resolutions has been done by R. Kemper, *Nationale Verfügung über natürliche Ressourcen und die Neue Weltwirtschaftsordnung der Vereinten Nationen* (1976), 24-48; also cf. J. N. Hyde, 'Permanent Sovereignty over Natural Wealth and Resources', 50 *AJIL* (1956), 854 ff.; S. M. Schwebel, 'The Story of the UN Declaration on Permanent Sovereignty over Natural Resources', 49 *ABAJ* (1963), 463 ff., also reprinted in International and Comparative Law Center (Southwestern Foundation Dallas, Texas) (ed.), *Selected Readings on Protection by Law of Private Foreign Investments* (1964), 699 ff.; K. N. Gess, 'Permanent Sovereignty over Natural Resources: An analytical Review of the UN Declaration and its Genesis', 13 *ICLQ* (1964), 398 ff.; P. J. I. M. de Waart, 'Permanent Sovereignty over Natural Resources as a Cornerstone for International Economic Rights and Duties', 24 *NILR* (1977), 304 ff.; for declarations made by Islamic States within forums of the OIC, see Declaration of Lahore, second Islamic Summit Conference (1974), reproduced in *Resolutions*, 42; see also other resolutions endorsed by the fifth ICFM (1974), the sixth ICFM (1975), and the eighth ICFM (1977), in *Resolutions*, 49–52, 59-61, 118 respectively.
9. According to Art. 2 (2) 'Each State has the right:

   (*c*) to nationalize, expropriate or transfer ownership of foreign property, in which case appropriate compensation should be paid by the State adopting such measures, taking into account its relevant laws and regulations and all circumstances that the State considers pertinent. In any case where the question of compensation gives rise to a controversy, it shall be settled under the domestic law of the nationalizing State and by its tribunals, unless it is freely and mutually agreed by all States concerned that other peaceful means be sought on the basis of the sovereign equality of States and in accordance with the principle of free choice of means.'

For a brief survey of the attitudes of developing countries reflected in the working group set up to draft the Charter, see Ipsen, 'Entwicklung zur "collective economic security" ', 20-3; also cf. K. M. Meessen, 'Völkerrechtliches Enteignungsrecht im Nord-Süd Konflikt', in W. Kewenig (ed.), *Völkerrecht und internationale wirtschaftliche Zusammenarbeit* (1978), 11-33, 13 f.

10. These arrangements are usually of a bilateral nature as efforts to conclude a multilateral convention on the protection of foreign property have so far totally failed, see Higgins, *Conflict of Interests*, 66-7; Greig, op. cit., 567; Polter, op. cit., 33-6, maintains that the OECD Draft Convention on the Protection of Foreign Property may be seen as 'die offizielle Einschätzung der Rechtslage seitens der OECD-Mitglieder (außer Spanien und die Türkei)', at p. 34; also cf. A. S. Miller, 'Protection of Private Foreign Investment by Multilateral Convention', 53 *AJIL* (1959), 371 ff.; M. J. van Emde-Boas, 'The OECD Draft Convention on the Protection of Foreign Property', 1 *CMLR* (1963/4), 265 ff.

11. By 1 Jan. 1983 the following OIC Member States had become signatories to the 'Investitionsförderungsvertrag' of the FRG: Bangladesh (not yet in force), Cameroun, Chad, Egypt, Gabon, Guinea, Indonesia, Iran, Jordan, Malaysia, Mali, Mauritania (not yet in force), Morocco, Niger, Oman (not yet in force), Pakistan, Senegal, Sierra Leone, Somalia (not yet in force), Sudan, Syria, Tunisia, Turkey, Uganda, and the Arab Republic of Yemen. Furthermore, Iran, Oman, Pakistan, and the Arab Republic of Yemen are parties to the US Treaty of Friendship, Commerce and Navigation, also known as Treaty of Amity and Economic Relations.

12. Cf. G. Schwarzenberger, 'The Principles and Standards of International Economic Law', 117 *RdC* (1966), i, 5 ff.; Wilson, *United States Commercial Treaties and International Law*, 6 ff.; R. R. Wilson, *The International Law Standard in Treaties of the United States* (1953); Alenfeld, op. cit., 24 ff.; Frick, op. cit., 83 ff.

13. Cf. statements made by delegates of Kuwait and Iran at the occasion of the formulation of the Charter of Economic Rights and Duties of States, UN Doc. A/C, 2/SR 1642 (411), and 1650 (452); see also Meessen, op. cit., 23, 31.

14. The Agreement has been drawn up among Member States of the Council of Arab Unity. Original signatory States were Jordan, Sudan, Syria, Iraq, Kuwait, Egypt, and the Arab Republic of Yemen. For a translation of the original Arabic text see UNCTAD Doc. TD/B/609/Add. 1, v. 15-17.

15. UNCTAD Doc. TD/B/609/Add. 1, v. 15.
16. Ibid., 16.
17. Resolution no. 648 (22nd), 3 Dec. 1973, ibid., 17-20. The document attaches two translations of the Resolution with slightly varying wording.
18. As per Art. VI amended by Resolution 648, ibid.
19. See UNCTAD Doc. TD/B/609/Add. 1, v. 106-25, containing an Annex on Settlement of Disputes (125-8) arising after cessation of the Corporation's operations, or arising between the Corporation and a country that has withdrawn from the Convention or a member that has lost its membership (Art. 34, para. 2) at p. 122.
20. See Art. 2 of the Convention, ibid., 106.
21. Cf. Art. 8, paras. (*a*), (*b*), and (*c*), ibid., 115-16.
22. Ibid., 107.
23. Cf. Dicke, op. cit., 127; Petersmann, *Wirtschaftsintegrationsrecht*, 138; Grieg, op. cit., 443; G. Schwarzenberger, *Der Schutz von Auslandsinvestitionen* (1969), 23; *AIOC* v. *SUPOR*, in 24 *ILR* (1955), 41; Menzel and Ipsen, op. cit., 334; Liemen, op. cit., 193.
24. Cf. 'Arbitral Award in the Dispute between Libyan American Oil Company (LIAMCO) and the Government of the Libyan Arab Republic, sole Arbitrator, Dr Sobhi Mahmassani, in 20 *ILM* (1981), 1-87, in which the Arbitrator comes to the conclusion 'that the right of a state to nationalize its wealth and national resources is sovereign, subject to the obligation of indemnification for premature termination of concession agreements', at 85; also cf. F. A. Mann, 'State Contracts and State Responsibility', 54 *AJIL* (1960), 587; C. F. Amerasinghe, 'State Breaches of Contracts with Aliens and International Law', 58 *AJIL* (1964), 882 ff.; R. Geiger, 'The Unilateral Change of Economic Development Agreements', 23 *ICLQ* (1974); 88 ff; K. G. Borchers, *Verträgen von Staaten mit ausländischen Privatpersonen* (1966), 103; Liemen, op. cit., 193, 196; Art. 4 of the *UNGA Res.* 1803 (XVII), 1962, reproduced in Brownlie, *Basic Documents*, 142; de Waart, op. cit., 311.
25. Cf. M. Lange and C. Uhlig, *Internationale Produktionskooperation in Jordanien* (1982), 5, 32; M. Lange and C. Uhlig, *Aspekte der Produktionskooperation in Syrien* (1982); C. Uhlig and M. Lange, *Internationale Produktionskooperation im Vorderen Orient: Joint Ventures und andere Formen der unternehmerischen Zusammenarbeit* (1983).
26. This opinion was expressed by the Randall Commission on Foreign Economic Policy in its 'Report to the President and the Congress' (1954), cited by Wilson, *US Commercial Treaties*, 21; Alenfeld, op. cit., 25 n. 17.
27. See Alenfeld, op. cit., 20 n. 12; Jüttner, op. cit., 257 ff., 272.
28. Alenfeld, op. cit., 19-20; Jüttner, op. cit., 259.
29. See R. Berger, 'Vermögensschutz im Ausland durch Investitionsförderungsverträge', 11 *AWD* (1965), 1-11; Jüttner, op. cit., 271.

30. Hereinafter cited as the Investments Agreement or simply Agreement. For text see Appendix III below.
31. The Member States are Kuwait, Morocco, Pakistan, Sudan, and Palestine; see Status Report, Doc. ICFM/13-82/EC/D, 11, 198.
32. Cf. Resolution No. 11/13-*E*, Signature and Ratification of the Agreement, thirteenth ICFM, 22-6 Aug. 1982.
33. Several capital-importing and capital-exporting Member States, however, have yet to sign the Agreement.
34. Cf. *Osborn's Concise Law Dictionary*, 35.
35. For the use of the term 'capital' in the General Agreement cf. Art. 1 discussed in ch. 4.3.2 and notes 57 and 58.
36. See definitions contained in Art. 1 (6) of the Agreement and dealt with in ch. 5.4.3.4.
37. *Osborn's Concise Law Dictionary*, 225.
38. Ibid., 295.
39. Ibid., 76.
40. Cf. G. Schwarzenberger, *Foreign Investments and International Law* (1969), 17; Wortley, *Expropriation in Public International Law* (1959), 8 ff.; in the case of intangible rights, such as good will, the OIC Agreement goes beyond the limits of customary international law that perceived 'good will' to be 'subject to inevitable changes' and, therefore, belonging to 'transient circumstances'. See Oscar Chinn Case, *PCIJ*, Series A/B, no. 63, 88; also cf. K. E. Bäulcke, 'Die materiellen Eigentumsschutzbestimmungen in den Verträgen der Bundesrepublik Deutschland' (1965), 37-8; White, *Nationalisation of Foreign Property* (1961), 49; Alenfeld, op. cit., 32; Frick, op. cit., 180.
41. For US Commercial Treaties, see Frick, op. cit., 111 ff.; for German Treaties, see Alenfeld, op. cit., 28 ff.; and Frick, op. cit., 178 ff.
42. OECD, *Draft Convention with Notes and Comments* (Paris, 1967), 45.
43. OECD, op. cit., 47.
44. Cf. Frick, op. cit., who interprets the term 'investment' occurring in the US Commercial Treaties as including direct as well as portfolio investments, 112; for the scope of the term *Kapitalanlage* used in the German treaty, see Alenfeld, op. cit., 30, who limits it to direct investments only.
45. See Art. 1 (6) of the Agreement which defines 'investor' and the discussion of this term in ch. 5.4.3.4 for a clarification of the situation to some extent.
46. For details on STOs and inter-developing country co-operation, see ch. 4.1 and n.13.
47. See reports compiled by BfAI (ed.), *Rechtsinformation: Kurzberichte zum Investitionsrecht der arabischen Staaten* (Mai 1982); *Kurzberichte zum Investitionsrecht schwarzafrikanischer Staaten* (Juni 1982), 15, 19, 21, 31, 35, 40, 46, 49; also cf. Lange and Uhlig, *Jordanien* and *Syrien*.

48. Cf. Wilson, *US Commercial Treaties*, 20-1; Alenfeld, op. cit., 19, 23; Frick, op. cit., 14; Jüttner, op. cit., 103, 115.
49. In fact, such an interpretation has been advanced in the case of West German investment agreements, see Frick, op. cit., who calls it a multilateralizing effect.
50. Cf. BfAI, *Kurzberichte zum Investitionsrecht der arabischen Staaten*, 23 ff., 38 ff., 52 ff.
51. Cf. Art. XXIV, para. 1 (*e*) of the US-German Treaty (1954), in Wilson, *US Commercial Treaties*, 348; see also Frick, op. cit., 109.
52. Cf. Art. 1 (*b*) of the OECD *Draft Convention*, 13, 18; also cf. Menzel and Ipsen, op. cit., 174.
53. Cf. Alenfeld, op. cit., 35-8, who also points out that in some FRG agreements special arrangements were made to restrict permission of work to be given by the host State only to experts and technicians, see op. cit., 89 and n. 154; also cf. Frick, op. cit., 114 ff. and 186 ff.
54. In practice some parties to bilateral treaties with capital-exporting countries, such as the FRG, have usually reserved the right to decide the extent of favourable measures and exemptions to be granted to individual investors according to the merits of each particular case. See Alenfeld, op. cit., 85, 88-92.
55. See G. Beitzke, 'Ordre Public', *WVR*, ii. 665-6; for similar provisions in the US Commercial Treaties, see Frick, op. cit., 116.
56. Cf. Art. V (1) of the US-German Treaty of Friendship, Commerce, and Navigation (1954), Art. 4 (1) of the German *Mustervertrag* for Investment Promotion, reproduced by Jüttner, at p. 384, and Art. 1 (*a*) of the OECD *Draft Convention*; see also Wilson, *US Commercial Treaties*, 113, 119; Frick, op. cit., 135-6 and 206 ff.; Alenfeld, op. cit., 108 ff.
57. See Notes on Art. 1 (*a*) of the OECD Convention (1967); also cf. Wilson, *US Commercial Treaties*, 119-20, who points out that all the bilateral treaties signed by the US up to the end of 1958 mention the standard of 'most constant protection and security, except the treaty with Muscat which refers to 'all possible protection and security'.
58. See Frick, op. cit., 136-7, 207, who mentions US Treaties concluded with Luxembourg and Belgium as containing the stipulation 'constant security therein through full legal and judicial protection', in Art. IV (1); also cf. E. H. Schwenk, 'Der neue Freundschafts-Handels- und Schiffahrtsvertrag zwischen der Bundesrepublik Deutschland und den Vereinigten Staaten von Amerika', in *JZ* (1957), 199.
59. See Schwarzenberger, *Foreign Investments*, 114-16; this opinion has been approved by Frick, op. cit., at 86 n. 51; for a discussion of the international minimum standard, see A. H. Roth, *The Minimum Standard* (1949), 111 ff.; E. M. Borchard, 'The Minimum Standard', *Proc. ASIL* (1939), 51-74; K. Doehring, *Die allgemeinen Regeln des völkerrechtlichen*

Fremdenrechts (1963), 23 ff.; Menzel and Ipsen, op. cit., 175 ff.; Brownlie, *Principles*, 524 ff.

60. *US* v. *Mexico UNRIAA*, iv. 60; also cf. Chevrou Case (*France* v. *Great Britain*) 1931, *UNRIAA*, ii. 1113, and in 27 *AJIL* (1933), 153, 160; Roberts Claim (*US* v. *Mexico*), 1926, *UNRIAA*, iv. 77; Brownlie, *Principles*, 525.
61. As Brownlie, op. cit., 525, takes this statement to be *the statement of the law*; the reasonableness of the statement lies of course in its objectivity, i.e., the test of the reasonable and impartial man.
62. As Amerasinghe, *State Responsibility for Injuries to Aliens*, 44, suggests; also cf. Roberts Claim, op. cit.
63. As suggested by Menzel and Ipsen, op. cit., 177; although a substantial number of States have become parties to the Covenant, only twelve Member States of the OIC have so far ratified or acceded to the Covenant; see Multilateral Treaties Deposited with the Secretary-General: Status at 31 Dec. 1982, UN Doc. ST/LEG/SER, E/2 (1983), 120.
64. See Wilson, *US Commercial Treaties* 6; Roesner, op. cit., 6; Frick, op. cit., 96, 123, 192 ff.; Alenfeld, op. cit., 47, 62; Schwarzenberger, 'The Most-Favoured-Nation Standard', 96 ff.
65. Ibid., 103; also cf. G. Schwarzenberger, 'The Province and Standards of International Economic Law', 2 *ILQ* (1948), 402-20; also cf. ch. 4.3.4 for the scope of the rule of 'equal and non-discriminatory' treatment, of which the 'most-favoured-nation' standard is an integral component.
66. Cf. Roesner, op. cit., 6-7 on the negative and positive formulations of the standard.
67. Cf. definition of 'most-favoured-nation' treatment in Art. XXV (4) of the US-German Treaty of Friendship, Commerce and Navigation; Jaenicke, 'Meistbegünstigungsklausel', 497 ff.; Schwarzenberger, 'The Most-Favoured-Nation Standard', 96 ff.
68. Cf. Roesner, op. cit., 86; Jaenicke, 'Meistbegünstigungsklausel', 501.
69. See also the examination of Art. 8 (*a*) and (*b*) of the General Agreement in ch. 4.3.4.
70. Jaenicke, op. cit.; Alenfeld, op. cit., 62; also cf. Art. 1 (*a*), clause 3 of the OECD' *Draft Convention* which reads: 'The fact that certain nationals of any State are accorded treatment more favourable than that provided for in this Convention shall not be regarded as discriminatory against nationals of a Party by reason only of the fact that such treatment is not accorded to the latter.'
71. In international commercial practice this would be the case, see R. C. Snyder, *The Most-Favored-Nation-Clause* (1948), 11 ff., 85 ff.; Schwarzenberger, 'The Most-Favoured-Nation Standard', 119; Frick, op. cit., 98.
72. As may be noted in bilateral treaties of the US and FRG; cf. Wilson, *US Commercial Treaties*, 9; Roesner, op. cit., 42; Frick, op. cit., 97-8, 193-4.

73. See Alenfeld, op. cit., 66; Dahm, *Völkerrecht*, 513; Bäulke, op. cit., 102, 112 ff.; Roth, op. cit., 102 ff.; Snyder, op. cit., 6, 9, 248.
74. Cf. Art. 13 (3) of the *Mustervertrag*, reproduced by Jüttner, op. cit., 390; Alenfeld, op. cit., 44; also cf. Art. 13 of the OECD *Draft Convention*, 55.
75. Although Art. 13 (3) of the German *Mustervertrag* generally stipulates a period of 20 years, in agreements concluded with Ethiopia, Sri Lanka, Chile, Iran, Sierra Leone, and Turkey the time-limit is fixed at 15 years and in those concluded with Pakistan, Senegal, and Thailand, the limit is 10 years. See Alenfeld, op. cit., 44; also cf. Art. 13 of the OECD *Draft Convention* which called for a time-limit of 15 years.
76. On the problem of 'creeping expropriation', see B. Weston, ' "Constructive Takings" under International Law: A Modest Foray into the Problem of "Creeping Expropriation" ', 16 *VJIL* (1975), 103-75; D. F. Vagts, 'Coercion and Foreign Investment Rearrangements', 72 *AJIL* (1978), 17 ff.; also cf. Art. 3 of the OECD *Draft Convention* which contains the wording 'measures depriving directly or indirectly', and comments thereto, 24-5.
77. See Alenfeld, op. cit., 108 ff.; Frick, op. cit., 135 ff., 206 ff., who points out that the US and FRG bilateral treaties are usually governed by general standards of protection, 137, 206.
78. See Art. 2 of the OECD *Draft Convention* and comments on the provision which deals with undertakings of a general nature, 19-21.
79. See UNCTAD Doc. TD/B/609/Add. 1, v. 17, containing Council Resolution no. 648/S-22, 3 Dec. 1973 amending Art. VI. See also ch. 4.4.1.
80. See Wortley, *Expropriation in Public International Law*, 38 ff.; White, *Nationalisation of Foreign Property*, 3, 43; Amerasinghe, *State Responsibility for Injuries to Aliens*, 123; also cf. Art. V (4) of the US-West German Treaty of Friendship and other references to 'expropriation' in US Commercial Treaties in Wilson, *US Commercial Treaties*, 337, 111 ff.; Frick, op. cit., 137 ff.; Brownlie, *Principles of Public International Law* (1979), 532.
81. I. Foighel, *Nationalisation* (1957), 19; see also White, op. cit., 41 ff.
82. See Amerasinghe, *State Responsibility*, 126-7; G. White, op. cit., 43.
83. For the text of the UNGA Resolution, see UN *Yearbook*, 16 (1962), 503 ff. and Brownlie, *Basic Documents*; the Charter of Economic Rights and Duties of States (Res. 3281 (XXIX), 1974) also uses in Art. 2 (2) *c* the terms 'nationalize, expropriate or transfer ownership of foreign property' as interrelated or even interchangeable as far as the legal consequences are concerned.
84. See Wortley, op. cit., 24-5; G. White, op. cit., 5 ff.
85. For the occurrence of the rule in US and FRG bilateral treaties see Wilson, *US Commercial Treaties*, 337, 111 ff.; Frick, op. cit., 141 ff. and 208 ff.; see also Art. 3 of the OECD *Draft Convention* which states in condition (i) 'public interest and under due process of law', 23.

86. Such as German Interests in Polish Upper Silesia Case, *PCIJ*, Series A, no. 7, 22; Walter Fletcher Smith Case, *UNRIAA*, ii. 917; for some other domestic and international decisions, see G. White, op. cit., 6-8; Amerasinghe, *State Responsibility*, 135-6.
87. G. White, op. cit., 146; Akinsanya, *The Expropriation of Multinational Property in the Third World*, 19, 201 ff.
88. For example, the Cuban Resolution No. 1 of 8 Aug. 1960, which implemented the Nationalization Law No. 851 of 6 July 1960, see M. Domke, 'Foreign Nationalization', 55 *AJIL* (1961), 600; also cited by Kronfol, *Protection of Foreign Investment*, 25.
89. See S. P. Metzger, 'Multilateral Conventions for the Protection of Private Foreign Investment, 9 *JPL* (1960), 40; Friedman, *Expropriation in International Law*, 140-2; G. White, op. cit., 146-50; Amerasinghe, op. cit., 137; Baade, *Permanent Sovereignty over Natural Wealth and Resources*, 3 ff., 23; Weston, 'The Charter of Economic Rights and Duties of States and the Deprivation of Foreign-Owned Wealth', 75 *AJIL* (1981) 439-40.
90. See Award in Dispute between Libyan American Oil Company (LIAMCO) and the Government of the Libyan Arab Republic, 12 Apr. 1977, Sole Arbitrator Dr. S. Mahmassani, reproduced in 20 *ILM* (1981), 1-87, 58, (hereinafter cited as the LIAMCO Award) in which the Arbitrator cites Friedman, op. cit., and G. White, op. cit., in support; Brownlie, *Principles of Public International Law*, 545, asserts that reference to 'public utility' causes confusion.
91. Even the most ardent supporter of the principle of public utility, the United States, came to the realistic conclusion that 'there is little authority in international law establishing any useful criteria by which a State's own determination of public purpose can be questioned'. See 'Restatement (Second) of Foreign Relations Law of the United States', §185, Comment (*b*), (1965), 553; also cited by Weston, 'The Charter of Economic Rights', 440 n. 15.
92. See ch. 4.3.4.
93. Cf. G. White, op. cit. 119 ff.; Brownlie, *Principles*, 539.
94. Amerasinghe, *State Responsibility*, 139, although the author does not elaborate on what he means by 'justice', it may be assumed that he is most probably referring to forms of arbitrary discrimination which are unjust and inequitable. See Kewenig, *Der Grundsatz der Nichtdiskriminierung*, i. 64; see also n. 97 below.
95. See M. McDougal, H. Lasswell, and L. Chen, *Human Rights and World Public Order: The Basic Policies of an International Law of Human Dignity* (1980), 738; see also Kewenig, *Der Grundsatz*, 43, who also holds that the 'minimum standard' in international law may be taken as a rule of customary international law.
96. Cf. *NV Verenigde Deli-Maatschapijen and NV Senembah-Maatschappij* v. *Deutsche Indonesische Tabak-Handelsgesellschaft mbH* (1959) cited by Domke, op. cit., 315; also cited by Amerasinghe, *State Responsibility*, 138-9.

97. Weston, 'Charter of Economic Rights', 445; see also O. Vicuna, 'Some International Law Problems Posed by the Nationalization of the Copper Industry by Chile', 67 *AJIL* (1973), 715, who underlined the concept of arbitrariness as embodying a 'profound moral judgment about what is just and unjust'. It is probably this idea which inspired Amerasinghe, *State Responsibility*, 139, to describe the basis of the rule of non-discrimination as a fundamental principle of justice.
98. See Award in the Dispute between *British Petroleum Exploration Company (Libya)* v. *Government of the Libyan Arab Republic*, 10 Oct. 1973, reproduced in 53 *ILR* (1979), 297 ff., and hereinafter cited as the BP Award, and the LIAMCO Award, reproduced in 20 *ILM* (1981), 1-87, see n. 90 above.
99. BP Award, 53 *ILR* (1979), 329; also cf. R. C. A. White, 'Expropriation of the Libyan Oil Concessions–Two Conflicting International Arbitrations', 30 *ICLQ* (1981), 1-19; for a discussion of all three Arbitral Awards (the third being the *Texaco Overseas Petroleum Co./California Asiatic Oil Co.* v. *Government of the Libyan Arab Republic (Merits)* (19 Jan. 1977, reproduced in an English translation in 17 *ILM* (1978), 3 ff. and hereinafter cited as TOPCO/CALASIATIC) see R. B. von Mehren and P. N. Kourides, 'International Arbitrations between States and Foreign Private Parties: The Libyan Nationalization Cases', 75 *AJIL* (1981), 476-552. It is interesting to note that in the recent AMINOIL Award, the Tribunal held that the nationalization of American Independent Oil Co. by Kuwait in Sept. 1977 was not a discriminatory measure (see 21 *ILM* (1982), 1019-20, paras. 87-8) although in his Separate Opinion, Sir Gerald Fitzmaurice suggests some subtle points which could be considered discriminatory (see 21 *ILM* (1982), 1052 n. 8.).
100. LIAMCO Award, 20 *ILM* (1981), 60; also cf. AMINOIL Award, n. 99 above.
101. See Weston, 'Charter of Economic Rights', 446-7; in making tentative statements on the present state of the law of expropriation some use the formulation 'Expropriations which are not for a public purpose, i.e., because they are discriminatory or arbitrary, are unlawful in international law' (see R. White, 'Expropriation of the Libyan Oil Concessions', 18) and tend to confuse the issues. Expropriations which may be for a public purpose can, nevertheless, be discriminatory or arbitrary.
102. See Upton Case (*US* v. *Venezuela*) Mixed Claims Commission (1903), 174; de Sabla Case, *UNRIAA*, vi. 366; see also Brownlie, *Principles*, 533, 544.
103. Amerasinghe, *State Responsibility*, 143; Akinsanya, op. cit., 30-41 for the position taken by Third World States on the issue of compensation, and 213 ff., for stipulation of the payment of compensation in nationalizing decrees issued by Third World States; for the texts of some nationalization decrees passed by Libya and Iraq, see 17 *ILM* (1978), 4 ff.; 11 *ILM* (1972), 847.

104. The *UNGA Res.* 1803 has been held to be a reasonably accurate reflection of customary international law. See TOPCO/CALASIATIC Award, 17 *ILM* (1978), 27-31, paras. 80-9; Weston, 'Charter of Economic Rights', 448; in the LIAMCO Award, 20 *ILM* (1981), 53, the *UNGA Res.* 1803 and 3281 (XXIX), 1974, were seen as 'evidence of the recent dominant trend of international opinion concerning the sovereign right of States over their resources, and that the said right is always subject to the respect for contractual agreements and to the obligation of compensation'. Brownlie, *Principles*; *also cf.* 543.
105. For its evolvement in the nineteenth century, see G. White, op. cit., 11 ff.; for the text of the Hull note, see 32 *AJIL* (1938), Supp. 184; for present status of the formula, see Brownlie, *Principles*, 533.
106. See Wilson, *US Commercial Treaties*, 116; Alenfeld, op. cit., 134 ff.; Frick, op. cit., 142-6, 216-20; see also Art. 3 (iii) of the OECD *Draft Convention*, 23.
107. G. White, op. cit., 12; OECD *Draft Convention*, 27; Alenfeld, op. cit., 144 ff.; Frick, op. cit., 144-5.
108. See OECD *Draft Convention* 27; Alenfeld, op. cit., 134ff.; Frick, op. cit., 143-4; G. White, op. cit., 13; Amerasinghe, *State Responsibility*, 150-2.
109. See OECD *Draft Convention*, 27-8; Alenfeld, op. cit., 140-2; Frick, op. cit., 145-7, 219-20; G. White, op. cit., 15-17; Amerasinghe, *State Responsibility*, 159-61.
110. On attempts by the US Delegate to assert such an interpretation, see UN Doc. A/C-2/SR 850 (326 ff.); also cited by Meessen, op. cit., 15 and n. 21; see also Schwebel, 'The Story of the UN Declaration on Permanent Sovereignty over Natural Resources', 463; see also Akinsanya, op. cit., 51 ff.; in their attitude towards this issue Third World States have remained consistent and within a decade of the passing of Resolution 1803, the same issue led to the failure to reach a consensus on the contents of Art. 2 (2) *c* of the Charter of Economic Rights and Duties of States, *UNGA Res*. 3281 (XXIX), 1974. See de Aréchaga, 'International Law in the Past Third of a Century', 302-3 who maintains that the drafters of the Charter intended only to avoid the inference that 'appropriate compensation ... in accordance with international law' necessarily means 'prompt, adequate and effective compensation'. One may, therefore, conclude that if 'appropriate compensation' is interpreted according to the classical formula then the formulation 'appropriate compensation should be paid' embodied in Art. 2 (2) *c* is an accurate statement of State practice; also cf. Brownlie, *Principles*, 544.
111. G. White, op. cit., 15.
112. See Dawson and Weston, op. cit., 751-3; see also Weigel and Weston, 'Valuation Upon the Deprivation of Foreign Enterprise', in Lillich, *The Valuation of Nationalized Property in International Law*, i. 3-39 (hereinafter cited as *Valuation*); on the demise of the Hull Formula see Dolzer, New Foundations of the Law of Expropriation, 557 ff.

113. Weston, 'Charter of Economic Rights', 454; R. B. Lillich and B. Weston, *International Claims: Their Settlement by Lump Sum Agreements* (1975), i. 207-56; Meessen, op. cit., 17-22; Dolzer, op. cit., 561 ff.
114. Some selected research done on the subject is cited herein: R. Lillich, *International Claims: Postwar British Practice* (1967); Lillich and Weston, *International Claims*; B. Weston, *International Claims: Postwar French Practice* (1971); C. F. Amerasinghe, 'The Quantum of Compensation for Nationalized Property', in *Valuation*, iii. 91 ff.; I. Seidl-Hohenveldern, 'The Valuation of Nationalized Property in Austria', in *Valuation*, i. 64 ff.; S. Freidberg and B. Lockwood, 'The Measure of Damages in Claims against Cuba', in *Valuation*, i. 117 ff.; Lillich, 'The Valuation of Nationalized Property by the Foreign Claims Settlement Commission', in *Valuation*, i. 95; O. Vicuna, 'The International Regulation of Valuation Standards and Processes: A Re-examination of Third World Perspectives', in *Valuation*, iii. 131 ff.; Lillich, 'International Law and the Chilean Nationalizations: The Valuation of the Copper Companies', in *Valuation*, ii. 120 ff.
115. 20 *ILM* (1981), 73. The question is whether it was an imperative general rule at any time before the war. The classical formula usually cited and held to be valid at the time Secretary of State Hull formulated it in his note to the Mexican ambassador (see Dolzer, op. cit., 558, who assumes it to have been the prevailing legal opinion at that time) is also open to question, cf. O. Schachter, 'Compensation for Expropriation', 78 *AJIL* (1984), 121, 122-4.
116. See Alenfeld, op. cit., 159.
117. Also cf. Brownlie, *Principles*, 543, who points out that Art. 2 (2) *c* of the Charter of Economic Rights and Duties of States does not deny the principle of compensation–a fact which has been overlooked by commentators.
118. See Alenfeld, op. cit., 145-8; Frick, op. cit., 221-2.
119. Cf. ch. 5.4.4.2.
120. Such as Bahrain, Kuwait, Qatar, Saudi Arabia, and the United Arab Emirates. Cf. the IMF 'Annual Report on Exchange Arrangements and Exchange Restrictions' (1983), 86, 294, 389, 401, 477-8.
121. Ibid., 3, 21.
122. Ibid., 34-6.
123. Ibid., 37, 39.
124. Out of a total of forty-five Member States of the OIC payments restrictions on both current and capital transactions form a regular feature of the exchange system in twenty-five Member States and payments restrictions on capital transactions only exist in one form or another in five Member States. Cf. IMF 'Annual Report' (1983), 524-9.
125. By the middle of 1983, the number of members of the IMF that had formally accepted obligations under Art. VIII, Sections 2, 3, and 4 of the

Articles of Agreement had risen to fifty-six, whereas eighty-eight Members were availing themselves of the transitional arrangements under Art. XIV, Section 2. Cf. IMF 'Annual Report' (1983), 7.

126. See Frick, op. cit., 157; in treaties concluded with Taiwan, Israel, Italy, and Uruguay, the host State may introduce exchange restrictions in order 'to assure the availability of foreign exchange for payments for goods and services essential to the health and welfare of its people', see Frick, op. cit., 161.
127. Frick, op. cit., 159.
128. See Alenfeld, op. cit., 73-80; Frick, op. cit., 230-1, however, comes to a diametrically opposite conclusion.
129. See Frick, op. cit., 224, 229.
130. Frick, op. cit., 226-8.
131. Cf. Art. 4 of the OECD *Draft Convention*, 29.
132. For the concept of imputability, see Amerasinghe, *State Responsibility*, 49-52; Menzel and Ipsen, op. cit., 356, 358 ff.; though the provision does not mention the responsibility of the host State for acts of private persons, there are some situations in which such acts may be imputed to the State, see Amerasinghe, op. cit.; Menzel and Ipsen, op. cit.; Brownlie, *Principles of Public International Law*, 439; it should, however, be noted that the International Law Commission has used the word 'attributable' instead of imputable, see 'Draft Articles on Responsibility of a State', *Yearbook*, ILC (1975), ii. 60, Art. 3 on 'Elements of an internationally wrongful act of a State.'
133. Liability is to be distinguished from the general responsibility of a State for wrongs imputable or attributable to its organs, see Amerasinghe, *State Responsibility*, 51, for further references and cases on the subject.
134. For the essentialness of this criterion, see Amerasinghe, op. cit., 55; however, Menzel and Ipsen, op. cit., 353, point out that damage or 'injury' is not an essential criterion as it is inherent in the wrongful act giving rise to international responsibility; also cf. *YBILC* (1971), ii. 223, in which the Commission states: 'under international law an injury, material or moral, is necessarily inherent in every violation of an international subjective right of a State'.
135. (Indemnity) Merits (1928), *PCIJ*, Ser. A, no. 17, 29.
136. See *YBILC* (1975), ii. 59; *YBILC* (1976), ii. part ii, 73 ff.; also cf. *YBILC* (1971), ii. 205, in which the Commission recognizes it as a deeply rooted principle of international law; Menzel and Ipsen, op. cit., 345.
137. See Brownlie, *Principles*, 431; Menzel and Ipsen, op. cit., 101, 343.
138. (1924) *PCIJ*, Ser. A, no. 2, 12; also cf. Barcelona Traction, Light and Power Company Case, *ICJ Rep.* (1970), 3 ff., para. 35.
139. See Barcelona Traction Case, *ICJ Rep.* (1970), para. 79; also cf. Administrative Decision No. V, *US* v. *Germany* (1924), Mixed Claims Commission, 7 *UNRIAA*, 119, for a differentiated opinion.

140. For provisions in US Commercial Treaties and German Investment Agreements, see Frick, op. cit., 167-71, 234 ff.
141. H. Lauterpacht, 'Survey of International Law in Relation to the Work of Codification of the International Law Commission'. Memorandum prepared for the UN Secretariat, UN Doc. A/CN, 4/1/Rev. 1, 10 Feb. 1949, 19-20, reproduced in E. Lauterpacht (ed.), *International Law being the Collected Papers of Hersch Lauterpacht* (1970), i. 445 ff., 469-71; also cf. *Steiner and Gross* v. *Polish State*' in 4 *Annual Digest of Public International Law Cases* (1927-8), 291; also see Brownlie, *Principles of Public International Law* (1979), 580-93, who considers the subject of procedural capacity to individuals in great detail, dealing with various examples.
142. For cases on material damages, see M. M. Whiteman, *Damages in International Law* (1937), i-iii; for moral injuries, see the Lusitania Case(s) (1922), *US* v. *Germany*, United States-German Mixed Claims Commission, Decisions and Opinions, 2127, also cited by Amerasinghe, *State Responsibility*, 55; on the measure of damages generally, see the Lusitania Cases (1923), 7 *UNRIAA*, 32; Chorzow Factory Case (Indemnity), Merits (1928), *PCIJ*, Ser. A, no. 17; 'Corfu Channel Case', *ICJ Rep.* (1949), 244; cf. further the Janes Claim (1925) 4 *UNRIAA*, 82; Brownlie, *Principles of Public International Law*, 463-4.
143. Cf. Friedman, *Expropriation in International Law*, 214; LIAMCO Award, 20 *ILM* (1981), 63; however, Professor Dupuy held a contrary opinion to that expressed in the LIAMCO Award and directed specific *restitutio* in the case of nationalizations of the interests of Texaco and Calasiatic, see TOPCO/Calasiatic, 17 *ILM* (1978), 1-37; this award has raised some critical points which have been adequately discussed by publicists, see A. A. Fatouros, 'International Law and the Internationalized Contract', 74 *AJIL* (1980), 139; R. White, op. cit., 16; support for *restitutio* in the case of Texaco and Calasiatic has, understandably, come from von Mehren and Kourides, op. cit., 544, who were counsels to Texaco during the arbitral proceedings. It is, nevertheless, the only case so far which has awarded *restitutio* in a case relating to nationalizations, see Akinsanya, op. cit., 29. The basis of Professor Dupuy's award are intrinsically connected with his support of the theory of the internationalized agreement in the case of concession contracts. For a critical analysis of this theory and its rejection, see Liemen, op. cit., 146-205; also cf. Brownlie, *Principles*, 549-51.
144. Cf. Art. 4 (3) of the German *Mustervertrag* reproduced by Jüttner, op. cit., 385; see also Alenfeld, op. cit., 161-2.
145. See chs. 4.3.2. n. 62 and 5.1.
146. See ch. 5.4.5.2.1. (*d*).
147. See Frick, op. cit., 164.
148. See M. Muslehuddin, *Insurance and Islamic Law* (3rd edn., 1979); E. Klingmüller, 'The Concept and Development of Insurance in Islamic

Countries', 43 *Isl. Culture* (1969), 27-37; O. Farrukh, 'Banking and Insurance in Relation to the Islamic Concept of Riba', in M. A. Khan (ed.), *International Islamic Conference* (1970), i. 123-9; A. Rahman, *Banking and Insurance—Economic Doctrines of Islam*, iv (1979).

149. See ch. 1.2.
150. See de Aréchaga, op. cit., 297; reference to the Charter is to *UNGA Res.* 3281 (XXIX), 1974.
151. Brownlie, 'Legal Status of Natural Resources in International Law', 269.
152. See International Law Association (ILA), 'Report of the Sixtieth Conference' (ILA Montreal Report), Montreal (1982), 197.
153. See K. Hossain and S. R. Chowdhury (eds.), *Permanent Sovereignty Over Natural Resources in International Law* (1984), Introduction, pp. xii-xiii.
154. See n. 150 above; this view is also supported by S. R. Chowdhury, 'The Concept of Permanent Sovereignty: Origin and Development', in Hossain and Chowdhury (eds.), op. cit., 38, who holds that the 'right of permanent sovereignty, emanating as it does from the right to self-determination, has the same status of *jus cogens* in contemporary international law'.
155. See Brownlie, 'Legal Status of Natural Resources', 269-70.
156. AMINOIL Award, 21 *ILM* (1982), 1021-2, para. 90 (2).
157. See de Aréchaga, op. cit., 298-9.
158. See LIAMCO Award, 20 *ILM* (1981), 61-2; the contention that indemnification should include *lucrum cessans* in cases where expropriation is unlawful *per se*, as Brownlie maintains (see *Principles*, 539) is difficult to support.
159. See Brownlie, *Principles*, 543.
160. As pointed out by Judge de Aréchaga, op. cit., 301.
161. For the application of a variety of compensation formulas, see S. R. Chowdhury, 'Permanent Sovereignty and its Impact on Stabilization Clauses, Standards of Compensation and Patterns of Development Co-operation', in Hossain and Chowdhury (eds.), op. cit., 42-5; D. Flint, 'Foreign Investment and the New International Economic Order', in Hossain and Chowdhury (eds.), op. cit., 144-81.
162. See Dolzer, op. cit., 567.
163. See 20 *ILM* (1981), 1-87, 30 ff., 47; also cf. ch. 2.6.

Bibliography

This is a selected listing of the principal sources used. Other sources, including incidental references to publications, documents, or treaties used as aids to highlight certain points, concepts, or arguments, may be seen in the notes directly pertaining to that particular context.

Abi-Saab, G., 'Wars of National Liberation in the Geneva Conventions and Protocols', 165 *RdC* (1979), iv. 353 ff.

Abou-El-Haj, R. A., 'Ottoman Diplomacy at Karlowitz', 87 *JAOS* (1967), 498 ff.

— 'Ottoman Attitudes Toward Peace-Making: The Karlowitz Case', 51 *Der Islam* (1974), 131 ff.

Abu-Suliman, A. H., 'Islamic Theory of International Relations in the Contemporary World' (Unpubl. doc. diss. Univ. of Pennsylvania, 1970).

Ahmad, A. M., 'Die Auseinandersetzung zwischen al-Azhar und der modernistischen Bewegung in Ägypten von Mohammad Abduh bis zur Gegenwart' (Diss. Hamburg, 1963).

Ahmad, A., *A History of Islamic Sicily* (Edinburgh, 1975).

Ahmad, K. (ed.), *Islam—Its Meaning and Message* (Leicester, 2nd edn., 1976).

— *Studies in Islamic Economics* (Leicester, 1980).

Ahmad, Z., 'Zakat and Economic Well-Being', 20 *Isl. Stud.* (1981), 23 ff.

Akbar, M., 'The Ailing World Made Better', *Isl. Lit.* (1949), 35 ff.

Akhtar, S., 'An Inquiry into the Nature, Origin, and Source of Islamic Law of Nations', 10 *Isl. Stud.* (1971), 23 ff.

Akinsanya, A. A., *The Expropriation of Multinational Property in the Third World* (New York, 1980).

Akwensioge, M. N., 'Die Organisation für afrikanische Einheit' (Diss. Tübingen, 1974).

Alenfeld, J., *Die Investitionsförderungsverträge der Bundesrepublik Deutschland* (Frankfurt, 1971).

Alexandrowicz, C. H., 'Mogul Sovereignty and the Law of Nations', 4 *IYIA* (1955), 316 ff.

— 'Treaty and Diplomatic Relations between European and South Asian Powers in the 17th and 18th Centuries', 100 *RdC* (1960), ii. 207 ff.

— *Introduction to the History of the Law of Nations in the East Indies, 16th, 17th, and 18th Centuries* (Oxford, 1967).

Ali, A. Y. *The Holy Quran: Text, Translation and Commentary* (Beirut, 1968).

Ali, M., *The Holy Quran: Translation and Commentary* (Lahore, 1928).

Amerasinghe, C. F., 'State Breaches of Contracts with Aliens and International Law', 58 *AJIL* (1964), 881 ff.

— *State Responsibility for Injuries to Aliens* (Oxford, 1967).

Anabtawi, M. F., *Arab Unity in Terms of Law* (The Hague, 1963).

Anand, R. P., *Compulsory Jurisdiction of the Internaitonal Court of Justice* (London, 1961).

— 'Role of "New" Asian-African Countries in the Present International Legal Order', 56 *AJIL* (1962), 383 ff.

— 'Attitude of the Asian-African States Towards Certain Problems of International Law', 15 *ICLQ* (1966), 55 ff.

— *New States and International Law* (New Delhi, 1972).

— (ed.), *Asian States and the Development of Universal International Law* (Delhi, 1972).

Anderson, J. N. D., 'The Significance of Islamic Law in the World Today', 9 *AJCL* (1960), 187 ff.

Al-Araby, M. A., 'Private Ownership of Property: The Ethical and Moral Injunctions of Islam: Part II', 54 *Isl. Rev.* (July-Aug. 1966), 26 ff.

— 'Governmental Injunctions: Part II', 55 *Isl. Rev.* (June 1967), 28 ff.

— 'Eight Islamic Rules Governing Private Ownership of Property: The Report to the Arab League in 1952 on the Question of *Zakah* and the Meaning of Property; Part III', 55 *Isl. Rev.* (July 1967), 30 ff.

Arangio-Ruiz, G., 'The Normative Role of the General Assembly of the United Nations and the Declaration of Principles of Friendly Relations', 137 *RdC* (1972), iii. 42 ff.

de Aréchaga, J., 'International Law in the Past Third of a Century', 159 *RdC* (1978), i. 1 ff.

Arnold, T., and Guillaume, A. (eds.), *The Legacy of Islam* (Oxford, 1931).

Asad, M., *The Message of the Quran: Translated and Explained* (Gibraltar, 1980).

Atiya, A. S., *The Crusade in the Later Middle Ages* (New York, 1938, 2nd edn., 1965).

— *Kreuzfahrer und Kaufleute: Die Begegnung von Christentum und Islam* (Being a translation of the author's *Crusade, Commerce, and Culture*, 1962) (Stuttgart, 1964).

Azami, M. M., *Studies in Hadith Methodology and Literature* (Indianapolis, 1977).

— *Studies in Early Hadith Literature* (Indianapolis, 1978).

Baade, H. W., 'Permanent Sovereignty over Natural Wealth and Resources', in R. Miller and R. Stranger (eds.), *Essays on Expropriation* (Columbus, 1967), 3 f.

Badr, G. M., 'Islamic Law: Its Relation to other Legal Systems', 26 *AJIL* (1978), 187 ff.

Ballantyne, W. M., *Legal Development in Arabia: A Selection of Articles and Addresses on the Arabian Gulf* (London, 1980).

Bassiouni, M. C., 'Protection of Diplomats under Islamic Law', 74 *AJIL* (1980), 609 ff.

Bäulcke, K. E., 'Die materiellen Eigentumsschutzbestimmungen in den Verträgen der Bundesrepublik Deutschland zur Förderung und zum Schutz von Kapitalanlagen im Ausland' (Diss. Würzburg, 1965).

Baumann, J., 'Neure Tendenzen in der Investitionsgesetzgebung der Entwicklungsländer', 5 *AWD* (1959), 237 ff.

Baysan, C., Karim, S., and Ugurel, I., 'An Evaluation of the United Nations' Conference on Least Developed Countries', 3 *JECIC* (Oct. 1981), no. 1, 5 ff.

Beitzke, G., 'Ordre Public', in *WVR*, ii. 665 ff.

Berger, R., 'Vermögensschutz im Ausland durch Investitionsförderungsverträge, 11 *AWD* (1965), 1 ff.

Beyer, S., *Der diplomatische Schutz der Aktionäre im Völkerrecht* (Baden-Baden, 1977).

BFAI (ed.), *Rechtsinformation: Kurzberichte zum Investitionsrecht der arabischen Staaten* (Cologne, May 1982).

— *Rechtsinformation: Kurzberichte zum Investitionsrecht schwarzafrikanischer Staaten* (Cologne, June 1982).

Bode, I., *Die Diskriminierungsverbote im EWG-Vertrag* (Göttingen, 1968).

Bohn, M., 'Die Kodifikation des Völkerrechts durch die General Versammlung der Vereinten Nationen' (Diss. Bonn, 1972).

Boisard, M. A., 'On the Probable Influence of Islam on Western Public and International Law', 11 *IJMES* (1980), 429 ff.

Borchard, E. M., 'The Minimum Standard of the Protection of Aliens', *Proc. ASIL* (1939), 51 ff.

Borchers, K. G., *Verträgen von Staaten mit ausländischen Privatpersonen* (Göttingen, 1966).

Boutros-Ghali, B., 'Le Principe d'égalité des états et les organisations internationales', 98 *RdC* (1960), ii. 1 ff.

— 'The Addis Ababa Charter', *International Conciliation* (Jan. 1964), no. 546.

— 'The Arab League (1945-1970)', 25 *Rev. Egypt.* (1969), 67 ff.

— 'La Ligue des états arabes', 137 *RdC* (1972), iii. 11 ff.

Bowett, D. W., *Self-Defence in International Law* (Manchester, 1958).

— 'International Law and Economic Coercion', 16 *VJIL* (1975/6), 245 ff.

Brandon, M., 'Legal Deterrents and Incentives to Private Foreign Investments', 43 *Trans. Grot. S.* (1957), 39 ff.

Brewer, W. C., 'The Proposal for Investment Guarantees by an International Agency', 58 *AJIL* (1964), 62 ff.

Brierly, J. L., *The Basis of Obligation in International Law* (Oxford, 1958, repr. Aalen, 1977).

— *The Law of Nations* (Oxford, 6th edn. by Sir Humphrey Waldock, 1963).

Broches, A., *International Investment Guaranties; Possibilities and Problems* (Proc. ASIL 1962), 81 ff.

Browne, E. G., *The Persian Revolution of 1905–1909* (London, 1910, repr. 1966).

Brownlie, I., *International Law and the Use of Force by States* (Oxford, 1963).

— *Principles of Public International Law* (Oxford, 3rd edn., 1979).

Brownlie, I., 'Legal Status of Natural Resources in International Law (Some Aspects)', 162 *RdC* (1979), i. 245 ff.

— *Basic Documents in International Law* (Oxford, 3rd edn., 1983).

Bukhari, M., Sahih al-Bukhari, trans. M.M. Khan (Medina, 1971).

Burke, J. (ed.), *Osborn's Concise Law Dictionary* (London, 6th edn., 1976).

Cahen, C., 'Commercial Relations Between the Near East and Western Europe from the VIIth to the XIth Century', in K. I. Semaan (ed.), *Islam and the Medieval West* (1980), 1 ff.

Caldwell, J. A. M., *et al.*, *Dustur: A Survey of the Constitutions of Arab and Muslim States* (Leiden, 1966); repr. with additional material from the *Encyclopaedia of Islam*, 2nd edn.

Castenada, L. *Legal Effects of United Nations' Resolutions* (New York/London, 1967).

Cattan, H., *Palestine and International Law: The Legal Aspects of the Arab Israeli Conflict* (London, 2nd. edn., 1976).

Chapra, M. U., *The Economic System of Islam: A Discussion of its Goals and Nature* (Karachi, 1971).

— 'Objectives of the Islamic Economic Order', in K. Ahmad (ed.), *Islam—its Meaning and Message* (1976), 173 ff.

— 'The Islamic Welfare State and its Role in the Economy', in K. Ahmad (ed.), *Studies in Islamic Economics* (1980), 143 ff.

Chejne, A., 'The Role of al-Andalus in the Movement of Ideas between Islam and the West', in K. I. Semaan (ed.), *Islam and the Medieval West* (1980), 110 ff.

Choudhury, G. W., *The Last Days of United Pakistan* (London, 1974).

Chowdury, S. R., *The Genesis of Bangladesh: A Study of International Legal Norms and Permissive Conscience* (London, 1972).

Corbett, P. E., Law and Society in the Relations of States (New York, 1951).

Dahm, G., *Völkerrecht* (Stuttgart, 1958-61), i-iii.

— 'Das Verbot der Gewaltanwendung nach Art. 2 (4) der UNO Charta und die Selbsthilfe gegenüber Völkerrechtsverletzungen, die keinen bewaffneten Angriff enthalten', *JIR* (1962), 48 ff.

Dawson, G., and Weston, B., '"Prompt, Adequate, and Effective": A Universal Standard of Compensation?' 30 *Fordham Law Review* (1962), 727 ff.

DEG (ed.), *Investitionen in Entwicklungsländern* (Cologne, 7th edn., 1980).

— *Geschäftsbericht 1981* (Cologne, 1982).

Degan, V. D., 'The Commission of Mediation, Conciliation, and Arbitration of the OAU', 20 *Rev. Egypt*. (1964), 53 ff.

Derpa, R. M., *Das Gewaltverbot der Satzung der Vereinten Nationen* (Bad Homburg, 1970).

Dicke, D.-C., *Die Intervention mit wirtschaftlichen Mitteln im Völkerrecht* (Baden-Baden, 1978).

Dischler, 'Präambel', in *WVR*, ii. 790 ff.

Dodge, B., 'The Significance of Religion in Arab Nationalism', in J. H. Proctor (ed.), *Islam and International Relations* (1965), 94 ff.

Doehring, K., *Die allgemeinen Regeln des völkerrechtlichen Fremdenrechts und das Verfassungsrecht* (Cologne/Berlin, 1963).

zu Dohna, B., 'Die Grundprinzipien des Völkerrechts über die freundschaftlichen Beziehungen und die Zusammenarbeit zwischen Staaten' (Diss. Kiel, 1973).

Dolzer, R., 'New Foundations of the Law of Expropriation of Alien Property', 75 *AJIL* (1980), 553 ff.

Domke, M., 'Foreign Nationalizations', 55 *AJIL* (1961), 585 ff.

Doo-Soon Ahn, 'Indigenisierungstendenzen und Joint Venture Praxis in ASEAN-Ländern', in K. Hottes and C. Uhlig (eds.), *Joint Ventures in Asien* (1983), 277 ff.

Dougherty, J. E., and Pfaltzgraff, R. L., *Contending Theories of International Relations* (Philadelphia, 1971).

Doxey, M. P., *Economic Sanctions and International Enforcement* (London, 1971).

EI (ed.), *Dustur: A Survey of the Constitutions of Arab and Muslim States* (Leiden, 1966).

Elias, T. O., 'The Commission of Mediation, Conciliation, and Arbitration of the Organisation of African Unity', 40 *BYIL* (1964), 336 ff.

— 'The Charter of the OAU', 59 *AJIL* (1965), 243 ff.

— *New Horizons in International Law* (Alphen, 1980).

van Emde-Boas, M. J., 'The OECD Draft Convention on the Protection of Foreign Property', 1 *CMLR* (1963/4), 265 ff.

Emerson, R., 'Self-Determination', 65 *AJIL* (1971), 459 ff.

Falk, R., 'The Iran Hostage Crisis: Easy Answers and Hard Questions', 74 *AJIL* (1980), 411 ff.

Al-Faruqi, I. R. A., *On Arabism, Urubah and Religion* (Amsterdam, 1962).

Fatouros, A. A., 'International Law and the Internationalized Contract', 74 *AJIL* (1980), 134 ff.

Fawcett, J. E. S., 'Intervention in International Law', 103 *RdC* (1961), ii. 347 ff.

Findley, C. V., 'The Legacy of Tradition to Reform: Origins of the Ottoman Foreign Ministry', 1 *IJMES* (1970), 334 ff.

— 'The Foundation of the Ottoman Foreign Ministry', 3 *IJMES* (1972), 388 ff.

Fitzmaurice, G., 'The Law and Procedure of the International Court of Justice 1951-1954: Treaty Interpretation and Other Points', 33 *BYIL* (1957), 203 ff.

Foda, E., *The Projected Arab Court of Justice: A Study in Regional Jurisdiction with Specific Reference to the Muslim Law of Nations* (The Hague, 1957).

Foighel, I., *Nationalisation* (London, 1957).

Ford, A., *The Anglo-Iranian Oil Dispute 1951–52: A Study of the Role of Law in the Relations of States* (Berkeley/Los Angeles, 1954).

Franck, T. M., and Rodley, N. S., 'After Bangladesh: The Law of Humanitarian Intervention by Military Force', 67 *AJIL* (1973), 275 ff.

Frick, H., *Bilateraler Investitionsschutz in Entwicklungsländern: Ein Vergleich der Vertragssysteme der Vereinigten Staaten von Amerika und der Bundesrepublik Deutschland* (Berlin, 1975).

Friedman, S., *Expropriation in International Law* (London, 1953).

Friedmann, W., *The Changing Structure of International Law* (London, 1964).

— and Pugh, R. C. (eds.), *Legal Aspects of Foreign Investments* (London/Toronto, 1959).

— and Kalmanoff, G. (eds.), *Joint International Business Ventures* (New York, 1961).

— and Beguin J. P. (eds.), *Joint International Business Ventures in Developing Countries: Case Studies and Analysis of Recent Trends* (New York/London, 1971).

Fyzee, A. A. A., *Outlines of Muhammadan Law* (London, 1955, 1960).

Gabrieli, F., 'The Transmission of Learning and Literary Influences to Western Europe', in P. M. Holt, A. K. S. Lambton, and B. Lewis (eds.), *The Cambridge History of Islam* (Cambridge, 1970), ii. 851 ff.

— 'Islam in the Mediterranean World', in J. Schacht and C. E. Bosworth (eds.), *The Legacy of Islam* (1974), 63 ff.

Gauhar, A. (ed.), *The Challenge of Islam* (London, 1978).

El-Gebali, S., 'Die OAPEC als Organisation zur Interessenvertretung der arabischen Ölländer in den internationalen wirtschaftlichen Beziehungen' (Diss. Kiel, 1981).

Geiger, R., 'The Unilateral Change of Economic Development Agreements', 23 *ICLQ* (1974), 73 ff.

Gess, K. N., 'Permanent Sovereignty over Natural Resources: An analytical Review of the UN Declaration and its Genesis', 13 *ICLQ* (1964), 398 ff.

Ghanem, H., 'The Asian-African Legal Consultative Committee: 1958', 14 *Rev. Egypt.* (1958), 63 ff.

Al-Ghunaimi, M. T., *The Muslim Conception of International Law and the Western Approach* (The Hague, 1968).

Gold. J., 'Developments in the International Monetary System, the International Monetary Fund, and international monetary law', 174 *RdC* (1982), i. 107 ff.

Goldziher, I., 'Djamal al-Din al-Afghani', in *EI* (new edn. 1965, repr. 1970), i. 416 ff.

Goltz, H., 'Voraussetzungen, Vorteile und Hindernisse privater Kapitalanlagen in Entwicklungsländer', *Der Betrieb* (1965), Beilage no. 20 zu Heft 46.

Goodrich, L. M., Hambro, E., and Simons, A. P., *Charter of the United Nations* (New York/London, 3rd edn., 1969).

Gräf, E., 'Die Übertragbarkeit abendländischer Rechtsordnungen auf islamische Ländern', 10 *WINS* (1965/7), 131 ff.

Green, L. C., 'New States, Regionalism and International Law', 5 *CYIL* (1967), 118 ff.

— 'The Tehran Embassy Incident—Legal Aspects', 19 *AdV* (1980/1), 1 ff.

Greig, D. W., *International Law* (London, 2nd edn., 1976).

Gross, L., 'The Case Concerning United States Diplomatic and Consular Staff in Tehran: Phase of Provisional Measures', 74 *AJIL* (1980), 395 ff.

Grzybowski, K., 'The Regime of Diplomacy and the Tehran Hostages', 30 *ICLQ* (1981), 42 ff.

Guillaume, A., *The Life of Muhammad, a translation of Ibn Ishac's 'Sirat Rasul Allah'* (Oxford, 1955).

Hahn, H. J., 'Elemente einer neuen Weltwährungsordnung', in W. Kewenig (ed.), *Völkerrecht und internationale wirstschaftliche Zusammenarbeit* (1978), 215 ff.

Hall, H. D., *Mandates, Dependencies and Trusteeships* (Washington, 1948).

Hamidullah, M., *The Muslim Conduct of State* (Lahore, 7th edn., 1977).

— 'The International Law of Islam', 39 *Isl. Rev.* (1951), no. 4, 8 ff.

— 'Theorie und Praxis des Völkerrechts im frühen Islam', 5 *Kairos* (1963), 100 ff.

— 'The Place of Islam in the History of Modern International Law', 2 *Hyderabad Acad. Stud.* (1940) 29 ff.

— *The earliest extant work on the Hadith: Sahifah Hammam Ibn Munabhih* (Paris, 10th rev. edn., 1979).

Hartmann, G., *Nationalisierung und Enteignung im Völkerrecht* (Berlin, 1977).

Hasan, A., *The Early Development of Islamic Jurisprudence* (Islamabad, 1970).

— *The Doctrine of Ijma in Islam* (Islamabad, 1976).

Hasan, S. A., 'Islamic Unity and World Co-operation' in M. A. Khan (ed.), *International Islamic Conference* (Islamabad, 1970),12 ff.

Hashem, Z., 'Some International Law Aspects of the Palestine Question', 23 *Rev. Egypt.* (1967), 63 ff.

Hatschek, J., *Der Musta'min: Ein Beitrag zum internationalen Privat- und Völkerrecht des Islamischen Gesetzes* (Berlin, 1920).

Heffening, W., *Das islamische Fremdenrecht bis zu den islamisch-fränkischen Staatsverträgen* (Hanover, 1925, repr. 1975).

Henkin, L., *How Nations Behave* (London, 1968).

Hess, M., 'Die Organisation der afrikanischen Einheit' (Diss. Marburg, 1967).

Higgins, R., *Conflict of Interests* (Chester-Springs, 1965).

— *The Development of International Law through the Political Organs of the United Nations* (London/New York/Toronto, 1963).

Hill, E., 'Comparative and Historical Study of Modern Middle Eastern Law', 26 *AJCL* (1978), 279 ff.

Hitti, P. K., *History of the Arabs* (London, 5th edn., 1953).

Hossain, K. and Chowdhury, S. R. (eds.), *Permanent Sovereignty Over Natural Resources in International Law: Principle and Practice* (London, 1984).

Hottes, K., and Uhlig, C., *Joint Ventures in Asien: Eine Form internationaler Produktionskooperation* (Stuttgart, 1983).

Houben, P., 'Principles of International Law Concerning Friendly Relations and Cooperation among States', 61 *AJIL* (1967), 703 ff.

Huang, T. T. F., 'Some International and Legal Aspects of the Suez Canal Question', 51 *AJIL* (1957), 277 ff.

Hudson, M. C., 'Islam and Political Development', in J. L. Esposito (ed.), *Islam and Development* (1980), 1 ff.

Hurewitz, J. C., 'The Europeanization of Ottoman Diplomacy: the Conversion from Unilateralism to Reciprocity in the Nineteenth Century', 25 *Belleten* (1961), 455 ff.

— 'Ottoman Diplomacy and the European State System', 15 *MEJ* (1961), 141 ff.

Hurewitz, J. C. (ed.), *The Middle East and North Africa in World Politics: A Documentary Record*, i. *European Expansion, 1535–1914* (Princeton, 2nd edn., 1975).

Hyde, J. N., 'Permanent Sovereignty over Natural Wealth and Resources', 50 *AJIL* (1956), 854 ff.

Hyder, K., *Equality of Treatment and Trade Discrimination in International Law* (The Hague, 1968).

ICE (ed.), *The Muslim World and the Future Economic Order* (London, 1979).

IDB (ed.), *Second Annual Report*, 1397 H (1976-7); Sixth Annual Report, 1401 H (1980-1) (Jeddah, 1976-81).

Ijalaye, D. A., 'Indigenization Measures and Multinational Corporations in Africa', 171 *RdC* (1981), ii. 11 ff.

Inalcik, H., 'Imtiyazat', in *EI*, iii. 1182 ff.

Ipsen, K., 'Entwicklung zur "collective economic security" im Rahmen der Vereinten Nationen?', in W. Kewenig (ed.), *Die Vereinten Nationen* (1975), 11 ff.

Jaenicke, G., 'Diskriminierung', in *WVR*, i. 387 ff.

— 'Gleichbehandlung', in *WVR*, i. 690 ff.

— *Der Begriff der Diskriminierung im modernen Völkerrecht* (Berlin, 1940).

— 'Meistbegünstigungsklausel', in *WVR*, ii. 479 ff.

Jeffery, A., 'The American Hostages in Tehran: The International Court of Justice and the Legality of Rescue Missions', 30 *ICLQ* (1981), 717 ff.

Jenks, C. W., *The Common Law of Mankind* (London, 1958).

Jessup, P. C., *A Modern Law of Nations* (New York, 1948, repr. Hamden, 1968).

— 'Enemy Property', 49 *AJIL* (1955), 57 ff.

— 'Diversity and Uniformity in the Law of Nations', 58 *AJIL* (1964), 341 ff.

— 'Non-Universal International Law', 12 *COLJTL* (1973), 415 ff.

Johnson, D. H. N., 'The Effect of Resolutions of the General Assembly of the United Nations', 32 *BYIL* (1955/6), 97 ff.

Johnson, H. S., *Self-Determination within the Community of Nations* (Leiden, 1967).

Jüttner, H., *Förderung und Schutz deutscher Direktinvestitionen in Entwicklungsländern* (Baden-Baden, 1975).

Kahf, M., 'International Trade Patterns of the Muslim Countries', in ICE (ed.), *The Muslim World and the Future Economic Order.* (1979), 199 ff.

Kannun, A., 'Private Property in Islam', 58 *Isl. Rev.* (Sept. 1970), 22 ff.

Karpat, K. H., 'The Transformation of the Ottoman State 1789-1908', 3 *IJMES* (1972), 243 ff.

Katzarov, K., *The Theory of Nationalization* (The Hague, 1964).

Kelsen, H., *The Law of the United Nations* (London, 1950; 1951, with Bound in Supplement).

Kelsen, H., and Tucker, R., *Principles of International Law* (1952; 2nd edn., New York/London, 1966).

Kemper, R., *Nationale Verfügung über natürliche Ressourcen und die Neue Weltwirtschaftsordnung der Vereinten Nationen* (Berlin, 1976).

Kerr, M., *The Arab Cold War 1958–1967: A Study of Ideology in Politics* (London, 1967).

Kewenig, W., *Der Grundsatz der Nichtdiskriminierung im Völkerrecht der internationalen Handelsbeziehungen. Band 1: Der Begriff der Diskriminierung* (Frankfurt, 1972).

— 'Gewaltverbot und noch zulässige Machteinwirkung und Interventionsmittel', in W. Schaumann (ed.), *Völkerrechtliches Gewaltverbot und Friedenssicherung* (Baden-Baden, 1971), 175 ff.

Kewenig, W. (ed.), *Die Vereinten Nationen im Wandel: Referate und Diskussionen eines Symposiums* 'Entwicklungslinien der Praxies der Vereinten Nationen in völkerrechtlicher Sichtœ' (Berlin, 1975).

— *Völkerrecht und internationale wirtschaftliche Zusammenarbeit: Referate und Diskussionen eines Symposiums* (Berlin, 1978).

Khadduri, M., *War and Peace in the Law of Islam* (Baltimore, 1955; 3rd edn., 1962).

— *The Islamic Law of Nations: Shaybani's Siyar* (Baltimore, 1966).

— 'The Islamic System: Its Competition and Co-existence with Western Systems', *Proc. ASIL* (1959), 49 ff.

— 'The Islamic Theory of International Relations and its Contemporary Relevance', in J. H. Proctor (ed.), *Islam and International Relations* (1965), 24 ff.

— *Islamic Jurisprudence: Shafi'i's Risala* (Baltimore, 1961).

Khadduri, H., and Liebesny, H. J., *Law in the Middle East* (Washington, 1955).

Khalid, D., 'Theocracy and the Location of Sovereignty', 11 *Isl. Stud.* (1972), 187 ff.

Khalid, D., *et al.*, *Reislamisierung und Entwicklungspolitik: Forschungsberichte des Bundesministeriums für wirtschaftliche Zusammenarbeit* (Bonn/Cologne, 1982).

Kipp, H., 'Das Verbot der Diskriminierung in modernen Friedensvölkerrecht', 9 *AdV* (1961/2), 137 ff.

Kletter, L., 'The Sovereignty of Jerusalem in International Law', 20 *COLJTL* (1981), 319 ff.

Kronfol, Z., *Protection of Foreign Investment* (Leiden, 1972).

Krüger, H., *Fetwa und Siyar: Zur internationalrechtlichen Gutachtenpraxis der Osmanischen Seyh ul-Islam vom 17 bis 19 Jh.* (Wiesbaden, 1978).

Kruse, H., *Islamische Völkerrechtslehre* (Bochum, 2nd edn., 1979).
— 'The Islamic Doctrine of International Treaties', 1 *ICLQ* (1954), 152 ff.
— 'Die Begründung der islamischen Völkerrechtslehre—Muhammad as-Saibani—"Hugo Grotius der Moslimen" ', 5 *Saeculum* (1954), 221 ff.
— 'The Notion of Siyar', 2 *JPHS* (1954), 16 ff.
— 'The Foundation of Islamic International Jurisprudence', 3 *JPHS* (1955), 231-67.
Kunz, J. L., 'Individual and Collective Self-Defense in Art. 51 of the Charter of the United Nations', 41 *AJIL* (1947), 872 ff.
— 'The Meaning and Range of the Norm Pacta Sunt Servanda', 39 *AJIL* (1945), 180 ff.
— 'Bellum Justum and Bellum Legale', 45 *AJIL* (1951), 528 ff.
— 'The Status of the Holy See in International Law', 46 *AJIL* (1952), 308 ff.
— 'Natural Law Thinking in the Modern Science of International Law', 55 *AJIL* (1961), 951 ff.
Kutzner, G., *Die Organisation der amerikanischen Staaten OAS* (Hamburg, 1970).
Landscheidt, T., 'Der Einfluß des Islam auf die Entwicklung der Temperamenta Belli im europäischen Völkerrecht' (Diss. Göttingen, 1955).
Lane, E. W., *An Arabic-English Lexicon*, book i, part 2 (Beirut, 1865, repr. 1968).
Lange, M., and Uhlig, C., *Aspekte der Produktionskooperation in Syrien: Materialien und kleine Schriften*, no. 94, Institut für Entwicklungsforschung (Bochum, 1982).
— *Internationale Produktionskooperation in Jordanien: Materialien und kleine Schriften*, no. 93, Institut für Entwicklungsforschung (Bochum, 1982).
Lewis, B., *The Emergence of Modern Turkey* (Oxford, 1968).
— 'Politics and War', in J. Schacht and C. E. Bosworth (eds.), *The Legacy of Islam* (1974), 156 ff.
— *Islam from the Prophet Muhammad to the Capture of Constantinople: A Documentary History* (New York, 1974), i. *Politics and War*.
Lewis, B., Pellat, Ch., and Schacht, J. (eds.), *Encyclopaedia of Islam (EI)* (Leiden/London, new edn., 1965).
Liebesny, H. T., 'Religious Law and Westernization in the Moslem Near East', 2 *AJCL* (1953), 429 ff.
Liemen, E., *Erdöl Produktionsverträge des Iran* (Tübingen, 1981).
Lillich, R. B. (ed.), *The Valuation of Nationalized Property in International Law* (Charlottesville, 1972, 1973, 1975), i-iii.
— 'Economic Coercion and the International Legal Order', 51 *Int. Aff.* (1975), 358 ff.
— 'Economic Coercion and the "New International Economic Order": A Second Look at some First Impressions', 16 *VJIL* (1975/6), 233 ff.
Lillich, R. B., and Weston, B., *International Claims: Their Settlement by Lump Sum Agreements*, vol. i (Charlottesville, 1975).
Lindemeyer, B., *Schiffsembargo und Handelsembargo* (Baden-Baden, 1975).

Lyons, U. and M. C., and Riley-Smith, J. S. C. (eds.), *Ayyubids, Mamlukes and Crusaders: Selections from the Tarikh al-Duwal wa'l-Muluk of Ibn al-Furat* (Cambridge, 1971), i. Translation.

Macdonald, D. B., 'Dar al-Islam', *HWI*, 89 ff.

Madani, N. O., 'The Islamic Content of the Foreign Policy of Saudi Arabia: King Faisal's Call for Islamic Solidarity 1965-1975' (Ph. D. thesis, Washington, 1977).

Mahmassani, S., 'The Principles of International Law in the Light of Islamic Doctrine', 117 *RdC* (1966), i. 201 ff.

Mallison, W. T., 'An International Law Appraisal of the Juridical Characteristics of the Resistance of the People of Palestine', 28 *Rev. Egypt.* (1972), 1 ff.

Mann, F. A., 'State Contracts and State Responsibility', 54 *AJIL* (1960), 572 ff.

Maududi, A. A., *The Meaning of the Quran: Arabic Text with Translation and Commentary* (Lahore, 1976; 5th edn., 1980), i-viii.

— 'Political Theory of Islam' in K. Ahmad (ed.), *Islam—Its Meaning and Message* (1976), 141 ff.

McDougal, M., Lasswell, H., and Chen, L., *Human Rights and World Public Order: The Basic Policies of an International Law of Human Dignity* (New Haven, 1980).

McWhinney, E., 'The "New" Countries and "New" International Law', 60 *AJIL* (1966) 1 ff.

— *The World Court and the Contemporary International Law-Making Process* (Alphen aan den Rijn, 1979).

Meessen, K. M., 'Völkerrechtliches Enteignungsrecht im Nord-Süd-Konflikt', in W. Kewenig (ed.), *Völkerrecht und internationale wirtschaftliche Zusammenarbeit* (1978), 11 ff.

von Mehren, R. B., and Kourides, P. N., 'International Arbitrations between States and Foreign Private Parties: The Libyan Nationalization Cases', 75 *AJIL* (1981), 476 ff.

Menzel, E., and Ipsen, K., *Völkerrecht* (Munich, 2nd edn., 1979).

Metzger, S. D., 'Multilateral Conventions for the Protection of Private Foreign Investment', 9 *JPL* (1960), 133 ff.

Miller, A. S., 'Protection of Private Foreign Investment by Multilateral Convention', 53 *AJIL* (1959), 371 ff.

Miller, R., and Stranger, R. (eds.), *Essays on Expropriation* (Columbus, 1967).

Misra, K. P., *The Role of the United Nations in the Indo-Pakistani Conflict* (Delhi, 1971).

Mosler, H., 'Zur Anwendung der Grundsatzartikel des Vertrages über die Europäische Gemeinschaft für Kohle und Stahl', 17 *ZaöRV* (1956/7), 407 ff.

Muhammad, V. A. S., *The Legal Framework of World Trade* (London, 1958).

Muslehuddin, M., 'Islamic Jurisprudence and the Rule of Necessity and Need', 12 *Isl. Stud.* (1973), 37 ff.

— *Philosophy of Islamic Law and the Orientalists* (Lahore, no date).

Muslim, A. H. A., *Sahih Muslim: Being Traditions of the Sayings and Doings of the Prophet Muhammad as narrated by his Companions*, trans. A. H. Siddiqi (Lahore, 1976), i-iv.

Naff, T., 'Reform and the Conduct of Ottoman Diplomacy in the Reign of Selim III, 1789-1807', 83 *JAOS* (1963), 295 ff.

Nanda, V. P., 'Self-Determination in International Law: The Tragic Tale of Two Cities–Islamabad (W. Pakistan) and Dacca (E. Pakistan)', 66 *AJIL* (1972), 321 ff.

Naqvi, S. N. H., *Ethics and Economics: An Islamic Synthesis* (Leicester, 1981).

Nawaz, M. K., 'Some Legal Aspects of Anglo-Mogul Relations', 5 *IYIA* (1956), 70 ff.

von Neumann-Whitman, *The US Investment Guaranty Program and Private Foreign Investment* (Princeton, 1959).

Nienhaus, V., *Islam und moderne Wirtschaft* (Graz, 1982).

Nolte, R. H. 'The Rule of Law in the Arab Middle East', 48 *MW* (1958), 295 ff.

Nwogugu, E. I., *The Legal Problems of Foreign Investments in Developing Countries* (Manchester, 1965).

Nussbaum, A., *A Concise History of the Law of Nations* (New York, rev. edn., 1964).

O'Connell, D. P., *International Law* (London, 2nd edn., 1970), i-ii.

— 'Independence and Problems of State Succession', in W. V. O'Brian, *The New Nations in International Law and Diplomacy* (New York, 1965), 7 ff.

OECD, *Draft Convention on the Protection of Foreign Property and Resolution of the Council of the OECD on the Draft Convention* (Paris, 1967).

Okoye, F. C., *International Law and the African States* (London, 1972).

Oppenheim, L., and Lauterpacht, H., *International Law* (London, i. 8th edn., 1955; ii. 7th edn., 1952).

Paust, J. J., and Blaustein, A. P., 'The Arab Oil Weapon—A Threat to International Peace', 68 *AJIL* (1974), 410 ff.

Pavithran, A. K., *Substance of Public International Law, Western and Eastern* (Bombay, 1965).

Penrice, J., *A Dictionary and Glossary of the Koran* (London, 1873, repr. 1979).

Peters, R., *Islam and Colonialism: The Doctrine of Jihad in Modern History* (The Hague, 1979).

— 'Djihad: War of Aggression or Defense', in *Akten des VII. Kongresses für Arabistik und Islam Wissenschaft* (Göttingen, 1976), 282 ff.

Petersmann, E. U., *Wirtschaftsintegrationsrecht und Investitionsgesetzgebung der Entwicklungsländer* (Baden-Baden, 1974).

— 'Völkerrechtliche Fragen der Weltwährungsreform', 34 *ZaöRV* (1974), 491 ff.

Phillips, 'Insurance of Overseas Investment–the Australian Scheme', in G. Starke (ed.), *The Protection and Encouragement of Private Foreign Investment* (1966), 119 ff.

Pikcthall, M., *The Meaning of the Glorious Quran: Text and Explanatory Translation* (Delhi, 3rd edn., 1981).
Pillay, K. K., 'Relations between the East Indian Company and Bengal', 5 *IYIA* (1956), 350 ff.
Pirzada, S. S.,'Islam and International Law', in A. Gauhar (ed.), *The Challenge of Islam* (London, 1978), 196 ff.
Polter, D. M. *Auslandsenteignungen und Investitionsschutz* (Berlin, 1975).
Potter, P. B., 'The Palestine Problem Before the United Nations', 42 *AJIL* (1948), 859 ff.
Proctor, J. H., (ed.) *Islam and International Relations* (New York, 1965).
Rahim, A., *Muhammadan Jurisprudence* (Lahore, 1911, repr. 1982).
Rahman, F., 'Implementation of the Islamic Concept of State in the Pakistani Milieu', 6 *Isl. Stud.* (1967), 205 ff.
— 'Economic Principles of Islam', 8 *Isl. Stud.* (1969), 1 ff.
Reiners, H., 'Die klassische islamische Staatsidee: Ihre moderne Interpretation und ihre Verwirklichung in den Verfassungsordnungen muslimischer Staaten' (Diss. Münster, 1968).
Rie, R., 'Europäisches Konzert', in *WVR*, i. 491 ff.
Rodinson, M., *Islam and Capitalism* (Hammondsworth, repr. 1977).
Roesner, P., 'Die Meistbegünstigungsklausel in den bilateralen Handelsverträgen der Bundesrepublik Deutschland' (Diss. Heidelberg, 1964).
Röling, B. V. A., 'Aspects of the Case Concerning US Diplomatic and Consuar Staff in Tehran', 11 *NYIL* (1980), 125 ff.
Röpke, W., 'Economic Order and International Law', 86 *RdC* (1954) ii. 207 ff.
Rosenstock, R., 'The Declaration of Principles of International Law Concerning Friendly Relations: A Survey', 65 *AJIL* (1971), 714 ff.
Rosenthal, E. I. J., *Islam and the Modern National State* (Cambridge, 1965).
Roth, A. H., *The Minimum Standard of International Law Applied to Aliens* (Leiden, 1949).
Roy, G., 'Is the Law of Responsibility of States for Injuries to Aliens a Part of Universal International Law?', 55 *AJIL* (1961), 863 ff.
Sahovic, M., 'Codification of the Legal Principles of Co-existence and the Development of Contemporary International Law' in M. Sahovic (ed.), *Principles of International Law Concerning Friendly Relations and Cooperation* (Belgrade/New York, 1972), 9 ff.
Salem, E., 'Nationalism and Islam', 52 *MW* (1962), 277 ff.
Sarwar, H. G., *Muhammad, the Holy Prophet* (Lahore, repr. 1974).
Sayegh, F. A., 'Islam and Neutralism', in J. H. Proctor (ed.), *Islam and International Relations* (1965), 61 ff.
Schacht, J. (ed.). *G. Bergsträsser: Gründzüge des Islamischen Rechts* (Berlin/Leipzig, 1935).
— *Origins of Muhammadan Jurisprudence* (Oxford, 1950).
— *An Introduction to Islamic Law* (Oxford, 1964).
— 'Islamic Law in Contemporary States', 8 *AJCL* (1959), 133 ff.

Schacht, J. 'Aman', in *EI*, i. 429 ff.

— 'The Schools of Law and Later Developments of Jurisprudence' in M. Khadduri and H. J. Liebesny, (eds.) *Law in the Middle East* (1955), 77 ff.

Schacht, J., and Bosworth, C. E. (eds.), *The Legacy of Islam* (Oxford, 1974).

Schachter, O., 'Compensation for Expropriation', 78 *AJIL* (1984), 121 ff.

Schieder, T., 'Pariser Friede von 1856', in *WVR*, ii. 737 ff.

Schulz-Thurmann, W., *Internationaler Garantiefonds für Auslandsinvestitionen: Auf der Suche nach einem Schutz des privaten Investors, Der Volkswirt* (1961), 2078 ff.

Schwarzenberger, G., *Foreign Investments and International Law* (London, 1969), also translated as *Der Schutz von Auslandsinvestitionen* (Cologne, 1969).

— 'The Principles and Standards of International Economic Law', 117 *RdC* (1966), i. 5 ff.

— 'The Province and Standards of International Economic Law', 2 *ILQ* (1948), 402 ff.

— 'The Most-Favoured-Nation Standard in British State Practice', 22 *BYIL* (1945), 96 ff.

Schwebel, S. M., 'The Story of the UN Declaration on Permanent Sovereignty over Natural Resources', 49 *ABAJ* (1963), 463 ff.

— 'Aggression, Intervention and Self-Defence', 136 *RdC* (1972), ii. 411 ff.

Schwelb, E., 'Neue Etappen der Fortentwicklung des Völkerrechts durch die Vereinten Nationen', 13 *AdV* (1966/7), 1 ff.

— 'Termination or Suspension of the Operation, of a Treaty as a Consequence of its Breach', 7 *IJIL* (1967), 309 ff.

Schwenk, E. H., 'Der neue Freundschafts-Handels- und Schiffahrtsvertrag zwischen der Bundesrepublik Deutschland und den Vereinigten Staaten von Amerika', *JZ* (1957), 197 ff.

Seidl-Hohenveldern, I., *Investitionen in Entwicklungsländern und das Völkerrecht* (Cologne/Berlin/Bonn/Munich, 1963).

Semaan, K. I. (ed.), *Islam and the Medieval West: Aspects of Inter-Cultural Relations* (Albany, 1980).

Seymour, R., 'The Investment Guaranty Program of the United States', *Proc. ASIL* (1962), 77 ff.

Shihata, I., 'The Attitude of the New States towards the International Court of Justice', 19 *IO* (1965), 213 ff.

— 'Destination Embargo of Arab Oil: Its Legality under International Law', 68 *AJIL* (1974), 591 ff.

Shukri, A., *The Concept of Self-Determination in the United Nations* (Damascus, 1965).

Siddiqui, M. N., 'Muslim Economic Thinking: A Survey of Contemporary Literature', in K. Ahmad (ed.), *Studies in Islamic Economics* (1980), 191 ff.

Skubiszewski, K., 'Use of Force by States', in M. Sørensen (ed.), *Manual of Public International Law* (1968), 739 ff.

Snyder, R. C., *The Most-Favored-Nation Clause* (New York, 1948).

Sørensen, M. (ed.), *Manual of Public International Law* (London/New York, 1968).

Starke, G. (ed.), *The Protection and Encouragement of Private Foreign Investment* (Sydney, 1966).

Steinberger, H., *GATT und regionale Wirtschaftszusammenschlüsse* (Cologne/Berlin, 1963).

Steindorff, E., *Der Gleichheitssatz im Wirtschaftsrecht des Gemeinsamen Marktes* (Berlin, 1965).

Strupp, K. and Schlochauer, H. J. (eds.), *Wörterbuch des Völkerrechts (WVR)*, 3 Bde. (Berlin, 2nd edn., 1960-2).

Subhan, A., 'Jihad and Islam', *Isl. Lit.* (1951), 5 ff.

Sureda, A. R., *The Evolution of the Right of Self-Determination: A Study of UN Practice* (Leiden, 1973).

Suzuki, E., 'Self-Determination and World Public Order: Community Response to Territorial Separatism', 16 *VJIL* (1975/6), 779 ff.

Syatauw, J. J. G., 'The Relationship between the Newness of States and their Practices of International Law', in R. P. Anand (ed.), *New States and International Law* (1972), 10 ff.

Tibawi, A. L., *A Modern History of Syria including Lebanon and Palestine* (London, 1969).

— *Anglo-Arab Relations and the Question of Palestine 1914–1921* (London, 2nd edn. 1978).

— *Arabic and Islamic Themes* (London, 1976).

— 'Christians under Muhammad and his First Two Caliphs', in *Arabic and Islamic Themes* (1976).

Tworuschka, M., *Die Rolle des Islam in den arabischen Staatsverfassungen* (Walldorf, 1976).

Tyan, E., 'Djihad', in *EI*, ii. 538 ff.

Udokang, O., 'The Role of the New States in International Law', 15 *AdV* (1971/2), 145 ff.

Uhlig, C., 'Industrial Production Cooperation as Instrument of Development Policy', in K. Hottes and C. Uhlig (eds.), *Joint Ventures in Asien* (1983), 1 ff.

Uhlig, C., and Lange, M., *Internationale Produktionskooperation im Vorderen Orient: Joint Ventures und andere Formen der unternehmerischen Zusammenarbeit* (Stuttgart, 1983).

Umozurike, U. O., *Self-Determination in International Law* (Hamden, 1972).

Vagts, D. F., 'Coercion and Foreign Investment Rearrangements', 72 *AJIL* (1978), 17 ff.

Veith, W., and Böckstiegel, K. M., *Der Schutz von ausländischem Vermögen im Völkerrecht* (Baden-Baden, 1962).

Verdross, A., 'Kann die Generalversammlung der Vereinten Nationen das Völkerrecht weiter bilden?', 26 *ZaöRV* (1966), 690 ff.

Vicuna, O., 'Some International Law Problems Posed by the Nationalization of the Copper Industry by Chile', 67 *AJIL* (1973), 711 ff.

Voigt, R. and Höhne, K., 'Antwort auf Leserfragen: Organisation der islamischen Konferenz', 26 *Deutsche Außenpolitik* (1981), 118 ff.

de Waart, P. J. I. M., 'Permanent Sovereignty over Natural Resources as a Corner Stone for International Economic Rights and Duties', 24 *NILR* (1977), 304 ff.

Waldock, C. H. M., 'The Regulation of the Use of Force by Individual States in International Law', 81 *RdC* (1952), ii. 451 ff.

Walker, H., 'Treaties for the Encouragement and Protection of Foreign Investment: Present US Practice', 5 *AJCL* (1956), 229 ff.

Wansborough, J., 'A Mamluk Commercial Treaty Concluded with the Republic of Florence, 894/1498', in S. M. Stern (ed.), *Documents from Islamic Chanceries: Oriental Studies III* (Oxford, 1965), 39 ff.

— 'The Safe-Conduct in Muslim Chancery Practice', 34 *BSOAS* (1971), 20 ff.

Watt, M., *The Influence of Islam on Medieval Europe* (Edinburgh, 1972).

Watt, W. M., and Cachia, P., *A History of Islamic Spain* (Edinburgh, 1965).

Weigel, D., and Weston, B., 'Valuation Upon the Deprivation of Foreign Enterprise: A Policy Oriented Approach to the Problem of Compensation under International Law', in R. B. Lillich (ed.), *The Valuation of Nationalized Property in International Law* (1972), i. 3 ff.

Weinschel, H., 'The Doctrine of Equality of States and its Recent Modifications', 45 *AJIL* (1951), 417 ff.

Weston, B., ' "Constructive Takings" under International Law: A Modest Foray into the Problem of "Creeping Expropriation" ', 16 *VJIL* (1975), 103 ff.

— 'The Charter of Economic Rights and Duties of States and the Deprivation of Foreign-Owned Wealth', 75 *AJIL* (1981), 437 ff.

White, G., *Nationalisation of Foreign Property* (London, 1961).

White, R. C. A., 'Expropriation of the Libyan Oil Concessions–Two Conflicting International Arbitrations', 30 *ICLQ* (1981), 1 ff.

Whiteman, M. M., *Damages in International Law* (Washington, 1937-43), i-iii.

Wilson, R. R., *The International Law Standard in Treaties of the United States* (Cambridge, Mass, 1953).

— *United States Commercial Treaties and International Law* (New Orleans, 1960).

Wolfke, K., *Custom in Present International Law* (Wrocław, *OR* Breslau 1964).

Wood, H. M., 'The Treaty of Paris and Turkey's Status in International Law', 37 *AJIL* (1913), 262 ff.

Wortley, B. A., *Expropriation in Public International Law* (Cambridge, 1959).

Wright, Q., 'The Middle East Problem', 64 *AJIL* (1970), 270 ff.

— 'The Goa Incident', 56 *AJIL* (1952), 617 ff.

Young, T. C., 'Pan-Islamism in the Modern World: Solidarity and Conflict among Muslim Countries', in J. H. Proctor (ed.), *Islam and International Relations* (1965), 194 ff.

Yalcintas, N., 'Trade and Cooperation among Muslim Countries,' in ICE (ed.), *The Muslim World and the Future Economic Order* (1979), 223 ff.

Zerr, H., 'Der Begriff der Diskriminierung im Vertrag über die Europäische Gemeinschaft für Kohle und Stahl' (Diss. Heidelberg, 1961).

Zimmermann, E., *Die Preisdiskriminierung im Recht der Europäischen Gemeinschaft für Kohle und Stahl* (Frankfurt, 1962).

Index

Note: Sub-entries are in alphabetical order except where chronological or page order is significant.